This book examines a range of nineteenth-century European accounts from the Pacific, depicting Polynesian responses to imported metropolitan culture, in particular its technologies of writing and print. Texts designed to present self-affirming images of 'native' wonderment at European culture in fact betray the emergence of more complex modes of appropriation and interrogation by Pacific peoples. Vanessa Smith argues that Pacific islanders called into question the material basis and symbolic capacities of writing, even as they were first being framed in written representations. Examining accounts by beachcombers and missionaries, she suggests that complex modes of self-authorisation informed the transmission of new cultural practices to Pacific peoples. This shift of attention towards reception and appropriation provides the context for a detailed discussion of Robert Louis Stevenson's late Pacific writings. The book argues that these texts can only be properly assessed as the products of a complex, cross-cultural interaction which throws into question assumptions about the unidirectional influence of metropolitan upon peripheral cultures.

CAMBRIDGE STUDIES IN NINETEENTH-CENTURY
LITERATURE AND CULTURE 13

LITERARY CULTURE AND THE PACIFIC

CAMBRIDGE STUDIES IN NINETEENTH-CENTURY LITERATURE AND CULTURE

General editors
Gillian Beer, *University of Cambridge*
Catherine Gallagher, *University of California, Berkeley*

Editorial Board
Isobel Armstrong, *Birkbeck College, London*
Terry Eagleton, *University of Oxford*
Leonore Davidoff, *University of Essex*
D. A. Miller, *Columbia University*
J. Hillis Miller, *University of California, Irvine*
Mary Poovey, *The Johns Hopkins University*
Elaine Showalter, *Princeton University*

Nineteenth-century British literature and culture have been rich fields for interdisciplinary studies. Since the turn of the twentieth century, scholars and critics have tracked the intersections and tensions between Victorian literature and the visual arts, politics, social organization, economic life, technical innovations, scientific thought – in short, culture in its broadest sense. In recent years, theoretical challenges and historiographical shifts have unsettled the assumptions of previous scholarly syntheses and called into question the terms of older debates. Whereas the tendency in much past literary critical interpretation was to use the metaphor of culture as 'background', feminist, Foucauldian, and other analyses have employed more dynamic models that raise questions of power and of circulation. Such developments have reanimated the field.

This series aims to accommodate and promote the most interesting work being undertaken on the frontiers of the field of nineteenth-century literary studies: work which intersects fruitfully with other fields of study such as history, or literary theory, or the history of science. Comparative as well as interdisciplinary approaches are welcomed.

A complete list of titles published will be found at the end of the book.

LITERARY CULTURE AND THE PACIFIC

Nineteenth-century textual encounters

VANESSA SMITH

King's College, Cambridge

CAMBRIDGE
UNIVERSITY PRESS

PUBLISHED BY THE PRESS SYNDICATE OF THE UNIVERSITY OF CAMBRIDGE
The Pitt Building, Trumpington Street, Cambridge CB2 1RP, United Kingdom

CAMBRIDGE UNIVERSITY PRESS
The Edinburgh Building, Cambridge CB2 2RU, United Kingdom
40 West 20th Street, New York, NY 10011-4211, USA
10 Stamford Road, Oakleigh, Melbourne 3166, Australia

First published 1998

Printed in the United Kingdom at the University Press, Cambridge

Typeset in 11/12½pt Monophoto Baskerville   [SE]

A catalogue record for this book is available from the British Library

Library of Congress cataloguing-in-publication data

Smith, Vanessa
Literary culture and the Pacific: nineteenth-century textual
encounters / Vanessa Smith.
p.   cm.
Includes bibliographical references and index.
ISBN 0 521 57359 9
1. European literature – 19th century – History and criticism.
2. Exoticism in literature.   3. Islands of the Pacific in
literature.   4. Culture conflict in literature.   5. Stevenson,
Robert Louis, 1850–1894 – Criticism and interpretation, a.   I. Title
PN761.S65   1997
809′.93329–dc21   97-7612   CIP

ISBN 0 521 57359 9 hardback

For Sybil Olsen,
and for Vivian and Sybille Smith

The impediment of tongues was one that
I particularly over-estimated.

Robert Louis Stevenson, *In the South Seas*

Contents

Illustrations

MAP

Acknowledgements

I have been able to draw on the criticisms and encouragement of a number of people in writing this book. Gillian Beer has supported the project from its inception and her advice and enthusiasm have been invaluable. Nicholas Thomas generously shared his knowledge of Pacific exchange practices, and suggested many helpful improvements on early drafts. Vivian Smith provided me with innumerable new points of reference. Markman Ellis read lots of versions lots of times, with patience and insight.

I would also like to thank, for their comments on all or parts of the work, for the input of their ideas, and for their friendship, Sybille Smith, Gabrielle Smith, Nicholas Smith, Sybil Olsen, Peter Wilson, James Mackenzie, Winifred Amaturo, Adrian Poole, Tony Tanner, Maud Ellmann, Peter de Bolla, Marilyn Strathern, David Richards, Sue Benson, Margaret Harris, Penny Fielding, George Pattison and Francis West. I am grateful to King's College, Cambridge for electing me to a Junior Research Fellowship in 1994, which allowed me to complete the manuscript in a warm interdisciplinary environment. Grants from the King's College Research Fund enabled me to explore archival and cultural resources in Australia, New Zealand, Samoa and Tonga. The Beinecke Rare Book and Manuscript Library and the Whitney Humanities Center at Yale invited me to present some of this material at a Robert Louis Stevenson centenary conference in October 1994, and funded a period of research among the Stevenson archives. In particular I would like to thank Vincent Giroud, curator of modern books and manuscripts, for his generosity and assistance. I must thank the librarians and staff of Cambridge University Library, the British Library, Princeton University Library, the State Library of New South Wales, the Mitchell Library, Sydney, the National Library, Canberra, and the

Alexander Turnbull Library, Wellington, for their efforts in locating material and for permission to reproduce illustrations. Finally, thanks to Josie Dixon and Hilary Hammond at Cambridge University Press for editorial guidance.

Some material from chapter 1 has previously appeared as 'Crusoe in the South Seas: Beachcombers, Missionaries and the Myth of the Castaway', in Lieve Spaas and Brian Stimpson (eds.), *Robinson Crusoe: myths and metamorphoses*, London: Macmillan, 1996.

Introduction: acts of reading

In early missionary accounts from the Pacific, the experience of religious conversion is repeatedly equated with the experience of learning to read. Initially, it is claimed, Pacific islanders regard the written and printed words as a form of magic. This is because they free communication from a range of relationships of personal mediation, abrogating dependence on the potentially unreliable human messenger. Polynesians are represented as enthusiastic pupils, eager to gain access to writing's occult power. However, they show a preoccupation with externals that effectively makes a mockery of literacy. Concerned to mimic accurately the procedure of reading, they master a performance of recitation that bears little relationship to competence. In describing this initial reception of writing, missionary accounts produce a variety of images of false reading: reading betrayed as mnemonics by a book held upside down; alphabets recited as incantations; fetishised texts.

A typical anecdote of this kind is included in the annals of the Reverend Aaron Buzacott's mission to Rarotonga. Describing Buzacott's experiences teaching Rarotongans in the early 1830s, his biographer writes:

Under the belief that the alphabet and the primary syllables were a series of cabalistic sounds and signs peculiar to Christianity, 'many of the natives were wont to congregate together in the cool of the day and chant over the lessons they had learned at school, just as they had been wont to chant their heathen songs. Some even imagined them to be *forms of prayer*, to be repeated in times of danger.' In illustration, an amusing story is told of an aged couple who resided near the mission-house, and who were greatly alarmed by the evening visit of a cat belonging to the native teacher. The cat's peculiar mew drew their attention to the door of their dwelling, and being pitch dark, they saw what they described as two balls of fire. The wife began to remonstrate with her husband for having anything to do with the new religion; for, without her consent, and contrary

1

to her wishes, he had attended the daily instructions. 'See,' said she, 'what your conduct has brought upon us! Here is this monster come from the teacher to visit us. Alas! we shall be destroyed.' Poor puss, hearing the sound of muffled conversation, became frightened too, and began to send forth some of her most terrific cries. 'Oh, Tiaki,' exclaimed the wife, 'say the prayers you have learned.' Both immediately dropped on their knees, and Tiaki began most earnestly to cry, '*B a, ba; b e, be; b i, bi; b o, bo*'. The cat flew home in terror at such unwonted supplications, leaving the aged couple very grateful for their deliverance, and profoundly impressed with the efficacy of the new cabalistic sounds.[1]

The aged couple are portrayed in a comically infantilised relationship to written language. Their knowledge of literacy remains grounded in oral practices. Letters take effect as a chant; they are perceived, not as the primary units of language, but as a self-contained code, a magical formula.

Such representations, however, merely serve as a backdrop against which the figure of the true reader-convert – a Polynesian who passes the initiation of schooling – is made to emerge. His, or less frequently her, genuine conversion is signalled, not by displays of reading, but by the evidence of a facility for interpretation. Where literalist conformity to words on a page poses the threat of mimicry, acts of translation and exegesis exhibit an ability to reconcile text to context, to illuminate old themes with local metaphors. It is appropriation, paradoxically, which demonstrates a grasp of essential meaning. The Reverend William Wyatt Gill's *From Darkness to Light in Polynesia*, first published in 1894, eulogises one such true reader: the preacher Mamae, of Mangaia. Mamae is described as 'well versed in Scripture, which he expounded with great originality and power, bringing his illustrations not from books or commentaries, but from Nature, and from events familiar to those whom he is addressing'. Gill goes on to cite 'specimens of the racy and characteristic illustrations with which he enlivened his discourse', for instance the following:

Hollow Professors. Some professors are just like empty calabashes. When a man wants a new calabash, he selects the biggest green one he can find, bores a hole in the top, and carries it to a stream, where it at once sinks to the bottom. After a few days he comes back, and finds the once heavy calabash light and floating, the soft pith and seeds inside all decayed, and easily got rid of. Alas! that the religion of many should too much resemble the green calabash. They cannot endure temptation. Ere long their profession proves to be hollow. Are they not like empty calabashes floating down the stream?

Sometimes, when a fisherman walks along the reef, peering into every pool and crevice in the coral for fish, he sees what seems to him to be a lobster, so perfect is its form even to its eyes, spines, and claws. No defect can be discovered. Cautiously he makes a grab at the supposed prize, when, lo! it proves to be but a cast-off shell! The lobster has gone.

Let us not be mere shells, but real living Christians.[2]

Where the false converts held to the letter of the printed word, the true convert recontextualises the biblical Word. Like the aged couple, Mamae translates text into oral discourse, but his poetic licence, his range of local reference, are sources of conviction and delight. The substitution of calabash and crab shell for the gospel imagery of cups clean on the outside and whited sepulchres, to illustrate a universal lesson about the distinction between surface appearances and inner substance, reinforces for Gill the absolute authority of the Christian Word to speak across cultures.[3]

The change of register between these two anecdotes is striking. The first establishes its comic status using a substantial degree of narratorial mediation. The reader is told at the outset that this is 'an amusing story', and the narrator shifts between quotation and commentary, employing italics and exclamation in order to direct the emphasis of the tale. The second aims for relative transparency (albeit using similar techniques of italicisation, exclamation, and the presentation of recollected direct speech), and is concerned instead to establish the authenticity and sincerity of the indigenous preacher's exegesis. The first anecdote is slapstick; words, or rather letters, are simply instruments in a scene of misguided activity. The second is pure discourse. Comedy, in the first instance, is at the expense of the protagonists. The 'humour', 'wit' and raciness that Gill highlights as features of Mamae's discourse are firmly within their author's grasp, and are indicative of his mastery of the Christian text. Both tales, however, exceed their telling. If the aged couple have confused spelling with spellcasting, nothing within the first anecdote actually corrects them. The devil-cat *is* exorcised by a recitation of the primer. Writing serves as an effective incantation, and the naïveté of the couple's view must be signalled, rather heavy-handedly, through the framework of commentary. The discourse of Mamae, on the other hand, is not unified. His two examples of false surfaces and hollow centres are antithetical: the crab shell is indeed a deceptive carapace, but the calabash in fact only becomes a useful object once it has been transformed into an empty vessel. The local references

that Gill is confident are employed to illuminate and recontextual-
ise the Christian Word, appear here to divide rather than confirm
the message, their metonymic frame of reference undermining
the preacher's metaphoric intentions. A discourse about mimicry
threatens to slip into mimicry, at the very moment that Mamae's
translation emerges as original rather than copy. These two, in
many ways archetypal, stories of false and true reading and conversion elude the framework of their delineation. If only the latter
authorises Polynesian interpretation, both contain elements of
implicit critique. The uninitiated reader makes a farce of written
authority; the licensed interpreter raises the spectre of the 'hollow
professor'.

In descriptions of the initial reception of writing such as
Buzacott's anecdote, European literate culture seeks to define
itself against Polynesian oral culture in terms of presence and lack.
'Natives' are depicted as making a comical attempt to enact a
literacy that they have failed to grasp. Stephen Greenblatt has
offered a perceptive account of the complex cultural self-
aggrandisement that informed missionary gifts of literacy and
salvation. He observes that

With very few exceptions, Europeans felt powerfully superior to virtually
all of the peoples they encountered. . . . The sources of this sense of superiority are sometimes difficult to specify, though the Christians' conviction
that they possessed an absolute and exclusive religious truth must have
played a major part in virtually all of their cultural encounters. On many
occasions, this conviction was bound up with what Samual Purchas in the
early seventeenth century called the Europeans' 'literall advantage' – the
advantage, that is, of writing.

Greenblatt discusses that most violent context of Christian conversion, the American 'New World', where the 'literall advantage'
formed only one element within a brutal European 'mobile technology of power'.[4] In descriptions of the initial reception of
writing from the Pacific, however, the rhetoric of literal superiority is deployed with less overweening confidence. The straining
evident in Buzacott's comic narrative, as the author betrays his
anxiety to re-establish a patronising control over Polynesians who
have appropriated, rather than been transformed by, literacy, is a
recurrent phenomenon within early Pacific accounts. Not only the
missionaries who made literacy a project, but the beachcombers,
travellers, and traders who regarded it as a form of distinction, reg-

ister in their writings the disconcerted sense that the culture of print, in new hands, threatens to escape them. There is a recurrent, if suppressed recognition that, with the transmission of literacy, the prerogative of interpretation has been surrendered. It is the Western authorial prerogative that is actively asserted in the description of Polynesian responses to writing: absurdist narratives which illustrate, anxiously, that the Polynesian reader remains the object of European writing.

The linked depiction of false and true interpretation is a feature of the earliest accounts of contact, in which 'texts' other than the written are read by Polynesian recipients. The relationships of early contact authorised the native interpreter. Europeans in the Pacific required an introduction to language and local knowledge: the local informant, mediator, translator, was always, in this context, a privileged reader, transmitting an authoritative account of an unfamiliar society. In return for this broad cultural access, Europeans boasted that they traded the mere metonymies of a developed material culture: parts that were ludicrously taken for wholes – bits of glass and cloth and metal. The tradition of portraying islanders' awe upon receiving their side of the bargain destabilises the equilibrium of exchange. The authority with which they are invested as true readers and interpreters of local culture is immediately displaced by a depiction of the native as false reader of metropolitan material culture and technologies. This is a slippery strategy: the reverent gaze of the Polynesian instates the European object even as it betrays naïveté. Thus, for instance, the Reverend John Williams claims that his introduction to Samoa was effected through the following speech made by a chief, Fauea:

'Let us look at *them*, and then look at *ourselves*; their heads are covered, while ours are exposed to the heat of the sun and the wet of the rain; their bodies are clothed all over with beautiful cloth, while we have nothing but a bandage of leaves around our waist; they have clothes upon their very feet, while ours are like the dogs';– and then look at their axes, their scissors, and their other property, how rich they are!'[5]

The role of the Samoan mediator, on whom the missionaries' reception is in fact dependent, is elided in a 'speech' which figures the sufficiency of the missionaries' property as testimony: its self-evidence. Objects become the texts of an object lesson whose binary oppositions serve to differentiate missionary from Samoan. In the absence of material possessions, Samoans are refigured as invalid and animal, their dress 'a bandage', their uncovered feet 'like the dogs" (perhaps in order emphatically to sublimate an implication of post-lapsarian materialism in the representation of missionary wealth). In fact, as Caroline Ralston has pointed out, at the moment of initial contact Williams describes, his own familiarity with Samoan language would not actually have been sufficient to translate Fauea's words.[6] The metaphors recorded here are ventriloquised rather than recalled; tribute is put into the chief's mouth. What Fauea's 'speech' attests to, then, is the missionary's desire to assert the authority of his culture at that very moment when his dependence on native authority is absolute. The indigenous translator, mediator between two distinct languages, is reduced to a cypher, who simply points to the visible, to objects that speak for themselves.

Texts of contact strain to reposition Polynesian interrogators as overawed admirers of European culture. In James Wilson's compiled account of the first missionary voyage to Tahiti, for example, a conversation is described as taking place between King Pomare II, a beachcomber interpreter and the missionary party:

Pomārre [*sic*] asked Peter many shrewd questions concerning the places and things he had seen on the voyage, and more particularly about the natives of Tongataboo, as the red feathers, and various manufactures from thence, had given them a high idea of that people. Nothing grows on Otaheite but what they mentioned, to know if they had the same; and whether they had good land, good canoes, and fine women. They also inquired much about the Marquesas, and spoke of the people there as being as far inferior to themselves in civilization as they really are to Europeans. However, they appeared highly delighted with the relation Peter gave them of these countries: but when he spoke of the wonderful things of Europe, they at first expressed surprise; but not being able to form conceptions of the things he related, their pleasure quickly slackened: whereas the people of the Friendly islands and Marquesas are in almost all things similar to themselves; alike in person, manners, and dress; are tattoued, have canoes, bread-fruit, cocoa-nuts, and plantains, as well as they; and without these articles they admit of no country to be really valuable, though they do not deny our superiority in everything else . . . I told him, that we were once in the same predicament, and knew nothing; but that good men brought the speaking paper into our country, and taught us to understand it, by means of which we learnt to know the true God, to build and conduct ships, and to make axes, knives, scissars, and the various things which he saw we possessed . . . It behoves him to send his children and the natives to attend to [missionary] instructions; for, if they neglected the present opportunity, no more good men would come to them, but they would remain in ignorance forever.

I believe he paid as much attention to this as lay in his power, and said it was my ty (good), and so went to sleep.[7]

The Tahitian side of this conversation consists of comparative ethnographic inquiry, which may have had a political subtext (Pomare proceeded, after seeking information about the sophistication of neighbouring Polynesian communities, to express concern at his country's lack of a navy, a progression that suggests that he held localised imperialist ambitions.) The missionaries respond to this practical questioning with an account of their own culture's development which is obfuscatingly simplified: with the wish-fulfilment of a fairytale, technologies are rendered as mysterious links between knowledge and power. The gap, then, between Pomare's immediate interest in local cultural comparison and the missionaries' desire to claim tribute to their own culture's complexity, constitutes the field of a familiar Western cultural self-projection.

The first section of this book looks at a number of complex representations of true and false reading in early written accounts from the Pacific. It argues that the confident manipulation of these figures conceals an inherent contradiction: the desire simultaneously and strategically to authorise and undermine the indigenous reader, in order to instate those European objects and technologies that were being subjected, during the early contact period, to a new context of reception. In this way, such accounts attempt to control elements of potential critique and appropriation in Polynesian responses to European culture. Nicholas Thomas has recently redirected academic attention towards a history of appropriation at the periphery of European empire. Combining evidence from ethnographic fieldwork with readings of the Pacific historical archive, he argues that the representation of Polynesians' desire for European material culture, which forms a discursive continuity between the evolutionary positivism of colonial accounts and the nostalgia of much post-colonial critique, 'takes the properties of artifacts and introduced items as self-evident: it is assumed that the advantages of new items are immediately manifest to natives.' European accounts of initial exchange in the Pacific testify to the instantly recognised hegemony of European technology, yet as Thomas reminds us, 'technology is

dependent upon cultural knowledge: even relatively specialised
tools do not have specific purposes inscribed in them, and purposes and uses are variously relevant and recognised.'[8] Existing
Polynesian political and economic agendas are the lost subtexts to
these accounts. Thomas does not deny that an imbalance of power
was established between European and local interests in the
Pacific, but he is concerned to describe the nuances of that relationship rather than its monolithic structure. He reconstructs an
early contact situation in which the meanings of objects are up for
grabs, their uses and value entangled between cultural systems; a
period before European hegemony – colonial and interpretative –
has been secured.

Thomas's developing concern has been with visual representations, and texts have not figured prominently among the culturally
translated objects he discusses.[9] Yet written and printed words
offer a problematic, and therefore illuminating, example of the
dialectic of cross-cultural appropriation. For if, as I have suggested,
that dialectic involves the simultaneous representation of the
Pacific islander as authoritative interpreter and naïve reader, it is
the mutual incompatibility of these two roles which is foregrounded when the act of reading becomes an explicit practice.
Depictions of the reception of writing, which figure a transition
from naïve ciphering to competent interpreting, place the contest
of authority that occurs in early contact scenarios within the framework of European pedagogic control. However, writing proves to
be a problematic paradigm that resists this kind of narrative
determination. The teleology according to which the Polynesian,
under missionary tutelage, moves from mimic to interpreter,
ceasing to misapprehend the book as touchstone and instead
valuing it as repository of truth, is disrupted by the patent interdependence of true and false reading practices as they are represented within such narratives. As my opening examples indicate,
the false reader could spell out writing's false promises, while the
true reader could be trusted to misinterpret.

The risk in privileging writing as a case study in the politics of
appropriation, however, is that this will be seen to replicate the
very assumption that it attempts to expose: reifying the advent of
writing as an extra-significant moment in the history of Pacific
cultures. While questioning European assumptions that writing
was received as revelatory and transformative in any unproblem-

atic way within Pacific societies, this book focuses on exchange practices, local politics and oral discursive models within the Pacific only to the extent that these practices are represented in a range of texts depicting cross-cultural encounters. It makes no claim to the status of ethnography, and is almost completely dependent on archival resources. It thus remains open to the charge of implying that the history of the Pacific only really begins with the event of contact; that writing was inevitably a hegemonic practice, and that the forms of cultural resistance available to Pacific islanders were simply responsive acts of reading, predicated upon texts imposed and narrated from elsewhere. Yet while it is true that the study of pre-literate societies can only be approached through an awareness of other economies, discourses and politics than the literate, it is equally the case that an understanding of these phenomena is inevitably, from our current perspective, mediated through representations that have their own political, economic and discursive agendas, and which are governed by particular rhetorical and generic conventions.

By focusing on the Polynesian reader within European accounts, this book seeks to pay something more than the conventional lip service to contexts of textual production; to make explicit the 'entangled' status of the very representations through which contact in the Pacific was initially portrayed to foreign readers. It argues that Pacific islanders called into question the material basis and symbolic capacities of writing even as they were first being framed within written representations. This is not, however, to postulate an authentic Pacific experience of reading that anticipates a hindsighted critique. If attention has shifted from European acts of material prestation to Polynesian contexts of reception, interpretation remains confined by the limitations and particular agendas of textual sources. My interest is instead in those tensions within narrative that register the difficulty of controlling representations of 'natives' with written culture at their fingertips and on their lips. Rather than attempting to reconstruct and evaluate an early contact scenario from textual sources whose ideological biases and inconsistencies are often blatantly apparent, my analysis remains within the framework created by these limitations. It concerns itself with those silences or resistances that betray the questions that Pacific subjects posed for European authors.

The first section of this book also focuses on the Europeans and Americans who brought their material culture and technologies, including the technology of writing, into this new context of reception. For if access to such cultural artefacts established an ostensible polarity between 'native' and 'foreigner', this encompassing opposition served to conceal hierarchies that fractured the identity of the foreign subject. In fact, some of the first Europeans and Americans to reside in the Pacific – the beachcombers discussed in chapter 1 – were themselves regarded as outcasts from their original societies, a significant indicator of their occluded status being illiteracy. As 'others', styling themselves at the periphery as subjects, they were involved in a process of subversive imitation that resonates with those destabilising elements of mimicry to be found in the responses of Pacific islanders to Western material and written culture. Their initial impersonations undermined the efforts of the next group of settlers – the missionaries who are the topic of the second chapter – to institute an authorised version of Western culture and subjectivity in the Pacific.

Subsequent chapters shift from the question of readership to examine conceptions of authorship as they became illuminated in the nineteenth-century Pacific context. My example here is a figure who perhaps embodied Victorian consensus on the romance of authorship – Robert Louis Stevenson. Stevenson spent the last six and a half years of his life either travelling or in residence in the Pacific islands. In June 1888 he departed San Francisco in the company of his mother Margaret Stevenson, his wife Fanny Van de Grift Stevenson, and her son Lloyd Osbourne. After extensive touring throughout Polynesia and Micronesia, Stevenson took up residence, in October 1890, in 'Vailima', a 400-acre property above the town of Apia, on the island of Upolu, Samoa. He remained there until his death, in December 1894, making several further trips within the Pacific, but never returning to America or to Europe. During these last years he produced an extensive and various body of writings: travel accounts, romances, realist novellas, fantastical short stories, history, ballads, poems, fables, essays, lectures, prayers, public and private correspondence, sketches and fragments. The more acclaimed historical romances of this period of his career (*The Master of Ballantrae, Catriona, Weir of Hermiston*) were sourced primarily from

Stevenson's Scottish background. In these novels he writes from
the Polynesian colonial periphery of a historicised Scotland,
located in a double past of individual memory and historical narrative. Thinking across time becomes recalling across distance,
entering history via reminiscence. Stevenson looks back consistently, in the romances, to a period before or during the eighteenth-century British exploration of the Pacific, when the place
from which he writes was only just entering the imagination of his
home society. These works, however, are not the focus of the
current study, which chooses instead to examine in detail those
texts – fictional and factual – in which he responded directly to the
Pacific context.

Stevenson's prolific literary output provided the capital to
finance his estate in Samoa, and it was therefore accompanied by
an obsessive interest in the practical and financial aspects of literary production. Concerned to maximise profits, he alternately
haggled with publishers over royalties or made immediate sales of
his copyrights.[10] His letters to his American publisher Edward
Burlingame return repeatedly to the issue of the International
Copyright Act, passed in July, 1891. The bill figures first as a
desired framework for his literary activities: 'Copyright . . . If that
bill ever passes, I shall revise the text of all my books'; 'pray goodness the Copyright Bill pass before the book is ready'; and subsequently as a reference point for measuring his elusive profit
margin: 'By the way isn't it about time the accounting stepped out?
. . . I am very curious to see the result of the Copyright Act.'[11]
Stevenson had tackled the issue of copyright in print some years
before he settled in the Pacific, in the articles 'American Rights
and Wrongs' and 'International Copyright'.[12] But in Samoa his
concern with literary profit was underscored by a renewed sense of
financial dependence on the workings of the publishing industry,
and was expressed in terms of novel images of peripherality. In a
manuscript written in late 1889 or early 1890, entitled 'Authors
and Publishers', he speculates on the degree of profit merited and
received by the different agents of the publishing trade – 'the
author, the publisher, the printer, the bookseller, the paper-
maker'. From a position of established reputation, he returns to
an incident from the earliest days of his career, depicting the difficulties of an inexperienced 'young author' deceived by his

publisher as to the success of his book's sales. Stevenson draws a significant equation between the author's ignorance of sales figures, and the ignorance of white illiterates in the Pacific:

Some firms (all honour to them) begin to send us returns . . . The late lamented Bully Hayes, the pirate of the Pacific, used to visit islands (where he was sure that nobody could read), the bearer of a letter, which he would obligingly read out himself to the local trader; and that innocent was usually convinced and handed out his oil. I have no curiosity to hear such letters read to me, for I have no idea whether they are read as they were written. I have no curiosity to receive extracts from my publishers' books, or even to see the books themselves; for I have no guess whether they mean what they profess to mean.[13]

The politics of literacy in the Pacific here offer Stevenson a model for describing the ways in which the culture of print attains the status of fetish. At the same time, such comparisons highlight, rather than diminish, his physical distance from the centres of literate culture. The author's typical exclusion from the practical and financial details of literary production is, for Stevenson in the Pacific, an insurmountable fact, which creates the sense of impotence manifested in this somewhat paranoid fantasy of withheld profit.

If this period was marked by the particular urgency with which Stevenson accommodated his writing to his perception of consumer demand, it was also one in which, ironically, he became increasingly alienated from his audience, his publishers, his reviewers, and his supporters within the British and American literary establishments. The texts which he produced were distanced in form and not simply in subject matter from the expectations of his metropolitan audiences. Apart from those historical romances already mentioned, which he continued to set in Scotland, the late works met with a generally unfavourable critical reception. In addressing this response, recent studies of Stevenson's Pacific fiction have focused on the issue of genre, noting a shift towards topics and conventions of representation associated with the practice of literary realism.[14] Since my own analysis gestures towards an alternative account of the late work, I will only briefly summarise here an argument that is itself currently being challenged within genre criticism by reassessments of Stevenson's legacy as a precursor of Modernist self-reflexivity.[15]

Stevenson's popularity coincided with a revival in the 1880s of romance writing, which was embraced as an alternative to the dominant novelistic practice of realism. In opposition to what was perceived as realism's fictional determinism – its grafting of authorial invention to the social text – romance was represented as dictated by the immediate desire for escapism and adventure: as the literary product of imaginative licence. The 1880s was a decade of intense debate within literary publications over the nature and purpose of fiction. In the pages of *Longman's Magazine, British Quarterly Review, Saturday Review, Cornhill Magazine, Contemporary Review* and *Nineteenth Century* authors and critics engaged in heated disputes over the relative merits of realist and romance writing.[16] The romancist argument presumed upon the universality of readerly desires, but the fantasies to which their favoured genre catered belonged typically to the territory of the male child. Late nineteenth-century romance fiction, viewed with post-colonial hindsight, has emerged as a genre that displays the limits, rather than the transcendent powers, of the Victorian imagination, vicariously fulfilling a wish for masculine conquest displaced into the context of Britain's expanding empire. As Robert Dixon notes: 'In literary debates the New Imperialism was associated with the revival of romance, which its champions claimed as a uniquely masculine preserve . . . They saw romance as serving to deflect attention away from the dangerous unpleasantness of realism, which fostered introspection, unmanliness and morbidity.'[17] Where the literature of realism placed the domestic setting under scrutiny, romance was a discourse of exotic settings. Within its fictional parameters the Pacific figured as an idealised adventure playground, realm of noble savages and cannibals, of shipwrecks and castaways.[18] As a practitioner of romance visiting the periphery of European empire, Stevenson's literary course was clearly mapped.

Stevenson's permanent move to the Pacific also changed for him the axes of the exotic and the domestic: the exotic became his domicile. In Polynesia he encountered, not the territory of romance, but the margins of the romance imagination. As Gillian Beer has noted: 'part of the delight of romance is that we know we are not required to live full-time in its ideal worlds. It amplifies our experience; it does not press home to us our immediate everyday concerns.'[19] Once Stevenson began to live full-time in Samoa, detailing his 'immediate, everyday concerns', he necessarily abandoned the exoticising imperatives of romance. He also explicitly embraced a new aesthetic. Instead of plotting adventures, he produced ethnographically authoritative accounts of island cultures, focusing strictly on nuances of dialect and local politics; rather than describing idealised landscapes and characters, he wrote stories that set forth the ugly legacies of colonial contact; ignoring the model offered by the standardised exploits of 'empire boys', he depicted the heroism of Polynesian chiefs negotiating the opportunities for allegiances of power instigated by European imperial competition in the Pacific.[20] In the mode of his realist literary contemporaries, Stevenson showed a concern for scientific accuracy when describing Pacific cultural practices, refusing to shy away from harsh or sexually explicit material. Oscar Wilde expressed the sense of betrayal Stevenson's Pacific writing provoked in initial readers when he lamented: 'I see that romantic surroundings are the worst surroundings possible for a romantic writer. In Gower Street Stevenson could have written a new *Trois Mousquetaires*. In Samoa he wrote letters to *The Times* about Germans.'[21]

This account of Stevenson's graduation from romancist to realist is interesting for the ways in which it replicates a general tendency in discussions of Western literature on the Pacific. Bernard Smith's *European Vision and the South Pacific* offers a compelling model of this development, arguing that, as the texts of exploration were succeeded by the documents of settlement and colonisation, an idealised vision of Polynesian 'noble savagery' was displaced by unromanticised, purportedly 'scientific' description. A discourse of the noble savage, elaborated most influentially by Rousseau, but drawn on widely by writers of the European Enlightenment who took cultural cues from the exploratory narratives of Bougainville and Cook, figured the Polynesian islands as an Antipodal paradise of bounty rather than labour, populated by idealised natives whose physical attractiveness attested to moral virtue, and whose unrepressed lifestyle was sustained by a diet of fallen fruits.[22] However in the nineteenth century constructions of noble savages were supplanted by what Smith refers to as 'the objective investigations of scientists, educated missionaries and travellers', whose writings took on the rhetoric of a new realism (a rhetoric that is residual in Smith's commentary).[23] If subsequent 'realist' descriptions of life in the Pacific were offered as eye-witness correctives to the speculative romance of noble savage theories, however, the two discourses reflect the shifting lens offered by European imperial objectives: the wide angle of exploration giving way to the close focus of commercial settlement. Stevenson's literary career, by many accounts, constitutes a compressed version of this same history: he moves from the composition of romances predicated on detachment from their subject matter, to an engagement with Polynesian life that is at once critical of and implicated by the colonial contract.

To interpret the changed perception of the authorial role evident in Stevenson's Pacific writings as simply a development from romance to realism, however, is to reiterate two oddly compatible assumptions. The first, reflecting the discursive objectives of nineteenth-century imperialism, proposes a shift from romancist to realist perceptions as inevitable to the experience of settlement in the Pacific. The second presumes that Stevenson's late works are always primarily metropolitan texts, to be situated first and foremost within British debates about genre and authorial politics. In both cases the specific questions raised by the Pacific context for the interlinked histories of Victorian imperialism and literary production become neglected. The second section of this book instead looks at Stevenson's late writings as transactions between the print cultures of the Pacific periphery and the Anglophone metropolis. It draws attention to the ways in which Stevenson, himself an alienated author, inquiring at a distance into the practical processes of literary production, repeatedly articulated in his writings the experience of Polynesians whose initiation into the culture of print was not merely the expression of desire for a new form of magic, but a reflection and interrogation of the ways that magic was valued within Western cultures keen to represent literacy as their most politically and economically loaded gift.

Stevenson travelled to Polynesia with a secure literary reputation and an established audience who perceived him as a writer of romance, entering an idealised setting which he had appropriated in advance through fiction. He is therefore to be distinguished from those other nineteenth-century authors – Mark Twain, Charles Warren Stoddard, and most famously Herman Melville – whose literary careers were initiated with travel anecdotes and tales based on adventures in the Pacific. The very sense of his achieved centrality within Anglophone literary culture, of the ease that he experienced in transforming his narratives to print, accentuated the difficulties he began to encounter with publication from the Pacific islands. His distance from centres of literary production and circulation impeded the processes involved in turning manuscript into printed text, leaving him dependent upon limited exchanges with metropolitan literary delegates. Transcription and publication became slow-motion, provisional and makeshift processes.[24] They lacked facility, were at every stage explicitly and self-reflexively material. Stevenson had chosen to settle in Samoa because of its position on the mail route between Sydney and San Francisco, which enabled a relatively direct correspondence with both America and Britain. For his biographer Graham Balfour, this practical decision was all part of the myth of Stevenson the author: 'An author, and especially a writer of novels, can dispense with many of the blessings of civilisation; the one thing absolutely indispensable is a regular and trustworthy mode of communicating with his printer and his publisher. Now in the matter of mails Samoa was exceptionally fortunate.'[25] Despite such foresight, Stevenson found that letters and proofs were repeatedly delayed or went missing, and complaints such as this one, from a letter to Charles Baxter, recur in the correspondence: 'Please remember always to register when you write; masses of my letters are lost and masses of yours: Sydney is a jawhole. For instance – I need not bother with instances: such is the grim fact, and must still be borne in mind.'[26] The reference here to a 'jawhole', into which printed matter is swallowed, perhaps indicates a subconscious equation of impediments to written exchange with the mouth, as locus of oral discourse. Certainly, the anxiety registered in his correspondence as he awaited the comments of friends, publishers and reviewers on manuscripts he consigned with misgivings to the unreliable Pacific mail service indicates Stevenson's heightened awareness at this stage of the interlocutory role of an audience in literary production. He was forced to experience a new provisionality in his relationship to writing, to encounter difficulty in straightforward material processes, to contemplate the frustration of potential erasure.

This combined awareness of writing as material process and as embedded in a context of exchange is precisely one which I argue more generally was foregrounded for written culture in its transmission to the Pacific context. Perhaps unsurprisingly then, Stevenson's writings emerge as among the most complex in the Pacific archive in their engagement with the figure of the literate Polynesian. By the time Stevenson wrote from this region, the indigenous reader was an irrefutable presence in even initial encounters with many Pacific cultures. When he arrived in Hawaii in 1889, Stevenson found himself among a population of readers, their heads bent to the latest publication, indifferent to the literary figure in their midst:

People . . . came and went, they talked and waited; they opened, skimmed, and pocketed half-read, their letters; they opened the journal, and found a moment, not for the news, but for the current number of the story: methought, I might have been in France, and the paper the *Petit Journal* instead of the *Nupepa Eleele*. On other islands I had been the centre of attention; here none observed my presence. One hundred and ten years before the ancestors of these indifferents had looked in the faces of Cook and his seamen with admiration and alarm, called them gods, called them volcanoes; took their clothes for a loose skin, confounded their hats and their heads, and described their pockets as a 'treasure door, through which they plunge their hands into their bodies and bring forth cutlery and necklaces and cloth and nails', and to-day the coming of the most attractive stranger failed (it would appear) to divert them from Miss Porter's *Scottish Chiefs*: for that was the novel of the day.[27]

Stevenson finds it necessary, to his mock disappointment, to depict an absorbedly literate, rather than exotically other, Hawaiian subject. Denied the immediate recognition of an exchange of gazes, the European subject instead finds himself at best the mediated object of written representation. The fictional *Scottish Chiefs* upstages a Scot in the flesh. The moment of contact, with its poetry of misrecognition, has passed: in its place, a more banal lack of recognition attests to different canons, different written agendas. The writer sees himself reflected, not as god or volcano, or even as stranger, but simply as one among many in a new community of readers. The ubiquity of the literate Polynesian does not guarantee the author an audience, but it continues to raise questions for authorship as symbolic and as material practice.

CHAPTER 1

'A gift of fabrication': the beachcomber as bricoleur

When the missionary James Hadfield published the narrative of the beachcomber William Diaper in 1928, under the title *Cannibal Jack: the true autobiography of a white man in the South Seas*, he emphasised the uniqueness of the record. In his introduction to the volume, Hadfield writes of the Pacific beachcomber population as a source of stories lost to publication. He recalls: 'One man with whom I was brought into close contact was endowed with such a gift of fabrication that no one who knew him gave credence to any statement he made. What a loss was here to the world of fiction and light literature!'[1] The small corpus of Pacific beachcomber texts emerges from the elusive context of oral narration to depict outlandish histories for a Western readership.[2] Its protagonists are escaped convicts, deserting sailors or itinerant traders who 'went native' in the Pacific during the pre-colonial period of the late eighteenth and early nineteenth centuries. However these exotics – for a brief period in Pacific history – also had an unlicensed authority. As the first Europeans and Americans to establish themselves within many island communities, beachcombers provided an initial model for Pacific peoples of the metropolitan subject. This chapter examines the ways in which the beachcomber both invented and compromised Western subjectivity in the Pacific.

Hadfield's term 'fabrication', which combines significations of manufacture and forgery, is a particularly resonant one. The position of the beachcomber within island communities was premised upon a privileged access to metropolitan techniques and objects of manufacture. As a limited number of European articles – both weapons and hardware – began to circulate in the islands, frequently brought by the beachcombers themselves, or traded by visiting ships, the value of individuals willing to remain within island societies, who understood how to repair and maintain these objects, was recognised. Skill and object were bound by an intimate relationship. Beachcombers were also mediators in initial trade relations between European and American shipping companies and island ports of call, combining the roles of trading master, pilot, interpreter, and overseer of working gangs. They served as representatives of both foreign and indigenous interests, interpreting two languages, and assisting in the interpenetration of two distinct economic systems: facilitating and manipulating exchange.[3]

Where beachcombers were initially equated with sophisticated material culture, as prized objects, this attitude was supplanted by a recognition of the authority of the beachcomber as able to elucidate and thus control the object. 'John Jackson', who joined the retinue of a Fijian chief in the 1840s, wrote of the pressure he felt at being regarded simply as an exotic item: 'As I observed that they still thought of and used me more as a novelty than a human being, I became dejected, melancholy, and dissatisfied with everything.'[4] The demonstration of technical proficiency could transform the experience of cross-cultural voyeurism into a reclamation of subjectivity and an assertion of authority. The equation of manual dexterity with cultural status, moreover, inverted the significance of skilled labour in the class system of the beachcombers' home society. In the eyes of the Pacific islanders, the beachcomber graduates from possessor to producer of superior technology – an inversion of the social hierarchy of capitalist production. Within their adopted communities, their skills and property functioned in the manner of what Pierre Bourdieu has termed 'symbolic capital', attaining a prestige value, which in turn became subject to fluctuations in exchange.[5] Yet the authority achieved by the beachcomber at the periphery was a tenuous one. Typically an absconder from his society, he could nonetheless serve as representative of that society in the median period of Pacific history between contact and colonisation.[6] As Greg Dening observes: 'In the eyes of the islanders [beachcombers] were as divorced from their social realities as their cargo was divorced from its means of production.'[7] However, within his home culture the beachcomber was an 'other' in class and often in racial terms. Generally of working-class, and sometimes of criminal background, frequently the unfit: sailors 'dumped because they were recalcitrant or poor workers or sick', his status as representative of European culture to Pacific societies was ultimately a forged identity.[8]

H. Stonehewer Cooper, in his popular work *Coral Lands* (1880), offered a social-Darwinian account of beachcomber culture. Cooper compared the beachcombers to the 'mean whites' of the southern United States, claiming: 'The beachcombers of the South Pacific are, taking them as a class, of a superior order to the almost extinct American caste referred to . . . For most of these men are of British stock, some of them with good yeomen's blood in their veins.' Cooper compares the beachcombers unfavourably, however, with 'some of the better class of white adventurers who roam from island to island in the wide Pacific', and writes: 'the comparatively harmless beachcomber is doomed; but some of the wanderers in the great South Sea are of a different stamp from . . . these classes.'[9] There was, in fact, an aristocracy among the beach-combers: a class of 'gentleman beachcomber', of whom Herman Melville – the only beachcomber whose narratives have achieved canonical status – is the most famous example.[10] Cooper repre-sents the typical beachcomber as a degenerate, who nonetheless reveals a fitness for survival:

They are hardy, healthy, powerful, and bronzed. They have the strength to lift a kedge-anchor, and to carry a load of perhaps 200 cocoa-nuts out of the forest in the heat of a noonday sun. They climb trees like apes, and can dive almost as well as the natives with whom they live. They wear no shoes, but go at all times barefooted on beaches of sharp gravel and reefs of prickly coral. Some of these men have as many as twenty children with huge frames and gipsy countenances. Their intellect is of a low order, and their morals very lax; but it is quite possible they may improve as they multiply, and they are multiplying very rapidly.[11]

Compared with the 'ape' and the 'native', the beachcomber is often an object of denigration in nineteenth-century accounts.

As functionaries of technological initiation in Pacific communi-ties, beachcombers had only a temporary authority: their skills were destined to become superfluous. They were aware of the pre-cariousness of their status, and attempted to hoard their talents. Archibald Campbell reports an attitude to the transmission of skills prevalent among the beachcomber community of Hawaii in 1809. When requested to manufacture a loom, King Kamehameha's chief carpenter

declined, from an illiberal notion held by many of the white people, that the natives should be taught nothing that would render them inde-pendent of strangers. He told the king he did not know how to make looms; upon which I undertook to make one myself; although, by doing so, I incurred the displeasure of many of my countrymen. Davis [another beachcomber] had a native servant called Jack, who worked as a taylor [*sic*], and was a very handy fellow. This man shewed much anxiety to observe how I proceeded; but his master told me by no means to allow him, as he was so quick he would soon learn to make a loom himself. When I said I had no wish to make it a secret, he replied, that if the natives could weave cloth, and supply themselves, ships would have no encouragement to call at the islands.[12]

That any hand can labour equally well is the source of threat of the 'very handy fellow'. Trade lacks signatory status; the manual labourer is always reduplicable. Here the significance of racial and cultural difference is subordinate to concern about the effective standardization of the worker. Alternatively William Diaper, employed as an overseer on a Fijian estate, distinguishes himself from the indigenous worker by his strict refusal to participate in manual labour. His policy intimates a similar consciousness that the labourer cannot maintain distinction: 'I never did *any* work, because by doing so I should lose prestige in the eyes of the Fijians; and when I ordered them to hurry along with their work, they would tell me to do it myself, seeing I was a working man like themselves!'[13]

Literacy was regarded by the beachcomber as an even more significant focus of contestation than other forms of knowledge, since it was a far from common acquisition. Continuing his discussion of the tendency among beachcombers to hoard their talents, Archibald Campbell claims: 'Another instance of this narrow way of thinking occurred, when a brother of the queen's, whose name I do not remember, but who was usually called by the white people John Adams, wished me to teach him to read, Davis would not permit me, observing, "they will soon know more than ourselves"'.[14] The initiation of the Polynesian into literacy threatens to produce not merely a replica, but a superior subject, who will 'know more than ourselves'. Campbell has not acquired a reciprocal oral mnemonic skill: he fails to recall Adams's Hawaiian name. His own atypical willingness to impart cultural knowledge is undoubtedly a reflection of the distinction with which his literacy endows him among the beachcomber community.

BEACHCOMBER TEXTS: FABRICATING AUTHORITY

If beachcombers were rigid about the transmission of trade secrets, their repertoire of skills was a model of flexibility. The beachcomber was a jack of all trades, and his fabrications were assemblages of materials to hand. He was literally a *bricoleur*. According to Claude Lévi-Strauss, the *bricoleur* is someone 'who works with his hands and uses devious means compared to those of a craftsman'.[15] In *The Savage Mind*, Lévi-Strauss adopted the notion of *bricolage* as a model for describing 'savage' creative processes. He contrasted the activities of the *bricoleur* with those of the engineer, who, he claimed, epitomised the conceptual mode of Western thought:

The 'bricoleur' is adept at performing a large number of diverse tasks; but, unlike the engineer, he does not subordinate each of them to the availability of raw materials and tools conceived and procured for the purpose of the project. His universe of instruments is closed and the rules of his game are always to make do with 'whatever is at hand', that is to say with a set of tools and materials which is always finite and is also heterogeneous because what it contains bears no relation to the current project, or indeed to any particular project, but is the contingent result of all the occasions there have been to renew or enrich the stock or to maintain it with the remains of previous constructions or destructions.[16]

Whereas the engineer works with concepts, which transcend or seek to overreach limitations of circumstance, the *bricoleur* works with signs, which are context-bound. Lévi-Strauss applied the notion of *bricolage* to a discussion of the formulation of myth in 'primitive' societies. By focusing his interpretation upon symbolic constructions, he evaded the economic implications of his model. Yet the opposition of a scientific mode of creation that transcends material circumstances, to a *bricolage* that recognises material limitation as the definitive term in production, is not simply a dichotomy between essential Western and 'primitive' mental paradigms. It is also a reflection upon the economic systems that form the contexts of those creative processes. When Lévi-Strauss writes

It might be said that the engineer questions the universe, while the 'bricoleur' addresses himself to a collection of oddments left over from human endeavours, that is, only a sub-set of the culture . . . The engineer is always trying to make his way out of and go beyond the constraints imposed by a particular state of civilization while the 'bricoleur' by inclination or necessity always remains within them[17]

he might well be contrasting the outward drive of imperial capitalist expansion during the nineteenth century with the cultural productions of the colonised, assembled from the remnants of cultures subordinated to that imperative. As Western *bricoleur*, producing objects and narratives that are makeshift rather than crafted, from materials to hand at the periphery of empire, the beachcomber straddles such distinctions between Western and native subjects. A figure of early contact, he epitomises a situation in which relationships of power and of material authority were as yet undefined; in which personal histories were fashioned around the histories of objects whose value and purpose remained to be determined.

Beachcomber accounts, equally, are experiments with different forms of authority. In his essay 'The Storyteller', Walter Benjamin links the production of narrative with a context of licensed workmanship. Benjamin's archetypal storyteller is the artisan, whose stories have, like the articles he fashions, a primary use-value. 'Every real story', he writes, 'contains, openly or covertly, something useful. The usefulness may, in one case, consist in a moral; in another, in some practical advice; in a third, in a proverb or maxim. In every case the storyteller is a man who has counsel for his readers.'[18] The virtue of the artisan model of production for Benjamin lies in its commitment to refinement, rather than reduplication. He takes as his model the connection between Western traditions of storytelling and of manufacture, depicting the story as a crafted object. But the narratives of the beachcomber were not carefully constructed artefacts.[19] They were cobbled together. Their value was not inherent but was largely determined by exchange: by the exotic value their experiences acquired when conveyed to a metropolitan audience. For the editors and publishers of the beachcomber texts, the recovery of the storyteller could not involve the affirmation of a traditional social order (albeit in the context of a critique of modern capitalist production) that it does in Benjamin's essay. The beachcomber was a more slippery subject, in whom the linked practices of manufacture and narration were compromised. A jack of all trades, his labour was provisional, a mimicry of the gradually acquired mastery of the initiated guildsman. His narrative is makeshift: frequently collaborative or aleatory. A mediator between Pacific and capitalist economies of exchange, his stories form part of a history of transcultural negotiation.

Cannibal Jack, a fragment of the autobiography of the beachcomber William Diaper, entered circulation as a gift. According to

the classic gift theory of Marcel Mauss, 'a gift creates a debt that
has to be repaid': Diaper's text consists of three extracts from an
autobiography of nineteen handwritten books, copied out and
presented to James Hadfield in a context of reciprocal obligation.[20] Hadfield had provided the beachcomber with a stock of
writing-paper, and he notes: 'I have no doubt that it was in thankful recognition of this that he asked me to accept an exercise book
closely filled with an account of some years of his adventurous life.'
The gift, however, is intended by its donor to introduce his work
into commodity circulation. Diaper hopes that the gaps in the narrative of extracts that Hadfield receives will stimulate the desire of
the reader, and so create a potential purchasing audience for the
complete work. He advertises that: 'this is a mere specimen of the
whole, and which will be for sale, providing this is accepted and
reasonably paid for'. The beachcomber narrative was, in fact,
rarely destined to become a profitable commodity. Hadfield has
subsequently learnt of the destruction of Diaper's remaining
papers in a fire: the gift fragment is, apparently, all that survives of
his story.[21]

It is for his anticipated readership that 'Cannibal Jack' feels it
necessary to justify himself as author. His narrative is prefaced with
the history of his nickname:

I suppose the reader will expect an explanation of how I, in the first place,
came in possession of that somewhat disgraceful-sounding sobriquet of
'Cannibal Jack', and which I have since taken as my *nom de plume*.

Well then, as it is now a long time ago since I first commenced
scribbling– some forty years– and among the rest, I named one book *Jack
the Cannibal Killer*, thinking perhaps, as everything is in a name, that it
would have the greater circulation, but instead of remaining at that, it
was, by some means or other, altered, and 'Cannibal Jack' became indelibly fixed upon myself.

Diaper recalls an earlier attempt to manipulate literary circulation,
which redounded to his discredit. Promoting himself as the hero
of English fairytale tradition, Jack the [Giant] Killer, he was rewritten as the horrific cannibal, who 'smells the blood of Englishmen'.
The namer was renamed, the writer 'indelibly' inscribed. Seeking
to tempt the literary consumer, he became redefined as the figure
of excessive, degenerate consumption. Diaper, however, has
reappropriated his epithet, converting oral reputation to self-nomination. The French term *nom de plume* reasserts his discursive

reach: he claims 'possession' of the profits of his sobriquet. In fact, the beachcomber typically embraced otherness as title. Hadfield mentions 'Dirty Jerry, who was proud of his first name and endeavoured to live up to it . . . The adjectival prefix of his name . . . fittingly qualified his dwelling', and William Churchward tells of 'Monkey Jack' among 'gentlemen . . . whose nicknames, though perhaps appropriate, would not look particularly well in print'.[22] The beachcomber discarded social identity with the adoption of the sobriquet. Metonymic rather than metaphoric, his self-christening asserted the priority of context over lineage.

For the reader of the printed book *Cannibal Jack*, Diaper's explanation is pre-empted by Hadfield's introductory remarks. Noting that 'In this story Diapea denies cannibalistic practices', Hadfield protests, 'I trust that I am not traducing his name if I suggest that in spite of this disclaimer it was the accepted opinion in the Islands that he had been addicted, as no doubt were not a few white men, to such practices.' The verb 'traducing' compounds reference to defamation and misrepresentation with associations of transference and translation, and indeed the reinscription of Cannibal Jack as object rather than subject of his title occurs with the transition from written to printed text. Between Pacific periphery and metropolitan centre, between transcription and publication, Diaper's narrative, 'A few Extracts from the autobiography of William Diapea, alias "Cannibal Jack"', is renamed *Cannibal Jack: the true autobiography of a white man in the South Seas.* As cannibal, Diaper is beyond the pale of both Western and colonial Pacific codes of behaviour, indulging in a practice that has fallen, when Hadfield writes, 'in such evil repute that no native ever cares to speak or think of it'.[23] William Arens has argued that the cannibal is a universal image for defining the limits of cultural subjectivity: 'the assumption by one group about the cannibalistic nature of others can be interpreted as an aspect of cultural boundary construction and maintenance. This intellectual process is part of the attempt by every society to create a conceptual order based on differences in a universe of often-competing neighboring communities.'[24] Yet it is precisely such boundaries that a figure like Cannibal Jack serves to destabilise. Where, in the Western imagination, the non-Western cannibal is regarded as betraying an unmastered primitivity, the white cannibal such as Diaper represents the degeneration of the civilised principle.

When the Reverend William Wyatt Gill encountered Jackson on the missionary ship *John Williams*, bound for Samoa, he observed that the beachcomber hid away to 'avoid the jibes and scorn of his fellow-sailors'. Gill subsequently discovered that Jackson's self-promoted reputation as a 'white cannibal' was responsible for 'the scorn under which he writhed'.[25] Cannibalism is the point of no return in 'going native', implicating the Western subject in appetite.

However, if the publishers of texts such as Diaper's are keen to recoup on an element of the scandalous, they have an equal stake in recovering a legitimate beachcomber author. To this end the different editors of the beachcomber texts emphasise both the truth status and the fictional qualities of these narratives: their realism and their romance. Owen Rutter promotes the beach-comber James Morrison as both creative writer and ethnographer, claiming that 'Morrison seems to have been a born writer . . . Wherever he went he had an insatiable curiosity, and the knack of recording exact information with a wealth of picturesque detail. His description of Tahiti and its people, the fruit of over two years' residence in close contact with the natives, is the earliest detailed account we have.'[26] Saul Reisenberg presents his subject, James O'Connell, as a consummate liar, but points out that inventiveness does not preclude anthropological authority: 'O'Connell's description . . . provides us with an exceedingly valuable ethno-graphic account of an as yet undisturbed culture.'[27]

Those beachcomber narratives published during the period of empire were claimed as contributions to a colonising will to knowledge. The experience of the typically errant beachcomber was thus aligned with the collective imperial endeavour. Peter Bays, a castaway for just eight days on the tiny island of 'Bittoa' (Vatoa), regarded his course as having been guided by the Providence of Empire:

Though an island so thinly inhabited can be of little worth in itself, yet having trade to Milekemba and other islands, Bittoa, or Turtle Island, might be an introduction to all the Fegees; and who knows how great a fire this little spark may kindle? I am willing to hope our very providential landing here, may one day terminate in a business of much greater importance than our preservation.[28]

Archibald Campbell's editor tailors the beachcomber's narrative to fit gaps in the expanding map of imperial knowledge:

In those parts of the work which relate to places already well known, the narrative is entirely confined to the personal adventures of the author; and had the editor been aware that so much had been recently written regarding Kamschatka (*sic*) and the Aleutian Islands by the Russian navigators, the description of those places would have been either altogether omitted, or much more condensed . . . The importance of the subject will account for the disproportion of that part which relates to the Sandwich Islands to the rest of the work. From the advantages they owe to their situation, placed midway between the continents of Asia and America; from the fertility of the soil, and the natural talents and industry of the natives, they promise to become by far the most important of the recently discovered islands in the Pacific Ocean.[29]

The colonial cause claimed the absconding beachcomber retrospectively, creating a use for his text that counterweighs the fear of redundancy evident in such passages. Like the beachcomber's usefulness to his adopted society, however, the value of such knowledge was always threatened with displacement.

ORALITY AND DUPLICITY: THE FABRICATED ACCOUNT

The typical beachcomber tale was an oral narrative, conveyed in conversation to a listener who translated it into print. This substitution was justified by the social unsuitability of the beachcomber for authorship. As former sailors, beachcombers were familiar with a Western oral tradition of yarning: on their islands they became initiates in Pacific oral traditions. William Mariner's *Account of the Tonga Islands* was composed by Dr John Martin. Mariner became stranded in Tonga when the privateer the *Port au Prince*, upon which he was making a first voyage as captain's clerk, was captured in the Ha'apai Islands in December 1806. He was spared in the massacre that took place due to the favour of King Finau 'Ulukalala, who adopted him as his son. Mariner spent four years in Tonga; his ability to operate the weapons confiscated from the *Port au Prince* rendered him instrumental in Finau's campaign of internal colonisation. Yet that very absorption in Tongan oral culture which rendered Mariner an ideal cipher, also left him an inappropriate author when he returned to Britain to tell his tale. Martin writes:

To my inquiries respecting his intentions of publishing, he replied, that having necessarily been, for several years, out of the habit either of writing or reading, or of that turn of thinking requisite for composition and arrangement, he was apprehensive his endeavours would fail in doing that justice to the work which I seemed to think its importance demanded: he modestly proposed, however, to submit the subject to my consideration for a future opportunity.[30]

James Smith, compiler of Campbell's *Voyage Round the World*, justifies his literary intervention with reference to Campbell's social disadvantages: his aim is 'to rescue much of what is true and extraordinary from the oblivion to which the obscure condition and limited powers of the narrator would have condemned it'. Smith describes an authorial role that is less transcription than ventriloquisation: 'In the execution of his task, simplicity and perspicuity are all that the editor has aimed at. The ornaments of style, which are generally misplaced in such relations, would have been particularly incongruous in the mouth of a common sailor.'[31] An identical practice was employed by English translators working from foreign accounts of the Pacific, which supports the idea that the compilation of the beachcomber's narrative for literary consumption was perceived to be a transformation as radical as that between different languages. The translator of Otto von Kotzebue's *New Voyage*, for instance, also outlines his project as a self-effacing act of ventriloquism:

The first object of the translator has been fidelity to his original: he has not sought to embellish, by superadded ornaments of style and colouring, the unaffected language of a plain, though well educated and accomplished seaman; he has merely endeavoured to put it into such natural and manly language as would become an English naval officer to write, and as an intelligent reader may peruse with satisfaction.[32]

Here there is a compatibility between the natural languages of the naval officer and the intelligent reader. Ventriloquism is more performative in the case of the beachcomber's editor. James Smith's literacy qualifies him accurately to represent Campbell's orality; his class credentials validate an act of mimicry. In the slippage between writing as distinction and as minimalised tool for the transliteration of voice, the text of the returned beachcomber registers the social context of its production.

Similarly, these editors anticipate a suspicion of narrative unreliability, whose foundation is primarily social. James Smith writes of Campbell: 'From the humble situation held by the author, a distrust may be entertained of his qualifications to relate the facts

which fell under his notice.' John Martin assumes that 'the reader
will naturally wish to be put in possession of some account of Mr
Mariner's education, &c. in order to judge better of his capabili-
ties as an observer and narrator'.[33] If literacy is the implicit qual-
ification for verbal testimony, the focus of suspicion is ultimately
the oral mode of narration as such. Editors avoided duplication
when seeking to compile beachcomber texts as contributions to
imperial knowledge, although repetition also provides a mode of
authentification, lending weight to an insubstantial oral testimony.
The ability to tell twice, the faculty of memory, could make an
honest man of the beachcomber. Martin writes of Mariner:

His memory is very retentive, and his account of things is exceedingly
correct and uniform: of this I have had numberless proofs, and one in
particular I shall mention. I happened to mislay the English version
which he had written out at his leisure, of the speech of Finow the king
on first coming into power: after a lapse of a few weeks, not finding it, I
was under the necessity of requesting him to write another, which he did
in the same method as before, by calling to his mind the original Tonga
in which it was spoken. Sometime afterwards I found the first, and was
much pleased to discover so little difference between them, that they
appeared almost like copies, which sufficiently evinced the correctness
with which he remembered the original Tonga, and at the same time furnished an instance of the characteristic uniformity of his expression in
his own language.[34]

Duplication is the mode of validation of a culture of print.
Martin suggests that it also has an authenticating value for oral
culture, referring to Tongans as 'a people who have no conception
of any method of noting down their ideas, and yet pride themselves upon the uniform accuracy with which they speak and pro-
nounce their language'; however research within oral societies
indicates that the concept of exact replication is a literate imposition on oral notions of retelling.[35] Archibald Campbell's recently
published voyage is cited by Martin as providing further confirmation of Mariner's account. He includes Mariner's written commentary on specific passages from Campbell's text, which are
paginated to enable cross-reference. Mariner's implication in the
culture of print is not only manifest in his representation here as
authoritative reader between texts, but also in the bias of the
ethnographic knowledge he marshals in response to Campbell.
Discussing orthographic discrepancies between the two accounts,

Martin notes: 'The king's name, here spelt '*Tamaahmaah*', is pronounced by Mr Mariner, and is expressed by our orthography
Támmeahméha . . . The editor, Mr Smith, in note, p. 210, remarks
the different modes of spelling and pronouncing this name,
employed by different travellers, and that the *C* and the *T* are
scarcely to be distinguished in the pronunciation of the language.'
Oral discourse has apparently produced an elusive subject,
doubled rather than duplicate. Where such discrepancies in fact
testify to misconstruction by the unaccustomed British ear,
Mariner explains the problem as one of transmission rather than
reception:

The fact is, there are few of the natives but who have lost some of their
front teeth, owing to an absurd custom of knocking them out as a
sacrifice . . . The consequence is, that their pronunciation, to the ears of
a foreigner, is exceedingly indistinct: they often confound the *r* and the
l, possibly from this cause; but their indiscriminate use of the hard *c* and
the *t*, Mr Mariner is convinced, arises from this source.[36]

Mariner's account produces a disabled native subject whose
cultural practices are mutually conflicting: self-mutilation
hindering oral communication. Yet this incapacity is only registered in the translation into print, where orthographic unity
becomes a significant requirement.

Missionaries, as transmitters of print culture to the Pacific
context, were better equipped to recognise that discrepancies in
spelling were a textual problem. The compilers of the account of
the first missionary voyage to the Pacific noted that

The want of a proper guide for the pronunciation of names used by the
South-Sea islanders, and the diversity of modes in which they have been
spelled by writers and compilers of voyages, have long been subjects of
complaint . . . The variety of journals from which extracts are given in the
narrative of Captain Wilson's voyage, has frustrated, in a great measure,
the endeavours that were used to adopt a uniform and distinct orthography throughout the volume.[37]

Local pronunciation is variegated in the signature texts of journals, whose references become confounding when the attempt to
produce an authoritative printed text requires a universalised
terminology. Yet missionaries were also quick to penalise native
speech practices, rather than their own ear, in accounting for
difficulties in language transmission. A nineteenth-century treatise for children on missionary activity in the Pacific represents the

missionary linguist as a careful student confounded by incomprehensible native speech:

When the natives talk, he endeavors to remember and write down the words they use. Then, as he has opportunity, he inquires what those words mean. Perhaps the people *jabber* so fast that they do not speak the words distinctly, and so he is not able to repeat properly what he has but half heard, and gets laughed at for his pains. At other times, when the meaning of a word is asked, the natives nod their heads in a peculiar way, and say they do not know. The missionaries are therefore obliged to follow them about from place to place, hoping at last to get some clew as to what they are seeking. This process of learning a language must be very tedious.[38]

Beachcomber texts, on the other hand, with their less confident relationship to textual authority, retained elements of exchange associated with spoken language. Mariner's attentive reading of Campbell's text inscribes the interlocutory and aggregative mode of oral discourse, redefining publication as dialogue: 'I shall mention the different subjects in the order in which they occur in Mr Campbell's book, paging them accordingly; and if that author, or his editor, Mr Smith, sees any thing in Mr Mariner's statements which he knows or believes to be incorrect, he will perhaps take an opportunity of stating his objections.' The preface to the second edition of the *Account of the Tonga Islands* provides 'an additional weight of testimony in favour of the facts related': the deposition of Jeremiah Higgins, a fellow surviving crew member of William Mariner's ship. Mariner and Higgins are the same age, and thus share the advantage of youth in acquiring the Tongan tongue. Martin writes:

it is not every European, whom accident or design may station in those islands for a few years, that can learn their language with accuracy; for the idiom is so different from our more civilised and artificial forms of speech, that it must be chiefly young persons, with minds very susceptible of the impressions of spoken language, and of the gestures accompanying it, that can readily accomplish this object without the assistance of an interpreter.

There is an implicit compatibility, in Martin's representation, between the youth of these subjects and of a Tongan culture figured as preserving 'the history of the earlier ages of mankind' and 'the infancy of human society'.[39]

Not all voices, however, have equal weight in such exchange.

Higgins lacks the social credentials that Martin represents as essential for ethnographic observation:

Being very young, he was one of the first who acquired a tolerable knowledge of the language; he practised their dances, and learned their songs; – and although he had not the advantage of those better opportunities which fell in Mr Mariner's way, and consequently is not so intimately acquainted, in certain points of view, with the political sentiments, and moral notions and habits especially of the higher classes of the natives, which the superior education of the latter, as well as his relative condition among the Tonga chiefs, rendered him more apt to acquire; – still, the information obtained from Higgins must undoubtedly be considered valuable, if only regarded as generally corroborative, and in a few instances somewhat corrective of Mr Mariner's statements.

Mariner's educational background gives him access to a superior class of Tongan, with whom, it is implied, he has a greater social compatibility than with his fellow Englishman Higgins. Higgins and his neighbour, 'Mr T. Woodman, a very respectable and intelligent farmer', serve to read and verify Mariner's account.[40] Martin provides the addresses of these two witnesses, and within the narrative, those of several other returned survivors of the *Port au Prince* massacre. Such information serves discreetly to signal the social identity of the testifying subject, mapping the beachcomber back into English society even as his text is claimed as a contribution to the imperial mapping of the Pacific.

If the impressionable youths Mariner and Higgins are represented as ciphers for Tongan cultural practices – as ideally receptive – they appear inept at the reciprocal function of oral discourse, transmission. Reticence, however, is recuperated as a symptom of authenticity. Martin writes of Mariner, 'He is rather taciturn than loquacious, and under ordinary circumstances much more inclined to speak of the events of his life as common occurrences than as interesting anecdotes, which happens no doubt from his early, frequent, and familiar intimacy with unusual situations.' Mr Woodman reports of Jeremiah Higgins: '"as he is a young man of a reserved disposition, the communications he made were always desultory, unconnected and confined"'. The pair seem to have lost their voices in translocation. Yet Martin continues: 'when, however, [Mariner] is animated with social converse, he furnishes descriptions that are very interesting and natural'. To elicit the text his subjects bear, the writer reinvokes the context of oral exchange, observing that 'When they spoke the Tonga language together, I noticed the similarity of their pronunciation and accent: when Higgins sang and exhibited some Tonga dances in the presence of several of my friends, whilst Mr Mariner also sang and beat time according to the native method, we were struck with the accuracy of the description of these amusements in the "voyages of Captain Cook"'. Martin recognises that to become audience to a traditional performance is the first stage in translating Tongan culture into print. The performance, the scene of validation within oral cultures, provides the ultimate authentication for textual representation: the oral and the written become mutually confirming. And if this demonstration serves primarily as testimony to the authority of Cook's original text, the tattooed body of the performing beachcomber, a Tongan imprint, in turn recovers the art of inscription for oral culture:

To give greater effect to the scene, Mr Mariner was dressed as represented in the frontispiece, and Higgins's only apparel was a sort of circular apron . . . He is beautifully tattowed from the hips nearly to the knees, agreeably to the custom of the Tonga people. Upon them it appears of a black colour, but upon a white man it causes the skin to resemble soft blue satin. The neatness, and I might almost say, the mathematical precision with which the pattern is executed, far surpasses the expectation of all who see it for the first time.[41]

The above description is, however, relegated to the subordinate text of a footnote, allowing print the last word. Appropriately, the representative of a textual culture is here seen to make the more effective printed impression.

The irony of the search for duplicate evidence was that this too could be forged. 'H. H. W.', the 1836 editor of James O'Connell's *A Residence of Eleven Years in New Holland and the Caroline Islands*, similarly produced the testimony of repetition as a guarantee of authenticity:

continued and frequent conversations with him, in which, assisted by others, we repeated trivial questions, and invariably received the same answers, soon disarmed us of all suspicion . . . He amused himself one day by writing a list of a couple of hundred words in the language of the Carolines, and their English signification. We preserved the paper, and, some days afterward, questioned him from it. His answers were invariably correct, evincing such a knowledge of the language as could only have been acquired by a long residence.[42]

Plate 1. 'Mr Mariner in the Costume of the Tonga Islands', frontispiece to John Martin, *An Account of the Natives of the Tonga Islands, in the South Pacific Ocean*.

However, O'Connell's twentieth-century editor subsequently reveals that in fact '30 per cent of his vocabulary appears either to belong to some other language or to be invented'. For the later editor, such duplicity reflects the dubious identity of the beachcomber narrator. He guesses at an unsavoury, perhaps convict past, which motivated O'Connell to reinvent himself in his account, producing in the process a fictive culture and language of Ponape.[43] The same vocabulary which 'H. H. W.' cited as authentication becomes the text in which O'Connell's second editor discovers inconsistency. In fact, the misnomers of O'Connell's account do serve metaphorically to describe the experience of the beachcomber. His cultural insularity, and consequent fragmentary, rather than communal, perception of the adopted space are figured in his erroneous insistence on referring to places on the mainland of Ponape as islands. The most significant gap in his terminology, the parts of the body – nineteen of those he lists are unidentifiable in Ponapean vocabulary – evokes a related effect of physical self-alienation.[44]

The question of unreliability could actually become accentuated by duplication of content. Two accounts of the wreck of the *Minerva* whaler in 1829 were eventually published; the first, in 1831, by the ship's sailing master, Peter Bays, and the second, between 1848 and 1850, by crew member John Twyning. The survivors of the wreck attained the island of Vatoa, where they remained together for ten days before splitting into two parties. Bays's party took to sea again, and reached Tongatapu, from which he eventually departed for New Zealand; Twyning was among those who remained at Vatoa for four months, before being taken to Lakemba. He ultimately spent nineteen years in Fiji, Wallis, Futuna and Tonga. Where Twyning becomes a beachcomber, Bays is only ever a castaway. The period of overlap in their stories is a briefly narrated beginning to Twyning's narrative; for Bays, a more limited experience must assume greater significance, in order not only to produce the substance of a text, but in doing so to recuperate what is an involuntary sojourn outside the familiar social realm. The inconsistencies between the two accounts represent a double standard.

Bays depicts his experiences as providential. His story points the moral: '*Man's extremity is God's opportunity.*' In his account, the biblical text supplants the text of the map as a guide for the castaways.

He claims that the *Minerva*'s incomplete maps are responsible for the wreck: 'had the shoal been laid down in our charts, it is almost impossible that we should have struck here'. Unlike these fallible texts, of which the 'latest edition' is requisite, the Bible provides enduring guidance. The map becomes erased: 'there was a chart of the Fegee and Friendly islands saved out of the wreck, but it was so sodden with salt water during the night, that it was totally defaced in the morning', and in the absence of this text the unmediated operation of a divine authorial hand is revealed: '[we prayed] that God would remember us now in our great extremity, and, as we had no chart to direct us, that he would send us such a wind, that we might be constrained to see his hand alone in the preservation of our lives'. Gathering momentum from supplicatory success, Bays announces the divine finale: 'God had hitherto manifested himself as our deliverer, without any help from man, – He will now, independent of human aid, show himself our preserver.' His experience produces substantial claims for the biblical text: 'whosoever is in the possession of a Bible cannot be poor: – he has a treasure within himself'. The representation of the Word as sustenance in a scenario of extreme physical suffering marks the absolute subordination of experience to discourse.[45] Twyning's subsequent version of events, however, casts doubt upon the veracity of Bays's narrative. Twyning suggests that the sailing master's actions during the shipwreck were self-serving.[46] The elision of personal agency involved in Bays's adoption of the providential narrative mode may incorporate an evasion of culpability. The production of a second witness, Twyning, reintroduces behind Bays's divine author the figure of the dubious narrator.

Fears of unreliability, then, were not only derived from a consciousness of the status of the narrator as social outsider. The beachcomber 'gone native' could also manifest the instability of those 'civilised' values that other Europeans and Americans were simultaneously endeavouring to inculcate throughout the Pacific islands, highlighting a recidivist potential within their own societies. The missionary George Vason was landed on Tongatapu as part of the London Missionary Society's Pacific initiative, in April 1797. A better convert than converter of the Tongans, Vason became the proprietor of a prosperous fifteen-acre estate, and participated in the civil wars that commenced in Tonga in 1799. The confessional text produced upon his return to England attempted to recuperate lapse as example. Vason's experiences are formulated by 'a clergyman of the established church', who describes his discreet interposition in the text's production as the conventional act of editorial ventriloquism:

The composer trusts . . . that in order to avoid circumlocution, and to render the Narrative more interesting, he may be permitted to use the first person instead of the third. By letting the Author relate his own life, while the writer only arranges the thoughts, and clothes them with language, the varying sentiments, sensations and motives, that actuated him in every changing circumstance and event, will be more exactly delineated.

This substitution attempts to close the fissure opened up by Vason's declension; the contingency of authorship reaffirms the unity of evangelical discourse. But the desire to 'clothe' is an ambiguous sign of the recovery of the Christian subject, the product of a post-lapsarian, as well as a renewedly civilised, impulse. The need to distinguish between 'established' and errant Christian effectively produces a divided authorial identity: 'Having said this of the Author, the composer begs leave to state of himself, that his principal design in this Narrative is, to promote the conversion of the heathen, and to give to missionary labours, the best direction by an impartial and genuine display of their present miserable and degraded state.'[47] The ambiguity here – are the heathen, or rather missionary labours, 'miserable and degraded'? – is of a type created by Vason's example.

The desire both to recuperate declension and to distinguish lapsed missionary and unregenerate heathen from Christian compositor and civilised society produces a conflicted narrative voice. The already divided functions of narrator and compiler are further multiplied in the preface into the trinity 'writer', 'Author' and 'composer'. At the conclusion of the narrative, the capitalised Author is revealed explicitly to be God: God occupies Vason's voice, and the unity of purpose of Father, prodigal son and spiritual amanuensis is declared:

If some soul should be guarded, by these memoirs, from yielding to negligence and presumption, either in distant climes, or in their own land; . . . the great wish of the Missionary, seduced abroad, and reclaimed at home, will be completed, and the design of the compiler of the narrative fully answered; and to the Triune Author of all good, shall be all the praise.[48]

Redemption is predicated upon a displaced subject: a reader on
the brink of declension. The final words of the text are given to 'an
eminent writer' – a generic title which, like that of the 'clergyman
of the established church', implies at once universality and self-
dissociation. His appendix offers a heavy-handed extrapolation of
the lessons of Vason's story, prompted by his perusal of the manuscript. The text's potential audience of lapsed Christians is recast
as an enclosed circle of discursive initiates, engaged in a project of
self-affirming reiteration.

Within the framework of Vason's narrative, distinction must also
be drawn between the circumscribed lapse of the missionary and
the typically errant beachcomber. The missionary party to which
he initially belongs are met at Tongatabu by three beachcombers,
Ambler, Conelly and Morgan, whose criminality they easily infer.
This trio were the first beachcombers to establish themselves in
Tonga. They were landed in a group of one seaman and five
convict stowaways from the American ship *Otter* in 1796.[49] The missionaries embody a new type of foreign subject in Tonga, threatening the hitherto unique representative status of the
beachcombers. In social terms, typical early missionaries actually
lacked superior prestige. Until the 1840s, they were recruited
from the 'mechanic', or lower middle and working classes – Vason
was employed before his conversion as a bricklayer – and espoused
an ethic of poverty.[50] Where the Christians perceive the distinction
between themselves and the beachcombers to be ethical, however,
for the latter it is social, and only to be circumvented by the fabrication of an exaggerated status of their own: '[The beachcombers]
gave it out, that they were persons of the greatest consequence,
that one was the king's son, the other a duke, or a great chief; but
that we were only of the lower class, and servants to them in our
own country.'[51]

In fact objects, rather than words, serve as the touchstones of
status. According to Vason, 'Whatever pretensions they made of
being dukes or princes, the natives had sense enough to conclude,
that if they were really men of rank, they would have received presents from their country, as well as ourselves. But as they had none
to bestow, they were treated with little respect.' The introduction
of the metropolitan article into circulation within Pacific gift
economies was a literal 'taking possession'; the first stage in the
expansion of commodity exchange into the peripheral context.

Yet property also introduced risk. The writer of the appendix perceives displays of material wealth to create a focus for intercultural aggression:

Voluntary poverty, and a trust in providence for daily bread, and a willingness to live like the natives, as to food, lodging, &c. is essential to the character of a missionary. To send him rich, (for European manufactures, however cheap and coarse are *riches*, among savages), is to expose him to robbers and murderers. He will have no safety, and feel that he has none, till he is reduced to that poverty, which he should at first have chosen.[52]

The first Europeans in the Pacific sought to achieve an authority informed by cross-culturally compatible notions of propertied class. The beachcombers' initial representative status did not, however, give them the freedom to invent lineage, since claims to rank required the substantiation of the gift. But the beachcombers and Tongans effectively mapped a set of roles, predicated on the status of otherness, which circumscribed those available to the missionaries who arrived subsequently: so missionaries are advised, above, to 'live like the natives', in order to prevent the Pacific islanders from adopting the type of the criminal beachcomber, and becoming 'robbers and murderers'.

Vason's experience of declension is contextualised by a further encounter with genuine lapse. The ship that eventually rescues him from Tonga returns another, unrepentantly nativised missionary from Tahiti to 'civilisation'. Although Vason evades any direct recognition of compatibility, this Mr Benjamin Broomhall cannot but provide him with an uneasy reflection:

my mind was not at ease, contrasting my own destitute situation with that of those around me, and ashamed of my exposed appearance among those who were more decently clothed (for I was still in want of many articles of dress), I began to reflect on my past strange life and conduct, and to look forward with shame and anxiety to a return to my native country.

It is the lapsed Christian who plays the Samaritan to Vason's fallen condition, donating him clothing, and so covering his nakedness as the compiler will later 'clothe' his history in text. Yet a final mirror encounter – occurring subsequent to this in the story, though situated earlier, and therefore less conclusively, within his narrative – reveals Vason to be indelibly inscribed by his Tongan experiences. While he is bathing in New York, wearing only the tattooing that 'bears so admirable a resemblance to a close dress that it might in some circumstances be taken for it', a youthful onlooker recognises an emperor with no clothes:

Some people not far off, who saw me enter the water, supposing that I was swimming in trowsers, came near to look at me. I remained in the water till they had walked away, but a boy about fifteen stayed till I came out: he looked at me with great surprise, as though he could not believe his senses, and upon coming nearer, exclaimed, 'I thought you had got some clothes on.' Others upon hearing him began to approach, and had I not put on my clothes, their curiosity also, it is probable, would have discovered equal cause for surprise.[53]

Vason is exposed in civilisation wearing the garb of an exotic culture; to clothe him or his narrative is not to cover spiritual nakedness, but the inscription of that culture.

Unlike the typical beachcomber, Vason has entered the exotic realm as ambassador to rather than absconder from civilisation. But the ultimate lesson of his mission is the necessity of preaching to the already colonially converted. Among the papers of his original missionary party is a statement concerning the abandonment of the Tahitian mission, which affirms the necessity of combining secular settlement with missionary enterprise: 'As a rational Object it is of great importance, as a Missionary Object, infinitely greater.'[54] Both Vason's text and appendix stress the importance to the missionary enterprise of encountering societies familiar with metropolitan values of civil law and the sanctity of property:

it is of vast importance to begin with places, in which, however uncivilised and sunk in pagan darkness, the laws and the police protect the persons and properties of men, without discrimination, from fraud, and violence; and where theft, robbery, and murder, meet with condign punishment; and where persecution for religion is the principal danger to which Missionaries are exposed.

Force must, it seems, precede discourse in encounters with peripheral societies. Vason's narrative threatens to reveal that cultures cannot integrate, that the missionary endeavour is a foreclosed one. The text inscribes a structural dislocation, between the periphery as the site of lapse and the metropolis as the source of the book of repentance, paralleled by the fissure between Vason's agency within the narrative and his expressed aim of producing a redeemed subject in the reader.

In the oral cultural context of Tonga, missionaries were forced

to translate their text into performance: 'We . . . availed ourselves
of every suitable opportunity to perform our daily worship, to sing
and pray, when they were present.'[55] Unable, in the initial absence
of a mutual language, to dictate significance, their enactments
produced the effect of pure theatre. The evangelical message was,
ironically, only retrospectively revealed to the Tongans by the
beachcomber William Mariner. As Martin reports: 'The king and
several other chiefs at the Tonga islands appeared quite surprised
when Mr Mariner informed them that the object of the missionaries had been to instruct them in the religion of the white people:
they had thought that the latter came to live among them merely
from choice, as liking the climate better than their own.'[56]
Counteracting this failure to communicate intention, Vason's text
is laden with exegesis. The writer's attempt to render his subject's
story as providential produces a stilted interweaving of narrative
with biblical quotation: 'We saw indeed "the wonders" of the Lord
"in the deep": we heard "the stormy wind arise", and it soon "lifted
up the waves" of the sea. We seemed to "be carried up to the
Heaven above", and now again to go down to "Hell beneath". "The
souls of some began to melt away for fear."' But the voice of belated
evangelism remains conflicted. Vason's overruling sin at the time
of his initial conversion to Christianity has been the use of profane
language: 'I was addicted to swearing and cursing.' This is recognised as a kindred practice by the beachcombers he encounters in
Tonga: 'Thinking we were as bad as themselves, they swore with the
fluency of abandoned seamen.'[57] Where Vason's conversion has
involved enforcing control upon his tongue, the legacy of blasphemy remains a shadow presence behind the text of confession.

It is as beachcomber rather than missionary that Vason in fact
achieves that ideal of civility espoused by his text. In the representation of Vason's secular estate in Tonga, the narrative
enshrines an image of ordered community: 'My little farm was a
garden throughout. Many came to offer themselves for workmen.'
This Edenic site is repeatedly described, with echoes of Milton, in
terms of an harmonious interweaving: 'sheltered on the outside
with a skilful intertexture of the branches of the plantain tree'; 'the
rows of sugar canes . . . embowered and entwined themselves so as
to form a shady walk'. The appropriateness of each element within
this tapestry in turn provides the basis of a natural law: a thief is at
one point 'detected by some other natives, who with great dexter-

ity, discovered that he was the person who had stolen some pines and plantains, by bringing the fruits to the trees, from which they had been robbed, and fitting them to the branches where they had been broken off'. It is within this ideal community that Vason becomes fluent in Tongan speech, achieving a correspondingly idealised level of communicative exchange. In the night-time communion of the male aristocrats of Tonga, he finds himself rendered the object of speculation: 'I have heard them for hours talking of us, our articles, dress, and customs, and entertaining each other with conjectures respecting the distance of the country, whence we came, the nature of it, its productions.' Yet it is in such conversation that an alternative to the fallen discourse of cursing or the misconstrued preaching of the missionaries is adumbrated: 'I have been delighted, for hours, in listening to these nocturnal confabulations, and often very much surprised and improved, by the shrewdness of their observations, and the good sense of their reasonings.'[58]

Since it proves impossible to have faith in a beachcomber narrator, duplicity emerges as a standard for authorship: Hadfield's 'gift of fabrication'. The beachcomber narrative has precedents in the eighteenth-century traditions of the 'rogue's tale', or criminal biography, in which criticism of the social status quo via the figure of the 'other within' was licensed and defused in the fictional context.[59] Yet the question of literary authenticity persists. H. Stonehewer Cooper repudiates as inauthentic the dominant representation of the beachcomber during the colonial period, claiming that 'The future of Polynesia, in a moral and commercial sense, seems to me to be a very important business problem with which sentiment has little or nothing to do. "Pretty" writing, comparing beachcombers to lotus eaters, or dwelling as some people have done exclusively on the poetical side that does unquestionably attach to their existence, is, to my mind, beside the mark.'[60] Cooper suggests that literary and colonial discourses conflicted rather than collaborated in representing the beachcomber. The translocation of the beachcomber from the periphery to the library shelf involved editors and publishers in a romance of character creation. Hadfield's transformation of Cannibal Jack's narrative from artefact to literary article, approximately eighty years after the events of his story took place, required the mediation of multiple frames. The book Hadfield received from William

Diaper in 1889, and which documents events occurring forty years prior to writing, was not published until 1928. On the first page 'a photograph of the book in which the autobiography was written' represents the weathered manuscript, textured rather than textual, artefact of another climate and the passing of time; evocative of the distances that the book has survived. A foreword is provided by H. de Vere Stacpoole, author of *The Blue Lagoon* (1908), whose own bestseller, like the typical beachcomber text, offered a mixed representation of licence and socialisation in its depiction of castaways upon a Pacific island. Stacpoole welcomes Diaper's maverick text into the selective adventure catalogue of his personal library: 'For my own part this book goes on the shelf beside Aloysius Horn's *Ivory Coast in the Earlies* and Melville's *Typee*, feeling sure, as I do, that neither Horn nor the author of *Omoo* would turn up their noses at the company of William Diapea.'[61]

It remains a body and a voice, rather than a text, that Stacpoole places on his shelves, an oral production that print evokes:

Mr Hadfield and the Publishers are to be congratulated on their rare good taste in preserving the original manuscript from the touch of any 'literary' hand. A page here and there may be cloudy, but any cloudiness is not of style but of speech; for Cannibal Jack does not write, he talks: he button-holes you, he belches in your face; when he has done, it is not the end of a book, but the stopping of a voice.

The foreword is followed by Hadfield's introduction, which highlights the contradictions inherent in the beachcomber's adoption of the authorial role. Diaper's voice is belatedly perceived as modern. His writing occurs between excess and constraint – between the private realm of eccentricity and the public world of material distribution: he has a 'mania for scribbling', but insufficient stationery. Like his book – a tattered artefact that finds a place in a distinguished library – Cannibal Jack represents literary authority in minimal garb, unconventional material. Hadfield writes: 'Altogether – despite his old and frayed apparel – he was a man of distinguished bearing. To make a general comparison of his appearance with one well known to us all, I would invite the reader to think of Mr Bernard Shaw.' Ultimately for its editor, Diaper's narrative achieves literary status as exemplary realism: 'Much as his story is reminiscent of Robinson Crusoe, he did not appear to me to be a member of the school of romanticists. His range of experience was so wide that he had no need to draw on his imagination, as did Defoe.'[62] The peripheral context of representation, rather than the tradition of the English romance, authorises the account of the beachcomber.

The redefinition of cannibal text as consumable product, of unorthodoxy as authorial, was not immediate. During the Victorian period, when Hadfield first encountered Diaper's manuscript, the voice of its author was inadmissible as literature: 'My regret on closing the book was that the writer had used such coarse language and described events in so realistic a manner as to preclude any thought of publication. I therefore stowed the MS. away with other derelict material.' Cannibal Jack must wait to find his audience not among the censorious Victorians, but in the modern century of a generation of grown-up Victorian sons: 'it would have remained in obscurity or have been destroyed had it not been unearthed and perused by one of my sons who reads every scrap of South Sea literature he can lay his hands on, and who clamoured for its immediate publication.' The publisher's postscript identifies this boy reader as the mature professional, Dr J. A. Hadfield, whose enthusiasm for South Seas stories may involve a nostalgia for the scenes of his youth. The literary reclamation of the beachcomber narrative for the genre of High Adventure locates the text in the paradoxical territory where the child is father to the man. Diaper himself equates his writing with procreation, claiming:

My acquaintances, who, by the by, seem to know as much of my antecedents as I do myself, have long since declared that I am the reputed father of 38 children, and 99 grandchildren, and so, that being the case, I shall in a very few years more be the great-grandfather of 999 – perhaps 1,000 – great-grandchildren, and if I live long enough for this to become a *fait accompli* . . . I think I shall then be entitled to gratulate [*sic*] myself on not having lived or written in vain.[63]

The heirs of Cannibal Jack – the end of his literary and personal endeavours, who 'entitle' him, where his own title renders him an object of reputation – are a posterity of cross-cultural subjects, with whom Hadfield's son, the 'boy' reader, implicitly claims kinship. Beachcombers' half-caste children often received a valuable inheritance: they were typically the first recipients of the beachcombers' carefully guarded technological knowledge. An instance of this restricted cross-cultural pedagogy is provided by William B. Churchward, who writes of the beachcomber John Stowes 'having well brought up a most respectable family, the sons to mechanical trades, the daughters being as well educated as the opportunities of the country permit'.[64] As H. E. Maude notes, 'few balked at imparting their skills to their own children who . . . tended to follow the occupations of their white fathers'.[65] The passing on of skills from the beachcombers to island populations occurred, not as immediate exchange, but with the merging of racial cultures across generations.

A further frame for Diaper's narrative is provided by the publisher's note, which narrows focus to the printed text. His publishing policy has been one of discretion. Print, he informs the reader, has attempted to imitate, rather than compose, manuscript: 'It has been thought better to leave even slips of the pen untouched, for these slips are often characteristic of the writer.' The postscript to this preface claims for Hadfield's text the authority of final word: it publishes a letter from a trader acquaintance of Diaper's, which establishes the death of the author and the destruction of his remaining papers. Yet Cannibal Jack's slippery hand destabilizes this claim to finality. A disparity persists between the orthographies of the trader's letter and the printed text: the former refers to John Diaper, where the latter is the work of William Diapea.[66] The survival of another fragment of Diaper's story under the pen name of Jackson – a precursor of which Hadfield's publishers remain apparently unaware – further complicates authorial identity.[67] 'Jackson', son of Jack, is both progeny and predecessor of Hadfield's narrator. The authorial subject is left irresolvably doubled and elusive, although the final foreword to the printed narrative, 'a slightly reduced facsimile of a page from the original manuscript', attests to the ultimate integrity of the authorial hand.

Where the beachcomber, as mediator of metropolitan knowledge in the Pacific, played a provisional role, as text he endures. The reclamation of his account mirrors the activity of beachcombing: publication transforms 'derelict material' – the cast-up manuscript – into object of potential value – the printed book. Diaper practised a comparable trade in Tonga:

I bought and begged all the books – new and old – I could lay my hands upon, restitched the old ones, and re-covered them with gaudy covers in the little book-binding press which I had myself made, and then placed them with new titles in my bookshelves, which I had also constructed myself, where they became the general attraction, and not one of these books left those shelves for less than the thousand per cent. profit.

Forged publication is just one of 'about fifty irons in the fire' which constitute Diaper's livelihood.[68] The scarcity of print at the periphery extends authorial licence to *bricolage*. Yet such substitutions reflect those involved in publishing Diaper's narrative at the metropolitan centre: the hawking of fragment as book; the reissuing of a story under a different name.

TEXT AND PERFORMANCE: THE RETURN
OF THE BEACHCOMBER

For those beachcombers who eventually returned to their country of origin, the book often served as an immediate means of self-support. Back home, the beachcombers lost their status as technological initiates, and were reinstated as the tools of technology. Never prodigal sons, they were restored from a lifestyle based upon the thrifty exploitation of a limited material legacy to an inheritance of labour. Those disabled by their experiences abroad were unfit for the types of manual activity to which their social backgrounds consigned them. Returned from cultures prepared to accept them as representatives of 'civilisation' to a home community that defined itself against the types of otherness they embodied, these beachcombers peddled their self-representations as unofficial publications, or 'mendicant' texts. Samuel Patterson, an American seaman who spent periods of time in Hawaii between 1803 and 1807, and was wrecked on Fiji in 1808, published two cheap editions of his narrative, at the expense of subscribers. Patterson's socio-educational background and crippled body disqualified him within his own culture. As he explains:

Deprived of the use of [my] limbs, . . . the publick will at once perceive there are but few employments to which [I] can resort with any hope of being useful. Having no opportunities for acquiring an education in early life, and having since I was ten years of age followed the seas, I of course am not fitted to pursue any of the mechanical or intellectual avocations of a sedentary nature, in which, had my education fitted me for an accountant, or had I been master of some trade, I might have succeeded in supporting myself.[69]

Patterson's story was compiled and endorsed by ministers of the gospel as a narrative of conversion. His experience was rendered exemplary: the beachcomber finding a use, despite disablement, as text, the subject of a sermon.

Archibald Campbell found that, despite having suffered an amputation prior to his sojourn in Hawaii, his disability did not prevent him from serving as representative white man at the highest level of Hawaiian society:

My appearance attracted the notice, and excited the compassion of the queen; and finding it was my intention to remain upon the islands, she invited me to take up my residence in her house. I gladly availed myself of this offer, at which she expressed much pleasure; it being a great object of ambition amongst the higher ranks to have white people to reside with them.

Upon his return to Edinburgh he was admitted to the infirmary, his wounds having never properly healed, but was, as his editor James Smith narrates, 'dismissed as incurable. [He] contrived to earn a miserable pittance, by crawling about the streets of Edinburgh and Leith, grinding music, and selling a metrical history of his adventures.' By Smith's intervention the 'incurable' was recuperated discursively; his mendicant text upgraded into a respectable publication. Yet it was ultimately as performer rather than as text that Campbell managed to improve his standard of employment. Smith concludes his biographical sketch: 'Being ambitious, however, of performing on a more dignified instrument, he has since learned to play on the violin; and he finds employment on board the steam-boats that ply upon the river Clyde, by playing for the amusement of the steerage passengers.'[70]

As performer, the beachcomber could maintain an identity in translocation, supporting himself by representing the culture from which he had come, even as he had in the Pacific islands. The practice of tattooing meant that the body of the repatriated white man often bore the inscription of an alien aesthetic, which could serve as the text of performance. Not simply of anthropological or artistic value, the tattoo was also the scandalous sign of degeneration. The architect Adolf Loos summed up a perception of scarification which was not simply the product of his own Modernist aesthetic, when he criticised the 'perverse and polymorphous sensuality of the man who "covers with tattoos his own skin, his boat, his paddle, in short anything he can lay his hands on"'. Loos claimed that where the tattooed Papuan 'is not a delinquent, . . . the modern man who tattoos himself is a delinquent or degener-

Plate 2. 'A Chieftain of Tongataboo', frontispiece to James Orange,
Narrative of the Late George Vason, of Nottingham.

ate'.[71] Jean Cabri, a beachcomber returned from his adopted
home in the Marquesas to Europe by Krusenstern's Russian
expedition to the Pacific, was initially appreciated as a cultural
artefact. He was taken by the Russians to Kamchatka, where he
proved an object of scientific curiosity. Initially he represented a
text rather than an actor. He had forgotten his native language
(French), and his body and face were almost completely scarified.
Indelibly inscribed and lacking the language for self-interpreta-
tion, he was a figure of indecipherability. Loss of an original
tongue was not an unfamiliar occurrence among beachcombers.
The first missionary party to Tahiti reported that a European they
encountered had forgotten his own language though he 'had not
been more than five years among the islands', and related this phenomenon to his illiteracy:

Perhaps something might be said in excuse for him; he never could read;
but had he possessed only a small share of literature, it is likely abstract
or speculative ideas would have sometimes arisen in his mind, to express
which, words of his native language connected with such ideas would naturally and of necessity recur, that of the islands being too penurious.[72]

In the Pacific, the beachcomber was required to perform
Western subjectivity. John Jackson, whom I earlier quoted as
expressing dissatisfaction with his status as foreign novelty, experienced a peculiarly telling alienation from his performative role,
when he witnessed a Fijian impersonation of the beachcomber at
a masquerade in Viti Levu. As he narrates:

An individual . . . took the character of a white man, and performed it so
well, that he caused great mirth. He was clothed like a sailor, armed with
a cutlass, and as a substitute for bad teeth (which is a proverbial characteristic of white men amongst these people), he had short pieces of black
pipe-stems placed irregularly, which answered very well. The nose of his
mask was of disproportionate length (which they also say is another
prominent feature, adding nothing to the beauty of white men). His hat
was cocked on three hairs, in the sailor fashion, and made from banana
leaves. In his mouth was a short black pipe, which he was puffing away as
he strolled about, cutting the tops of any tender herb that happened to
grow on either side . . . This mimicking sailor acted his part cleverly, and
paid no attention whatever to decorum, but strutted about puffing away
at his pipe as unconcerned as though he was walking the forecastle. He
detached himself from the crowd, flourishing his cutlass about and
gaping alternately in all quarters, as though he was a stranger just arrived,
when some of the masqueraders reminded him that he was in the pres-

ence of Tui Dreketi. He immediately asked who Tui Dreketi was, and could not be made to understand, till some of them looked in the direction the king was sitting, when he pointed (which is greatly against the rules), and asked if that was the 'old bloke', walking up to him bolt upright and offering his hand, which the king smilingly shook. The sailor then told him that he had better take a whiff or two with him, as it was the best tobacco he had smoked for many a day. The king, willing to make the best of the amusement, took the pipe, the spectators making the air ring again with their shouts and laughter, 'Vavalagi dina, dina sara' (a real white man, a real white man).[73]

There is much to enjoy in this passage, with its depiction of the performers' canny recognition of foreign insensitivity to local etiquette, and of the contests of authority that take place at contact. Displaced into the context of mimicry, a transgression and indirect interrogation of Fijian society's own boundaries of authority, as well as of Western cultural narcissism, becomes licensed. The Fijians' ability to measure the gap between the white man's degenerate appearance and his assumption of the role of bearer of the Western gift, tobacco, offers an uncomfortable reflection for the beachcomber Jackson, which he attempts to evade by himself acting as translator and exegete, playing cultural insider, while identifying the object of satire as 'a stranger just arrived'. Returned beachcombers such as Jean Cabri adopted an equally alienated performative relationship to their former identity when they returned to Europe. He exhibited his tattoos and Marquesan dancing and played cannibal charades for the high society of Moscow and St Petersburg, exploiting a self-objectifying relationship with the ranks of the society in which he had been washed up.[74]

But exhibition was ultimately a creative role for Cabri. The pictogram of his body became the pretext for invention: 'a gift of fabrication'. He ended up performing at fairs in Brittany and Paris, producing a text as supplement to his act, in which he elaborated his status as other. As Greg Dening discovered:

He had a small pamphlet written about himself, no doubt to distribute with his exhibition as he wandered through the *départements* of France. He billed himself in the pamphlet as 'Judge of Nukuhiva'. . . . It was a showman's licence and his pamphlets, reprinted with slightly different details for each of the cities he visited, bent the truth in other ways.[75]

The variations between these mendicant texts reflect the beachcomber's perception that identity could be rewritten with change of location. He had become author of the text he physically bore, reinterpreting it performatively. Cabri's fabrications also made their way into legitimate publications, undermining the authority of other writers, even as he offered them the story they desired. Robert Ker Porter met Cabri in Moscow in 1806, and incorporated a sentimental version of the beachcomber's tale into his published volume of travel letters, brimming with references to his own sympathetic tears, and including 'an almost Shandean digression' on the subject of Cabri's tattoos.[76] Porter's sister Jane also wrote a story based on the experience of Cabri. Bill Pearson defines the genre of Cabri's tale in Porter's rendition as 'both genteel and sentimental, in the rhetoric of the Gothic novel'.[77] In transmitting his narrative to a metropolitan literary audience, Cabri participates in rewriting realism as romance, reportage as sentimental fiction. It was only when his voice had been finally silenced that science could propose to repossess him as artefact. After his death, museums at Valenciennes proposed keeping his tattooed hide for display and scientific examination.[78]

James O'Connell, the consummate beachcomber self-fabricator, invented himself in performance. O'Connell made his name as 'The Tattooed Man' after returning from the Pacific to the United States in 1835. He performed in circuses until his death in 1854, like Cabri producing accompanying mendicant publications. His editor Saul Reisenberg suspects that O'Connell's tattoos were a disguise, reprinting a body inscribed with convict brands. The inflicted text of the tattoo itself remains open to accusations of forgery. According to Reisenberg, the tattooing operation which O'Connell describes in his narrative, involving incision with shells, and colouring with charcoal and berry juice, was not authentically Ponapean. Circus-goers reported that his upper body, including his face, was incised with blue–black and red welts. Reisenberg concludes that:

If red designs were seen, and if any of them were on the chest, possibly the descriptions are of another man who performed under O'Connell's name, as was sometimes the case in those days among rival circuses, when a successful act would be imitated and the name taken as well. But it could also mean that James might have thought it necessary to enhance his exhibition value by improving on the Ponapean style.[79]

The beachcomber performer is author rather than genuine anthropological artefact, embellishing his text. But lacking a copyright, his work is once again impossible to authenticate; duplicate rather than signature. It is precisely in the space between representation and fabrication that the beachcomber subsisted, both at the periphery and back within metropolitan society. His productions – the manufactured object, the book, the performance, the tattoo – bear the traces of this double design.

CHAPTER 2

Lip service and conversion

The beachcomber was metropolitan representative to the Pacific by proxy; the missionary was representative by project. The declared aim of missionary enterprise was the moral transformation of 'heathens' or 'cannibals' into 'civilised' Pacific citizens. Yet the initial impediments to communication raised by the absence of a common tongue meant that this ambition was realised in material terms before it was realised in the spirit. The first stage of the missionary project was an external transformation: the clothing of the native, the importation of the artefacts of 'civilisation'. The introduction of sophisticated material culture was posited as a metaphor for spiritual 'improvement'; a mere outward manifestation, which under the circumstances of contact attained the status of primary sign. This order of priority, however, left evangelical discourse fissured. Jean and John Comaroff's description of the relationship between the advent of missionary teaching and the advent of capitalism in Africa could equally be applied to the Pacific context:

The impact of Protestant evangelists as harbingers of industrial capitalism lay in the fact that their civilizing mission was simultaneously symbolic and practical, theological and temporal. The goods and techniques they brought with them . . . presupposed the messages and meanings they proclaimed in the pulpit, and vice versa. Both were vehicles of a moral economy that celebrated the global spirit of commerce, the commodity, and the imperial marketplace.[1]

The missionary was involved in the introduction of goods that were to serve simultaneously as testimonies to Christian superiority. The status of material and symbolic gifts is a significant theme in Christian theology. Its tensions are apparent in the parable of the talents, which teaches that spiritual capital only matures if one recognises the imperative to invest gifts and account for returns.

By making explicit the link between material and spiritual economies, the discourse of missionary contact spelled out Christian metaphor, espousing a physically evident conversion. But this externalist emphasis in turn rendered the notion of salvation vulnerable to mimicry.

The notion of mimicry as subversion was theorised by Homi Bhabha in his virtuoso essay, 'Of Mimicry and Man', in relation to the distinction between the theory and practice of colonial administration. Bhabha argued that the project and discourse of colonialism were fissured by the conflicting desire 'for a reformed, recognizable Other, *as a subject of a difference that is almost the same, but not quite'*. The conflicted desire to produce colonial subjects and institutions whose identity confirmed their originals, while maintaining an equally affirming sense of difference and distinction, was matched by an ambivalence registered in the colonial imitation between mimicry and mockery. Bhabha describes the politics of this ambivalence as follows:

It is from [the] area between mimicry and mockery, where the reforming, civilizing mission is threatened by the displacing gaze of its disciplinary double, that my instances of colonial imitation come. What they all share is a discursive process by which the excess or slippage produced by the *ambivalence* of mimicry (almost the same, *but not quite*) does not merely 'rupture' the discourse, but becomes transformed into an uncertainty which fixes the colonial subject as a 'partial' presence. . . . The success of colonial appropriation depends on a proliferation of inappropriate objects that ensure its strategic failure, so that mimicry is at once resemblance and menace.[2]

The evangelical mission was the archetypal 'reforming, civilizing mission'. Missionary documents are strained by incompatible desires to produce converts at once recognisably Christian (resemblance), and yet residually other (menace). Simple imitation, in societies such as those of the Pacific, where oral mnemonic skills were traditionally cultivated, could not provide adequate testimony of conversion. Yet the forms of cultural translation by which Pacific islanders represented Christianity upon their own terms threatened to transform its message beyond recognition.

In this chapter I turn first to two early missionary accounts, which are each representative of a different relationship of exchange with particular Pacific communities: John Williams's

Missionary Enterprises, and William Ellis's *Polynesian Researches.* John Williams promoted the metropolitan object as sign of spiritual advancement: a material testimony. William Ellis brought to the Pacific that most successful of technological testimonies: the culture of print. Print, of course, represents the traditional Christian bridging point between the spiritual and the material: the site at which the Word of inspiration is made text. Ellis's example focuses a range of issues concerning the relationship between tangible and intangible spiritual gifts. In discussing Williams's case before Ellis's, I reverse historical chronology in favour of paradigm. The printing press in fact arrived at the Society Islands, site of the earliest evangelical endeavours, some years before Williams began to make contact with island groups such as the Cooks and Samoa. Generally, however, the book was the culminating, rather than the initial example of cultural advancement proffered by missionary evangelists. The earliest missionaries to the Pacific were selected for their mechanical, rather than literary skills. Outlining the qualifications of initial candidates, Thomas Haweis wrote: 'These are usually not literary Men, tho a few of good attainments in knowledge have offered themselves', claiming that the directors of the society were 'Not . . . persuaded that deep attainments in literary pursuits in all Missionaries will be so essential to the great Object we have in view, and not having any prospect, that a Member of this Sort Sufficient for our purposes could be procured'.[3] The primacy of the Society Islands on the missionary agenda, however, lead to the introduction of literacy there earlier than in other regions of Polynesia.

The two missionary texts that I have chosen to examine offer typical but nuanced accounts of initial relationships of exchange. In both cases, I discuss the ways in which Christian discourse is fractured and exposed by those same assumptions that were deemed necessary to transmit its tenets to the Pacific context. I focus on the context of reception depicted in these accounts: on representations of audiences and classrooms, in which it is repeatedly the indigenous interrogator who draws attention to the inconsistencies and fissures within evangelist discourse. In the second half of the chapter I look at two explicit forms of local commentary that arose from missionary contact: the authorised mediation of native preachers, and the unauthorised critique of cult leaders. I suggest that the boundaries between official and illicit discourse are often less apparent in their content than they are in form.

MISSIONARIES AND TRADE: THE CASE OF JOHN WILLIAMS

The transmission of the Christian Word to the Pacific was a task divided between several missionary groups. The London Missionary Society (LMS: founded in 1795, and known simply as the Missionary Society until 1818) first sent missionaries to Tahiti, Tonga and the Marquesas in the *Duff* in 1796–7. These parties left Polynesia under political threat, but the LMS resumed its Tahitian mission in 1811, with the support of King Pomare II. In 1822 the first Wesleyan missionary arrived in Tonga. Wesleyan activity spread to the Lau Islands and Samoa, but the rival interests of the LMS forced their withdrawal from Samoa in 1836, and they did not return until 1857. The American Board of Commissioners for Foreign Missions established a mission in Hawaii in 1820, and expanded into Micronesia after 1851. The Board ceased sending missionaries to Hawaii after 1854. Roman Catholic missionary activity commenced in Hawaii in 1827, and in Tahiti by 1841. The Mormon church also established a mission at Tahiti in 1844, and gained influence in Tubuai and the Tuamotus.[4]

Multiple orthodoxies meant multiple interpretations. Missionary practice was often politicised and rivalrous – for instance, English Protestant missionaries openly opposed French Catholic expansion into the Society Islands, for a combination of nationalistic and religious reasons.[5] It was the awareness that such divisions undermined the claim to represent a universal discourse which led missionary groups to negotiate for separate spheres of influence within the Pacific. John Williams, who was of LMS allegiance, remarked

upon the desirableness of every Society having a distinct sphere of labour among a heathen people. Much as I should rejoice in being associated with an Episcopalian, a Baptist, or a Methodist brother, who did not attach primary importance to secondary objects, yet the interests of every Mission, especially in the earlier stages of its progress, seem to me to require another line of conduct. The natives, though comprehending but very imperfectly our objects, would at once discern a difference in the modes of worship, and their attention would of necessity be divided and distracted.[6]

In turn, boundaries of missionary influence came to reflect pre-existing political divisions between different Polynesian chiefdoms. In Samoa, for instance, Williams gained the support of the high chief Malietoa, who exploited the foreigners' understanding of unified rule to instate himself as king in their eyes. He was then able to increase his prestige within Samoa as the first recipient of European firearms and hardware. Subsequently other chiefs, seeking similarly enhancing foreign connections, authorised beachcombers to act as their own 'spiritual' directors, exposing the politics of conversion. Local political claims could quickly unravel years of missionary labour. The missionary George Brown recorded despairingly in his diary the sudden defection of one district in Savai'i, Samoa, from LMS to Methodist allegiance, resisting the admission that religious preference was political rather than personal:

In the evening I was stunned with a letter sent to Mr Pratt by Mr King telling him to let me know that Vaitaimuli have all turned over to them. It quite upset me and I was very nearly ill from its effect. I cannot imagine how people can act thus. Such an act of black ingratitude I never expected to find in Samoa . . .

After service I went to Palauli and saw the Chiefs who have left us. They say they have no fault against me but simply wish to have one lotu in their villages. This of course is a lie but my hands are clean. They have shewn the blackest ingratitude but I leave it all to God.[7]

The reiteration of the word 'black' here may indicate a more than metaphoric status, signalling the missionary's sudden alienation from the Samoans, who are no longer flock, but differently coloured, incomprehensibly motivated, and other.

This chapter focuses primarily on LMS evangelical activity, which predominated in the Pacific at least until 1860. This group incorporated various denominations of British Protestantism, consciously aiming to subsume metropolitan conflict and dissent in the presentation of a united evangelical front at the periphery. An 'Address to Christian Ministers, and all other Friends of Christianity, on the subject of Missions to the Heathen' by Dr David Bogue, the initial advocate of a London Missionary Society, pointed out that 'the increase of union and friendly intercourse

among Christians of different denominations at home, is one of
the happy effects which will immediately flow from an institution
of this nature', while Thomas Smith, in his *History and Origin of the
Missionary Societies,* claims that the LMS,

unfettered by sectarian peculiarities, and desirous of merging party
names in one grand combination for the diffusion of divine light through
a barren and benighted world, extended the hand of cordial fellowship
to all the genuine friends of the Redeemer; and erected a banner,
beneath which both ministers and private Christians of evangelical
sentiments but of different denominations might, without the slightest
sacrifice of religious principal, concentrate all their energies with a view
to the spread of the everlasting gospel, the exaltation of a crucified Jesus,
and the eternal salvation of immortal souls.[8]

John Williams's career as a missionary was an ascent of the rungs
of capital.[9] He rose from 'godly mechanic' to shipbuilder, chief
advocate of missionary participation in trade, and ultimately ship
owner. An increase in social credential was broadly typical among
the LMS during the nineteenth century. The earliest missionaries
were artisan evangelists known as 'godly mechanics'. Their perceived task was to transmit a combined gospel of biblical and technical instruction. Among the first missionary party to Tahiti,
mechanical talents were valued over literary proficiency: 'We were
desirous to obtain some possessed of literary attainments, but
especially to procure adepts in such useful arts and occupations as
would make us most acceptable to the heathen in that state of inferior civilization to which they were advanced.'[10] After 1840 this
policy gave way to the education of 'gentleman missionaries'.[11]
The shift was partly due to Williams's personal influence. His
Missionary Enterprises – a book whose title links the missionary
project with capital venture – concludes with a call to the active
participation of the upper classes in missionary work. Williams
sent fifty advance copies to selected members of the British aristocracy, soliciting their support for a cause hitherto perceived to
be the province of the lower middle classes.[12] However, as Niel
Gunson has pointed out, Williams's own self-fashioning had a
secular telos. His appropriate inheritor was his son John Williams,
who accompanied his father to Samoa in the ship *Camden* in 1838
and established himself as Apia's first resident trader. Indeed, the
missionaries who travelled from England with the pair complained
of a conflict between commercial and spiritual interests, claiming
that 'one third of the "Camden" was occupied by goods belonging

to John Williams, Junior . . . It was even suggested that Williams planned it so "that the missionaries should be under the necessity of purchasing things from his son John"'.[13]

Certain of the objects that cluttered the *Camden*, however, were intended to serve evangelical purposes. Williams brought from England a magic lantern, the donation of a well-wisher. As his biographer Ebenezer Prout records, when asked what gift would be of service to his project,

Mr Williams replied, that as the Romish priests were on their way to the islands with electrifying machines, and other philosophical apparatus, by which they expected to impress the natives with their preternatural power, he thought he might legitimately, if it were necessary, turn their weapons against themselves; and as he intended, on the voyage, to translate Fox's Martyrology, he should like to illustrate it by the magic lantern. [His benefactor] procured for him a large instrument, and in addition to numerous other slides on Scripture, English and natural history, ordered a series to be well executed from the best plates in the Martyrologist's work, representing the tortures and deaths of the faithful confessors of Protestant Christianity.[14]

The lantern was a gift cannily selected by Williams in the confidence that objects were the tools of his intentions. The same 'apparatus' which is witchcraft and weapon in Catholic hands is to become legitimate and useful in his own. Yet even as Williams harnesses the instrument to his didactic project, the topic of martyrdom threatens a confusion with Catholic doctrine, so that 'Protestant' must be introduced as a term of distinction. Other missionary groups were more cautious about distancing themselves from what were perceived as secular technologies. Kotzebue reported the response of the American Mission in Hawaii to the prospect of a magic lantern exhibition: 'Lord Byron had brought with him from England a variety of magic lanterns, puppet-shows, and such like toys, and was making preparations to exhibit them in public, for the entertainment of the people, when an order arrived from Bengham to prevent the representation, because it did not become God-fearing christians to take pleasure in such vain amusements.'[15]

Williams establishes a representation of the naïve indigenous audience, reporting in correspondence:

I may here inform you of the prodigous interest the exhibition of the magic lantern produces. At the natural history slides they are delighted; the kings of England afforded them still greater pleasure; but the

Scripture pieces are those which excite the deepest interest . . . The birth of Christ, Simeon taking the Saviour in his arms, and the flight into Egypt, indeed all that had a reference to the Saviour, excited prodigous interest: but when the plate of the crucifixion was exhibited, there was a general sobbing, their feelings were overcame, and they gave vent to them in tears.

The redefinition of the false instrument as true becomes registered in the body of the Samoan subject, whose tears attest to an unfeigned response. A comparable awe is exhibited by Williams's early biographer, who describes the lantern as 'powerful and perfect': an appropriate representative of the divine.[16] Such a response is a reflection of the relative historical novelty of the lantern at the time Prout writes, as well as of his subject's particular reverential attitude to technology. As Asa Briggs notes, even at a somewhat later period wonderment at the illusionistic powers of technology was manifest in metropolitan responses to the magic lantern, when it was employed for similar purposes of religious didacticism: 'The magic lantern was a favourite device in Sunday Schools (and in temperance societies) on both sides of the Atlantic and was often thought of as a marvel.'[17]

Williams, however, is concerned repeatedly to emphasize a distinction between native naïveté and European know-how. Ironically, he thus becomes implicated in a worship of technology that he ascribes to Pacific islanders. Throughout *Missionary Enterprises* he records testimonials to the impact of the object, in which Polynesians give expression to a purportedly self-evident equation between European material advantages and spiritual advancement. A telling discrepancy between Williams's account and that of a fellow missionary is indicative of his predisposition towards representing Polynesian enthusiasm for foreign techniques of manufacture. When Aaron Buzacott took over from Williams as preacher at Rarotonga, he gave a display of his abilities as blacksmith. According to Williams, 'the very day after they landed, Mr Buzacott, who is an excellent mechanic, put on his apron, turned up his sleeves, and began to work at the forge. On seeing this, the people were much delighted, especially [the chief] Makea, who exclaimed, "This is the man for us; this is the man for us."'[18] In Buzacott's version of the same events, however, the Rarotongan is rendered speechless, and it is Williams who associates his technical skill with his fitness as missionary representative:

'The eyes of the older missionary filled with tears of joy, for the art of Vulcan did not come easily to his hand; and turning to the chief, who was looking on in mute astonishment, he put his hand upon Mr Buzacott's shoulder, and exclaimed in the native language, "This is the man we want."'[19]

In Williams's account the emphasis of local witness is repeatedly upon visible signs. Earlier I discussed another example of purported wonderment, in which Williams claimed that the Samoan chief Fauea drew attention to the distinction between the clothed European, and his own people with 'nothing but a bandage of leaves around our waist'. Yet Williams's deployment of figures of dress and nakedness is inconsistent. In the preface to *Missionary Enterprises* he asserts that his writing gives evidence of its authenticity by betraying, in its clumsier constructions, the author's commitment to preserving the naked and unrefined testimony of native speech:

[The author] has preserved the dialogues in which much of his knowledge was obtained, and has not spoken for the natives, but allowed them to speak for themselves. In doing this, he has carefully avoided the use of terms and phrases which are current among nations more advanced in the scale of intelligence and civilisation . . . and he has been equally careful to convey native ideas in the phraseology and under the figurative garb in which they were expressed.[20]

Here the dressing up of the native is not advocated: language preserves its natural 'figurative garb'. Williams is confident that, both in their symbolism and in their transparency, the Polynesian languages will serve him as witness; that, like their sophisticated opposite, that 'philosophical apparatus' the magic lantern, indigenous sign systems can be appropriated to the narrative of his enterprise. Yet as I noted earlier, testimonials to metropolitan technology such as Fauea's 'speech' have a fictive status, since their 'transcription' is predicated on an initiation into language unavailable to Williams in the first-contact situations he depicts: they represent, above all, a fantasy of European self-aggrandisement.

Where Williams assumes his own ability to measure the Polynesian subject both in spirit and appearance, oppositions between material and spiritual, external and internal, also present contradictions within his text. He writes of an incident where some teachers at Rarotonga have been disrupted by 'the yelling of a person who pretended to be inspired, and who, like the heathens of old, endeavoured to support his pretensions by distorting his features and speaking in an unnatural tone'. They respond by feigning a naïve and potentially violent literalism, proposing 'to take out their knives, and demand that they should be allowed to make an incision and search for the great god Tangaroa, who, he said, was within him'. The capacity for critique is not, however, credited to the uninitiated Polynesian. After witnessing the production of whitewash by missionaries, the islanders of Aitutaki, according to Williams, 'were so surprised and delighted at its softness and whiteness, that they actually whitewashed their hats and native garments, and strutted about the settlement admiring each other exceedingly'.[21] Their actions incorporate an ignored commentary upon the false promise, implicit in missionary discourse, that metropolitan techniques can transform natives into white men. Whether cutting through to false interiors or offering the promise of converted surfaces, Williams has faith in the capacity of objects to serve him as touchstones, their powers of reference contained by the symbolic framework of his own evangelical agenda.

Williams's text displays its author's unquestioning faith in his ability to shift between metaphoric and material planes of reference, to ventriloquise his subjects, to speak at once symbolically and practically. Language strains to accommodate incompatible levels of signification: property becomes parable. Williams reports that one Raiatean teacher taxed his vocabulary in attempting to authorise the practices of missionary commercialism, announcing to his congregation:

'I have been seeking a name by which to call the property thus subscribed, and I think it may be called *Property to seek lost souls*. Are not the souls of those living in darkness lost souls? and is not this property the means by which they will obtain the light of life? It is the thought of *lost souls* that animates good people in their labours. They do not collect property for themselves; *it is for lost souls*. We give property for every thing. If we want a canoe, we give property for it; if we want a net, we give property for it; and are not lost souls worth giving property to obtain?'[22]

The clumsy length of the neologism '*Property to seek lost souls*' registers the difficulty of reconciling material with spiritual goals. Where the gospels' 'fishers of men' set aside the instruments of their trade to labour at the saving of souls, here the fisherman's tools – canoe and net – are implicitly equated in value with the soul.

The defining achievement of Williams's career was the building of a ship, the *Messenger of Peace*, from local materials at Rarotonga in 1827. This triumph of *bricolage* has been recuperated by his biographers to literary models, perhaps as a substitute for literary criticism of his narrative itself. According to Prout, Williams's inspired text transcends actual criticism of style: 'With scarcely an exception, the reviewers drank into the spirit of the work . . . In the production upon which they pondered, there was a record of facts and feelings too sacred for the exercise of cold investigation, or mere critical acumen. As though they trod on holy ground . . . extracts and eulogy, instead of dissection and discussion, formed the staple of their critiques.'[23] Gavan Daws reinvokes *Robinson Crusoe*: 'as he told it, the tale was as good as anything out of the life of Robinson Crusoe', a model which Ebenezer Prout had earlier claimed Williams surpassed: ('Defoe never ascribed to the hero of his romance any achievement so wonderful').[24] *Robinson Crusoe* was the textbook of nineteenth-century self-sufficiency. In autodidactic isolation upon his island, its hero 'improv'd my self in this time in all the mechanick Exercises which my Necessities put me upon applying myself to', gradually acquiring most of the traditional English trades. In the absence of certain crucial tools, his apprenticeship is equally one in improvisation and substitution: he mimics, rather than simply implements, the modes of manufacture of his home culture. Crusoe approaches his technical training theoretically, although it is imposed by practical necessity. He explains: 'I went to work; and here I must needs observe, that as Reason is the Substance and Original of the Mathematicks, so by stating and squaring every thing by Reason, and by making the most rational Judgment of things, every Man may be in time Master of every mechanick Art.'[25] As shipbuilder, Williams was similarly forced to fabricate tools for his task. In attempting to manufacture a pair of bellows, however, he came to recognise the inadequacy of available theoretical literature to the peripheral context:

I examined publications upon mechanic arts, Dictionaries and Encyclopaedias, but not one book in our possession gave directions sufficiently explicit for the construction of so common an article; and it appears to me a general deficiency in all the works I have seen on the useful arts, that instructions and explanations sufficiently simple are not supplied, by which an important and useful object may be accomplished by means less complex than the machinery of civilised countries.

Williams finds it necessary to recover an earlier stage in the history of manufacture, where the links between stages of construction were made explicit: his practice is metonymic. Yet the ship, a miraculous assemblage of objects made to serve for others, is also a testimony to its author's powers of metaphoric substitution:

a perforated stone for a fire iron, . . . a pair of carpenter's pincers for our tongs. As a substitute for coals, we made charcoal from the cocoanut, tamani, and other trees . . . As a substitute for oakum, we used what little cocoa-nut husk we could obtain, and supplied the deficiency with dried banana stumps, native cloth, or other substances which would answer the purpose. For ropes we obtained the bark of the hibiscus . . . For sails we used the mats on which the natives sleep . . . Aito, or iron wood, answered remarkably well for the sheaves of blocks.[26]

Where metropolitan objects served Williams as miraculous evidence of Christian superiority, the building of a ship at the periphery is, by the same teleology, miraculous to a metropolitan readership. Prout writes:

Had we seen him at Rarotonga, and, without knowing the man, heard him avow his design, who would not have condemned it as one of the wildest and most impracticable dreams that had ever beguiled a disordered imagination? For what was it? It was to build a ship without a knowledge of the art, without the implements essential to the undertaking, without the aid of a single artificer, and even without the requisite materials.[27]

In the Polynesian context, where 'miraculous' feats of seamanship formed the history of settlement in the islands, Williams's 'impracticable dream' may have seemed less remarkable. As Ian Campbell points out, 'During the time of European contact some Pacific islanders were found to have craft which are properly called ships: twenty-five or more metres in length, built of planks fastened securely with ropes of coconut fibre, propelled at least in the western half of the Pacific by huge fore-and aft sails which were very efficient.'[28] A similar shipbuilding project to Williams's had in fact been adumbrated by Tahitians (with more consciously imperialist intent) at the time of first contact with European missionaries. When Captain Wilson and the crew of the *Duff* departed Tahiti they noted that King Pomare and his chiefs were 'purpose building a vessel of one hundred or one hundred and fifty tons, capable of visiting all the islands around them; for which they have materials of every kind, plenty of timber, and able workmen'.[29] The missionaries do not appear to express surprise at the scope of this ambition, nor the capacity of local materials to meet its requirements. In Prout's metropolitan account, Williams figures as Romantic overreacher – a fevered dreamer. Yet the building of the ship is also the elaboration of Williams's role as 'godly mechanic' – the capable artisan.

The ship served Williams in his project of evangelical colonisation. He declared himself thwarted by the fragmentary geography of Polynesia: 'For my own part, I cannot content myself within the narrow limits of a single reef; and, if means are not afforded, a continent would to me be infinitely preferable; for there, if you cannot ride, you can walk; but to these isolated islands a ship must carry you.'[30] He intended, with the ship, to subordinate that geography to the universalist logic of Christian discourse: to join islands into continents, to walk on water. The name *Messenger of Peace* signals the ship's function as bearer of the Word. Yet it is the medium which effectively becomes the message. Williams succeeds in constructing a symbol, rather than simply an instrument, of his enterprise. As Niel Gunson writes: 'The central motif in the pattern of John Williams' life must always be the Ship . . . Besides its obvious utility, the Ship was also, for Williams, both a symbol of material success and of escape.'[31] The ship is repeatedly represented as miracle of the man-made, as symbol of Williams's project and testimony to his authorship; it therefore loses impact as testimony to a divine Maker, to the handiwork of Providence. Williams does himself briefly acknowledge divine instrumentality as ultimately preserving the *Messenger of Peace*, claiming that

We never reflect upon our voyage from Rarotonga without feeling our obligations to a kind and protecting Providence. It will readily be conceived, that a vessel built under the circumstances I have described, very insufficiently fastened with iron, caulked with the bark, and covered partly with lime, and partly with gum from the bread-fruit tree, instead of pitch, was not calculated to sustain the buffetings of many storms.[32]

Yet even here he slips into detailing once again the processes of construction, implying the triumph of the man-made. In the account of Aaron Buzacott, on the other hand, who Williams himself acknowledged was a blacksmith of superior skill, the *Messenger of Peace* is depicted as an unsatisfactory fabrication, held together by a prayer: 'There can be little doubt that they owed their safe voyage quite as much to the special care of the Lord of winds and waves as to the sea-worthiness of the schooner.'[33] But in other versions of the shipbuilding narrative, and in particular his own, Williams himself fulfils the providential role. As Prout eulogised the enterprise: 'He [was] compelled not only to invent some things, but almost to create others (for may not his new combinations truly bear his name?)'[34] Materials and technology are never simply instrumental: they function as signs within the framework of Williams's personal mythology.

Since objects were always significant for Williams, the conversion of other cultures involved the appropriation of their artefacts to his narrative. Missionary policy demanded the desecration of Polynesian 'relics of idolatry' as (paradoxically) a material sign that such objects had ceased to signify.[35] Williams describes three practices regarding former objects of Rarotongan worship: 'Some of these idols were torn to pieces before our eyes; others were reserved to decorate the rafters of the chapel we proposed to erect; and one was kept to be sent to England, which is now in the Missionary Museum.' The demand for ritual vilification is a violent reflection of the more confident forms of appropriation of Polynesian artefacts, which are subsumed, *bricolage* fashion, within the texture of the Christian building, or decontextualised within the museum. Both the latter are conscious gestures of misinterpretation. Williams continues, regarding the idol transported to Britain:

It is not, however, so respectable in appearance as when in its own country; for his Britannic Majesty's officers, fearing lest the god should be made a vehicle for defrauding the King, very unceremoniously took it to pieces; and not being so well skilled in making gods as in protecting the revenue, they have not made it so handsome as when it was an object of veneration to the deluded Rarotongans.[36]

The further act of desecration by the officers of Empire leaves the artefact devoid of genuine ethnographic interest: it continues to signify, in the context of the Missionary Museum, only to its subordination within the narrative of missionary conquest.

Christopher Herbert has noted a 'strong undertow of ambivalence that is manifest in the missionaries' code of "participant observation"' within Pacific cultures.[37] On the one hand, missionary accounts are motivated by the desire to represent Polynesian societies as degenerate, and therefore in urgent need of salvation and civilisation; yet on the other hand, they are the product of a nascent anthropologising impulse to record the interwoven complexity of alternative cultural systems, and thus pay a grudging homage to their self-sufficiency. Missionary attitudes to the natural productions of the Pacific reflect a related ambiguity. In his *Polynesian Researches*, William Ellis represents the landscape and produce of Tahiti as offering a natural testimony to divine authorship: 'Amid the unrestrained enjoyment of a bounty so diversified and profuse, it is hardly possible to suppose that the divine Author of all should neither be recognised nor acknowledged.'[38] Part of Ellis's own perceived task is to voice the connection between creation and creator. Yet the natural history he provides in fact testifies to the bounty of the Tahitian environment, to a native abundance in addition to which any gifts that the missionary can offer must figure as supplementary. The breadfruit and coconut, for instance, which fulfil a variety of purposes, in a single tree providing building materials, food and drink, and so providing a 'staff of life' for Pacific islanders, emerge in Ellis's and other missionary accounts as symbols of earthly plenitude rather than signifiers of the divine hand.[39] Williams confidently slips from question to exclamation when declaring the force of the natural as theological example: 'Is it possible to reflect upon the wonderful adaptation of the fruits of the earth to the climate where they grow, and the circumstances of man, without exclaiming, "How manifold are thy works, O God! in wisdom hast thou made them all!"' The breadfruit and coconut, multipurpose products, are embraced as ideal exempla by Williams, always keen to promote Christianity through the testimony of the useful object. But they remain unredeemed cultivations, bearing witness to the self-sufficiency of the Pacific environment.[40]

On his return to Europe, Williams testified to the wonders of Polynesian produce and craftsmanship. In the private sphere, he is represented as attempting to create an authentic context for the reception of Pacific artefacts. Prout reports that, when within intimate circles back in England, the curiosities which [Williams] had brought from the islands were drawn from their hiding places, and the various contents of several cases covered the table or the floor. A singular medley of idols, dresses, ornaments, domestic utensils, implements of industry, and weapons of war, formed so many subjects of remark; and not unfrequently, Mr Williams arrayed his own portly person in the native tiputa and mat, fixed a spear by his side, and adorned his head with the cap of many colours, worn on high days by the chiefs; and, as he marched up and down his parlour, he was as happy as any one of the guests whose cheerful mirth he had thus excited. To this exhibition he would add explanations of each relic; naming and sometimes describing the island from which he obtained it; the past history and present state of its inhabitants; the use of the object, or the customs connected with it; and various other interesting particulars. In general these interesting statements were crowned by a donation of some curiosity which had awakened special interest; and that his visitors might taste, as well as see the good things of Polynesia, jars of native preserves, either of the banana or some other Polynesian fruit, were opened for their gratification.[41]

Here the violent theatre in which idols were desecrated before a missionary audience is replaced by a comic missionary performance. Unlike the Missionary Museum with its mis-assembled artefacts, Williams's exhibits are accompanied by adequate contextualising information. Indeed, Williams not only describes but reinvokes a Pacific context. He arrays his 'portly person' in island costume, and introduces the Polynesian object into a new sphere of circulation through the practice of gift exchange. There is an illicit aspect to such occasions: the objects are 'drawn from their hiding places' into the circle of initiates, who witness Williams attired between fetishism and drag, and achieve 'gratification' in the consumption of exotic fruits. But this in turn signals a translation of experience that moves beyond voyeurism: Williams's audience are invited not merely to look on, but to taste.

Williams's faith in the object as primary cross-cultural signifier did not preclude a facility in oral communication. Prout in fact links Williams's appreciation of objects with his ability to acquire vocabulary, claiming that, 'Accustomed to mark, not merely the general outline, or the broad surface of surrounding objects, but their distinctive peculiarities, and less obvious, but most interesting features, he was enabled to present more graphic delineations, and to report conversations with greater accuracy than most men.'[42] Williams's perception of objects as signifiers – in terms of their differences from other objects with which they are linked contextually – provides him with a model for the acquisition of foreign linguistic structures. On a figurative level, his appreciation of Polynesian metaphor is partly based on its materiality of reference: 'Their *proverbs* and *similes*, generally drawn from familiar objects, are often very striking and appropriate.'[43] Ultimately, however, Williams's recognition of the subtle differences that inform Polynesian languages is subordinated to his desire to affirm the universal authority of Christian discourse. Lecturing to a chief of Atiu on 'the folly of idolatry', Williams cites Isaiah 44:16–17: 'with part thereof he roasteth roast, and is satisfied; and the residue thereof he maketh a god, and worshippeth it, and prayeth unto it, and saith, Deliver me, for thou art my God.' According to Williams:

Nothing could be better calculated to make an impression on the mind of an intelligent South Sea islander than these inimitable verses of inspired truth; indeed the effect is likely to be far greater than that produced on the mind of an English reader. The natives have two words, not very much unlike, but expressive of opposite ideas, – *moa* and *noa*, the *moa* meaning sacred, and *noa* the very reverse of sacred. All that pertains to the gods is the superlative of *moa*; and all that pertains to food, and the cooking of food, the superlative of *noa*. The idea now, for the first time, darted, with irresistible force, into the mind of Roma-tane; and he perceived at once the excessive folly of making a god and cooking food from one and the same tree, thus uniting two opposite extremes, the *moa* and the *noa*.[44]

The language of Atiu has, it is claimed, a revelatory potential. In fact, Western lexicons borrowed a term from Polynesian languages to describe the complex relationship between the sacred and the unclean. *Tabu* (taboo) is one of the few Polynesian words to have been actively, rather than anthropologically, incorporated into the English language. As James Frazer acknowledged: 'The term Taboo is one of the very few words which the English language has borrowed from the speech of savages.'[45] In Williams's account, Roma-tane's recognition that the contradictory significations *moa* and *noa* could not subsist in juxtaposition signals the abolition of ambiguity resulting from the Pacific encounter with missionary discourse. The Western adoption of the term *tabu*, however, involves the acknowledgement that a Polynesian word can hold in tension ambiguities unreconciled in the Western imagination. A term developed in an oral cultural context allows Western societies to describe their unwritten laws. Freud draws attention to the ambivalence of the term 'taboo' in *Totem and Taboo,* observing that 'The meaning of "taboo", as we see it, diverges in two contrary directions. To us it means, on the one hand, "sacred", "consecrated", and on the other "uncanny", "dangerous", "forbidden", "unclean".'[46] By providing a way of naming customs and cultural resistances, it could be argued, the Polynesian word assisted in rendering the Western subject anthropological. For Williams, however, the very language of Atiu implicitly deauthorises local cultural practices, and attests to the universality of Christian law.[47] Polynesian discourse proves to be less a language of context than a reinscription of the absolute Word.

MISSIONARIES AND PRINT: THE CASE OF WILLIAM ELLIS

Unable ultimately to compete with traders in winning over Pacific islanders with material inducements, missionaries instead offered the gift of direct participation in the literate world economy. Missionaries were responsible for the introduction of a culture of print into Polynesia, setting up presses in all the major island groups during the course of the nineteenth century. William Ellis manned the first LMS press at Moorea: between June 1816 and May 1817 he claimed to have printed 9,000 books, after which the press was taken to Huahine, in the Leeward Islands. Presses were established in Tahiti in 1818, in Honolulu in 1822, in Tonga in 1831, in Rarotonga in 1834, in Fiji and Samoa in 1839, and in Micronesia by the 1860s.[48] Missionary printers combined religious with secular publishing priorities, printing the first Polynesian alphabets, scripture and hymn-books, school texts and codes of laws. The literate bias of historians has tended to telescope the Polynesian recognition of the value of literary culture. G. S. Parsonson, for instance, claims that Pacific islanders 'grasped the fact that the real difference between their culture and the European was that theirs was non-literate, the other literate. The key to the new world with all its evident power was the written word.' Parsonson asserts that Polynesians 'appear to have realised' that not only literate culture as such, but the acquisition of the English language, 'would have enlarged the range of their ideas'.[49]

As Stephen Greenblatt has pointed out, however, 'Monuments to writing are built by writers: from the midst of the system within which our knowledge of the world is organized, we take legitimate pleasure in our own tools.'[50] In fact, rather than evidencing a swift abandonment of traditional cultural practices in favour of 'grasped' methods of literacy, the early contact period was remarkable for the flexibility and incisiveness with which Pacific islanders incorporated the printed word into local symbolic and political frameworks.

Literacy enables the kinds of cultural boundary-crossing upon which conversion depends. As Jack Goody has pointed out,

Literate religions . . ., at least alphabetically literate ones, are generally religions of conversion, not simply religions of birth. You can spread them, like jam. And you can persuade or force people to give up one set of beliefs and practices and take up another set, which is called by the name of a particular sect or church. In fact the written word, the use of a new method of communication, may itself sometimes provide its own incentive for conversion, irrespective of the specific content of the Book; for those religions are not only seen as 'higher' because their priests are literate and can read as well as hear God's word, but they may provide their congregation with the possibility of becoming literate themselves.[51]

Goody points to a slippage that frequently occurs between transmission and reception of literate religions. Missionary accounts, as I noted in my introduction, equate the spread of literacy with the task of conversion. Yet in reception, the order of priority implicit in this equation is often reversed. Literacy becomes the message, rather than the medium; an end in itself, which may, however, necessitate an attendant conversion. The attempt to suppress this recognition strains the written accounts of missionaries engaged in the propagation of the (written) Word.

In his own book, *Polynesian Researches*, William Ellis emphasizes the distinction between printed word and object in missionary transactions. Ellis establishes an opposition between the false promise of the object and the true promise of the Word, as these gifts redound to the missionary enterprise. He points out that missionaries were in fact ill-equipped to play a lavish role within Pacific gift economies. He stresses that no material inducements were offered at his school in Huahine to encourage literacy: 'We made no presents to those who were our scholars . . . We offered no reward to anyone for learning, and held out no prospect of personal or temporal advantage to our pupils and hearers', contrasting this to a policy of largesse, which he claims would produce only mimic converts:

Had our means been ample, and had we, on landing, or when inviting the attention of the chiefs and people to the objects of our proposed residence among them, liberally distributed presents of cloth, ironmongery, &c. or even engaged in part to support the children that would receive our lessons, the chapel would undoubtedly have been well attended, and the scholars preportionably multiplied; but then it would have been only from the desire to receive a constant supply of such presents.[52]

The printed word is, for Ellis, the touchstone of the true convert. As he describes the composition of classes at the mission school at Eimeo (Mo'orea), 'Aged chiefs and priests, and hardy warriors, with their spelling-books in their hands, might be seen sitting, hour after hour, on the benches in the schools, by the side, perhaps, of some smiling little boy or girl, by whom they were now thankful to be taught the use of letters.'[53] Writing is represented as a labour which, in contrast to the capacity of the material gift to confer immediate privilege, equalises subjects, inverting traditional hierarchies of authority. Prout similarly describes a levelling of Tahitian hierarchy that takes place with the introduction of writing: 'Chiefs and raatiras, hoary men and lisping children, the mother with her suckling at the breast, and the once cruel priests of Oro, whose hands, now holding the primer or the Gospel, had been often stained with the blood of human sacrifices, were seen sitting upon the same form, spelling the same words, and mutually availing themselves of each other's aid.'[54] Yet transcription also introduced new hierarchies, serving as a form of distinction within missionary practice. The writing down of the names of converts was an initial stage in discipleship, allowing missionaries 'to become personally acquainted with [converts], and to exercise over them a guardian care, which they could not do without knowing their names, places of abode, &c'.[55] To become the object of writing is the first step by which the Pacific islander acquires individual subjectivity in missionary perception.

Otto von Kotzebue, the most forthright critic of missionary practice in the Pacific, observed the appropriation of writing to the expression of hierarchy when he visited Hawaii. On entering the residence of Queen Ka'ahumanu he found

The stairs were occupied from the bottom to the door of the Queen's apartments, by children, adults, and even old people, of both sexes, who, under her Majesty's own superintendence, were reading from spelling-books, and writing on slates – a spectacle very honourable to her philanthropy. The Governor himself had a spelling-book in one hand, and in the other a very ornamental little instrument made of bone, which he used for pointing to the letters. Some of the old people appeared to have joined the assembly rather for example's sake, than from a desire to learn, as they were studying, with an affectation of extreme diligence, books held upside down.

The patronising representation of Polynesians of different age and status rendered equals by a common wish to achieve literacy echoes the missionary accounts. However, the image of the stair-case subtly figures a continued hierarchy: the eager pupils remain ranked before the queen's doors. Kotzebue later encounters a Hawaiian who spells out the political subtext of such tableaux. Kaahumanu has issued a decree, that all persons above eight years of age be brought to the capital to be taught reading and writing. The countryside has become destitute, as commoners camp in the streets of Honolulu and attend school. Kotzebue narrates:

I met a naked old man with a book in his hand, whom my companion addressed, and knowing him for a determined opponent of the new system, expressed his surprise at his occupation, and enquired how long he had been studying his alphabet. With a roguish laugh which seemed intended to conceal a more bitter feeling, first looking round to make sure that he should not be overheard, he replied, 'Don't think that I am learning to read. I have only bought the book to look into it, that Kahumanna may think I am following the general example; she would not otherwise suffer me to approach her, and what would then become of a poor, miserable, old man like me? What is the use of the odious B A, Ba? Will it make our yams and potatoes grow? No such thing; our country people are obliged to neglect their fields for it, and scarcely half the land is tilled. What will be the consequence? There will be a famine by and by, and "Pala, Pala" will not fill a hungry man.'[56]

The earnest mimicry of the earlier passage, with its students faking reading 'books held upside down', is displaced here into an articulate critique of the way in which literacy had begun to operate as a means of social advancement, at the same time undermining traditional systems of production and relationships to the land.

Ellis is in fact unable to divorce representation of the value of the written word from a recognition of its material status. In pro-

moting writing among the Society islanders, missionaries emphasized its material qualities, pointing out that it would enable them
to 'preserve whatever they heard that was valuable, by making it
fast upon the paper'. Ellis records that, with the printing of scripture, 'a small equivalent' was demanded in return for the book
(earlier spelling-books had been distributed free), 'lest from the
circumstance of their receiving them without payment, they
should be induced to undervalue them'. The price, 'a small quan-
tity of cocoanut oil', merely covered the costs of production. Ellis
writes: 'This was not done with a view of deriving any profit from
the sale of the books, but merely to teach the people their value;
as no higher price was required than what it was supposed would
cover the expense of paper and printing materials.'[57] At a stage
when Pacific produce had not yet entered global circulation, the
value of the oil, which Ellis stresses is 'the article they could most
easily procure', was a matter simply of estimate. Value is symbolic,
rather than economic: the price signifies value itself, not the specific value of the book as commodity. Yet the necessity of expressing symbolic value in economic terms in turn implies that the
language of exchange, rather than the transcendent language of
scripture, is the true universalising discourse.

The materiality of the text was registered in the constraints upon
its production in the Pacific. Local materials were made to accommodate to the shape of the book. With insufficient paper, ink and
binding to meet demand, Ellis unsentimentally recalls, 'it was
quite amusing to see goats' dogs' and cats' skins collected to be
prepared for book-covers. Sometimes they procured the tough
skin of a large dog, or an old goat, with long shaggy matted hair
and beard attached to it, or the thin skin of a wild kitten taken in
the mountains.' He writes of how the Tahitians 'prepared pieces
of native cloth with great care, and then, with a reed immersed in
red or purple native dye, had written out the alphabet, spelling,
and reading lessons, on these pieces of cloth, made with the bark
of a tree'.[58] Representations of an enthusiastic spirit of substitution
are standard in early missionary accounts: Williams writes, in a
similar vein, of the ingenuity of Rarotongan schoolchildren in producing equivalents for slate and pencils from flakes of stone and
sea-urchins' spines.[59] In their purported anxiety to acquire the
culture of print, the islanders evidence a genius for *bricolage* akin
to Williams's own in constructing the *Messenger of Peace*. If their

acceptance of substitute materials suggests a recognition of the transcendent, non-material value of scripture however, conventional instruments of printing could equally well be converted to serve secular purposes. Ellis records that, during the period of civil unrest before Pomare established control in Tahiti, the mission houses were ransacked, and books and printing equipment refashioned as weaponry: 'Every implement of iron was converted into a weapon of war. The most valuable books were . . . distributed among the warriors for the purpose of making cartridge papers, and the printing types were melted into musket balls.'[60] The material of the book was appropriated, and not merely imitated.

Ellis's own reciprocal initiation into Tahitian language occurred via the printed word. He writes: 'I found the composing, or setting, of the types for the Tahitian books, the best method of acquiring all that was printed in the language. Every letter in every word passing repeatedly, not only under my eye, but through my hand, I acquired almost mechanically the orthography.' Ellis acquires language through eye and hand, rather than ear and tongue: as object, rather than discourse. He hesitates to equate the activity of typesetting with composition, however, and instead represents the performative context as the proving ground of authorship: 'I had never so deeply felt the responsibility of my situation, and my insufficiency for the work, as I did on the day when I delivered my first native discourse.'[61] Oral performance was the context in which missionaries most frequently expressed self-doubt. George Brown, for instance, confided to his journal touching fears about the inadequacy of an early sermon before his Samoan congregation:

Preached at Palauli from Isaiah XXX 21 and from the same here in the evening. Was much cast down and dispirited on account of the nervous impediments in my speech which I felt very much to day. I never feel it scarcely until I begin to read the Lesson and then I get so nervous that I can scarcely proceed. I am determined to make it a special subject of Prayer to God. I am certain it can be overcome & pray that I may be enabled to overcome what may prove an hindrance to my Work.[62]

Hymn-books, which preserved an oral context of reference, were, according to Ellis, found to be 'acceptable to the people, who are exceedingly fond of metrical compositions, their history and traditions having been preserved in a metrical kind of ballad'. He in fact suggests that Polynesian oral culture is continuous with the earliest apostolic tradition: 'the promulgation of the gospel by the living voice . . . has been regarded as the first great duty of a Missionary, according with his very designation, the principle design of the institution under whose patronage he is engaged – the practice of the apostles and first Missionaries, and the spirit as well as the letter of the Divine commission.' However, exemplary missionary conduct as described by Ellis remains what amounts to an imitation of the effect of print: 'a full, plain, and explicit statement of his objects in the commencement of his work, and a uniform reference, in all his subsequent conduct.'[63]

In the Pacific, the Word initially took effect deictically. The inception of printing at Eimeo was theatre. Pomare II was invited both to compose the first page of type and to print the first sheet on 30 June 1817, with attendant ceremony. Ellis describes a stage framed by the tiers of a Tahitian audience desirous of spectacle:

The printing office was daily crowded by the strangers, who thronged the doors, &c. in such numbers, as to climb upon each others backs, or on the sides of the windows, so as frequently to darken the place. The house had been enclosed with a fence five or six feet high; but this, instead of presenting an obstacle to the gratification of their curiosity, was converted into a means of facilitating it: numbers were constantly seen sitting on the top of the railing; whereby they were able to look over the heads of their companions who were round the windows.

Enclosure is 'converted' to performance space. Pomare, lacking technical confidence, abjures an audience: 'the door was closed, and the small window next the sea darkened, as he did not wish to be overlooked by the people on the outside.'[64] Rather, it is the printed word itself that becomes spectacle: 'the first sheet was shewn to the crowd without, who, when they saw it, raised one general shout of astonishment and joy.'[65] The scene was made much of in reviews of *Polynesian Researches*, which took up a comparison drawn by Ellis with metropolitan demonstrations of novel technologies: 'The excitement is likened to what the English felt at witnessing, for the first time, the ascent of a balloon, or the movement of a steam-carriage . . . For several weeks before the first portion of the Scriptures was finished, the district in which the printing-house stood resembled a public fair.'[66]

Performance, however, had a dubious heritage in Tahiti. It was traditionally the prerogative of the Arioi society, a troupe of actors associated with the god Oro, whose members practised compulsory abortion and infanticide. According to Ellis, the Arioi 'appear to have placed their invention on the rack, to discover the worst pollutions of which it was possible for man to be guilty, and to have striven to outdo each other in the most revolting practices'. The Arioi were consummate performers, whose licensed status allowed them to criticise Tahitian social practices and religious institutions. 'The priests, and others', Ellis reports, 'were fearlessly ridiculed in these performances, in which allusion was ludicrously made to public events.' They had earlier confounded the first missionaries to Tahiti by appearing to combine incompatible qualities of nobility and degeneracy: 'They are the finest persons we have seen, are said to have each two or three wives, which they exchange with each other; and inhumanly murder every infant that is born among them . . . They never work; live by plunder; yet are highly respected, as none but persons of rank are admitted among them.'[67] Ellis claims that the Arioi made superlative converts: 'Many of them have been the most regular and laborious teachers in our schools, and the most efficient and successful native Missionaries.' By stressing effortful labour, in contrast to former virtuosity, Ellis attempts to distinguish between genuine and false performances. Yet the qualities demanded of Christian discipleship were also requisite for initiation into the Arioi society, where 'After a considerable trial of his natural disposition, docility and devotedness . . . if [the would-be member] persevered in his determination to join himself with them, he was inaugurated with all the attendant rites and observances.'[68]

The Arioi explicitly represent the threat of mimicry. Ellis counters the potential interchangeability of their illicit and redeemed performative roles by emphasising an absolute opposition between former and converted selves. He claims that

No sooner did these deluded, polluted, and cruel people, receive the gospel of Christ, the elevated sentiments, sacred purity, and humane tendency of which, convinced them that it must have originated in a source as opposite to that whence idolatry had sprung, as light is to darkness, than the spell in which they had been for ages bound was dissolved, and the chains of their captivity were burst asunder.

However, the immutability of print here, ironically, undermines the claim to conversion, marking the Arioi indelibly as initiates of the illicit society from which they have been reclaimed: 'I have heard several wish they could remove from their bodies the marks tataued upon them, but these figures remain too deeply fixed to be obliterated, and perpetually remind them of what they once were.'[69]

If there is no way of distinguishing genuine from mimic convert, signs are rendered provisional, without the authority to discriminate. The missionary account is fissured by double standards: what in one case serves as evidence of the true is in another sign of the false. For instance Ebenezer Prout quotes a letter from John Williams, in which Williams represents reiteration as duplicitous, claiming that 'in all the islands they commit so much Scripture to memory, from merely hearing it, that unless frequently and carefully examined, they will repeat chapter after chapter so correctly, and appear to read with such fluency, as completely to deceive any one'. Here Polynesian oral mnemonics play at literate notions of intelligibility. Yet when writing of Williams's own character as public speaker, Prout makes reiteration the sign of authenticity, by which the genuine speaker is to be distinguished from the actor changing masks: 'there was as little variety in his words, as in the incidents themselves, which he employed on most public occasions. He exhibited the same facts in the same form; the figure seldom changed its drapery, or its adornments . . . He never did act a part, and never could.'[70]

Where public profession has an ambiguous status, it is the private act of worship that becomes the most significant register of conversion. Ellis recounts how the first Tahitian recruits to Christianity were identified, when a missionary overheard the rhythms of Christian prayer uttered in a novel tongue:

It was not a few detached sentences that were spoken, but a continued address; not in the lively tone of conversation, but solemn, as devotion; or pathetic, as the voice of lamentation and supplication . . . O, what hallowed music must have broken upon his listening ear, and what rapture must have thrilled his soul, when he distinctly recognised the voice of prayer, and heard a native, in the accents of his mother-tongue, with an ardour that proved his sincerity, addressing petitions and thanksgivings to the throne of mercy.[71]

Whereas reading could be faked – the image of the book held upside down as clue that memory is substituting for comprehension, oral only imitating literate culture, is standard in missionary accounts – here, the tongue offers no cover. Sincerity reveals itself through tone rather than semantics, to the ear before the eye. The earlier missionary fulfils the desire of Ellis's own text, to recognise, beyond the threat of conscious imitation, the true convert, the 'unconscious author'. The praying voice described here belonged to a former 'inmate' (presumably servant) of a house established at Matavai by the first LMS evangelists. This Tahitian kept alive the memory of the Christian forms to which he was exposed, after the departure of the missionaries from Tahiti. His worship is consummate, unauthorised imitation, recuperated as the genuine, first by missionaries wearied from years of unsuccessful labour, and retrospectively by a writer whose text exhausts its repertoire of images of authentic conversion, as it registers the shadow presence of mimicry.

The book as sign was central to narratives of conversion: the particular missionary texts in which such narratives were contained, however, figured in a somewhat ambiguous relationship to this symbolic text. Two years after *Polynesian Researches*, Ellis published a work entitled *A Vindication*, which defended the activities of missionaries against printed attacks by travellers and explorers such as von Kotzebue. Ellis's defence was two-pronged, drawing attention to missionary work in converting islanders into readers, and also to the authority of missionaries, as residents among the islands and students of their languages, to write about the Pacific. Noticing the appearance of an article unfavourable to missionary activities, Ellis writes

I shall content myself with asking [the writer], in reference to one of his assertions, if he has never heard that the knowledge of *reading* is possessed by the majority of the population, and that the New Testament is translated and widely circulated amongst the people? If he has read of these effects of Missionary labour, to say nothing of others, will he, in the face of such facts, declare that the Tahitians have not made 'one step towards raising' themselves '*to the rank of Christians?*' Or is *reading*, in the opinion of his school, one of the '*vices*' which the natives have borrowed from civilization, by which it is dishonoured?

He discusses another review whose author 'evinces his critical displeasure against the Missionaries, for spelling the names of the principle islands, in the Society and Sandwich groups, as they are pronounced by the natives, and for not adhering to the orthography employed by the editors of Cook's Voyages'. Ellis points out the ludicrousness of asserting the orthography of Western texts over local pronunciation, commenting that 'the authority of the natives ought surely to have some weight in adjusting such a ques-

tion'. Here, it is by association with the Pacific islander as cultural
authority that the missionaries' ethnographic authority is asserted.
As insiders, missionaries are able to provide accurate linguistic and
ethnographic data on Pacific cultures, unlike the 'foreigners, hur-
rying over the countries they visit', whose texts reveal 'the blunders
which it is scarcely possible to avoid, under the disadvantages to
which such transient visitors are exposed'.[72] On the one hand, Ellis
defends the missionaries as agents of change, and on the other, as
preservers of a cultural record, the incompatibility between these
two roles reflected in the division between the Pacific islander as
reader (and therefore also text of missionary enterprise) and the
missionary as writer of texts for metropolitan consumption.
Equally, it is the preservation of speech that justifies missionary
written accounts, but it is the institution of literacy, and by implication the destruction of oral cultural values, that validates missionary activity in the Pacific.

If the book emerges within Ellis's account as a symbol of an
unstable missionary authority, Ellis's own book is itself a text of
scholarly and physical substance. The second volume of *Polynesian
Researches* is a largely synchronous account of the 'mythology, traditions, government, arts, manners, and customs of the inhabitants'
of the Society Islands: a compendium of anthropology, history,
natural theology and sermon. Both Christopher Herbert and
Nicholas Thomas have defended the (*avant la lettre*) anthropological status of nineteenth-century missionary accounts such as
Ellis's. Herbert claims that 'the two large and scholarly volumes of
Ellis's *Polynesian Researches* offer a cornucopia of detailed ethnographic information regarding Tahitian crafts, . . . religion, art,
architecture, games, domestic customs and so forth. This
enthralling text is our authoritative source for knowledge of early
culture in the society islands.'[73] Thomas argues that the missionary task of transcribing Polynesian languages slid naturally into
other forms of anthropological inquiry: 'In some instances, missionaries' diaries make it clear that obtaining lists of words led
them to other topics such as names of deities, and to other activities such as compiling censuses.'[74] As counterweight to the synchronous compendium of the second volume, the first volume of
Polynesian Researches offers a diachronous narrative of missionary
activity, incorporating a pieced-together history of early evangelical labours in the Pacific. Ellis reproaches earlier missionaries for
failing to trust in the outcome of their narrative, and thus to keep

any written record of its daily development. By neglecting the authorial task, they have inadvertently deprived themselves of an evangelical tool:

[They] did not, at the time, prepare a full and particular account of the work which, under God, they had been instrumental in effecting: . . . lest subsequent events should disappoint the anticipations which present favourable appearances might originate . . . It cannot be doubted that the world has been thereby deprived of a full record of events, intimately connected with the destinies of the people among whom they transpired, and with the propagation of the gospel in the most distant parts of the world, during every future age of the Christian church.[75]

As first printer to the Pacific islands, Ellis takes responsibility for the production of an initial written historical record, reconstructing the origins of his enterprise.

THE INDIGENOUS MINISTRY: THE PREACHING OF THE CONVERTED

If true and false Polynesian readers are relegated to amusing or reaffirming anecdotes within missionary accounts, they achieved autonomous identities in the roles of native preacher and cult leader during the nineteenth century. In the remainder of this chapter, I will examine the significance and political force of these two opposed models of appropriation. Indigenous preachers were the licensed other, trusted to bear the authorised Christian message. The LMS began sending missionaries from the Society Islands to other areas of the Pacific after 1820. The Wesleyans, Presbyterians and American missionaries also employed Polynesian teachers. Their role was figured in conflicting terms within missionary rhetoric, as both initiative and conclusive. They were referred to as 'pioneers', and expected to use their influence to break down traditional religious systems. Their task was to prepare the way for better qualified white missionaries, and they often risked their lives as the vanguard of culture contact. At the same time, an indigenous ministry was also perceived to be the future of missionary enterprise in the Pacific. For many LMS missionaries, writes Niel Gunson, 'the whole object of mission work was to raise up an effective native agency, on the assumption that the generality of the people could only understand Christianity in their own terms, and in the language of their own experience'.[76]

Their mixed allegiance, to the discourse they bore, and to the cultural framework in which their mission took place, rendered indigenous teachers both fit and suspect mediators. The most common form of Polynesian missionary defection was sexual lapse. John Williams regarded the curbing of traditional physical practices – both bodily decoration and sexual licence – as the special work of Polynesian 'pioneers': 'All their lesser evil customs you will endeavour to cast down, going in a State of Nudity or nearly so, cutting and scratching themselves in seasons of grief – tatooing their bodies. Eating raw fish, their lewd dances etc.'[77] Surface transformation was regarded as a prelude to spiritual conversion. Declension was, in turn, a reassertion of cultural loyalties, which forced a recognition that changes in outward appearance, within cultures with traditions of performance, often amounted to no more than a switching of roles.

Initially selected for their literary proficiency, as well as dedication, indigenous preachers had simultaneously the useful ability to negotiate those variations in Polynesian idiom which complicated the task of transmission for the foreign missionary. They represented both printed and oral cultures to each other. The types of innocent duplicity that could arise from such a combined authority are indicated by William Ellis:

[A] source of perplexity resulted from the injudicious methods of the native teachers, who at first, in their zeal to encourage and assist their scholars, repeated to them every word in the columns of spelling, and their lessons, so frequently, that many of their pupils could repeat from memory, perhaps, the whole of the book, without being able to read a single line. When they took the book, it was only necessary for them to be told the first word or sentence in a chapter, in order to their repeating the whole correctly, even though the book should be open at some other part, or the page be placed bottom upwards.

False reading, then, was apparently encouraged by this mimic tutelage. Ellis converts the preachers' error into an affirmation of the value of the Word, claiming that 'The matter of the lessons, they . . . thought was the great thing to be remembered',[78] and thus representing the teachers as only too literal in their methods. Kotzebue, however, was scathing about the level of exegetical authority that could be attributed to ill-trained Polynesian teachers, claiming that 'In Russia, a careful and diligent study at schools and universities is necessary to qualify any one to be a teacher of religion. The London Missionary Society is more easily satisfied; a half savage, confused by the dogmas of an uneducated sailor, is, according to them, perfectly fitted for the sacred office.'[79] Ellis, in turn, was less literal in his understanding of pedagogic qualifications, writing in his *Vindication*

That none of the native teachers have received a university education, and that some of them have been unfit for their work, is not denied; but they have all been capable of communicating instruction in reading, writing and arithmetic, and mechanical arts, to the tribes among whom they have gone; and of teaching the plain and essential principles of religion; and that they have manifested many instances of noble Christian devotedness; endured much persecution; been exposed to imminent danger, or great distress; have persevered, notwithstanding, and that by their means many thousands of the inhabitants of adjacent and distant islands have renounced idolatry, embraced Christianity, and become a comparatively temperate, industrious and happy people – is equally undeniable.[80]

Yet the threat of mimicry was implicit in the translated orthodoxies of indigenous missionaries, as well as in the heterodox appropriations of cults. Indeed, sects such as the Mamaia of Tahiti, whose doctrines were formulated by lapsed teachers, were the inverted product of such pedagogical authority. The Polynesian missionary, looking simultaneously in two cultural directions, was always a potentially two-faced delegate.

Polynesian preachers occupied a role 'between mimesis and mimicry', to adopt a formulation of Homi Bhabha's.[81] They were given an intermediary status within the hierarchy of otherness in the Pacific: the brown mediator between the civilised white missionary and the black and savage Melanesian or the primitive Micronesian. As Nicholas Thomas has pointed out, the Melanesia/Polynesia distinction has served as a structuring device within European accounts of the Pacific since the period of exploration. Melanesian languages, skin-colour and political organisation are repeatedly compared unfavourably with their Polynesian counterparts. Thomas contends that 'Polynesians were upheld by nineteenth-century writers because the women seemed attractive, because they had made a step or two closer to our own exalted state of civilisation, and because they displayed some readiness to adopt a variety of western goods and practices, which Melanesians conservatively and intransigently resisted.'[82] An anecdote in William Churchward's *My Consulate in Samoa* illustrates the way in which, amid this discursive ambivalence, the indigenous missionary role could slip into parodic colonialism. Churchward cites the examples of several graduates of the Malua Institute in Samoa, a training college for native pastors, who, he claims, 'feeling the great power over their more ignorant countrymen that education has given them, cannot curb their ambition, and beyond their missionary influence assert a sort of temporal authority'.

HEATHEN RAW MATERIAL.

Plate 3. 'Heathen Raw Material', from George Cousins, *From Island to Island in the South Seas: or The Work of a Missionary Ship.*

In one case a pastor was expelled from his Samoan parish, and went to the Ellice Islands, which he formally annexed for Samoa. Churchward writes: 'On arrival, he hoisted the Samoan flag, and at once proceeded in the most free and easy manner to tax and fine the islanders all round – his idea of the duties of a Viceroy.'[83]

A rare example of indigenous missionary self-representation, *The Works of Ta'unga*, attests to the contradictions inherent in the Polynesian pastor's intermediary identity. Ta'unga, a teacher from Rarotonga, was the exemplary convert: literate and technically skilled. He was among a group of teachers who travelled on the *Camden* in 1842 from Rarotonga to Samoa, the New Hebrides and the Loyalty Islands, where he took up a posting in Tuauru, on New

CHRISTIAN TEACHERS (RUATOKA AND HIS WIFE).

Plate 4. 'Christian Teachers (Ruatoka and his Wife)', from George Cousins, *From Island to Island in the South Seas: or The Work of a Missionary Ship*.

Caledonia. After five years in Melanesia he returned to Samoa, where he ministered for two years at Upolu and twenty-one years at Manua. In 1879 he returned to Rarotonga, where for the remainder of his life he engaged in translation work. Ta'unga was the progeny of Williams's missionary enterprise: bearing his knowledge of the biblical Word and metropolitan object across the sea borders of Polynesia, into the threatening territory of

Melanesia, where Williams had met his death on the shores of Erromanga in 1839.

Ta'unga's writings reinscribe the discourse of otherness. He regards the black complexion of Melanesian peoples as 'a heathen appearance', and their nakedness as evidence of savagery. He initially perceives New Caledonian speech to be animalistic, claiming: 'It is a strange language, it sounds like the noise made by turkeys.' He labels Melanesians as cannibals. William Arens has questioned the documentary status of Ta'unga's reports of anthropophagy, arguing that accusations of other societies' cannibalism are a mode of intercultural self-differentiation, and lack any provable validity.[84] However as Gananath Obeyesekere points out, 'Arens does not deal with the dialogical nature of cannibalistic discourse, and he does not recognise the possibility that where there is fantasy there could be slippage into reality and from there into human institutions.'[85] That Ta'unga's accusations of cannibalism are a mode of distancing Melanesian practices does not preclude authenticity, and indeed the striking similes he employs to describe cooked human flesh – 'the fingernails of the hand stood up like the tentacles of an octopus'; 'when a man is alive he has a human appearance, but after he is baked he looks more like a dog, as the lips are shrivelled back and his teeth are bared' – may surely testify to a realist as much as a fantasist imagination. Ta'unga also betrays his alienation from traditional Polynesian cultural practices. He resists recognising the conventional values exhibited in Samoan insistence on reciprocal obligation, evaluating gift exchange in defamiliarised moral terms: 'Their goodness was not the same as ours. Theirs was rather strange, because they coveted articles in exchange to pay for the food they brought us.' He employs a trope of misappropriation familiar from early European accounts of contact, reporting 'They came out naked. Buzacott took aside those who were only dressed in *tikoru* and girded them with lengths of cotton cloth. But they did not take any notice, they just took the cloth off and some of them tied it around their heads.'[86]

Ta'unga's later years were devoted to the work of translation. He produced a vocabulary of the Tuauru language, and collaborated with William Wyatt Gill on the translation of the Bible into Rarotongan. While he thus served as emissary of print, his translations, punctuated by gaps and repetitions, register the inability of writing to negotiate subtle differences between Pacific languages. As Ron and Marjorie Crocombe observe:

The only orthography he knew was that used by his European teachers for reducing the Rarotongan language to writing. Only about fifteen letters were used and many of the forms and sounds used in the Tuauru language . . . were quite foreign to Rarotongan. When Ta'unga wrote Tuauru words therefore (and he was probably the first person ever to do so) he had to use the letters which had the nearest equivalent value in Rarotongan.

Read in translation, Ta'unga's writings cannot be confidently assessed: however the providential thesis seems particularly blunt within his narrative. The victory of the chief of Tuauru in battle, for instance, is explained as the instant gratification of prayer by a visible sign: 'The reason for the defeat was that a younger brother of the chief of our district prayed to Jehovah above . . . "Give us success in this battle, that we may see evidence of your power."' Such interpretative conviction was undermined in the event. Ta'unga lists a series of diseases that visited the population of Tuauru: dysentery, an affliction of the knees, stomach sickness, mumps, 'a sickness affecting the eyes and then one affecting the back and the sickness which caused extreme weakness'. While such cumulative affliction has resonances of the plagues of Egypt, it was open to an alternative interpretation that endangered the missionary enterprise. Ta'unga reports: 'They blamed us saying that we brought all sorts of diseases to their island, and began to show bad feelings against us.'[87]

Ultimately, despite his commitment to received Western values, Ta'unga's mission was subject to forms of local religious appropriation that are indistinguishable from those of subversive cult leaders. The name *Ta'unga* is the traditional Rarotongan title for men with a specialist knowledge of matters of religion and ritual. His record is not solely the printed document: in the Samoan and Rarotongan cultural imaginations he attained a mythic status. His editors report various legends about Ta'unga still current in Samoa, including one claiming that he died one night and came to life the following morning. At Mauke he is credited with two miracles: having produced and later relieved a famine after some possessions had been stolen, and having cursed a vessel that was subsequently lost at sea, after the captain refused to spare him wine for communion. If such stories have obvious sources in the gospels, they also incorporate customary religious allegiances. According to the second legend, only one passenger survived the destruction of the ship off the coast of Mangaia: a woman who was protected by the assistance of a sea monster with which she had a totemic relationship.[88] Imported theology subsisted in juxtaposition with traditional elements of faith, failing to dispossess the latter of their authority.

CARGO CULTS: THE PREACHING OF THE UNCONVERTED

Missionaries contended with, on the one hand, confounding literalism, and on the other, freedom of symbolic interpretation in response to the objects and texts that they brought to the Pacific. Both these modes of reception emerged as strategies of resistance and subversion in the activities of cargo cults during the nineteenth century. Cargo cults, whose practices of worship are focused upon the anticipation of cargo of supernatural origin, have in the twentieth century been chiefly a Melanesian phenomenon.[89] However during the course of the nineteenth century cult activity was registered throughout the islands of Polynesia. The most politically significant of these movements were the cult of the female prophet Hapu of Hawaii, which developed after 1825, the more militant Hawaiian movement of Kaoni of the later nineteenth century, the Papahurihia movement among the New Zealand Maoris during the 1830s, the Tahitian Mamaia sect, which flourished during the 1820s, and the Samoan cult of Siovili, which achieved notoriety in the 1830s.[90] In an impressive recent study of another late nineteenth-century cult, the Tuka movement of Fiji, Martha Kaplan argues that the 'cargo cult' is a phenomenon of the Western colonial imagination, substantiated primarily in the archives of colonial administration where the term describes practices that were not in themselves formally distinct from traditional ritual–political practice, or from the activities of Christian converts.[91] Jukka Siikala has noted that cult practices were largely a response to missionary doctrine on property: 'the attitude similar almost to the worship of foreign wealth characteristic of cargo cults was in fact typical in the early stages of missionary work in Samoa'.[92] I focus here on the activities of two cults: the Siovili cult and the Mamaia sect. Samoa and Tahiti, where these two movements held sway, were important spheres of influence for, alternately, John Williams's object-led evangelical crusade, and William Ellis's promulgation of the printed Word.

The Siovili cult centred around the visionary Siovili, a Samoan who mimicked the status of foreigner that initially distinguished the missionary. During the 1820s Siovili made several trips aboard whaling and trading vessels to Tonga, the Society Islands, and possibly as far as New South Wales, acquiring some Tahitian and English during the course of his travels. According to the missionary George Turner, converts to Siovilism validated their religion in terms of its 'foreignness': 'They did not like to be called *heathen*, and wished to be able to say to a Christian teacher, or a friend who might warn them of their danger, "Don't speak to me. I have got a *foreign* religion as well as you."'[93] Siovilian rites reflected the simultaneous insider–outsider status of their leader, melding Christian and Polynesian religious practices. Members were strict keepers of the Sabbath, built their own churches, and emphasized prayer, whose content could however consist of a reversion to traditional incantations. Siovili's title expresses an interweaving of the imported with the traditional. It originated from the prophet's particular skill in the use of the *vili*, or Samoan drill, and was translated as 'Joe Gimlet' by LMS missionaries.[94] While the allusion to technical prowess reflects Williams's equation of spiritual authority with technical proficiency, the instrument from which Siovili derived his name was a local one.

Williams and the LMS missionaries in Samoa had, as I noted earlier, allied themselves politically with the powerful chief, Malietoa. Competition among other Samoan chiefs to establish equivalent connections with foreigners was subsequently intense and, according to George Brown, undiscriminating: 'The consequence was that any chief who had a white man living with him could have a "lotu" of his own "just like Malietoa".'[95] Malietoa's main rival, Mata'afa, sought to gain prestige through allegiance with a 'foreigner' by endorsing Siovili's religion against the teachings of the missionaries. In denouncing Siovili as insufficiently foreign, Williams was compelled to re-examine the principle metaphor of his own enterprise, that of the ship. He told the Samoans: 'perhaps the man might have been to Tahiti, but he had never united himself to any missionary there, consequently all the knowledge he had gained on the voyage was in pulling ropes on board ship; he was an ignorant and wicked man, his system was folly and deceit, and he was contemptible and unworthy of regard'.[96] Apparently, only contact with missionary discourse can endow shipboard experience with symbolic authority: unlike Williams's own flights of substitution in constructing the *Messenger of Peace*, Siovili's humble 'pulling ropes' is non-transcendent. In fact it is a hyper-literalism, a refusal to recognise the metaphoric status of much missionary discourse, which gives the force of critique to the mimic practices of cargo cults such as Siovili's. Siovili 'hymns' are rhythmic cumulations of foreign objects:

> Behold, come is Siovili,
> A man-of-war will present itself on the sea,
> With knives and musket-balls,
> And ramrods.
> Oh run in haste to be saved,
> She will bring us blue beads;
> How long is our ship on her watery way.[97]

The objects that formed an aspect of Williams's testimony and the ship that brought them are brought into the framework of performed verse, within which it becomes tempting to interpret them as metaphors. Yet the ultimate referent here is an anticipated physical event, the arrival of cargo. Metaphoric appropriation is only a stage in a foretold process of material transformation. Cargo cult poetics expose the slipperiness of missionary discourse, where the object is proffered as sign only to be retracted as symbol.

The propensity of Siovilians to mimic the forms of Christian worship in conjunction with traditional Samoan content, asserting identity even as they asserted difference, made their denunciation a complex task for the missionary. Williams, as quoted earlier, had found Rarotongan concepts of *moa* and *noa* particularly compatible with Christian distinctions between the sacred and the profane. However, the refusal of cult members to acknowledge the inherent profanity of their mimicry – if missionaries attempted to instruct them in Christian worship, they claimed to be Christians

already – produced shriller, less assured assertions of this distinction. 'To the missionaries', writes J. D. Freeman, 'the Siovilians
were the "poor deluded votaries" of a "kind of blasphemous half-
heathenism", and their "mongrel system" the "most extraordinary
corruption of Christianity".'[98] Missionaries were confronted by the
incompatibility of their desires, on the one hand, to retain the
sacredness of appropriated forms, and on the other, to expose the
profanity of alternative content. According to Siikala, 'imitation of
papalagi [white man's] behaviour without any precise contentual
correspondence was a feature of Siovilian rites'.[99] Missionaries
responded by reappropriating Siovilian culture. Just as traditional
Polynesian idols were frequently incorporated into the architecture of Christian buildings, so Siovili churches were ultimately
handed over to the missionaries in Samoa, providing a space
within which the ascendent discourse of Christianity was dissemi-
nated.

In certain instances, however, Siovilian appropriations threatened to supersede their Christian 'originals'. The missionary
Alexander Duff, commenting on a similar pattern of reception to
evangelical teaching in India, expressed his frustration that 'every
native term which the Christian missionary can employ to communicate the Divine truth is already appropriated as the chosen
symbol of some counterpart deadly error'.[100] Samoan traditions
offered a frame of reference to certain phenomena that had
receded to purely symbolic status within the European imagination. As Siikala observes, 'One of the paradoxes repeatedly con-
fronting the missionaries in the field sprang from the fact that they
proclaimed a religion in which the descriptions given in the basic
work, the Bible, of religious behaviour were more familiar to the
listeners than they were to the proclaimers.'[101] An aspect of
Siovilian literalism was thus cultural: biblical 'miracles' such as
direct revelation, spirit possession and speaking in tongues could
be taken literally by the members of a society within whose religious traditions these manifestations were recognisable phenomena. The missionaries, lacking comparable access to such
immediate forms of spiritual experience, suspected pure performance. The Siovilians became known as *lotu manava*, or the
ventriloquist's cult, a reference, Freeman notes, 'to the distorted
utterances of possessed mediums'. Siovili endorsed a return to

traditional Samoan costumes, and revived a sexual theatrics that had been denounced by the missionaries: polygyny, night-dancing, tattooing and the cultivation of long hair by males were all condoned.[102] This in turn lent an illicit aspect to all their traditionalist 'performances' in missionary eyes.[103] The biblical sign of authenticity, the possessed spirit, became the sign of a degenerate mimicry.

The shift from prophet to healer movement was a trend among nativistic cults. The body served as staging ground in the performance of faith. Initial encounters between missionaries and Pacific islanders were tussles to appropriate the providential, as displayed in visitations of ill-health and purportedly miraculous recovery. The following anecdote, from the voyage of the *Duff*, portrays Benjamin Broomhall using the occasion of his own illness to introduce a novel explanatory system to the Tahitians:

Brother Broomhall, through fatigue, and catching cold, had one day a sharp feverish attack. One of the priests told him this sickness was inflicted on him by the Otaheite Eatōoa, who was angry, and would kill him. Broomhall said he was not at all afraid of their god, who was a bad god, or rather no god; that our Jehovah sent it, and would remove it the next day. The saying instantly spread among the natives; and brother Broomhall began to fear he had spoken too hastily and unthinkingly of his speedy recovery, and that God might be dishonoured if his illness increased: he therefore looked up earnestly to God in prayer to heal him. The priest came to him again and again, as he turned in his bed, and asked of he should be well to-morrow? he said, he trusted his God would restore him. He had a refreshing night's sleep, and on the morrow found himself recovered, and rose. Many of the natives that day questioned him if he was well, and seemed astonished at his recovery. The priest, among the rest, desired to know if the Pretanee [British] God had sent away the sickness; he said, Yes; and took this occasion to speak to them about their superstitions, and urged that the gods which he and his deluded followers worshipped were no gods; but the priest insisted that they had gods, and a great many, and that they prayed to the good ones to keep away the bad ones; and if he did not bless the food, the bad gods would enter into the men and kill them.[104]

The allusion to a specifically Christian discourse of resurrection is perhaps an attempt to resolve the tension within this anecdote, between the missionary's impulse to dismiss the naïveté of Tahitians who seek supernatural causes for events that have a

straightforwardly practical explanation (fatigue), and his oppor-
tunistic substitution of Christian authority within an already
strongly established structure of providential belief.

The willingness of early missionary evangelists to interpret
illness, as well as natural phenomena such as storms and tidal
waves, providentially, left them open to discredit, when these
'signs' proved too capricious for the theological explanation.
Frederick Bennett, reported, when he visited Tahiti in the early
1830s, that the Society islanders had become

staunch ultra-contagionists: they consider that all diseases are infectious,
and should they so far overcome their prejudice as to attend upon a sick
relative, they will on no account use domestic utensils in common with
him. Upon the same principle, also, they find an exotic origin for nearly
all their disorders, leaving us in doubt, (if their traditions of imputed diseases are to be believed,) how the aborigines terminated their existence,
unless by violent death or extreme old age.[105]

As it became apparent that Europeans were more typically bearers
of disease than wealth from over the seas, cults such as Siovili's
offered the traditional remedy of faith-healing. An old woman in
Siovili's party claimed to be possessed by the spirit of Christ, or
'Seesoo Alaisah'. She sat behind a curtain in her house at night,
and the sick came to be cured by the touch of the divine hand. Her
performance collapsed the boundaries of theatre: the curtain
remained closed, but the actress made physical contact with her
audience. Faith-healing was one of several instances in which cults
displayed their willingness to stake their promises in the eventual.
'Seesoo Alaisah' named a date for the return of Christ, ordering
her followers to weed their family graves in preparation for the
raising of the dead. As provision for a subsequent future was rendered unnecessary, 'the taro plants were to be plucked up and
thrown away, bananas were to be destroyed, and the pigs to be
killed and cooked'.[106] The specified day arrived and passed, was
twice postponed, and the prophetess died, giving the lie to her
claims.

The situating of symbolic events within the realm of real time,
although leaving the claims of cult prophets open to disproof, also
subverted the authority of the biblical text: predicting the moment
of narrative closure that would render the book redundant.
Similarly, the claim of access to direct revelation circumvented the

mediation of the Bible. It was where cults such as Siovili's took a worshipful attitude to the printed word that their mimicry could be represented as a mockery by the initiates of print. According to Siikala: 'The sacred character of the books and respect for the secret knowledge they contained was so obvious that one missionary interpreted books as the real idols of the Siovilians.' Siovili used certain texts as props in his visionary performances, holding an English book before him during services and imitating the act of reading by, Siikala writes, 'muttering some unintelligible jargon'.[107] Here the missionary convention of describing comical natives caught out reading books upside down achieved its nemesis. Siovili's sacred text was initially a copy of the *Rambler*; this was subsequently exchanged, Freeman reports, 'for a treatise on rail-roads which had a flashy red cover, and [was] therefore calculated to inspire his flock with additional reverence for their priest'.[108] The implication here is that Siovili is dupe of an uneven exchange transaction, incapable of recognising generic distinctions, of making judgments of literary taste. The gap between mimicked form and altered content loses its threat, reduced to the sign of illiteracy. At the same time, an element of critique remains implicit in Siovili's recognition of the increased prestige value of a text about metropolitan industry. Similarly Evara, the leader of the twentieth-century Papuan cult known as Vailala Madness, would refer to 'a novel of 244 pages, entitled "Love and the Aeroplane", with on its cover a vivid portrayal of a flying machine with a man and a woman precariously attached to it by a rope'.[109] From the slim literary pickings of the periphery, visionaries selected texts that reflected not simply proletarian tastes, but an awareness of the value of technological reference.

Homi Bhabha has discussed the appropriation of the book by the indigenous subject in terms of the concept of 'hybridity'. Bhabha cites an instance from the account of the catechist Anund Messeh, who engaged in distributing Bibles in India early in the nineteenth century. Messeh found that his converts would accept the absolute authority of the Christian story only at the expense of its European mediation: they claimed direct access to revealed truth:

'These books,' said Anund, 'teach the religion of the European Sahibs. It is THEIR book; and they printed it in our language, for our use' . . . 'How can it be the European Book, when we believe that it is God's gift to us?

He sent it to us at Hurdwar.' 'God gave it long ago to the Sahibs, and THEY sent it to us' . . . The ignorance and simplicity of many are very striking, never having heard of a printed book before; and its very appearance was to them miraculous.[110]

Where it is acknowledgement of the authority of the specifically 'European Book' that is overtly resisted, Messeh interprets this response as a simple failure to understand the way in which books work as such. He thus recuperates an indirect testimony to the authority of the culture of print, and specifically to European modes of mediation. As Gauri Viswanathan comments: 'Christianity provides at once the frame of reference and the rules of recognition for the acceptance of its own authority.'[111] Yet Christian discourse remains compromised. The revelation received here by the natives of Delhi is cargo cult, image worship, satisfying the demand for a sign. As Bhabha writes elsewhere, 'In the ambivalent world of the "not quite/not white", on the margins of metropolitan desire, the *founding objects* of the Western world become the erratic, eccentric, accidental *objets trouvés* of the colonial discourse – the part-objects of presence . . . And the holiest of books – the Bible – bearing both the standard of the cross and the standard of empire finds itself strangely dismembered.'[112]

The level of overt criticism implicit in Siovili's use of the book as prop remains subject to reconstruction. The Mamaia movement of Tahiti, on the other hand, which possibly provided the model for Siovili's religion, produced an explicitly politicised commentary on the material base of print culture. The founder of the movement was a native deacon named Teau, known for his devotion, who in 1826 declared himself possessed by the spirit of Jesus Christ, and proclaimed the commencement of the Millennium. Another deacon, Hue, supported Teau's claims. They rapidly achieved a following throughout the Society and Cook islands. Mamaia was an Antinomian sect, preaching the transcendence of law, and endorsing sexual freedom and the production of alcohol. Prophesying was practised by *peropheta*, or prophets, who claimed to be possessed by, among other biblical characters, Peter, John, Mary and Gabriel. According to Siikala: 'The Mamaia prophets tried in every way to copy the behaviour of the Old Testament prophets, even down to their outward appearance. They had long beards and they prayed without ceasing.' By combining Antinomian ethics with New and Old Testament role-playing, the

Mamaia expressed their disregard for biblical teleology. As deacons, the Mamaia leaders had been selected by the Christian mission for their outstanding skill in literacy. Among the indigenous population they were reputed 'to know all the books there were in Tahiti'.[113] They claimed that the distinction between their religion and Christianity was one between the black book – the Bible – and a new white book of their revelations. Yet their doctrine was a subversion of the book. The *peropheta* criticised the missionary policy of demanding payment for the printed word from the perspective of a Tahitian ethics of exchange. They claimed access to direct revelation, memorised, rather than read, texts, and emphasised the efficacy of solitary prayer.

While the Mamaia offered a directly articulated critique of missionary practices, the battle-ground between missionaries and *peropheta* remained the space of metaphor. Niel Gunson has noted that Christianity most effectively colonised the Tahitian imagination as a metaphoric discourse: 'The Tahitians were obviously fond of figurative and parabolic language. The missionaries encouraged this, and their sermons were often rich with similes and metaphors . . . Speakers at missionary meetings vied with one another in the use of similes.'[114] Gunson suggests that the name *mamaia*, which signifies 'unripe fruit, or fruit that falls from the tree before it is properly ripe and is considered by the natives good for nothing' was 'a label . . . derived from a figurative analogy in a missionary's sermon'. If the bountiful fruits of Polynesia served missionaries such as Ellis and Williams as natural theological exempla, the *mamaia* were its antithesis: fruit turning sour in the mouth; natives speaking back to their missionary mentors. For missionaries, the name implied that the cargo cult's promise of bounty would fail to achieve fruition. The Mamaia in turn inverted theological modes of figuration, exposing their inconsistencies. They read biblical truths as metaphoric, and took Christian metaphor literally. According to the account of the missionary John Orsmond, 'They professed (1) that their leader was at the time of inspiration really God (2) that the missionaries are all liars in as much as they state that the soul never dies (3) that hell fire is figurative and not real (4) that men ought to eat and drink abundantly and take any wife they long for that the land may be full of people.' The Mamaia refused to participate in the ordinance of the Lord's Supper, expressing the belief that the bread and wine were really the blood and body of Christ. Their reading of the Christian ceremony converted the missionary to the cannibal other, in the manner of Protestant denunciations of the Catholic doctrine of the host.[115]

The authority of the Christian mission was eventually reasserted, over the perverse poetics of Mamaia critique, through the medium of the body. During a smallpox epidemic in 1841 the *peropheta* refused vaccination, trusting in the power of their religion to resist and cure disease. '"Why vaccinate?" they mockingly asked the missionaries. "Was not the Son of God pierced for us according to what the teachers say and must we be pierced over again?"'[116] Their mockery involved an, in this instance fatal, literalisation of a biblical sign – the wounds of Christ – which in the Western religious imagination survives as a purely symbolic trace. They were discredited and for the most part annihilated, though the Mamaia sect appears to have survived in a reduced and definitively othered form. According to oral evidence collected by Gunson, some members may have persisted with their practices in certain valleys in the regions of Papeete and Puna'auia well into the twentieth century. From outspoken critics they became the uncanny subjects of rumour, their performance a self-erasure – they 'wore black *pareus* and white shirts in order not to be seen and . . . behaved in the manner of poltergeists, throwing knives or stones at those who came along the paths'. Their commentary was no longer intelligible: '"You cannot understand their language. You could certainly hear it, but it was like grunting, grunting, you would not know what it meant . . . Yes, perhaps like animals, though real speech, real speech it was."'[117] For the LMS missionaries, the Mamaia's loss of political force through the ravages of disease was a 'special dispensation of Providence'. Such an outcome made manifest divine Authorship and the ascendency of their religion's exegetical framework. Yet it was precisely this kind of interpretative confidence that cult strategies of misreading had thrown irrevocably into doubt.

Beachcombers as well as Pacific islanders mimicked the ascendent missionary enterprise. During the early nineteenth century a proliferation of 'sailors' sects' throughout the islands represented themselves as alternatives to missionary teaching, or, more compromisingly, as versions of Christian discourse, preparing the way. They achieved particular success in Samoa where, as

I. C. Campbell notes, 'in contrast to other island groups the demand for a foreign religion preceded intensive contact with the West'.[118] On his second voyage to Upolu, John Williams found that his mission of conversion had been anticipated by the activities of two Englishmen. He describes his meeting with these apostate John the Baptists:

thinking that it would afford me pleasure, they began to describe their exploits in turning people religion, as they termed it . . . Having asked how they effected their object, one of them said, 'Why, Sir, I goes about and talks to the people, and tells 'em that our God is good, and theirs is bad; and when they listens to me, I makes 'em religion, and baptizes 'em.' 'Sure,' I exclaimed, 'you baptize them, do you? how do you perform that?' 'Why, Sir,' he answered, 'I takes water, and dips my hands in it, and crosses them in their foreheads and in their breasts, and then I reads a bit of prayer to 'em in English.' 'Of course,' I said, 'they understand you.' 'No,' he rejoined, 'but they say they knows it does 'em good.'[119]

The missionary counters the beachcomber travesty with his own mimicry. Williams's practice of quoting 'direct' exchange – in this case, uneducated speech – situates the beachcombers in terms of their class background. His *faux naif* questions allude to the exploitative and performative aspects of their activities. The beachcombers assume that their lay mission will give Williams 'pleasure', but their explicit recognition that form rather than content, theatre rather than text, constitute the evangelical message, is more than the missionary cares to acknowledge. Countering this implication, Aaron Buzacott's account of a later Samoan beachcomber's evangelistic performance presents the unwillingness to offer exegesis in accompaniment to the sacred text as a key distinction between the beachcomber's mimicry and missionary practice:

a young man . . . had assumed the title of Tangipo, the night crier. In a native hut he erected a rough pulpit, and upon this placed and kept some old books, which he had brought on shore with him. These he styled sacred books, which he allowed to be uncovered only on Sundays. In imitation of the evangelists, he persuaded the people to assemble for worship on the Lord's-day. The service consisted on the part of the hearers, in bowing to the sacred books, which he did not deign to explain to his audience. He managed to be regarded as the high priest of his lotu, or religion, and as such was held in high repute, and liberally supported by his disciples, of whom there were a few in several villages.[120]

The beachcomber is generally an exaggerated other within the missionary text. More often represented as a figure of extreme violence than as mimic preacher, he provides a type of theatre akin to that of traditional Polynesian priestly religions. Williams fantasises a tableau in which a beachcomber 'seated himself upon a kind of stage, smeared with blood, and surrounded with the heads of his victims. In this state, his followers would convey him on their shoulders, with songs of savage triumph, to his own residence.' Despite their excessive violence, these monsters are perhaps less threatening than are the charlatan pastors to the missionary enterprise: objects, rather than subjects, of worship. Of another such renegade, Williams narrates: 'The chief for whom he was fighting entertained so high an opinion of his bravery, that he cut off his head, . . . and it was said that he worshipped it as his *etu*.'[121]

Yet the beachcomber was also capable of providing an informed critique of missionary practices. Williams writes of an escaped convict who

ingratiated himself into the favour of the chiefs and people by telling them that they were selling their hogs and provisions at a price far too small, in receiving but eight or ten yards of print, &c., for a pig, whereas, in England, one joint was sold for more than they obtained for the whole; and that the Missionaries, from interested motives, were keeping them in the dark upon these subjects . . . Inflated with ideas of his own importance, he drew up a list of every article they had to dispose of, with the price attached.

This calculated critique nonetheless retains an element of theatre: 'he . . . carried his insolence so far, that one week-day afternoon, he entered the chapel and upbraided [the Missionary] with not having told the people to demand higher prices for their property'. The performance has uncomfortable echoes of Christ's denunciation of the temple money-changers. Unlike the sailor preachers, this figure must be recognised by Williams as 'certainly a well educated and clever rogue', who illustrates for the islanders, with facts and figures, the double standard inherent in the colonial economic contract. In the face of literate criticism, Williams resorts to a refusal to read, claiming, punningly, that 'a document from a rogue was beneath my notice'. The islanders put the beachcomber to trial by cargo, concluding 'that, if the man would bring his ships with his black coats and beautiful shawls, he should have all the pigs and arrow-root in the island; but if his ships, his black coats, and shawls, were only in his mouth he was a liar, and unworthy of regard'.[122] The beachcomber, unlike the missionary, is unable to produce objects to substantiate his discourse: he is undermined by the very economic relation he has attempted to expose.

CHAPTER 3

'Other people's books': Stevenson's Pacific travels

The first section of this book has examined a variety of early written accounts depicting the reception of metropolitan objects and technologies within Pacific cultures. Focusing primarily on the representation of writing and print, both as items and methods of exchange, I have argued for the emergence of a Pacific context of appropriation and interrogation, even from within texts concerned to present self-affirming images of 'native' wonderment at Western culture. The next chapters move from the broadly textual to the more specifically literary implications of this suggestion. I turn to the case of a particular author, Robert Louis Stevenson, who produced a body of literature for metropolitan consumption from the Pacific in the late nineteenth century. At this stage, the majority of Pacific cultures were relatively familiar with writing: Stevenson's travels among the islands were in part an ironised authorial quest for that reflecting, elevating gaze of wonderment familiar from earlier accounts of contact. In fact, that degree of investment in his writing came most explicitly for Stevenson from the context that he had left behind – the British literary establishment. Stevenson was perhaps the late nineteenth-century writer who most embodied a European romantic myth of authorship. It was the metropolitan mythologisation of writing, rather than its Pacific projections, that his example serves to interrogate.

Stevenson's Pacific travels were envisaged as a book. When he departed for the Marquesas from San Francisco in the yacht *Casco*, on 28 June 1888, his American agent Samuel Sidney McClure had already obtained a commission from the New York *Sun* for a series of letters describing his anticipated adventures. McClure had also organised serialisation in the English press: the net earnings of the correspondence were to amount to $15,000. Stevenson worked on his 'South Seas' material during the journey on the *Casco*, which

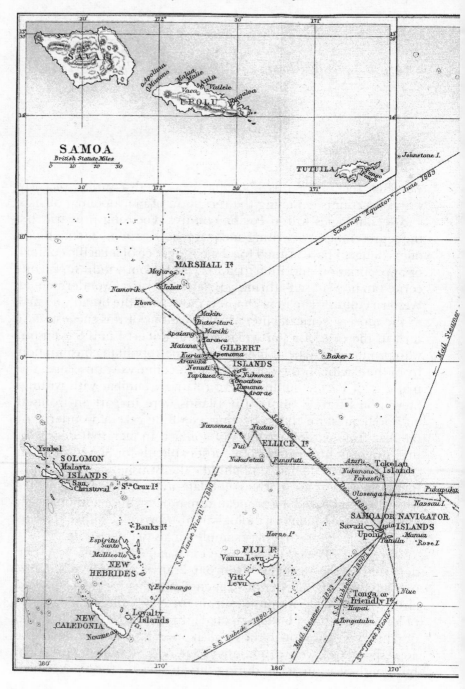

Map 1. A map to illustrate Robert Louis Stevenson's

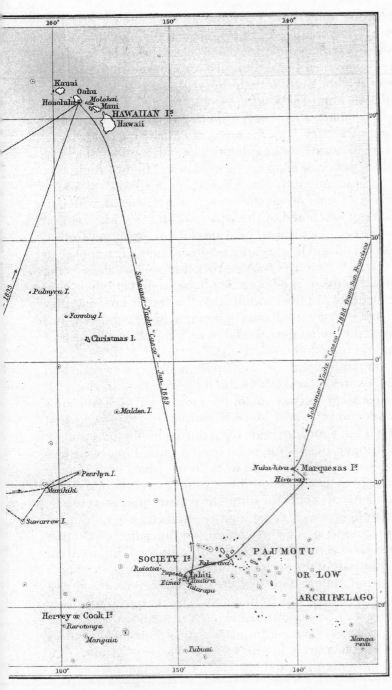

life in the South Seas, from *In the South Seas*.

took him throughout French Polynesia, and to Hawaii, and during his travels on the trading steamer *Equator*, among the atolls of Micronesia. His correspondence makes clear, however, that from the earliest stages he imagined his project in terms of the encompassing text of a book rather than the fragmentary text of letters.

An initial version, *The South Seas*, was printed as a copyright edition in November 1890. Stevenson instructed that the printed copy be sent on to New York for serialisation, writing to McClure: 'what you are to receive is not so much a certain number of letters, as a certain number of chapters in my book. The two things are identical but not conterminous. It is for you to choose out of the one what is most suitable for the other.'[1] The changed format of the text was not welcomed by the editors of the *Sun*, who refused to take the letters as per the original agreement. As Sidney Colvin, Stevenson's friend and literary adviser, described their response in a letter to Charles Baxter, 'The New York Sun people, after seeing the first instalments of the South Sea book, repudiate their contract with McClure, on the grounds that the stuff is not what they asked for: that is to say, not letters of incident and experience, hot and hot from the scenes described, but only the advance sheets of a book, and rather a dull book at that.'[2]

Colvin sympathised with the *Sun*'s editors. Stevenson's wife and stepson also expressed misgivings about the 'South Seas' material. Indeed, *In the South Seas* was one of the most vexed of Stevenson's literary productions: at each stage negatively received by its first readers, it did not appear in book form during his lifetime, and, as Roger Swearingen notes, 'the complicated publishing history of *The South Seas* as a distinct single work shows [that] both in contents and order of arrangement it was subject to continual evolution in the hands of others for some thirty years after Stevenson's death'.[3] Yet criticisms were revealingly contradictory. According to Colvin, the complaint of the commissioning editors was that Stevenson's travel account was too heavily authored. Rather than writing as transparent transcription, 'letters of incident', leaving a tangible imprint, 'hot and hot', of the tropics, Stevenson sent the *Sun* fragments of what was undeniably a book; one whose very unreadability attested unequivocally to its textuality. Yet it was in fact less an over-assertive authorial presence than his refusal to deliver his Pacific travels in the expected Stevenson authorial format that most disappointed his readers' expectations.

Stevenson's 'South Seas' writings signified book before story: moreover, they did not even claim the status of original book, of first word. Rather than inventing an Adamic role of first Pacific author, free to name what he saw as he pleased, he acknowledged the pre-existence of a Pacific library, and insisted upon reading before he wrote. In a letter from Honolulu, dated 21 May 1889, Fanny Stevenson writes:

Louis has the most enchanting material that any one ever had in the whole world for his book, and I am afraid he is going to spoil it all. He has taken it into his Scotch Stevenson head, that a stern duty lies before him, and that his book must be a sort of scientific and historical impersonal thing, comparing the different languages (of which he knows nothing, really) and the different peoples, the object being to settle the question as to whether they are of common Malay origin or not . . . And I believe there is no one living who has got so near to them, or who understands them as he does. Think of a small treatise on the Polynesian races being offered to people who are dying to hear about Ori a Ori, the making of brothers with cannibals, the strange stories they told, and the extraordinary adventures that befell us; – suppose Herman Melville had given us his theories as to the Polynesian language and the probable good or evil results of the missionary influence instead of *Omoo* and *Typee* . . . Louis says it is a stern sense of duty that is at the bottom of it, which is more alarming than anything else. I am so sure that you will agree with me that I am going to ask you to throw the weight of your influence as heavily as possible in the scales with me . . . otherwise Louis will spend a good deal of time in Sydney actually *reading up* other people's books on the Islands.[4]

Stevenson is represented here as engaging in an excess of primary reading. For the immediacy of encounter he has substituted the mediation of theory; his first-hand authority becoming dissipated in his willingness to defer to prior texts. Travel writing always involves a wrestling with predecessors, a trope of debunking. The traveller embarks with preconceptions or questions formulated from the stories that circulate around a destination. Gradually these are displaced by the traveller's own story. Yet the threat with Stevenson in the Pacific, as Fanny envisaged it, was that he would fail to discard his textual baggage: indeed, that he would accumulate more and more *en route*. Travel was drawing him into, and not away from, the library.

Fanny's criticisms of Stevenson's methods recall those levelled by early practitioners of ethnographic fieldwork against Victorian 'armchair' anthropology.[5] Although he is on the scene, Stevenson is effectively losing contact. He remains within the library, drawing up a comparative treatise, rather than producing a text of personal experience. Fanny's idea of fieldwork is, however, salacious rather than scientific. What Stevenson should be extracting from his immediate encounters are details of the 'extraordinary' rather than the everyday: cannibals made brothers; intimacy with the other. In a letter from Samoa, dated January 1890, she offers a comic portrait of her husband falling between two incipient anthropological stools:

I suppose Lloyd has described my desperate engagements with the man of genius over the South Sea book. Many times I was almost in despair. He had got 'Darwin on the Coral Insect' – no, Darwin was 'Coral Reefs'; somebody else on Melanesian languages, books on the origin of the South Sea peoples, and all sorts of scientific pamphlets and papers . . . Instead of writing about his adventures in these wild islands, he would ventilate his own theories on the vexed questions of race and language. He wasted much precious time over grammars and dictionaries, with no results, for he was able to get an insight into hardly any native tongue. Then he must study the coral business. That, I believe, would have ruined the book but for my brutality. We had stopped when cruising . . . at a most curious and interesting Island. We were all going ashore together, but to my surprise Louis refused to start with us, but said he would follow in a second boat. Lloyd and I spent several hours wandering over the island, having some odd adventures and seeing many curious things. But no Louis. At last we gave him up and went down to the beach to return to the ship. There was that gentleman on the reef, halfway between the ship and the shore, knee-deep in water, the tropical sun beating on his unprotected head, hammering at the reef with a big hatchet. His face was purple and his eyes injected with blood. 'Louis, you will die,' I cried, 'come away out of the sun quickly.' 'No' he answered, 'I must get specimens from this extraordinary piece of coral. I can't take the whole of it, for it's too heavy, but after two hours' hard work I have got off bits showing the different sorts of formation. I still haven't got all there is to be got, and the work is so hard nobody will help me.' He then showed me the fragments that he wished me to take to the ship; for dinner, fatigue, nothing should get him away from the important discoveries he was making. I looked at his specimens with contempt. 'Louis,' I said, 'how ignorant you are! Why, that is only the common brain coral. Any schoolboy in San Francisco will give you specimens if you really want them.'[6]

Stevenson, the would-be ethnographer and naturalist, theorist of remote languages, collector of exotic specimens, is here reduced to no more than the ludicrous figure of the English tourist, who lacks a gift in foreign tongues, runs about at midday without a hat on, and whose Old World ignorance can be shown up by an elementary degree of New World savvy. The role of the 'man of genius' is to weave story magically, without labour, and instead he engages in cumbersome study and superfluous manual activity. The author has become the clown.

In both the extracts from Fanny's correspondence, Stevenson's recognition of his lack of authority figures as a failure to do justice to the immediate exoticism of their Pacific encounters. His bookishness is a deficiency of engagement: comparative linguistics takes him away from oral exchange; Darwin on 'Coral Reefs' does not enable him to recognise simple coral formations. Fears are expressed that Stevenson is losing a contest of appropriation: rather than recuperating the novelty of the Pacific to the idiosyncrasies of his personal style, his energy is dissipated upon a variety of new interests that position him as student of Pacific culture rather than master of literary production. Any generically specific conception of authorship collapses in these responses, to be replaced by the figuration of authorship as performance, threatened by a comic loss of authority.

In this chapter I want to explore, through relatively detailed readings of the different sections of *In the South Seas* and of some of his less well-known or fragmentary late writings, the various authorial roles that Stevenson adopted in order to negotiate his Pacific material. By mapping quite specifically the ways in which his projected authority fluctuates with shifts of location, I argue that, for Stevenson, being in a novel environment was always primarily about constituting himself as an authorial subject: a task which, however, involved becoming aware of the ways in which exotic environments were resistant to, rather than simply available for, inscription.

THE MARQUESAS: ART AND CANNIBALISM

Stevenson confronts directly the relationship between authority and communication in the second chapter of *In the South Seas*. Dismissing, or perhaps confirming, Fanny's scathing comment that 'he was able to get an insight into hardly any native tongue', he confidently asserts,

The impediment of tongues was one that I particularly over-estimated. The languages of Polynesia are easy to smatter, though hard to speak with elegance. And they are extremely similar, so that a person who has a tincture of one or two may risk, not without hope, an attempt upon the others.

And again, not only is Polynesian easy to smatter, but interpreters abound. Missionaries, traders, and broken white folk living on the bounty of the natives, are to be found in almost every isle and hamlet; and even where these are unserviceable, the natives themselves have often scraped up a little English, and in the French zone (though far less commonly) a little French–English, or an efficient pidgin, what is called to the westward 'Beach-la-Mar', comes easy to the Polynesian; it is now taught, besides, in the schools of Hawaii; . . . and will almost certainly become, the tongue of the Pacific.[7]

Stevenson's confidence that he can master communication in this new context is predicated upon a willingness to embrace partiality and mediation: the intercultural language of pidgin as official tongue. Indeed, he must invent a new verb, to *smatter*, for the type of linguistic competence required: a verb suggestive of the landscape of islands rather than continents, embracing the poetry of hybridity, rather than the authority of bilingualism. He recognises the kinds of complex indebtedness in post-contact Pacific languages that I have sketched in the first two chapters of this book: the importance of intermediary figures such as beachcombers and missionaries to cross-cultural communication and interpretation; the ways in which the taught language of literacy remains grounded in the give and take of spoken exchange.

Yet this playful, deauthorising attitude to language is predicated upon other, ambiguous forms of authority. 'But to be able to speak to people is not all', Stevenson continues. Communication is facilitated by alternative relationships of power. As 'showman of the *Casco*', he is curator of a floating museum of metropolitan artefacts. He reiterates the scenario, familiar from the literature of first contact, of natives lost in wonderment at a superior material culture:

The men fathomed out her dimensions with their arms, as their fathers fathomed out the ships of Cook; the women declared the cabins more lovely than a church; bouncing Junos were never weary of sitting in the chairs and contemplating in the glass their own bland images; and I have seen one lady strip up her dress, and, with cries of wonder and delight, rub herself bare-breeched upon the velvet cushions. (11)

This catalogue of Marquesan responses to the *Casco*'s luxury fittings recites a mini-history: here Stevenson briefly attains the authority of the original European, and outdoes those other predecessors, the missionaries, in showing off a cabin 'more lovely than a church'. With glib cultural assurance, he depicts Polynesian bodies thrown into ludicrous reflection by the yacht's highly furnished interior: the face in the mirror is described as a 'bland image', unworthy of poetry, which appears nonetheless to have a hypnotic effect on the naïvely fetishistic Marquesan; the novelty of velvet produces an autoerotic display that reveals the flimsiness of civilised costume. Yet as 'showman', Stevenson is performer as well as curator, and exchange in this context goes beyond the inscription of material relations. He recognises that he is object of the Marquesan gaze, and that the very items that he places on display are effectively refigured, when perceived differently by an audience unfamiliar with their attributes. A showing of his family photograph album produces in Stevenson an effect of alienation, and in an Antipodean reversal, he tropes the once-familiar as exotic: 'this sober gallery, their everyday costumes and physiognomies, had become transformed, in three weeks sailing, into things wonderful and rich and foreign; alien faces, barbaric dresses'(11).

If there is an element of self-conscious cultural imperialism to the role of luxury traveller, Stevenson also has access to a marginal subjectivity, which he represents as a more legitimate basis of cross-cultural communication. 'It was', he claims, 'perhaps yet more important that I had enjoyed in my youth some knowledge of our Scots folk of the Highlands and the Islands.'(12) He posits a kinship between Scottish and Polynesian oral traditions, drawing attention to similarities in pronunciation such as 'the elision of medial consonants' and the 'catch'. More politically, he documents a comparable history of colonisation and the circumscription of cultural practices, and recognises a mutual tradition of celebratory violence that develops under such historical circumstances. This relativism, however, turns out to be merely a pretext for the production of an ethnographic account of Marquesan custom:

When I desired any detail of savage custom, or of superstitious belief, I cast back in the story of my fathers, and fished for what I wanted with some trait of equal barbarism: Michael Scott, Lord Derwentwater's head, the second-sight, the Walter Kelpie, – each of these I have found to be a killing bait; the black bull's head of Stirling procured me the legend of *Rahero*; and what I knew of the Cluny Macphersons, or the Appin Stewarts, enabled me to learn, and helped me to understand, about the *Tevas* of Tahiti. The native was no longer ashamed, his sense of kinship grew warmer, and his lips were opened. (13)

Stevenson's language betrays the unevenness of such attempts at cross-cultural barter. Compatible anecdotes are proffered in the spirit of the hunt, eliciting information duplicitously, in the manner of hypnotism. An apparently even exchange remains weighted in favour of the materially stronger culture.

A relationship of unequal status, then, lurks behind apparent discursive equilibrium; and a mutual self-alienation displaces an overt display of material advantage. It is this awareness of the shifting and non-essential value of authority that was manifest in Stevenson's complex attitude to his own authority as writer, anxiously noted by the first readers of his 'South Seas' material. *In the South Seas* is a text precisely about how it might be possible to write the Pacific islands. In his own account of his methodology, Stevenson embraces a performative, rather than writerly, attitude to communication. He shifts between the characters of the ethnographer and the wealthy traveller, or rehearses the hybrid languages of Polynesia, playing a role rather than asserting an identity, and embracing a mediated and partial access to the foreign. Where his first readers depicted Stevenson's methods of cross-cultural inquiry as cumbersome and laborious, his neologism for the acquisition of language, to 'smatter', suggests a ludic attitude to the relationships between discourse, authority and identity.

Stevenson had departed for the Pacific with literary expectations. While in San Francisco, he was introduced to the writings of Herman Melville by Charles Warren Stoddard, a writer who had himself made three journeys to Hawaii and one to Tahiti. According to Jenni Calder, Melville 'had first brought the Pacific within literary perspectives. Louis read him enthusiastically, whetting his appetite for the experiences that were soon to be his.'[8] Stoddard, who had published several volumes of tales based on his Pacific experiences, including the popular *South Sea Idyls* and *The Island of Tranquil Delights*, was himself not unaware of the biases of literary travel. The protagonist of 'The Island of Tranquil Delights' arrives in Tahiti 'saturated with romance. I fed on the nectar and ambrosia that drop from the pens of Herman Melville, Jules Verne, Mayne Reid and the rest.' Gradually a first-hand experience of Tahitian culture displaces the false images he has imbibed with such literary lotus-eating, and his collection of literary reference books is relegated to the tool-chest of the *bricoleur*: 'the circulating library that a literary tramp would be most likely to cling to in adversity'.[9] Stoddard's first collection of Pacific stories had been published shortly before he became secretary to Mark Twain in London. Twain's own career as a writer was launched with the series of twenty-five sponsored weekly letters he wrote from Hawaii in 1866, for the Sacramento *Union*.[10] Early in 1888 Stevenson had met Twain in New York.

Yet Stevenson becomes critical of his preliminary 'South Seas' reading once he arrives on the scene. In the Marquesas, language encountered only in print, in Melville's *Typee*, is heard as speech, exposing Melville's writing as inaccurate transcription. 'Take the valley of Hapaa', writes Stevenson,

known to readers of Herman Melville under the grotesque mis-spelling of Hapar. There are but two writers who have touched the South Seas with any genius, both Americans: Melville and Charles Warren Stoddard; and at the christening of the first and greatest, some influential fairy must have been neglected: 'He shall be able to see,' 'He shall be able to tell,' 'He shall be able to charm,' said the friendly godmothers; 'But he shall not be able to hear,' exclaimed the last. (25)

A false textual image is displaced by an immediate sensory impression. Melville, the literary forefather, becomes infantilised as the ear undermines the pen. By placing Melville within the framework of folklore, as an incongruous Sleeping Beauty, Stevenson plays with the notion of romanticisation. Yet this is more than a ritual father-killing, making way for the play of Stevenson's own authorial imagination. The kind of expectation that provoked Fanny's incredulity in her letter to Colvin: 'Suppose Herman Melville had given us his theories as to the Polynesian language . . . instead of *Omoo* and *Typee*' informs Stevenson's criticism of Melville. In his own chapters on the Marquesas, Stevenson includes a table of six Polynesian languages, drawing attention to the minute differences, almost invisible in a written text – the change of a vowel or the elision of a consonant – that achieve significance in pronunciation. These tables signal typographically the extent to which Stevenson was prepared to disrupt the smooth development of his narrative with ethnographic data.

Stevenson's description of his first encounter with the Marquesans exemplifies what Mary Louise Pratt has termed 'the classic Polynesian arrival scene'. Its topoi of initial contact are mirrored in the opening passages of Raymond Firth's ethnographic classic *We, the Tikopia*. Firth, confronted by the approach of Tikopian canoes to his sailing ship, manned by 'men . . . bare to the waist, girdled with bark-cloth, large fans stuck in the back of their belts, tortoise-shell rings or rolls of leaf in the ear-lobes and nose, bearded, and with long hair flowing loosely over their shoulders', reflects upon the difficulties of anthropological classification: 'I wondered how such turbulent human material could ever be induced to submit to scientific study.'[11] Stevenson expresses a comparable sense of frustration when he is made the object of the Marquesan gaze: 'as I sat writing up my journal, the cabin was filled from end to end with Marquesans . . . regarding me in silence with embarrassing eyes . . . A kind of despair came over me, to sit there helpless under all those staring orbs' (8). He holds the Marquesans responsible for this failure of communication, claiming he felt 'a kind of rage to think they were beyond the reach of articulate communication, like furred animals, or folk born deaf, or the dwellers of some alien planet' (8). The use of the infinitive here implies an effort of will: Stevenson thinks the Marquesans into objecthood, and re-establishes his authority. In fact it is Stevenson's party who have failed to respond to the communicative overtures of the Marquesans, who speak all too fluently an acquired language of trade: 'all talking, and we could not understand one word; all trying to trade with us, who had no thought of trading' (7). The evocation of a first-contact situation, in which the native displays a naïve delight in over-valued trinkets, slides into the disappointed recognition of a post-lapsarian paradise. By 1888, the Marquesan experience of barter with Europeans in fact went back over a century.[12] The islanders present an 'embarrassing' reflection of Western exchange values, appearing to be motivated by an unmitigated market instinct.

For Stevenson, the Pacific islands are a site of physical recuperation. Yet the revivification of the author has a mortifying reflection in the ravages of imported disease among Polynesian populations, which according to Stevenson are responsible for a decline in local cultural production.[13] He claims: 'The whole body of Marquesan poetry and music was being suffered to die out with a single dispirited generation' (29). The use of the word *body* makes explicit the link between physical well-being and cultural production, despite the implication, in 'dispirited', of a failure of artistic inspiration.[14] In Stevenson's account, the depiction of a primitive fascination with the metropolitan object serves to reinstate the superiority of a colonising culture exposed as infective, degenerate. The Marquesans are represented as enacting the death wish of primitive peoples confronted by Western cultural supremacy. According to Stevenson, 'The coffin, though of late introduction, strangely engages their attention. It is to the mature Marquesan what a watch is to the European schoolboy.' The coffin is here presented as a cult object, desire for which produces psychosomatic effects. Disease is refigured as 'rather of the will than of the body' (28): the foreign object can then be represented as cure, revivifying both body and artistic practice: 'a Marquesan, dying of this discouragement – perhaps I should rather say this acquiescence – has been known, at the fulfilment of his crowning wish, on the mere sight of that desired hermitage, his coffin – to revive, recover, shake off the hand of death, and be restored for years to his occupations – carving *tikis* (idols), let us say, or braiding old men's beards.' Alternatively, cannibalism is held by Stevenson responsible for the proscription of Marquesan art. He claims that 'it formed the hire of the artist . . . The civil power, in its crusade against man-eating, has had to examine one after another all Marquesan arts and pleasures, has found them one after another tainted with a cannibal element, and one after another has placed them on the proscript list' (82). If, as William Arens has argued, societies label other cultures cannibal in order to 'define their sense of worth and draw the line between contemporary civilisation and barbarism', within Stevenson's account cannibalism displaces, even as it mirrors, the feeding of foreign disease upon the Marquesan body.[15]

Fanny Stevenson's correspondence offers an interesting commentary on this relationship. Her gender gives her access to a privileged understanding of the relationship between custom and fashion, which in turn enables her to interrogate essentialist

notions of savagery and to show how costumes, objects and
posturings position individuals in the theatrics of cultural
exchange. Writing to Colvin from the Marquesas, she asserts: 'that
they are cannibals may be true, but that is only a freak of fashion
like the taste for decayed game, and not much more unpleasant'.
She describes how the Western object has come to serve in, rather
than transform, savage practices:

In the next island we are going to visit, a man whom the whole population hated was killed for vengeance. The question was how should every
man have a taste of his enemy without the authorities finding out. This
was solved by filling matchboxes with the cooked flesh, and passing them
about. I think the combination of the civilized matchbox and the 'long
pig' very interesting.

The transformation from savage to civilised is a simple change of
costume: 'When we first arrived there they swarmed over the vessel
like flies, clothed in breech cloths and tattooing only. For their
farewell visit the beachcomber had made them all white trousers
and shirts. Every man was as clean as a new pin, and shining with
cocoanut oil, their finger nails, even, as carefully looked after as
our own.' It is as easily inverted:

Lloyd has had given him by a native woman an ornament to wear in the
war-dance. It is composed of locks of women's hair made into a sort of
gigantic fringe. As many as ten women were killed to make this ghastly
adornment, their bodies being cooked for the dancer's feast. I am glad
to tell you that quite suddenly Louis's health took a change for the better,
and he is now almost as well as ever he was in his life.[16]

The unselfconscious slide from the description of an artistic practice predicated on the destruction of the body, to comments on the
revivification of Stevenson the artist, again inscribes a relationship
between the discourse of savage degeneracy and the romance of
authorship at the periphery.

Stevenson also acknowledges that certain canny Polynesian performances suit themselves to foreigners' expectations. He tells the
story of a Marquesan who, for the benefit of a British plantation
superintendent, 'picked up a human foot, and provocatively
staring at the stranger, grinned and nibbled at the heel'(92).
Playing the cannibal, the Marquesan strategically manipulates an
image of difference in order to intimidate his audience: equally,
the foreigner could respond with a performance of power in order

to establish a tenuous authority. Threatened during subsequent wars between rival Marquesan chiefs, the same settler gathered together 'three other whites . . . and (what was their best defence) ostentatiously practised rifle shooting by day upon the beach. Natives were often there to watch them; the practice was excellent; and the assault was never delivered.' (94) Stevenson remains susceptible to the kinds of ambiguity that such liminal performances generate. As his party say farewell to the Marquesas, he offers a portrait of 'an incurable cannibal grandee': unlike the author, an unrecuperated figure. As a final image of duplicitous native identity, he juxtaposes the extended hand, sign of an achieved cross-cultural friendship, with the human hand as cannibal delicacy: 'His favourite morsel was the human hand, of which he speaks today with an ill-favoured lustfulness. And when he said good-bye to Mrs Stevenson, holding her hand, . . . he wrote upon her mind a sentimental impression which I tried in vain to share.' (119)

THE PAUMOTUS: MAPPING AND WRITING

Recent studies of the literature of travel have represented travelling as primarily a written experience. In an impressionistic essay entitled 'Travel and Writing', Michel Butor exhaustively unpacks the literal and metaphoric connections between the activities of writing, reading and travelling.[17] To read and to write are forms of mental excursion: equally, to travel is to read the signs of landscape, and to inscribe the traces of an itinerary upon its surface. In Butor's account, travel is implicitly the prerogative of the literate. Only literate travellers can appreciate the subtext of the travel experience, its simultaneous frame of reference on the page and within the library. Dean MacCannell, in his celebrated study *The Tourist*, discusses the ways in which 'markers' – texts such as plaques or brochures, as well as reproductions such as souvenirs – effectively create sights for the tourist imagination. Travel is not experienced until it has become mapped by the marker.[18] As Jonathan Culler elaborates:

Not only do they create sights; when the tourist encounters the sight, the markers remain surprisingly important: one may continually refer to the marker to discover what features of the sight are indeed significant; one may engage in the production of further markers by writing about the sight or photographing it . . . In each case the touristic experience involves a production of or participation in a sign relation between marker and sight.[19]

In trying to avoid the futile cycle of the search for authenticity, and to embrace instead the retrospective condition of modernity, critics such as MacCannell privilege textual representation.[20] Their analyses instate literacy as the ticket to travel: non-literate cultures can only ever be the objects of accounts produced and assessed according to such assumptions.

Among the atolls of Polynesia, Stevenson must negotiate with travel that threatens to be unwritable. The 'low island' landscape of the Tuamotu archipelago (which he refers to as 'the Paumotus') presents an impediment to authorial appropriation: physical minimalism. A barren and unimposing setting, the atoll represents a limited topic, 'offering to the eye, even when perfect, only a ring of glittering beach and verdant foliage, enclosing and enclosed by the blue sea'(124). The senses are disappointed. Here is a painting 'robbed of all its colour', a sculpture that offends a sense of proportion: 'an inconsiderable islet, flat as a plate upon the sea, and spiked with palms of disproportioned altitude'(126). Stevenson represents atoll life as lotus-eating bleached of gratification: 'I have spent since then long months upon low islands; I know the tedium of their undistinguished days; I know the burden of their diet.'(126) He describes the atoll of Fakarava as a 'frail barrier . . . a mere causeway in the sea, of nature's handiwork, yet of no greater magnitude than many of the works of man'(129). The causeway between reaches of sea, like writing, is a mark threatened with erasure. Despite its barrenness, the atoll represents a feminine geography: its shape a ring, drawing downwards in its centre to a watery space. Here the writer's subject matter must be something more than meets the eye.

Initially, Stevenson takes up the role of naturalist, describing a detail that emerges on close inspection. Difference is located in the realm of the microscopic: 'the two beaches do certainly abound in life, and they are strangely different'(135). In the lagoon are smooth waters and white shells; on the ocean side, rough surf, and 'variety and brilliancy' of marine life. He devises an experiment: 'Collect the shells from each, set them side by side, and you would suppose they came from different hemispheres; the one so pale, the other so brilliant; the one prevalently white, the other a score of hues.' (136) By describing the lagoon ecology first, Stevenson implies that the atoll's strip of land effectively colours and creates life, although it could equally be inferred that the lagoon encircled by the atoll offers a bleached, dead reflection of the oceanscape. The voice of the naturalist here recalls that of Phillip Gosse, the father of Stevenson's contemporary and friend, Edmund Gosse, whom the latter portrays in *Father and Son,* practising natural theology on the coast of Devon.[21] But authorship in the atolls is *bricolage* rather than revelation: Stevenson's fellow-traveller between the beaches' 'hemispheres of difference' is the hermit crab, a 'nasty little wrecker, scavenger and squatter'.

To make literature, rather than natural history, in the atolls, Stevenson adopts a genre that invests absence with significance: that of the fantastic. The details that the naturalist uncovers provide the uncanny elements of horror story: 'It adds a last touch of horror to the thought of this precarious annular gangway in the sea, that even what there is of it is not of honest rock, but organic, part alive, part putrescent; even the clean sea and the bright fish about it poisoned, the most stubborn boulder burrowed in by worms, the lightest dust venomous as an apothecary's drugs.' (138) Disease in this context is sinister rather than tragic, part of a bizarre plot in which degeneracy undermines virility: 'Early in the morning, it is narrated, aged and malicious persons creep into the sleeping village, and stealthily make water at the doors of the houses of the young men. Thus they propagate disease; thus they breathe on and obliterate comeliness and health, the objects of their envy.' (150) Unseen, observing presences populate the atolls in Stevenson's imagination: 'the *Casco* sailed by under the fire of unsuspected eyes. And one thing is surely true, that even on these ribbons of land an army might lie hid and no passing mariner divine its presence.' (129) A narrative of terror can be uncovered below the surface of the atoll. Stevenson tells the tale of the disappearance of some children on the islet of Hao. Searchers, alerted by 'the brown hand of a human being issu[ing] from the ground', discovered a cave in which 'sixteen cannibals were found crouching among human bones and singular and horrid curiosities'. This horror story even has a personal resonance: Stevenson's name is inscribed in the identity of the victims, 'the two young sons of a Captain Steven' (148).

Stevenson returns to the role of ethnographer, seeking out and inscribing legend. His comparative wealth serves as a touchstone, enabling him simultaneously to locate and to disqualify stories of horror. The atoll of Fakarava is deserted when the *Casco* arrives, yet the empty island magically produces a population when Stevenson provides a feast. His gift enables him to become master–narrator and mimic of local myth: 'In view of low island tales, and that awful frequentation which makes men avoid the seaward beaches of an atoll, some two score of those that ate with us may have returned, for the occasion, from the kingdom of the dead.'(140) Stevenson also establishes a difference between private and public morality among the Tuamotuans: 'three at least, who had refused at the festival, greedily drank rum behind a door'(152). In the event, the feast he holds comes to 'haunt' him. An old man dies of exhaustion: Stevenson is indirectly responsible for swelling, as well as summoning, the ranks of the dead. He witnesses the progress of the death with the detached titillation of a writer recognising a subject: 'the human tragedy reduced to its bare elements, a sight beyond pathos, stirring a thrill of curiosity'(157).

Stevenson's play with the invisible in the Tuamotus is founded upon an unequal material relationship, and displays levity toward local tradition. Yet he comes to recognise the value of such tradition in creating a cultural repository for what have proved to be the unwritable atolls. Oral tales are acknowledged to be consummate fantastic narratives, and Stevenson concedes to become the collector, rather than the writer, of 'graveyard stories'. This involves an exchange of tales in which his own stories are subordinate, serving merely as prompts for Tuamotuan narration. Reviewing the superstitions of his own culture in a new light, Stevenson comments 'no Polynesian seems at all to share our European horror of bones and mummies.' The perception exemplifies the type of reciprocal critique that he gestured towards when, seeking detail of 'savage custom' in the Marquesas, he 'cast back in the story of my fathers, and fished for . . . some trait of equal barbarism'(13). In the Tuamotus, legend reshapes the landscape: 'To one who conceives of these atolls, so narrow, so barren, so beset with sea, here would seem a superfluity of ghostly denizens.' The atoll's physical barrenness becomes spiritual fertility: cultures reinvent their territories.

THE EIGHT ISLANDS: OTHERNESS AND IDENTITY

In Hawaii, Stevenson is confronted by a simulacrum society: a successfully Westernised Pacific island. In a desire to differentiate the text of his own experience from that of the tourist multitude, he becomes implicated in a search for authenticity, attempting to locate a traditional Hawaiian culture beneath the veneer of appropriated modernity. Richard Handler and Jocelyn Linnekin have isolated two strands to the retrospective construction of tradition within modern Hawaiian culture: the recognition of persisting rural practices, and the selective reclamation of myth.[22] Stevenson investigates both these aspects of the traditional. He chooses to sojourn in Hookena, a village that is reputedly 'uninhabited by any white, the creature of pure native taste' (179). And he explores Hawaiian history, revivifying a tradition of heroic achievement.

Yet as he goes unnoticed in a society that successfully mirrors European dress, housing and cuisine, Stevenson continues to regret an original exchange of gaze between Hawaiian and British subjects. The explorer provides a measure for the failed originality of his experience. In a passage that I quoted earlier, he measures the difference between his own reconstructed first-contact scenario, and the impact of genuine initial cross-cultural encounter:

One hundred and ten years before the ancestors of these indifferents had looked in the faces of Cook and his seamen with admiration and alarm, called them gods, called them volcanoes; took their clothes for a loose skin, confounded their hats and their heads, and described their pockets as a 'treasure door, through which they plunge their hands into their bodies and bring forth cutlery and necklaces and cloth and nails'. (183)

The lament here for the passing of empire's age of exploration, and its dialectic of otherness, is not for the loss of an objectified 'native' subject of description. Rather, Stevenson elegises an experience of European objectification within the Hawaiian metaphoric imagination.[23] Marshall Sahlins has suggested that a particular mythical framework was responsible for the reception of Captain Cook's party in Hawaii as divine visitation. According to Sahlins, the novel appearance of Cook was interpreted as the cyclical reappearance of the god Lono, the Hawaiian imagination refiguring 'discovery' as eternal return: 'Cook was a tradition for Hawaiians before he was a fact.'[24] Stevenson desires a comparable experience of mythologisation: to recognise his own difference, returned to him by the gaze of the other.

In a debate that has achieved its own mythical status, Gananath Obeyesekere has challenged Sahlins's reconstruction of the context of Cook's assassination, suggesting that Hawaiian recourse to the defence of mythology was a strategic measure, giving the sanction of religious difference to a political action. Obeyesekere accuses Sahlins of reconstructing a version of Hawaiian history which privileges what is in fact an imperialist myth of the explorer as deity: 'Sahlins's anthropological narrative of the life and death of Cook is . . . a continuation, albeit unwitting, of the European myth of the apotheosis of James Cook.'[25] Sahlins has returned Obeyesekere's attack by arguing that attributions of political rationalism equally impose a Western framework of motivation upon Hawaiian actions.[26] The contest between the attribution of political realism and cultural mythologisation has precedents in the nineteenth century. Where Stevenson recreates a myth of first-contact wonderment, his literary predecessor in Hawaii, Mark Twain, was aware of the relationship between identification and mythologisation. In a letter written for the Sacramento *Union*, entitled 'Story of Captain Cook', he attempts, like Stevenson, imaginatively to re-enter the Cook narrative. He writes:

I went and stood in the edge of the water on the flat rock that took away his life, and tried to picture in my mind the doomed man struggling in the midst of the multitude of exasperated savages – the men in the ship crowding to the vessel's side and gazing in anxious dismay towards the shore- the – But I discovered that I could not do it.

Twain's conclusions are unromanticised: 'Plain unvarnished history takes the romance out of Captain Cook's assassination, and renders a deliberate verdict of justifiable homicide.'[27]

Repeatedly in Hawaii Stevenson is confronted by false façades. In a village on the Kona coast he comes across a modern house, imposing from without, but hollow inside:

One [house] arrested my attention; it stood on the immediate verge of a precipice: two stories high, with double balconies, painted white, and showing by my count fifteen windows . . . In the lower room, which I entered, there was not a chair or table; only mats on the floor, and photographs and lithographs on the wall. The house was an eidolon, designed to gladden the eye and enlarge the heart of the proprietor returning from Hookena; and its fifteen windows were only to be numbered from without.

Sahlins has discussed the place of the 'civilised house' in what he terms 'the political economy of grandeur' during an earlier period of European–Hawaiian relations. He describes the networks of chiefly competition which gave rise to a practice of 'the accumulation of deluxe items [which] outran any possibility of personal consumption'.[28] In Stevenson's account of the showcase mansion, such local political significances are ignored, nor does he draw attention to those ways in which architecture has been made to incorporate a meld of European and traditional Polynesian building styles. Instead, the difference in the double is established, and it ceases to disconcert. The Hawaiian is refigured as the dupe of surfaces: 'That is the way with natives; they spend money on the outside.' (191) In fact, according to Gavan Daws, it was settler taste that was most often responsible for the production of second-rate copies of European and American architectural styles in Hawaii during the later nineteenth century.[29]

Equally, however, Hawaiian copies can cast their originals into doubt. A lithograph of Nelson on the wall of the many-windowed house encapsulates a history of the global expansion of capital. Stevenson comments: 'I thought it a fine instance of fame that his features and his empty sleeve should have been drawn on stone in San Francisco, which was a lone Mexican mission while he lived; and lettered for a market in those islands, which were not yet united under Kamehameha when he died.' (192) Nelson has, like Cook, achieved an enviable fame in Hawaii. Yet Stevenson wonders if the British hero might not also be an empty image, devoid of significance, reduced to a purely decorative function: 'And then I had a cold fit, and wondered after all if these good folk knew anything of the man's world-shaking deeds and gunpowder weaknesses, or if he was to them a "bare appelation" and a face on stone.' He is relieved to find the owners of the household familiar with Nelson's story: 'he was known as a character of Romance!' (192) Romance, Stevenson's own favoured fictional genre, resuscitates the imperial hero in the bland epoch of the colonial simulacrum.

In contrast to the surface complexity of the modern 'eidolon', the historic 'city of refuge' becomes for Stevenson the site of an internal significance invisible from without; of an enshrined narrative. Dean MacCannell has analysed the central importance of back or inner regions to the tourist's pursuit of the authentic. Where the front of the tourist site is regarded as a space of performance, and therefore inherently false, the back or inside is regarded as the locus of the genuine, behind the scenes. As MacCannell observes: 'Just having a back region generates the belief that there is something more than meets the eye; even where no secrets are actually kept, back regions are still the places where it is popularly believed they are.'[30] 'The city of refuge' at the same time represents a commentary upon this search for authenticity. Once they had passed within the sanctuary of the city, accused or persecuted Hawaiians were formerly regarded as having been absolved of their crimes. Stevenson's desire to retrieve story from the city implicates him in the very act of penetration against which its function was defined; exposing hidden subjects within the walls. He justifies his intrusion as restoration rather than penetration, constructing his own version of this site against the purportedly glancing account of the missionary William Ellis. Ellis's visit has been closer to the authentic. At the time he wrote, 'the temple still preserved some shadow of its ancient credit and presented much of its original appearance' (196). However primacy is not, in this instance, invoked with regret. The missionary had insisted upon viewing the forbidden. Stevenson quotes Ellis: '"We endeavoured to gain admission to the inside of the house, but were told it was strictly prohibited . . . However, by pushing one of the boards across the doorway a little on one side, we looked in."' (197)[31] Yet he has failed to perceive artefacts of significance: 'Thus the careless eyes of Ellis viewed and passed over the bones of the sacrosanct Keawe.'

Of particular historical interest to Stevenson is the figure of Queen Ka'ahumanu, the ruler responsible for instigating that programme of Westernisation which has ultimately left him with his diminished sense of difference and authority. A cultural innovator, Ka'ahumanu instituted *'ai noa* ('free eating'), breaking the long-established Hawaiian *tabu* against the consumption of specified foods. Yet her radicalism aligned itself with American missionary doctrine – the breaking of *tabu* was accompanied by public baptism of the more powerful chiefs – thus immediately instating an alternative, foreign set of cultural codes and *tabu*s.[32] The ambiguity of her position, as cultural reformer and agent of colonialism, reflects her position as high-ranking female. Jocelyn Linnekin points out that

The tabu eating restrictions were most in conflict with the status of chiefly women, who had high *kapu* rank but were at least theoretically susceptible to death at the hands of men for eating certain foods or entering certain places . . . Interaction with powerful tabu-breaking foreigners intensified the contradictions inherent in the system, but even before Cook's arrival Hawaiian women– particularly chiefly women – had cultivated some disdain for the tabus.[33]

Stevenson portrays Ka'ahumanu as a figure who bridges gender roles. He has earlier branded contemporary Hawaiian culture castrated, claiming that Hawaiians have degenerated from 'a warlike and industrious race' (186), and now prefer civil service to 'manly occupation' (187). By contrast, he elegises Ka'ahumanu's female virility: 'while she was thus in person an emblem of womanly charm, she made her life illustrious with the manly virtues'. (203)

The lepers of Kona represent the most problematic embodiment of that alterity which Stevenson seeks in Hawaii. They expose the desire for difference as the desire for a partial, incapacitated other, and place Stevenson in attitudes of ineffectual paternalism and recoil. The leper's is the distorted reverse face of Hawaii's Westernised society: a horrific litmus of contact. The consistent excision from editions of *In the South Seas* of the letters Stevenson wrote about his visit to the lazaretto on the island of Molokai reflects, perhaps, a refusal by editors to acknowledge that the leper has anything other than supplementary status in the romance of Stevenson's Pacific travels.[34] The standard version simply records an encounter with a leper girl who is about to depart from Kona for the segregated leper colony. In this anecdote, Stevenson takes up the voice of medical authority, and its discourse of emotional restraint. He prescribes rules for reading the lepers, prefacing this section of his narrative with an endorsement of the law: 'The scenes I am about to describe, moving as they were to witness, have thus an element of something weak and false. Sympathy may flow freely for the leper girl; it may flow for her mother with reserve; it must not betray us into a shadow of injustice for the government whose laws they had attempted to evade.' (207) Stevenson offers medical injunctions to a potentially sympathetic audience, advising his readership against the same level of response exhibited by the islanders to the spectacle of the leper girl's mother, who has turned a scene of pathos into an opportunity for public performance. Yet his warning, with its resonance of freak-show disclaimers, underscores the very theatricality it deplores.

Stevenson claims to have witnessed a performance of emotion. He records staging, costume and music: 'both the doors were open. In front, a circle of some half a dozen women and children sat conspicuous in the usual bright raiment; in their midst was a crouching and bowed figure swathed in a black shawl and motionless; and as I drew more near, I was aware of a continuous and high-pitched drone of song.' (207) Within this context of display, the daughter is depicted as pathetically attempting self-concealment: 'covered from eyesight, . . . it was painfully plain she would conceal, if possible, her face'.(208) A 'genuine' pity for the leper girl emerges against the framework of a 'false' exhibitionism. The veiled centre of performance, she is the ultimate image of an inner significance behind false appearances. Stevenson is moved to a gesture of charity. Yet in the Hawaiian context, this involves becoming implicated, despite himself, in ceremony: 'I was about to make [the gift] in silence. The confounded expression of the school-master reminded me of where I was. We stood up, accordingly, side by side before the lepers; I made the necessary speech.' If, in Americanised Hawaii, Stevenson has initially regretted the advent of global homogeneity, the image of the artist offered by the operatic mother performing over the body of the leper girl, the embodiment of his desire for a difference to represent, reconciles him to the roles of colonial benefactor and ventriloquist of Western law.

BUTARITARI: STAGING AUTHORITY

In Kiribati, or as he knew it, the Gilberts, Stevenson reaches the periphery of the periphery. Among the islands of Micronesia, the tail-end explorer of a post-contact Pacific can claim authority as the last, if not the first, witness of cultural authenticity: 'yet ten years more, and the old society will have entirely vanished. We came in a happy moment to see its institutions still erect'.(214) Leaving behind the luxury yacht *Casco* in Hawaii, the Stevenson party takes its passage aboard 'a pigmy trading schooner, the *Equator*' (213), abandoning the voyeuristic detachment of the tourist and entering into the traffic of commerce. H. E. Maude has defined the contribution made by traders to nineteenth-century Pacific literature in terms which evoke the synthesizing methodology of comparative anthropology. He compares their role to that of resident beachcombers and missionaries, who might in turn be regarded as the antecedents of the ethnographic fieldworker:

Admittedly the sea traders were unable to give the detailed accounts of life ashore which we find in the best works of the local residents, but they compensated by their ability to observe and compare societies and individuals on many islands and groups, by being less given to parochial or sectarian bias, and frequently by visiting localities beyond the horizon of the most venturesome expatriate settler.

Maude suggests that the relationship between trader and Pacific islander was a performative one, dictated by local practices. He points out that traders 'had to ascertain and conform to local mores and etiquette, as well as to the consumer preferences of their customers, if they were to succeed in their ventures. Though the traders frequently had to pay the pipers, it was the islanders who in reality called the tunes.'[35] The trading relationship typifies the dialectical exchange between Europeans and Pacific peoples during the nineteenth century. While traders promoted the expanded circulation of metropolitan commodities and capital, their degree of success was in turn dictated to an extent by local cultural objectives, and not simply by global market forces.[36] In his travels in Kiribati on board the *Equator*, Stevenson explores the two sides of the trader's contract: the allegiance to empire, and involvement in the local politics of cultural performance.

The Stevensons take up residence in the appositely titled 'Wightman compound'. (227) It is a property which came, after their sojourn, into the possession of the Pacific Islands Company of Sydney and London. An article in the *Pacific Islands Monthly*, written by the trader who resided in the house after the Stevensons, notes that the literary author briefly occupied a space destined to be filled by the representatives of international trading interests: when phosphate of lime was discovered on nearby Nauru, 'in adjustment of business interests and joint working of the deposits, the property passed to der [*sic*] Jaluit Gesellschaft, of Hamburg'.[37] From his balcony Stevenson watches the population pass by in a parade. His post of observation in turn falls within the purview of other gazes. The whole island lies under the encompassing view of the toddy-cutters: 'look where you will, above or below, there is no human presence, only the earth and shaken forest. And right overhead the song of an invisible singer breaks from the thick leaves . . . All round the isle, the toddy-cutters sit on high, and are rocked by the trade, and have a view far to seaward.'(228) The local police force controls a more threatening régime of visibility: 'all must lie – I was about to say within doors, of a place where doors, and even walls, are an exception . . . Only the police themselves go darkling, and grope in the night for misdemeanants.'(230) The Stevensons are also observed by a degraded beachcomber, whose 'white, handsome face (which I beheld with loathing) looked in upon us at all hours across the fence'.(232) Butaritari is characterised a multilayered voyeurism which destabilises individual authority.

In his role of participant observer, Stevenson embarks on a narrative of anthropological resonance: 'the tale of a tapu', reporting how a period of debauch unravels imposed civil distinctions among the islanders: 'the whole polity – king, magistrates, police, and army joining in one common scene of drunkenness'(238). Yet events as he describes them occur primarily in the genre of romance. Stevenson claims to enter the frame of a boy's own story: 'we were travellers, folk that had come far in quest of the adventurous; on the first sign of an adventure it would have been a singular inconsistency to have withdrawn'(242). Like the typical Victorian adventure tale, this narrative is steeped in the discourse of imperialism. Stevenson plays the role of colonial authority: mendaciously represented as 'Queen Victoria's friend (who was soon promoted to be her son)'(245), he acquires an initial immunity from threat. Yet the rhetoric of the 'child of Empire' meets with perfunctory respect from the islanders. Consigned to his own compound, Stevenson occupies the illuminated stage of his verandah, only to be forcibly reminded that he is not immune to the violence of this real-life romance narrative. As he sits writing, a stone is hurled from the dark outside, space of an invisible audience. Inscription is interrupted: 'Three inches to one side and this page had never been written.'(246) Authorial detachment is no longer possible: the act of writing has become a direct target of interracial aggression.

Stevenson responds in romancist terms, making a series of stirring speeches which theatricalise the rhetoric of empire. He
desires to replace passive acceptance of a part with determined
activity, and marshalls the settler community for battle. In a stagey
scene in the house of Mr Muller, patron of the tavern *The Land We
Live In*, he occupies the spotlight with a call to action, demanding
that Muller cease selling alcohol to the islanders: 'All the light . . .
struck full in my face, but Mr Muller stood in shadow' (249).
Muller misaddresses him in response as 'Mr Stevens' (249), reinforcing the sense of an acting of roles. Stevenson convinces his
fellow character to join him in taking charge of plot: 'I don't mind
much about losing that life you talk so much of; but I mean to lose
it the way I want to.' (250–1) A romance of masculine heroics is
enacted, catering to the desires of a schoolboy readership: 'my
family . . . bubbled with delight at the approach of trouble; and we
sat deep into the night like a pack of schoolboys, preparing the
revolvers and arranging plans against the morrow' (252). However
anticipation is deflated; the population of Butaritari resumes
order without the necessity for any acts of heroism. King
Tebureimoa re-establishes the *tapu* on alcohol which alone
enforces respect within his community, and romance is consigned
once more to the realm of rhetoric.

Stevenson subsequently depicts two alternative viewing spaces
which displace the political theatre he has obliquely described.
The competitive musical performances of the islanders of
Butaritari and Little Makin offer him the romance narrative he has
desired: 'Then came the alarm of war, and a great battle, of which
for a time the issue was doubtful; but the hero conquered, as he
always does.' (257) This is the theatrical only tenuously recuperated from the political: eventually order collapses as rules are
broken by the vanquished Butaritari troupe. Stevenson recipro-
cates with two showings of the magic lantern he has brought with
him from Hawaii. This simple device, donated, along with a set of
biblical slides, by a Protestant missionary, appears to have been a
ready substitute for a state-of-the-art machine that Stevenson
ordered in a letter to Charles Baxter from Honolulu:

Another thing we shall want out at Sydney is full advertisements and price
lists of *really fine* magic lanterns. The idea is to begin the panorama there,
and when it is ready, carry it to some of the islands in style, and get more
stuff for it; thus making it feed itself. Can you send us . . . price lists of A1

magic lanterns for public performances, full rigged for cities and metropolises; and receive the benediction of the *Island Nights Entertainment Troup.* Walk up, ladies and gentlemen! Wish we had Henley here; bet he could learn to sing second: besides we could put him in a glass case, as a specimen *Beritani.* The object of the present show is to take the place of the yacht, as something to interest and amuse the natives.[38]

As this letter indicates, the subjects and audience of the magic lantern were intended to shift with change of location: in the Pacific, it would display that strange other, the 'Beritani' (Britisher) to 'interest and amuse' Polynesians; in 'cities and metropolises' it would represent the exoticism of the Pacific islander in a photographic panorama assembled during the course of travel.

Although the lantern shows were offered as impromptu contributions to the performance festival, in a context of cultural exchange, Stevenson was effectively the bearer of an instrument of evangelical instruction. The biblical slides were shown in the Butaritari church, presided over by the Hawaiian missionary, Maka. However the missionary is unable to make the most of the evangelical opportunity, since he is not a gifted performer: 'Maka, in the opinion of his aggrieved wife, did not properly rise to the occasion. "What is the matter with the man? Why can't he talk?" she cried.' (260) Maka fails to create a text adequate to accompany the miraculous gift of the slides, and instead the images speak for themselves:

whether he did ill or well, the exposure of these pious 'phantoms' did as a matter of fact silence in all that part of the island the voice of the scoffer. 'Why then,' the word went round, 'why then, the Bible is true!' And on our return afterwards we were told the impression was yet lively, and those who had seen might be heard telling those who had not, 'O yes, it is all true; these things all happened, we have seen the pictures.' The argument is not so childish as it seems; for I doubt if these islanders are acquainted with any other mode of representation but photography; so that the picture of an event (on the old melodrama principle that 'the camera cannot lie, Joseph,') would appear strong proof of its occurrence. (234)

Stevenson writes in counterpoint to the missionary's commentary, invoking the Old Testament primal scene against Maka's presenta- tion of New Testament images: 'I stood for some while unobserved in the rear of the spectators, when I could hear just in front of me a pair of lovers following the show with interest, the male playing the part of interpreter and (like Adam) mingling caresses with his lecture.' (260) Interpretation is figured as a form of masculine display – with Maka chastised by his wife for exegetical ineptitude.

Stevenson stands aloof from the circle of evangelical initiation, the viewer of a metaperformance. His gaze encompasses simultaneously audience, images and their mode of production, his lack of involvement contrasting with the implicitly sexualised responsiveness he observes in the audience: 'chance rays of light struck out the earnest countenance of our Chinaman grinding the hand organ; a faint glimmer showed off the rafters and their shadow in the hollow of the roof; the pictures shone and vanished on the screen; and as each appeared, there would run a hush, a whisper, a strong shuddering rustle, and a chorus of small cries among the crowd' (265). Yet he cannot remain completely detached from Maka's failure of discursive authority. He is conscious that the lantern show is the least fine of his productions; a shoddy imposition upon a superlative musical event, which redefines cultural competition as one between media, rather than between performers. When a company of rehearsing islanders absconds to watch the slides, the triumph of imported technology over indigenous performance is represented as a victory over, above all, Stevenson's own aesthetic values. His description of the rehearsal is imbued with nostalgia for the genuine. Performance is here grounded in a healthful physicality, registered on multiple sensory planes: 'the hot clean smell of the men and women striking in my face delightfully' (259). The preference of the troupe for the visually delusory 'phantoms', as the slide images are named, is a victory of spirit over flesh at the expense of culture – an ironic staging of the practice of missionary intervention. Moreover, the islanders' faith in the documentary status of the slide images proceeds not from naïve wonderment at foreign technology, but from familiarity with imported forms of representation. The metropolitan object speaks for itself. In the arena of free-appropriation, the exegete and the author are rendered redundant.

APEMAMA: THE RULER AS SUBJECT

The final destination of Stevenson's travel account is the atoll of Abemama, realm of the absolute monarch, Tem Binoka. H. E. Maude has provided a historical account of the two late nineteenth-century rulers of Abemama, Tem Baiteke and his son, Tem Binoka, and of the régime that they established. 'In the face of European cultural pressures that had overrun the whole of Polynesia and Micronesia', Maude writes, 'they had maintained the political, economic, and social integrity of their territory from the beginnings of European contact to virtually the end of the nineteenth century, selecting and accepting from the European only such ideas and material goods as appeared to them of value, and these strictly on their own terms and not those dictated by the dominant race.' Maude describes a society whose contact with European imperialism was regulated and mediated by its rulers. Europeans resided only as employees of the high chiefs, and for specified periods; trade and importation were strictly controlled, and foreign religious and secular innovations were initially prohibited or made the prerogative of the ruler.[39] As Stevenson notes, Tem Binoka was checked when he ventured into empire-building and export: 'Maiana once paid him tribute; he once fell upon and seized Nonuti: first steps to the empire of the archipelago. A British warship coming on the scene, the conqueror was driven to disgorge, his career checked in the outset'; 'Ships of his have sailed as far as to the colonies. He has trafficked direct, in his own bottoms, with New Zealand. And even so, even there, the world-enveloping dishonesty of the white man prevented him.' (281) Yet Tem Binoka remained able to guard the boundaries of Abemama against colonial intrusion.

Tem Binoka's policy of exclusion created the realm of Stevenson's desire: a territory not yet penetrated by the European, unexplored and undescribed. He describes Abemama as 'a close island, lying there in the sea with closed doors; the king himself, like a vigilant officer, ready at the wicket to scrutinise and reject intrenching visitors. Hence the attraction of our enterprise; not merely because it was a little difficult, but because this social quarantine, a curiosity in itself, has been the preservative of others.' (283) Yet Stevenson is no ethnographic fieldworker: he arrives aboard a trading schooner, and is met by a trader king whose greed for foreign souvenirs mimics his own desire authentically to experience another culture. In the dialectic of trade, the withheld is not always the genuine: 'Thwart the king and you hold him. His autocratic nature rears at the affront of opposition' (280); 'Among goods exported specially for Tembinok' there is a beverage known (and labelled) as Henessy's brandy. It is neither Henessy, nor even brandy.'(282) Maude comments, 'Binoka was convinced that in the European culture lay a talisman which he was determined to possess . . . For years the warehouses of Australia, England and Germany were culled by astute trading firms for some gadget which Binoka might still lack, it being well known that no price would deter him from acquiring it on sight.'[40]

Maude implies that Tembinok' is the dupe of a cargo cult mentality, and thus the victim of foreign trading agendas. Yet he also depicts traders pushed to the extremes of inventiveness in order to accommodate their products to the king's taste. According to Stevenson, Tem Binoka lacks the palate of the connoisseur, which would enable him to distinguish between Henessy and a false concoction. But, as Jean Baudrillard observes in a recent essay, the fanaticist collecting in which the king engages transcends such distinctions:

the collector partakes of the sublime not by virtue of the types of things he collects . . . but by virtue of his fanaticism. This fanaticism is always identical, whether in the case of the rich man specialising in Persian miniatures, or of the pauper who hoards matchboxes. This being so, the distinction one might be tempted to make between the collector as connoisseur – one who adores objects because of their beguiling singularity and differentness – and the straightforward collector, whose passion is to fit his acquisitions into a set or series, breaks down.[41]

Stevenson recognises in Tem Binoka (a rich man who hoards matchboxes), a curator with the eye of a surrealist:

House after house, chest after chest, in the palace precinct, is already crammed with clocks, musical boxes, blue spectacles, umbrellas, knitted waist-coats, bolts of stuff, tools, rifles, fowling-pieces, medicines, European foods, sewing-machines, and what is more extraordinary, stoves: all that ever caught his eye, tickled his appetite, pleased him for its use, or puzzled him with its apparent inutility. (279)

Both use and exchange values become irrelevant to the king: in his museum of foreign artefacts, the practical equipment of the European colonial enters a catalogue of the exotic. It is worth noting here that the catalogue of items which Stevenson collected during his Pacific travels displays a reciprocal tendency to fetishise the everyday. Stevenson collected an array of Polynesian necklaces, fans, combs, currency, practical tools, items of dress and cooking implements which were auctioned by his stepdaughter after his death. A note in the sale catalogue draws attention to the ways in which objects achieve different values and significances in different contexts: 'At every meeting of a ceremonious nature gifts are given and received, and although the visitor may see little use or value in what he receives, the gift sometimes represents the most precious possession of the giver.' The composers of the catalogue are keen to assert, however, that the acquisition of foreign goods was in Stevenson's case free of the taint of trade:

In his travels, Stevenson carried no goods for trade purposes and bought very little from the natives, but he received from the various native rulers many gifts of ceremony and tokens of affection, and of such the present collection of Island handicraft is principally made up. In his book on the South Seas he tells how he had received as gifts objects he desired, after having tried in vain to buy them.[42]

Three items received from Tem Binoka – Gilbert Island corselets, normally worn in battle – represent the most prized Pacific acquisitions in the sale catalogue.

Tem Binoka may indeed be seen as a type of anti-connoisseur, whose collecting can challenge norms of taste and assumptions of value. John Elsner and Roger Cardinal depict the archetypal maverick collector as follows:

Outside the boundaries of social recognition arises the myth of the pioneering, the experimental collector whose vocation may be to parody orthodox connoisseurship, to challenge the expectations of social behaviour, even to construct a maverick anti-system. The supreme pioneer is the totalizing collector, the 'completist', like Noah. Such a collector can brook no constraint, can show no hesitation, in the compulsion to possess a complete category in each and every of its variations.[43]

Maude denies Tem Binoka's collecting the capacity for such obsessive critique, representing it, instead, as slavishly imitative, and suggesting that there is an element of cultural abdication in the king's purported 'determination to ascertain and copy the conventions of civilised European society'.[44] Yet this neglects those elements of *bricolage* and mimicry in Tem Binoka's appropriation of foreign cultural forms and objects, which emerge strongly in Stevenson's account. Stevenson portrays the king as a role-player, whose changes of costume ignore and ironise European conventions of dress: 'Now he wears a woman's frock, now a naval uniform; now (and more usually) figures in a masquerade costume of his own design: trousers and a singular jacket with shirt tails.' (278)

Stevenson's sojourn in Abemama serves the king's own, unspecified purposes: 'it was by our talk that we gained admission to the island; the king promising himself (and I believe really amassing) a vast amount of useful knowledge ere we left.' (286) Stevenson depicts a relationship of ethnographic exchange. Tem Binoka uses the information he acquires to assess accounts by previous Western informants:

It was my part not only to supply new information but to correct the old. 'My patha he tell me,' or 'White man he tell me,' would be his constant beginning. 'You think he lie?' Sometimes I thought he did. Tembinok' once brought me a difficulty of this kind which I was long of comprehending. A schooner Captain had told him of Captain Cook; the king was much interested in the story; and turned for more information – not to Mr Stephen's Dictionary, not to the *Britannica*, but to the Bible in the Gilbert Island version (which consists chiefly of the New Testament and the Psalms). Here he sought long and earnestly; Paul he found, and Festus, and Alexander the coppersmith: no word of Cook. The inference was obvious: the explorer was a myth. (304)

The king uses the Bible to interrogate other Western sacred truths. A practised reader, he cross-references between the Bible and the history of exploration, highlighting the incompatibility between spiritual and imperial narratives. Captain Cook, a figure invested throughout *In the South Seas* with an unrecuperable primacy, is reduced by Tem Binoka to a logical fiction.

If Tem Binoka, as supreme trader, subjects European objects to interrogation, Stevenson is reciprocally invited to test the traditional power of the local artefact. Becoming ill, he offers his body as a touchstone for Kiribati medical practices. A first attempt to rid him of his cold by 'devil-work' is ineffectual, but the use of the powerful 'medicine box' eventually promotes a successful cure. Stevenson becomes activated by a desire for possession which reflects Tem Binoka's earlier documented eagerness to acquire items of trade. He confesses 'my appetite for curiosities (not usually very keen) had been strangely whetted by the sacred boxes' (320), and he offers exorbitant sums for its purchase. His association with the all-powerful monarch enables him at last to achieve his goal, and the box returns to England as a gift to the anthropologist Andrew Lang: to become part of the metropolitan museum of empire. Yet once, as owner, he gains access to its secret, Stevenson is confronted by objects whose significance remains beyond his comprehension: 'now I had my box, and could open it and look within. It contained a miniature sleeping-mat and a white shell'(325). Their purpose proves to be reductively metonymic, rather than profoundly symbolic: 'Tamaiti, interrogated next day as to the shell, explained it was not exactly [the god] Chench, but a cell, or body, which he would at times inhabit. Asked why there was a sleeping-mat, he retorted indignantly, "Why have you mats?"'

Stevenson enters a relationship of patronage with Tembinok', in which artistic pursuits are reduced to the activities of a leisured class: 'While some of the party would be away sketching, Mr Osbourne and I hammered away at a novel. We read Gibbon and Carlyle aloud; we blew on flagolets, we strummed on guitars; we took photographs by the light of the sun, the moon, and flash-powder; sometimes we played cards.'(289) He attempts to miti-gate the impression of dilettantism that emerges here by depicting writing as manual labour – 'hammering'. But his authorship is reflected in the king's own original and critical use of language. Tembinok''s sayings are recognised as potentially symbolic: he speaks an oracular English 'so different from ordinary "Beach de Mar", so much more obscure, expressive, and condensed.'(283) 'His vocabulary is apt and ample to an extraordinary degree'(303), and he is even represented as literary critic: 'Asked what his songs were about, Tembinok' replied, "Sweethearts and trees and the sea. Not all the same true, all the same lie." For a con-densed view of lyrical poetry (except that he seems to have forgot the stars and flowers) this would be hard to mend.'(296) Tembinok' is the first topic of discourse in his realm: 'There is one great personage in the Gilberts: Tembinok' of Apemama: solely conspicuous, the hero of song, the butt of gossip.'(275) As absolute ruler, he also controls expression: '"Here, in my island, *I* 'peak," he once observed to me. "My cieps no 'peak – do what I talk."'(284)

Within the closed community of Abemama, Stevenson achieves a semblance of that first contact which he has repeatedly sought. Yet in Tembinok''s realm he is forced to recognise the mutual implication of such authorial fantasies with a régime of power. As guest of Abemama's monarch, Stevenson is identified with an élite. He has negligible contact with Tem Binoka's subjects: 'We saw but little of the commons of the isle . . . Many villagers passed us daily going afield; but they fetched a wide circuit round our tapu, and seemed to avert their looks.'(305) Tem Binoka mimics, but also effectively embodies, an imperialist presence. He supervises the building of Equator city, a special compound in which the Stevensons are to reside, in colonial costume: 'a pith helmet on his head, a meerschaum pipe in his mouth'(287). His host's grand gesture enables Stevenson to play out a further fantasy of primacy: the founding of the city. Yet he is aware that his town is a desecrating presence, a 'devastation'(287). The primacy he experiences in Abemama is merely an experiment in imperialism, of which, by desiring to play first author, he has become the subject: distanced from, rather than in contact with, island life. Desire for self-erasure becomes the corollary of his original desire for authenticity. Stevenson fantasises the eradication of the signs of his presence immediately after describing the founding of the town:

the improvised city, where we were to stay two months, and which – so soon as we had done with it – was to vanish in a day as it appeared, its elements returning whence they came, the tapu raised, the traffic on the path resumed, the sun and the moon peering in vain between the palm-trees for the bygone work, the wind blowing over an empty site. (288–9)

The erasure of every other trace will at the same time leave Stevenson's written text as sole material sign of this last-contact encounter.

STEVENSON AND THE MISSIONARIES PUBLICATION AND LIBEL

In the South Seas is only the most familiar of Stevenson's non-fictional writings from the Pacific. A body of published and unpublished literature surrounds this text, encompassing the authorised and the slanderous, fiction and field notes, which explores, implicitly, and frequently explicitly, the limits of writing in the late nineteenth-century Pacific context. The most notorious item in this collection is 'Father Damien: an open letter to the Reverend Doctor Hyde of Honolulu'. Written in Sydney in February 1890, the letter is a denunciation of another letter, penned by the American Congregationalist missionary Charles McEwen Hyde, which had been published initially in the San Francisco religious paper the *Occident*, but was encountered by Stevenson in reprinted form in the Sydney *Presbyterian* of 26 October 1889. Hyde's letter was a response to enquiries by the Revd H. B. Gage concerning the Catholic missionary Father Damien. Damien had achieved the reputation of a martyr after his death from leprosy, contracted while ministering to the lepers of Molokai. In his letter, Hyde played devil's advocate, depicting Damien as 'a coarse, dirty man, headstrong and bigoted', and 'not a pure man in his relations with women'.[45] Stevenson's 'open letter' drew attention to the materially comfortable lifestyles of the dominant Protestant missionaries in Hawaii, contrasting these with Damien's physical self-denial and suffering. His defence of the priest was presented as an attempt to reconstruct Damien's features, eroded, he implied, by words as well as by disease: 'substituting once for all a creditable likeness for a wax abstraction'.[46]

The letter was initially printed privately. Fanny Stevenson later recalled: 'My husband hired a printer by the day, and the work was rushed through. We then, my daughter, my son, and myself, were set to work helping address the pamphlets, which were scattered far and wide.'[47] Her reminiscences of printing as family activity develop the contradiction inherent in the notions of private publishing and 'open letter'. An advance copy of the document was sent to the *Ka Elele Hawai'i*, a Hawaiian newspaper published in English and Hawaiian. Another was sent to the *Scots Observer*, and it was subsequently reproduced widely, in full and in extract. Stevenson was self-conscious about the potentially libellous status of the text. In a note accompanying a copy of the book he asks Charles Baxter, in his private role of friend, to recognise the spirit behind an intervention which, in his public capacity as lawyer, he could only condemn: 'Enclosed please find a libel: you perceive I am quite frank with my legal adviser; and I will also add it is *conceivable* an action might be brought, and in that event *probable* I should be ruined. If you had been through my experience, you would understand how little I care; for upon this topic my zeal is complete and, probably enough, without discretion.'[48] Later 'Father Damien' was reprinted as a book, for which Stevenson vehemently refused any profits, writing to the publisher Andrew Chatto: 'The letter to Dr Hyde is yours, or any man's. I will never touch a penny of remuneration; I do not stick at murder, I draw the line at cannibalism, I could not eat a penny roll that piece of bludgeoning had gained for me.'[49] He claims here that his letter is public property, and rejects the implication of personal gain.

Stevenson's shifting presentation of the 'Father Damien' piece as public exposure and as private engagement was foregrounded and replicated in responses to his letter. Dr Hyde had apparently written in the context of what he regarded as a private exchange with Reverend Gage. Gage betrayed the contract of privacy by making Hyde's letter public within the Protestant press. Stevenson's authorial reputation and relationship with publishing establishments enabled him to broadcast Hyde's 'off the record' comments further afield, to an international literary audience. In a letter to the *Pacific Commercial Advertiser*, a correspondent signing themselves 'Fair Play' drew attention to the unsolicited nature of this publicisation:

Dr Hyde writes a short, hasty letter to a friend, which is published without his knowledge or consent. This, Mr Stevenson, without informing himself as to whether the publication was authorized or not; without making any enquiry into the truth of its allegations; without even giving himself the trouble to deny them; makes the text of a six-column invective against Dr Hyde, an invective, the brutality and grossness of which are set in a glaring light by the most powerful English in which it is clothed. It is no excuse to say that Stevenson did not know the letter was not intended for publication. He ought to have informed himself. It was not merely private in form, but bore all the internal evidence of that character. It was, on the face of it, not intended for publication, and this circumstance ought to have put Mr Stevenson on his guard.[50]

The correspondent argues that Stevenson has shifted uncritically between the roles of naïve reader and literary authority. Neglecting the format of the text before him and producing an excessive commentary, he has translated a document of declarative brevity, without literary merit, into a lengthy literary piece.

This focus on an elision of readerly and authorial identities recalls complaints levelled by the first readers of *In the South Seas*. However, whereas in that instance it was argued that Stevenson, with too much preliminary reading, had taken the romance out of the Pacific, here it is asserted that he has, with insufficiently nuanced interpretation of written evidence, created a romance. 'Fair Play' continues: 'Stevenson, the extravagant romancer, the worshipper of heroes and heroic actions, came to these tropic shores in search of new literary material; . . . he thought he had struck a bonanza in Father Damien.' Within his open letter Stevenson overtly plays the role of romance hero, figuring his engagement with Doctor Hyde in chivalric terms: 'I rejoice to feel the button off the foil and to plunge home.'[51] Yet 'Fair Play' concludes that Stevenson has in this instance overstepped the limits of genre: 'Mr Stevenson is not a novelist, but a romancer, and . . . he feels himself, as little in this letter as elsewhere, bound down to the actual facts of life. It is safe to say that the Dr Hyde of this latest effusion is as purely the creature of the author's imagination, as the Mr Hyde of his famous extravaganza.'[52]

Arthur Johnstone, a Hawaiian resident who wrote one of the many parasitical Stevenson memoirs published after the author's death, discusses the 'Father Damien' incident at length. He argues that the term *slander* encompasses both public and private discourse, and draws attention to the duplicity of attempts to maintain a public/private distinction. He mentions two articles published in the *Hawaiian Gazette* in defence of Hyde, in both of which 'it is explicitly pleaded that Dr Hyde's letter was private, and published without his knowledge or consent'. Johnstone berates 'the falsity underlying flimsy moral makeshifts of the class which tacitly assumes the right to make injurous statements in private correspondence that otherwise would not be tolerated without positive proof'.[53] He reproduces two authoritative public documents in order to demolish the nebulous text of slander: a report submitted in 1887 by an official 'of tried probity and integrity' to the Board of Health at Honolulu, which tested and refuted the claims against Damien, and Damien's own report of 11 March 1886, to the Board.

It is the elusive figure of rumour, however, that unravels the texts surrounding Hyde's attack on Damien. Each of these authors reserves their strongest terms of scorn for evidence accumulated by attention to gossip, yet each is implicated in the web of scandal. Stevenson refers to Hyde as one 'busy to collect, so bold to publish, gossip on your rivals'.[54] However he acknowledges that he has heard the same accusations that Hyde makes in print levelled at Damien in bar-room gossip:

This scandal, when I read it in your letter, was not new to me. I had heard it once before; and I must tell you how. There came to Samoa a man from Honolulu; he, in a public-house on the beach, volunteered the statement that Damien had 'contracted the disease from having connection with the female lepers'; and I find joy in telling you how the report was welcomed in the public-house. A man sprang to his feet; I am not at liberty to give his name, but from what I heard I doubt if you would care to have him to dinner in Beretania Street. 'You miserable little –' (here is a word I dare not print, it would so shock your ears).[55]

Stevenson plays with the distinction between the sanctity of print and foul speech, linking this with the gap that separates Hyde's exclusive residence from the non-élite environment of the bar, whose customers he later terms 'a rude knot of beachcombing drinkers'. Hyde's slanders have already been published abroad, in that declaratively public space, the public house, where the response of a coarse man breaks down the distinction between gentlemen of appearance and of feeling, also transgressed within Stevenson's portrait of Damien.

The correspondent of the *Pacific Commercial Advertiser*, however, simply reiterates this distinction by drawing attention to the low-life context in which Stevenson is prepared to figure himself in the open letter. He claims that Stevenson 'intimates that prurient gossip must furnish a favorite topic of conversation in Dr Hyde's family; a contemptible insinuation coming strangely enough from any gentleman, – doubly strange here, – since it seems to apply much better to its Bohemian author, who, from his own account, heard the story from a drunken rowdy in a barroom, than it does Mr Hyde'. Even as he denounces the practices of the 'Bohemian author', the correspondent falls under his authorial power, and slips into a reference to 'Mr [rather than Dr] Hyde'. The majority of the adjectives in his professedly unliterary letter are expended on the figure of rumour: 'prurient gossip', 'insulting innuendoes', 'common rumour', 'infamous libel'. Arthur Johnstone also takes issue with 'slanderous gossip', again translating a distinction in language into a social distinction: he refers to 'lewd stories springing from that class of degenerate persons whose vulgarity festers in isolated communities'.[56] He contrasts the false 'mouthings of vulgar men' with the truth elicited by the 'keen-eyed officer of the Board of Health', and claims of the latter's authoritative report: 'even when reduced to a skeleton of words his statement will be found to be an armoured refutation of the accusations either purposely or inadvertently uttered'.[57] His metaphors reinvoke the physical body, the most poignant text of the Damien story, which has become simply a subtext within a debate about public and private discourse.

Stevenson's relationship to the various forms of Christian discourse available in the Pacific was a contradictory one. Publicly, he
is represented as approving of missionary practice. In an address
read before the Women's Missionary Association and members of
the General Assembly of the Presbyterian Church of New South
Wales, he depicts himself as a convert to missionary activity, claiming 'I had conceived a great prejudice against Missions in the
South Seas, and I had no sooner come there than that prejudice
was at first reduced, and at last annihilated. Those who deblatter-
ate against missions have only one thing to do, to come and see
them on the spot.'[58] The shift in his attitude paralleled the change
in Stevenson's status, from tourist to settler in the Pacific. His
'Prayers: written for family use at Vailima' locate the practice of
Christian worship within the paternalist organisation of the
Vailima property. Fanny Stevenson explains that the word 'family'
is used to refer, not in the familiar Victorian sense to the immediate domestic circle, but to the entire community of 'retainers'
upon the estate. The Samoan, according to Fanny 'but a larger
child in most things', is said to have adopted Christian prayer as a
form of superstition, receiving reassurance from an act of chant-
ing which reflects 'no real conception of the words'. The introduction of Christian worship, then, is not effectively a transmission of
sense, but an institution of ritual. For Stevenson, by contrast,
prayer is claimed to have been an assertion of individual voice:
'With my husband, prayer, the direct appeal, was a necessity.' Yet
Fanny also represents evening prayer as a Samoan-inspired
custom, and the services at Vailima as culturally composite: 'hymns
were set to ancient tunes very wild and warlike and strangely at vari-
ance with the missionary words'. The Bible is, moreover, appropriated as a cypher for direct political commentary. Fanny recalls,
'Once I remember a look of surprised dismay crossing the countenance of Tusitala when my son, contrary to his usual custom of
reading the next chapter following that of yesterday, turned back
the leaves of his Bible to find a chapter fiercely denunciatory, and
only too applicable to the foreign dictators of distracted Samoa.'[59]
Underlying the reassuring repetition of discourse is a subtext of
subversion in which settlers and Samoans are figured as mutual
participants, fellow interpreters.

Stevenson took lessons in the Samoan language from a missionary at Apia, the Reverend S. J. Whitmee, and practised by reading

the Samoan Bible.[60] The lists of vocabulary which he made are
revealingly composite of biblical and political allusions. Surviving
manuscripts include translations of scripture passages accompanied by corrections in the hand of his tutor. However, the Samoan
terms of which Stevenson took note tended to signify in the local
political rather than the biblical context – for example: 'Fatataiga,
a sitting together cross-legged, the chiefs and heads of families',
'Palagatete, shaking mud, to be unsettled politically.'[61] Pencilled
on the back flyleaf of his copy of *A Grammar and Dictionary of the
Samoan Language,* by the Revd George Pratt, are notes in Samoan
in Stevenson's hand, which appear to be towards an address to a
gathering of chiefs.[62] Among his jottings is a page devoted to the
distinctions characterising chiefly discourse, Stevenson noting
that, 'He [the chief] is addressed, referred to and described in a
particular language.'[63]

In a speech that Stevenson delivered to the students at the
Malua missionary college in Samoa, spiritual becomes political
admonition. Initially he makes the distinction between true and
false converts familiar from missionary literature:

I was on an island not very far from here, where they are trying to teach
them French, for the government there is a French government. Show
any of the young men, some written French, and they would read it out
aloud with a good pronunciation, never stumbling; ask them what any of
it meant, and they held their peace; they did not understand one word;
they read as parrots speak.[64]

Throughout the speech he opposes the falsity of 'the letter that
kills' to the truth of action, arguing that the Samoan pastors will
make a mockery of the Word that they profess to teach unless they
are seen also as attempting to live by its precepts. His own speech
is distinguished from the false 'letter' by its representation as oral
discourse – a form of words which bridges the gap between letter
and action: 'I come here and speak to you – good words, I think,
honest words.' When Stevenson goes on to recommend specific
projects for the missionaries he addresses, the notion of action
takes on an explicitly political relevance. He advises them to
preach against the sale of Samoan lands to foreigners, and makes
reference to the prevention of imported disease and to the need
to struggle against unjust imprisonment. In this context, his allusions to the duplicity of the letter become an implicit critique of
the duplicity of colonial law. His relativised account of the differ-

ence between text and action breaks down distinctions between the European as author and the native as dupe of law, suggesting instead that action as a form of ultimate literalism is the means to make law serve its subjects: 'It is good to make laws, and good to keep them; but let us remember that a law in itself is but a form of words, as the mark of a tapu was only a bunch of cocoanut or a piece of mulberry bark. What makes either strong is something in the heart of the people.'

MYTHMAKING: MIMICKING PACIFIC TRADITIONS

At the opening of his largely unpublished travel account 'A Malaga in Samoa', Stevenson delights in the plurality of forms of expression available to a group of Samoan rowers:

As they went they kept up a scarce intermitted minstrelsy: now a hymn in Samoan, now one of Shelley's in English, now a mere jingle of Samoan rhymes at which they would all laugh aloud like children for its very silliness, anon an imitation of all the birds in the bush: owl, pigeon &c, and then back to one of the regular narratives or at least topical songs of the race.[65]

The Samoans juggle, mimic and fragment imported and local traditions, taking private pleasure from what is also an act of performance. If the Samoan rhymes seem to occupy a slightly subordinate position in this list of genres, denigrated as child's play, the imitation of bird calls anticipates and defuses the familiar trope of native mimicry as parroting. This facility in simulating and melding traditions was something which Stevenson in turn sought to mimic during his travels. To the annoyance of those who wished him to play author rather than audience in the Pacific, he proved to be an eager collector of local myths, songs and stories. Among his papers are numerous transcriptions, primarily of Tahitian material. Occasionally a translation of Stevenson's is set next to a Tahitian text in another hand, probably that of the chief Ori a Ori, of whom Stevenson was a guest in Tahiti.[66] Ori a Ori was a member of the tribe of the Tevas, into which Stevenson was adopted during his stay. The pair exchanged names: according to one correspondent, Stevenson was effectively subjected to a double rechristening: 'the chief calling himself "Rui", there being no "L" in the Tahitian alphabet'.[67]

The distinction between Polynesian tradition as self-representation and as metropolitan construction is reflected in the two ballads Stevenson published from the Pacific, 'The Song of Rahēro' and 'The Feast of Famine'. Both poems are supported by a scaffolding of annotation, but where the former lays claim to ethnographic authenticity, the latter mimics that authenticity. 'Rahēro' is subtitled 'A Legend of Tahiti', and Stevenson draws attention to the minimalism of his own authorial role and the polyphony of the poem's construction: 'This tale, of which I have not consciously changed a single feature, I received from tradition . . . I have heard from end to end two versions; and as many as five different persons have helped me with details'. The context of composition is conjured up by a manuscript sheet among Stevenson's papers in which Ori a Ori records the songs of the Tevas's clan gathering.[68] 'Rahēro' is dedicated to Ori a Ori, in verse which alludes to the reciprocity of oral exchange – 'In every tongue and meaning much my friend' – and is signed 'with the name you gave'. Stevenson's annotations to the published poem testify that he directed this composition primarily to the literate Tahitian. Pointing out that he has named the king of Paea inaccurately, he adds:

This note must appear otiose indeed to readers who have never heard of either of these two gentlemen; and perhaps there is only one person in the world capable at once of reading my verses and spying the inaccuracy. For him, for Mr. Tati Salmon, hereditary high chief of the Tevas, the note is solely written; a small attention from a clansman to his chief.

The subtitle of 'The Feast of Famine', 'Marquesan Manners', signals, on the other hand, its status as mimicry. Stevenson presents this ballad as a foil to the genuine text, 'Rahēro', referring candidly to the poetic licence he has taken: 'It rests upon no authority; it is in no sense, like "Rahēro", a native story; but a patchwork of details of manners and the impressions of a traveller.'[69]

Both poems are occupied with the connection between feasting and death. 'Rahēro' narrates a legend of clan foundation. The chief of Paea, a weak clan, uses his fertile land to cultivate a superabundance of produce. Tempted by greed, the clan of the Tevas approaches him peacefully, and he first feeds them and then carries out a massacre while they are stunned with feasting, thus fulfilling a promise he has made to a grieving woman who wishes to gain revenge on the Tevas for the death of her son. Rahēro alone escapes, and taking a woman from Paea, departs to repopulate the lands of the Tevas. 'The Feast of Famine' is a more prurient account of a cannibal feast during a time of famine in the Marquesas. It figures a frenzied priest in the familiar guise of native parrot – 'like a parrot, ruby-eyed', and two lovers who are willing to break tabu and enter a forbidden forest in order to escape cannibal sacrifice. Eventually the entire clan are left at the mercy of their enemies, since cannibal appetites lead them to destroy the hero as he comes to warn them of attack, and render them sluggish and ill-prepared for self-defence. Yet while these poems can be seen to represent true and false versions, the former revealing an insider's knowledge, the latter betraying an outsider's fetishising, their sequential publication breaks down such distinctions. Instead, Stevenson highlights the way in which writing about the Pacific must negotiate between local and external perspectives, neither of which is finally authoritative or authentic.

CHAPTER 4

Piracy and exchange: Stevenson's Pacific fiction

In a series of unpublished Imaginary Dispatches, probably written in 1885, Stevenson adopted a variety of roles, including those of the explorer Henry Morton Stanley, of 'Banzaboo' (prime minister of 'the Cannibal Islands') and of a reporter at a meeting of 'The American Pirates Trades Union', in order to parody the hypocrisy of policy. The interleaving of satiric pieces on the topics of colonialism and copyright establishes a parallel between the ironies and inconsistencies of imperialist and literary exploitation, while the 'American Pirates' dispatch exposes the unstable association of republican sentiments with free-trade ethics:

The chairman opened the meeting with an address in which he said 'Ladies and Gentlemen, the liberties of this free and mighty land are being interfered with. The greedy Britisher envious of our cuteness wishes to secure our birthright. (hisses and groans.) He says in a disgusting and insulting manner that if we want books we must pay for 'em (groans), but no gentlemen we won't stand it (applause). Shall the downtrodden and perfidious Briton trample on one of our Great Institutions?'[1]

The ludic dispatches were written some years before Stevenson placed himself at the periphery of print and of empire in the Pacific, yet they anticipate an intermeshing of concerns which is less heavy-handedly present in his late fiction. The novels and short stories that Stevenson published from and also set in the Pacific mediate anxieties about the material basis of literary production through an exploration of the narrative modes and forms of authority available in this peripheral context. These texts express a concern about those interconnections between discursive and commercial exchange that are implicit in their own production.

THE WRECKER AS BEACHCOMBER NARRATIVE

Writing to Will Low, the American painter to whom he dedicated *The Wrecker*, some time after the novel's publication, Stevenson posed a question about the value of artistic labour:

And then the problem that Pinkerton laid down: why the artist can do nothing else? is one that continually exercises myself . . . I think of the Renaissance fellows, and their all-round human sufficiency, and compare it with the ineffable smallness of the field in which we labour and in which we do so little. I think *David Balfour* a nice little book, and very artistic, and just the thing to occupy the leisure of a busy man; but for the top flower of a man's life it seems to me inadequate. Small is the word; it is a small age, and I am of it. I could have wished to be otherwise busy in this world. I ought to have been able to build lighthouses and write *David Balfours* too.[2]

Addressed to Low, such sentiments harbour an element of nostalgia. The pair had been members of the Barbizon artist's colony for periods during the years 1875 to 1877, at a time when, Low reminisced later, they 'were more intent upon learning our respective trades than in producing finished works of art'.[3] In those days, uncommitted to singularity of artistic endeavour and less concerned with the benefits of protectionism, they were part of a group who formed 'The Barbizon Free-Trading Company, Unlimited' whose planned activities included sailing a yacht and trading in sealskins.[4] Four of the company, including Stevenson, also bought shares in a barge, which was never used.[5] In his letter to Low, Stevenson goes on to compare himself unfavourably with Fielding the 'active magistrate' and Richardson the 'busy book-seller', and to wish that his own curriculum did not exclude the work of his father and grandfather, both engineers, whose light-house constructions guard the coasts of Scotland.[6] Yet perhaps more apposite than the activities of earlier canonical authors to Stevenson's ideal of the literary jack of all trades was the local example of the Pacific beachcomber. As I observed earlier, the beachcomber author is a figure defined by multiple projects, from the technical to the performative. In *The Wrecker* the beachcomber offers an implicit model for a sustained investigation of the modes of labour that accompany and define artistic production.

The Wrecker was the second of three novels that Stevenson wrote in collaboration with his stepson, Lloyd Osbourne.[7] Like the collaborative projects of the novel's protagonists, Loudon Dodd and Jim Pinkerton, Stevenson and Osbourne's joint authorship was a business venture. Osbourne's American citizenship gave their writing the protection of United States copyright laws prior to the International Copyright Act of July 1891. The profits of *The Wrecker* were intended to contribute to the purchase of a trading schooner that Stevenson and his family planned to operate between the islands of the South Pacific. Where Loudon Dodd's artistic pursuits are supported by Pinkerton's business activities, Stevenson's art was to finance an enterprise of trade. In a letter to Henry James he refers to the novel as 'a machine', but also as a piece of, possibly dubious, craftsmanship, in which he practises 'the curious (and perhaps unsound) technical manoeuvre of running the story together to a point as we go along, the narrative becoming more succinct and the details fining off with every page'.[8] Aspiring to a writing that is one of several ventures, Stevenson produces a text whose labour is a shifting term, neither simple mechanics nor pure artistry.

The Wrecker tells the story of Loudon Dodd's various attempts to find suitable employment on the spectrum between art and labour. His father, James Dodd, a millionaire businessman who finishes life a bankrupt, sends his son to Muskegon Commercial Academy. Here, in what amounts to an education in exchange-value, Dodd participates in gambling games with 'college paper' and ledgers, experiencing accelerated shifts of fortune which serve only to convince him that 'the whole traffic was illusory'.[9] His own ambitions are unspecifically 'artistic'. His father is involved in the planning of the new city of Muskegon, and, in a brief affiliation with paternal aspirations, Dodd engages in an autodidactic pursuit of architecture. This phase of the novel has echoes in Stevenson's biography: Stevenson had himself initially studied engineering in the tradition of his 'family of engineers', and then completed a law degree as a compromise between his literary aspirations and his father's professional ambitions for him. Dodd's description of his architectural pursuits could equally describe Stevenson engaged in the study of engineering: 'I threw myself headlong into my father's work, acquainted myself with all the plans, their merits and defects, read besides in special books, made myself a master of the theory of strains, studied the current prices of materials.' (23) (Stevenson acknowledged in a letter to Edward

Burlingame that, although his protagonist was based primarily on Will Low, 'Much of the experience of Loudon Dodd is drawn from my own life.'[10])

Dodd's father agrees to send him to Paris to study sculpting, intending him to put artistic training to a practical purpose in designing the façades of public buildings in the city of Muskegon. On his way to the Continent, Dodd visits his maternal relatives in Edinburgh. He finds favour with his grandfather, Alexander Loudon, a former stonemason whose shoddy workmanship is, however, inimical to Dodd's artistic pretensions. When Alexander takes him on a tour of some houses he has fabricated, Dodd comments: 'I have rarely seen a more shocking exhibition: the brick seemed to be blushing to the walls, and the slates on the roof to have turned pale with shame; but I was careful not to communicate these impressions to the aged artificer at my side.' (29) After his father's bankruptcy and death, a gift of money and later posthumous bequest from his grandfather enable Dodd to escape the curse of labour in his Uncle Adam's grocery business. The paternity of a businessman who can only appreciate art as engineering and the legacy of an incompetent *bricoleur* provide an insecure foundation for Dodd's artistic pursuits. Jim Pinkerton, the combined businessman–*bricoleur* who takes over the burden of Dodd's maintenance, is in part a reincarnation of these father-figures.

Pinkerton, Dodd's closest friend in Paris and erstwhile benefactor, is a jack of all trades. Pinkerton cannot understand the exclusive devotion which characterises Dodd's artistic ambitions, while Dodd defines his singular pursuit against the multiplicity of Pinkerton's endeavours: 'this was not an artist who had been deprived of the practice of his single art; but only a business man of very extended interests' (46). Pinkerton has numerous 'irons in the fire' (98). He has been a 'tin-typer', or travelling photographer, with a sideline in ethnography:

As he tramped the Western States and Territories, taking tin-types . . . he was taking stock by the way, of the people, the products, and the country, with an eye unusually observant and a memory unusually retentive; and he was collecting for himself a body of magnanimous and semi-intellectual nonsense, which he supposed to be the natural thoughts and to contain the whole duty of the born American. (42–3)

He has found employment as a railroad-scalper, a trade whose essence, Dodd explains, 'appears to be to cheat the railroads out

of their due fare'(43), and while in Paris acts as foreign correspondent for an American newspaper. Back in San Francisco, his
projects multiply: he hawks brandy, keeps an advertising office,
charters a boat for fishing parties, refurbishes condemned vessels,
and has a tenth share in 'a certain agricultural engine'.(98) He
promotes a public lecture upon Dodd's return to the United States
from Paris, and organises what become notorious weekend
picnics, with Dodd acting again as showman.

The portrait of Pinkerton, Stevenson's correspondence attests,
was in fact based upon a figure from the world of metropolitan
publishing: his American literary agent Samuel Sidney McClure.[11]
Stevenson regarded McClure as something of a shyster, and
worried about the risks he might have engendered by placing his
literary fortunes partly in McClure's hands. In the year that *The
Wrecker* was published, he wrote to Charles Baxter from Samoa: 'I
fear the solvency of the Great McClure must be a-totter. This will
leave me in a dreadful hole, for I have no idea my money will have
been kept separate as he proposed; the being is too Pinkertonish
for that.'[12] However Pinkerton's dubious 'irons in the fire' range
beyond the literary, recalling the projects of the beachcomber
William Diaper, who writes in his autobiography:

I had about fifty irons in the fire at once, and not one of them burnt. I
supplied as many as thirty or forty ships in the season during the year, with
pork and vegetables at quite a thousand per cent. profit . . . Even the red
chilli-peppers which grew wild all round, I employed the boys and girls
to gather them in bushels, and then bottled them up in vinegar which I
made myself from the ripe bananas, and sold hundreds of bottles to the
foremast hands of all these ships . . . Another source of wealth or income
was the way I used to receive the officers and crews of the ships when they
came on shore for liberty. I always treated them to a picnic or '*al fresco*'
meal under the nice shady branches of the tree which stood on the green
where I used to spread the good things of the whole island.

There are certain immediate dissimilarities between the activities
of the metropolitan and the Pacific *bricoleur*. Pinkerton's ventures
are purely entrepreneurial, where Diaper accompanies promo-
tion with manual labour. Diaper's profit margin is more arbitrary.
Yet both are portrayed as engrossed in the romance of business
venture, rather than in acquisition: in the narrative, rather than
the artefacts, of enterprise. Pinkerton is described as 'representing
to himself a highly coloured part in life's performance . . . Reality
was his romance; he gloried to be thus engaged'(97), while Diaper

claims to have been absorbed by the process of accumulation rather than the question of profit: 'I neglected nothing with which I could make money, not so much for the love of it – as I did not at that time any more than now worship it – as for the amusement it gave me in accumulating it.' Pinkerton's funds are perpetually in circulation: 'No dollar slept in his possession; rather, he kept all simultaneously flying, like a conjurer with oranges.' (98–9) Diaper's profits change shape within the chameleon economy of barter: 'if not money, perhaps [payment was] a "hickery" shirt, worth to me quite two dollars, as I could convert all these things into pigs, which in the end meant money'.[13] Both Pinkerton and Diaper of course include textual production among their business ventures.

Pinkerton involves Dodd in the purchase of an exorbitantly priced wreck, the *Flying Scud,* which has come up for sale in San Francisco under mysterious circumstances, and which he suspects of containing an illicit cargo of opiate. Dodd is sent aboard another ship, the *Norah Creina,* to the Pacific island of Midway where the wreck lies abandoned, to endeavour to secure this anticipated treasure. Here, engaged in the anti-aesthetic labours of 'wrecker', taking apart the *Flying Scud,* Dodd attains manhood. Rather than single-minded and sedentary artistic pursuits, he comes to celebrate *bricolage,* and a masculine world of manual labour:

if things had gone smooth with me, I should be now swollen like a prize-ox in body, and fallen in mind to a thing perhaps as low as many types of the *bourgeois* – the implicit or exclusive artist . . . The dull man is made, not by the nature, but by the degree of his immersion in a single business . . . The eternal life of man, spent under the sun and rain and in rude physical effort, lies upon one side, scarce changed since the beginning.

I would I could have carried along to Midway Island with me all the writers and the prating artists of my time. Day after day of hope deferred, of heat, of unremitting toil; night after night of aching limbs, bruised hands, and a mind obscured with the grateful vacancy of physical fatigue. (232–3)

This speech recalls another eulogy to physical labour, within Stevenson's correspondence from Samoa. Writing to Sidney Colvin about his work weeding and path-breaking on the Vailima estate, he observes of himself:

To come down covered with mud and drenched with sweat and rain after some hours in the bush, change, rub down, and take a chair in the verandah, is to taste a quiet conscience. And the strange thing that I remark is this: if I go out and make sixpence, bossing my labourers and plying the cutlass or the spade, idiot conscience applauds me: if I sit in the house and make twenty pounds, idiot conscience wails over my neglect and the day wasted.[14]

In a letter from which I quoted in my introduction, Oscar Wilde comments acerbically on such relishing descriptions of physical exertion: 'To chop wood with any advantage to oneself, or profit to others, one should not be able to describe the process . . . Stevenson merely extended the sphere of the artificial by taking to digging.'[15] He suggests that the elevation of toil is the ultimate literary illusion. Stevenson's self-conscious espousal of the benefits of manual labour transforms the sought escape from literary dilettantism into a literary activity.

The Wrecker's questions about the material base of aesthetic pursuits and the value of artistic enterprise as measured against forms of manual activity surface repeatedly in Stevenson's meditations, published and private, on the art of writing. Perhaps because he was conscious of having broken with the practical tradition of his 'family of engineers', and of having been dependent on his father's financial support to establish his literary career, Stevenson was impelled to interrogate the validity of literature as labour. This concern had a wider frame of reference, however, within later nineteenth-century literary debate. There was, as Kenneth Graham has observed, a utilitarian emphasis to Victorian defences of the novelist's art.[16] The image of the novelist as craftsman, and of writing as technical labour, was a critical commonplace: Trollope's *An Autobiography* famously referred to the novelist as a cobbler, whose method was mechanical.[17] Such metaphors reflect anxieties about the capacity of literature to function as a means of support for its producers. Stevenson wrote, less solemnly, in a letter of July 1883:

you will never weary of an art at which you fervently and superstitiously labour . . . Forget the world in a technical trifle . . . Bow your head over technique. Think of technique when you rise and when you go to bed. Forget purposes in the meanwhile; get to love technical processes, to glory in technical successes; get to see the world entirely through technical spectacles, to see it entirely in terms of what you can do.[18]

The emphasis on the technical here is rhetorical, even incantatory, rather than a materialist critique. Repetition culminates in the aurally pleasurable but ludicrous 'technical spectacles': this is still

playful, rather than laborious, writing. However Stevenson's subsequent experiences publishing texts from the Pacific served to
defamiliarise the 'literature as labour' commonplace; his distance
from metropolitan centres slowing down and rendering practically explicit the processes of literary production.

Rather than any materially valuable cargo, Dodd retrieves from
the *Flying Scud* a wealth of story. He locates evidence that the crew
who had been rescued from the ship was in fact a cast of interlop-
ers. Ascertaining their true identities, Dodd uncovers the history
of a fellow-dilettante, Norris Carthew, whom he recognises as,
effectively, his double. Carthew has early in life been cast off by his
father and sent to Australia as a remittance man. There he is
redeemed, like Dodd, from an emasculated existence by entry into
the communal, physical world of masculine labour. He takes up
work on a railway gang, and then joins a group of friends aboard
the ship *Currency Lass* on a trading venture in the Pacific. They
begin with excellent fortune in Butaritari, where they are able to
make an inflated profit on the sale of their cargo. However luck
changes when the mast of their ship splits in mid-ocean, and they
are forced to take to the lifeboat and make for Midway. This island,
which they have been misled by their ship's directory to believe
supports an active coaling station, turns out to be a barren guano
deposit. The appearance of the *Flying Scud* offers a conditional
promise of rescue: the captain of the ship demands that the group
hands over the huge spoils of its trading venture in return for
removal from Midway. In an outbreak of extreme violence, the
crew of the *Currency Lass* massacres the crew of the *Flying Scud*. This
explains the substitution of identities which has taken place upon
the ship's return to San Francisco. Dodd's attempts to uncover the
true history of the wreck are initially motivated by a plan to blackmail Carthew, and thus to turn story directly into profit. However
a growing sense of recognition encourages him to refigure his role
as that of Carthew's ally. For Carthew, the achieved world of masculine activity has tipped over into violence. Dodd retrieves a
balance by in turn converting the destructive activity of 'wrecker'
into the reconstructive role of storyteller.

The interdependence of constructive and destructive forms of
masculine physicality is an assumption that informs the collected
literature of the Pacific beachcomber. And there are further
echoes to suggest that the types of labour and alterity explored in

The Wrecker are influenced by this local model. The two vessels upon which Dodd and Carthew achieve manhood, the *Norah Creina* and the *Currency Lass*, are both makeshift constructions: *bricolage*. The former has been rushed through overhauling in San Francisco, and the latter is precariously reassembled from a state of dilapidation: 'she sold . . . a shade above her value as old junk; and the three adventurers had scarce been able to afford even the most vital repairs. The rigging, indeed, had been partly renewed, and the rest set up; [the] old canvas had been patched together into one decently serviceable suit of sails; [the] masts still stood, and might have wondered at themselves.' (357–8) Their respective crews are similarly cobbled together. The latter's includes a genuine *bricoleur*. 'Richard Hemstead . . . had an odd-job-man's handiness with tools.' (357) The crew members of the *Currency Lass* reappear in San Francisco like beachcombers returning to metropolitan society: under false names, telling a duplicitous story, the captain sustaining an injury which prevents him from signing authorship of his testimony. It is the *bricolage* nature of the typical ship's crew in the Pacific – its members material-to-hand, occupying a particular function for the space of a journey – which produces the narrative motivation of *The Wrecker*, enabling the perplexing substitution of one crew for another.

Dodd ultimately achieves a patronage less emasculating than those which he rejects during the course of the novel. In the prologue, he arrives in the Marquesas as the partner of his double, Carthew. In this role he continues to represent the supported dilettante: the ship he runs upon Carthew's capital is a floating gallery of *objets d'art*, rather than the beachcomber's *objets trouvés*, and he distinguishes himself from the beachcomber by its furnishings: '"His money, my taste," said Dodd. "The black walnut bookshelves are old English; the books all mine – mostly Renaissance French. You should see how the beach-combers wilt away when they go round them, looking for a change of seaside library novels. The mirrors are genuine Venice; that's a good piece in the corner. The daubs are mine – and his; the mudding mine."' (6) Unlike William Diaper's swap-library of refashioned books on handmade shelves, Dodd's books and bookshelves are collector's pieces. Nonetheless, this assemblage retains the character of *bricolage*: part the work of his hands, part appropriation, uniting artefacts from a variety of contexts. In the epilogue,

Stevenson enters the frame of one of Dodd's projects. Like the editors of the beachcombers' 'mendicant' texts, he is represented as using his literary authority to bring Dodd's narrative into print. Yet neither Dodd's associations with Carthew nor with Stevenson are further instances of straightforward patronage. Once in possession of the narrative of *The Wrecker*, Dodd has attained a valuable item of exchange – Carthew's secret, and Stevenson's story – with which he can negotiate upon his own terms. In fact, Dodd successfully attains what Stevenson and Osbourne hope to earn from the writing of the novel: a vessel for trade among the islands.

Dodd, like the beachcomber, has pursued a wide range of dubious types of employment, which provide the material for his narrative: wrecker, opium-smuggler, blackmailer, '"It's rather singular," said he, "but I seem to have practised all these means of livelihood."'(10) It is the multiplicity, rather than singularity, of Dodd's operations which characterises him as *bricoleur* rather than dilettante. His arrival in the prologue is viewed through the eyes of another type of beachcomber, reminiscent of Jean Cabri or James O'Connell: 'the famous tattooed white man, the living curiosity of Tai-o-hae'(2). This figure is an icon of alterity – tattooed, cannibal: 'he would hear again the drums beat for a man-eating festival; perhaps he would summon up the form of that island princess for the love of whom he had submitted his body to the cruel hands of the tattooer'. Yet this 'so strange a figure of a European' also defines Stevenson's authorial practice in *The Wrecker*. Like the tattooed man, whose 'memory would serve him with broken fragments of the past', Stevenson draws upon the different contexts of his varied experience – Paris, San Francisco, the Marquesas – to produce a narrative that is also a *bricolage*.

In the novel's epilogue, Stevenson explains to Will Low the 'genesis and growth'(425) of a book which is in fact less an organic production than an assemblage. In the early 1920s, Low was to develop into a major composition a sketch he had made of Stevenson while the pair were living in the artists' colony of Barbizon. One commentator referred to the painting as his 'affectionate answer, perhaps, to Stevenson's epilogue in 'The Wrecker''.[19] Low also published for private circulation a book describing the genesis and growth of this artwork. Ambiguously entitled 'Concerning a Painting of Robert Louis Stevenson', this text slips between representing Stevenson as subject and as implicit author of his portrait. Low's commentary is heavily conscious of his sitter's development from student into renowned literary figure, preceding the maturation of his sketch into a finished artwork. His painting is now a posthumous memorial, deriving interest and authority primarily from its subject, even as it, like Stevenson's epilogue, draws from a shared pool of memories that continue to situate the two artists as novices and equals. Yet Low's pamphlet also offers an exhaustive description of artistic composition: of the conceptualisation and realisation of a project of representation. The distinction between the aesthetics espoused by his text and *The Wrecker*'s epilogue is effectively one between composition and *bricolage*. The epilogue describes a narrative developed from yarning. The task of writing is figured as manual craftsmanship: 'the scaffolding of the tale had been put together. But the question of treatment was as usual more obscure.' (425) Its finished product is a fabricated article, a piece of weaving, rather than a precious artwork:

The tone of the age, its movement, the mingling of races and classes in the dollar hunt, the fiery and not quite unromantic struggle for existence with its changing trades and scenery, and two types in particular, that of the American handyman of business and that of the Yankee merchant sailor – we agreed to dwell on at some length, and make the woof to our not very precious warp. (426)

This plot summary incorporates a range of projects and contexts of activity familiar from beachcomber accounts. The authors also represent literary production as oral exchange, a depiction which somewhat belies facts. Stevenson and Osbourne's formal collaboration involved sequential writing and revision: much discussion of the project took place in correspondence while Lloyd was in Europe settling the family's affairs, Stevenson complaining at one time to Lloyd: 'This is the hell of collaboration half the world away.'[20] Commenting later on literary collaboration, Stevenson suggested that this type of authorship presses at the limits of oral communication: 'The great difficulty of collaboration is that you can't *tell* what you mean. I know what kind of an effect I mean a character to give – what kind of *tache* he is to make; but how am I to tell my collaborator in words.'[21] Nonetheless, in the epilogue the authors are keen to place the genesis of their story in a productive oral context. Here the beachcomber narrative offered an implicit answer to the problems of construction which the novel posed. The authors refer to their aim of uniting the complex plot of detective fiction with the detail of daily life: romance with realism. They succeed in creating an aleatory text, in which disparate narratives build into a story, simultaneously bringing a variety of contexts into play. As I argued in chapter 1, part of the appeal of the beachcomber narrative lay in the dubious status of the account, in the challenge it offered the reader of sifting true story from tall tale. In the conflicting and yet duplicate histories of Dodd and Carthew, two non-singular artists, or beach-comber-*bricoleur*s, Stevenson's longstanding preoccupation with the double, the *alter ego*, is remodelled at the periphery.

THE EBB-TIDE: CONVERTING BEACHCOMBER TO MISSIONARY

With the writing of *The Ebb-Tide*, the process of collaboration between Stevenson and Lloyd Osbourne broke down. Stevenson's account, in correspondence, of the construction of the novella stresses a division of labour. Osbourne drafted the first four chapters in 1889/90. Stevenson rewrote this section with little emendation, and then set the work aside until 1893, when he completed the story with 'The Quartet'. After serialisation in Britain in *Today* (11 November, 1893–3 February 1894), and in the United States in *McClure's Magazine* (February–July 1894), adverse reviews lead Stevenson to consider deleting Osbourne's name from the book's cover: erasure, rather than signature of authorship seemed in this instance more likely to serve Osbourne's literary reputation. Stevenson described the writing of the novel as a debilitating labour, rather than the playful construction of a *bricolage*: 'it has been such a grind! . . . I break down at every paragraph, I may observe, and lie here, and sweat, and curse over the blame thing, till I can get one sentence wrung out after another.'[22] Both Stevenson and his reviewers characterised the subject matter of *The Ebb-Tide* as waste material, a failed literary transaction: 'Of grace, virtue, beauty, we get no glimpse. All we have in exchange is a picture of the fag-ends of certain useless and degraded lives.'[23]

The writing of *The Ebb-Tide* was a failure of *bricolage*: a grinding labour, bringing together parts that failed to cohere, producing waste material, rather than a useful new object. *The Ebb-Tide* is the tale of the demise of the beachcomber narrative. Where *The Wrecker* represented the beachcomber, implicitly, as a figure of enterprise, *The Ebb-Tide* portrays the beachcomber explicitly as a figure of waste. Pinkerton, the archetypal *bricoleur* of the earlier novel, is a speculator with the projective energy of the New World citizen, the American democratic subject. *The Ebb-Tide* instead depicts the implication of the Pacific beachcomber within the class values of Old World society. The novel tells the stories of three beach-combers, each representing a different tier of the British class system. Robert Herrick is an Oxford-educated son of the prosper-ous middle classes, whose family has become bankrupt; Davis has been a merchant sea captain; and Huish is a Cockney who was once a clerk. The class origins which I argued earlier were temporarily suspended for Europeans in the pre-colonial context of the early nineteenth-century Pacific, are depicted in *The Ebb-Tide* as return-ing to subjugate the beachcomber during the colonial period.

The class status of the three beachcombers is defined, in the absence of material possessions 'on the beach', by the types of narration in which they engage. They shelter within the ruins of the old calaboose at Papeete in Tahiti, a building in which Herman Melville had earlier been held on the charge of mutiny.[24] Their context, then, links them to the production of the canonical beachcomber texts, *Typee* and *Omoo*. Yet despite their proximity to a literary heritage, the types of narration and writing in which the three beachcombers of *The Ebb-Tide* engage fail to achieve author-ity, and are fragmentary and self-enclosed. Huish, who is ill, demands to be entertained with a yarn. Herrick responds by invok-ing an *Arabian Nights* scenario, in which a magic carpet transports the beachcombers back to metropolitan society. As each takes up the tale, the backgrounds of the three are defined by their fan-tasies of home yarned at the periphery; by the metonymies, par-ticularly of food, through which class represents itself as personal taste. In this version of the *Arabian Nights* the other is not the Oriental, but the returned beachcomber, gazing upon British society as outsider.

Davis remains the closest of the trio to the model of the enter-prising beachcomber, and it is he who instigates the most practical of narrative activities. He earns breakfast by dancing and singing English musical favourites to a group of Polynesian sailors, a per-formance which is the residue of the beachcomber's earlier role as cross-cultural translator. He also engages the other two beach-combers in a letter-writing project, begging writing implements from the British consul. Inspired by reminiscence, he suggests that they each write to loved ones at home in England. The letters that they produce are romanticised accounts of their present life: South Seas fictions. However only Huish is comfortable with the role of duplicitous narrator. Davis and Herrick, conscious of the gap between a fictional romance and the reality of their situation, are reluctant, guilty authors: 'Now they would write a word or two, now scribble it out; now they would sit biting at the pencil end and staring seaward; now their eyes would rest on the clerk, where he sat propped on the canoe, leering and coughing, his pencil racing glibly on the paper.'[25] Huish produces a generic romance tale in which he claims to have made his fortune: 'I wrote to her and told her 'ow I had got rich, and married a queen in the Hislands, and lived in a blooming palace.'(192) His pronunciation slurs the Pacific islands with the Scottish Highlands that were the setting of Stevenson's own romances. Huish's story reinvokes those of an earlier generation of beachcombers – of figures such as William Mariner, whose tale of adoption into the Tongan aristocracy is the material of romance. However, in the era of Pacific colonialism, romance is figured as degenerate. Huish's facility with this type of writing is indicative of his unredeemed nature, and his text is reviled and destroyed: 'the clerk reached out his hand, picked up the letter, which had fallen to the earth, and tore it into fragments, stamp and all'(192).

Herrick's productions, on the other hand, reflect a classical education, and are the antithesis of the beachcomber's *bricolage*. He lacks the 'gift of fabrication', so that his ventures into numerous professions have acquired for him the name of 'incompetent' (175). He is distinguished by his library rather than by his manual productions, carrying 'a tattered Virgil in his pocket'(174). Herrick holds on to this artefact of a 'dead tongue', even while he lives, surrounded by a double oral heritage, among yarning sailors in Polynesia. Where Cannibal Jack's library was one of his many successful enterprises, Herrick's book is a further testimony to his incompetence – a text he is able neither to circulate nor to subsist upon:

Certainly, if money could have been raised upon the book, Robert Herrick would long ago have sacrificed that last possession; but the demand for literature, which is so marked a feature in some parts of the South Seas, extends not so far as the dead tongues; and the Virgil, which he could not exchange against a meal, had often consoled him in his hunger. (174)

The name Robert Herrick alludes, of course, to the author of *Hesperides* (1648), and like the verse of the Carolinean poet, Herrick's 'literary' productions are effete, self-conscious pieces. He inscribes his own epitaph – the 'famous phrase' from Beethoven's Fifth Symphony, and a line from the *Aeneid* – on the calaboose walls that once housed Melville, and which have since become decorated with the cave paintings of the other, Polynesian and European: 'The crumbling whitewash was all full of them: Tahitian names, and French, and English, and rude sketches of ships under sail and men at fisticuffs.' (193) Where the *bricolage* productions of the beachcomber were adaptive to context, Herrick's chosen form of writing, the epitaph, is static, expressing a determination to endure, to leave a sign. He takes pleasure in the incongruity of his inscription, in the social distinction his quotations imply: '"So", thought he, "they will know that I loved music and had classical tastes. They? He, I suppose: the unknown, kindred spirit that shall come some day and read my *memor querela*. Ha, he shall have Latin too!"' (194) The reader he fantasizes is singular, rather than communal: he prides himself on writing a language of few initiates. But bathetically, his actual audience turns out to be Davis, who incorporates Herrick's solipsistic, congealed quotation into plot. By coincidence, the captain figures, Herrick's inscription was made at the very time at which he himself succeeded in securing a new venture for the three beachcombers: to crew the contaminated ship *Farallone*, with its cargo of champagne, to Australia. Davis brings Herrick's dead fragments of language into line with active enterprise, invoking the providential thesis:

'About how long ago since you wrote up this truck?' he asked.
'What does it matter?' exclaimed Herrick. 'I daresay half an hour.'
'My God, its strange!' cried Davis. 'There's some men would call that accidental: not me. That . . .' and he drew his thick finger under the music – 'that's what I call Providence.' (196)

Herrick's impotence marks a demise in the figure of the gentleman beachcomber, of whom Melville is the canonical precedent. Like Herrick, Melville was the son of a prosperous merchant who went bankrupt, forcing his son to seek employment on board whaling ships cruising the Pacific. T. Walter Herbert has argued that Melville's South Seas fictions betray 'the complex psychology of the failed patrician'.[26] In *Omoo,* Melville depicts a ship's crew comprised of similar types to the *Ebb-Tide*'s three protagonists. The captain, an educated Cockney, is like Herrick, 'in no wise competent'. The mate Jermin prefigures Davis: a capable seaman with a weakness for strong drink. But the most authoritative figure aboard this vessel is Dr Long Ghost, a character in the model of the gentleman beachcomber, who carries similar cultural baggage to Herrick: 'he quoted Virgil, and talked of Hobbes of Malmsbury, beside repeating poetry by the canto, especially Hudibras'. Long Ghost converts literary fragment into active narrative, rather than the dead text of epitaph. He is a teller of stories and a singer of songs: 'he had more anecdotes than I can tell of. Then such mellow old songs he sang, in a voice so round and racy, the real juice of sound. How such notes came forth from his lank body was a constant marvel. Upon the whole, Long Ghost was as entertaining a companion as one could wish.'[27] For *The Ebb-Tide*'s trio, by contrast, a general failure of enterprise is signalled by the exhaustion of narrative possibility that marks their aleatory or shallow creative endeavours.

Davis's proposal is an attempt to revive the beachcomber in a project of active speculation. The authors of *The Ebb-Tide* turn to the type of plot which motivated *Omoo* and *The Wrecker,* seeking to create a profitable story from the waste material of the three beached protagonists. In the prologue to *The Wrecker,* Loudon Dodd boasts of his involvements in a series of duplicitous speculations, as wrecker, smuggler, and blackmailer. The common product of these ventures is narrative. Dodd and Pinkerton gamble upon the story that lies hidden in the mysterious wreck of the *Flying Scud,* and the tale within their tale is the wealth that they eventually recover. In the first half of *The Ebb-Tide,* Davis proposes a parallel set of projects: to smuggle the *Farallone*'s cargo of champagne, to wreck the ship and claim from the profits of insurance using blackmail, to intimidate the owner of the pearl island upon which they alight. Yet in this novel such ventures are ill-fated: the twists of plot offer only a series of dead-ends. As the only men in Papeete willing to sail the ship *Farallone* despite a risk of infection, the trio are marked as doomed subjects, gambling with death. Possibilities recede, like an ebb-tide, leaving the beachcomber

washed up, a useless object rather than a fabricator. The novel
Lloyd Osbourne begins by rewriting the plot of *The Wrecker* is laid
aside, becomes waste material, exhausted like its protagonists.
When Stevenson takes up the thread of narrative again in 'The
Quartet', introducing the character of Attwater, the owner of the
pearl island, he recycles this waste material in a new *bricolage*.
However, it is the figure of the missionary as represented by
Attwater, rather than of the beachcomber, who provides the
authority for continuation: who offers to make something of the
legacy of the beachcomber.

Each of the trio takes up the threads of narrative without
success, grasping and then surrendering the reins of authorship.
Herrick's 'incompetence' is indicated by his inability to assume
control until the very conclusion of the story. The more resource-
ful plotting of Davis, already mentioned, meets its match in
Attwater. He hands authority over to Huish, who formulates a
desperate plan to destroy Attwater using a bottle of acid. The
bottle is a significant image in *The Ebb-Tide*, emblematising the
emptying out of meaning that accompanies closure of speculation.
The cargo of champagne aboard the *Farallone* initially represents
bounty to the three beachcombers. These bottles, however,
contain wine turned to water.

'Illo!' said Huish. 'Ere's a bad bottle.'

He poured some of the wine into the mug: it was colourless and still.
He smelt and tasted it . . . The mug passed round; each sipped, each smelt
of it; each stared at the bottle in its glory of gold paper as Crusoe may
have stared at the footprint; and their minds were swift to fix upon a
common apprehension. The difference between a bottle of champagne
and a bottle of water is not great; between a shipload of one or the other
lay the whole scale from riches to ruin.

A second bottle was broached . . . Still with the same result: the contents were still colourless and tasteless, and dead as the rain in a beached
fishing boat. (226–7)

Where Crusoe, the mythical beachcomber hero, encountered the
sign of presence, the footprint on the sand, the three latter-day
beachcombers are confronted by the sign of absence, water, the
featurelessness of which is verified by each of their senses. The
bottle of luxury becomes the bottle of despair, to be substituted by
Huish's bottle of bile. In the stories of castaways on desert islands,
bottles assume significance as bearing final messages; ultimate

authorial statements. Huish's last-resort bottle of acid, on the other hand, serves a horrific project of erasure, signalling the expiration of the beachcomber plot.

Attwater's pearl island is a space replete with poetic possibilities: an appropriate setting for the figure who emerges as the dominant authorial presence within the narrative. Stevenson depicts the atoll landscape as one of deceptive minimalism and metaphoric abundance, recalling his description of the Tuamotus in *In the South Seas*. It exhausts Herrick's limited poetic capacities:

> He tortured himself to find analogies. The isle was like the rim of a great vessel sunken in the waters; it was like the embankment of an annular railway grown upon with wood: so slender it seemed amidst the outrageous breakers, so frail and pretty, he would scarce have wondered to see it sink and disappear without a sound, and the waves close smoothly over its descent. (237)

I suggested earlier that the atoll represents a feminine geography within Stevenson's island vocabulary. Herrick's poetic failure is perhaps due here to the attempt to impose masculine similes upon a feminine landscape. The atoll is both fertile, producing a wealth of pearls, and barren, its population recently annihilated by an epidemic, and it is this ambiguous signification that Attwater's own sermonising fails to reconcile. For of course his pearl island is not simply a physical space: it is also a missionary colony, and an exegetical text.

If Attwater's are the ascendent poetics of *The Ebb-Tide*, this development reflects a post-contact Pacific historical teleology. The missionary's authority and influence defeat the projects of the superseded beachcomber. Robert Irwin Hillier has compared the character of Attwater to those missionaries whom Stevenson lionized in his correspondence from the Pacific: George Brown of Samoa, Shirley Baker of Tonga, and James Chalmers of New Guinea. Hillier claims that 'the similarities between Attwater and actual missionary figures are sufficient to demonstrate that Stevenson regarded Attwater as heroic'.[28] Yet rather than simply endorsing the missionary as hero, Stevenson represents in the figure of Attwater the dominance of evangelical discourse: a discourse which, in the later nineteenth-century Pacific, prospered through association with colonial policy. Attwater's are the poetics of absolute authority. He is introduced just as the beachcombers' fund of invention becomes exhausted: 'They had no plan, no story prepared.' (240) He terrifies Herrick with his godlike omnipresence: '"He knows all, he sees through all; we only make him laugh with our pretences – he looks at us and laughs like God!"' (271) He refers to himself consistently using the indefinite pronoun *one*, describing his actions in the third person in a self-consciously writerly fashion. He claims to be 'a plain man and very literal' (259), but his speech is imbued with the classical education of the later nineteenth-century 'gentleman' missionary.

In Attwater's confrontation with Huish, the aristocrat defeats the proletarian, and literacy overcomes orality. Attwater prides himself on being a winnower of souls, on providing in his island colony a context in which both Polynesian and Western subjects may find an opportunity to prove their worth. However, his is the touchstone of class: 'The presence of the gentleman lighted up like a candle the vulgarity of the clerk.' (242) During his first encounter with Attwater, Huish reverts to an oral performance described as innately 'savage', but redolent of Cockney culture, singing 'a piece of the chorus of a comic song which he must have heard twenty years before in London: meaningless gibberish that, in that hour and that place, seemed hateful as a blasphemy: "Hikey, pikey, crikey, fikey, chillinga-wallaba dory."' (248) Huish's nonsense is a sound poem, an echo: it is blasphemous in its very non-literacy. Attwater, in turn, subtly denigrates Huish by reading rather than speaking his name. He titles Huish 'Mr Whish', pronouncing the Cockney self-nomination *Uish* as it might be written rather than as it must be heard. Attwater mimics orality by consciously over-articulating. By contrast, Huish's plan to destroy Attwater involves manufacturing a duplicitous letter of truce which is a piece of transcribed speech. It is distinguished within Stevenson's text by its typeface, which is further fractured by apostrophes marking verbal ellipses: 'I 'ave deputed my friend and partner, Mr J. L. Huish, to l'y before you my proposals, and w'ich by their moderytion, will, I trust, be found to merit your attention. Mr J. L. Huish is entirely unarmed, I swear to Gawd! and will 'old 'is 'ands over 'is 'ead from the moment he begins to approach you.' (290) Huish fetishises the unfamiliar written text: 'Huish read the letter with the innocent joy of amateurs, chuckled gustfully to himself, and reopened it more than once after it was refolded, to repeat the pleasure.' (290) The contest between beachcomber and missionary is depicted as one between two discursive modes: the beachcomber's linked to British working-class oral traditions, and the missionary's to the advent of literacy.

Attwater's literal-mindedness expresses his commitment to the Old Testament paradigm of earthly vengeance and reward. However, his favoured mode of discourse is the New Testament poetics of parable. He offers the unnerving redemption of a place within sermon. The populace of his island, decimated by disease, are resurrected as the subjects of story. He tells the beachcombers a morality fable of opposite types, former inhabitants of the atoll to whom he refers as Obsequious and Sullens. The pair represent two colonial caricatures, the mimic and the silent slave. Their public faces have deceived Attwater: the subservient figure in fact proves duplicitous, while the silent native is revealed to be loyal in his motives. The discovery of their true identities comes too late to save the pair from their master's swift and destructive judgement. The fable depicts a régime of absolute power based on insufficient perception; however other aspects of Attwater's authority illustrate an alternative model of control, which finds explicit statement in Stevenson's public comments on missionary policy.

In the lecture from which I quoted earlier, entitled 'Missions in the South Seas', Stevenson focuses on the necessity of adaptation to context. He urges missionaries, in their encounters with Pacific cultures, 'to seek rather the point of agreement than the points of difference; to proceed rather by confirmation and extension than by iconoclasm'.[29] It is the ability to negotiate between the culture of his origins and that of his adopted context which renders Attwater an insurmountable force. At a dinner party for the beach-combers, he displays his authority through his masterful appropriation of Polynesian cuisine, serving dishes which utilise the island's natural delicacies:

They sat down to an island dinner, remarkable for its variety and excellence: turtle-soup and steak, fish, fowls, a sucking-pig, a cocoanut salad, and sprouting cocoanut roasted for dessert. Not a tin had been opened; and save for the oil and vinegar in the salad, and some green spears of onion which Attwater cultivated and plucked with his own hand, not even the condiments were European. (261)

Attwater is a missionary liberated from dependence on the metropolitan article. In this context, his ability to manipulate that slippery signifier, the bottle, is only a supplementary sign of control: 'Sherry, hock, and claret succeeded each other, and the *Farallone* champagne brought up the rear with the dessert.' (261)

By appropriating the beachcomber's strategy of cultural interaction, once the beachcomber has become an exhausted force, the missionary in turn achieves ascendency in the Pacific. Attwater has stored up a treasure-trove of material for *bricolage* in a house on his island

which stood gaping open on the afternoon, seiz[ing] on the mind of Herrick with its multiplicity and disorder of romantic things. Therein were cables, windlasses and blocks of every size and capacity; cabin windows and ladders; rusty tanks, a companion hatch; a binnacle with its brass mountings and its compass idly pointing, in the confusion and dusk of that shed, to a forgotten pole; ropes, anchors, harpoons, a blubber-dipper of copper, green with years, a steering-wheel, a tool-chest with the vessel's name upon the top, the *Asia*: a whole curiosity shop of sea-curios, gross and solid, heavy to lift, ill to break, bound with brass and shod with iron. (250)

Attwater goads Herrick to make metaphor from this material: '"only old junk! And does Mr Hay find a parable?"' (250). The beachcomber is conscious, however, of his poetic enervation. When Herrick eventually offers himself to Attwater it is as another object cast up by the tide, unable to fashion anything from himself, but hoping to serve as an element in the missionary's *bricolage*: '"Can you do anything with me? . . . I am broken crockery; I am a burst drum; the whole of my life is gone to water; I have nothing left that I believe in, except my living horror of myself . . . I put myself, helpless, in your hands."' (279)

The union of the beachcomber and the missionary represents a powerful force, and was espoused by Stevenson in his lecture on missions. There he recommends that the missionary attempt to recognise, rather than antagonise, the beachcomber:

Too many missionaries make a mistake . . . when they expect, not only from their native converts, but from white men (by no means of the highest class) shipwrecked or stranded at random in these islands, a standard of conduct which no parish minister in the world would dare to expect of his parishioners and church-members. There is here, in these despised whites, a second reservoir of moral power, which missionaries too often neglect and render nugatory . . . The trader is therefore, at once by experience and by influence, the superior of the missionary. He is a person marked out to be made use of by an intelligent mission.

Stevenson's polemic describes Herrick's plot: 'Sometimes a very doubtful character, sometimes an exceedingly decent gentleman, he will almost invariably be made the better by some intelligent and kindly attention, for which he is often burning, and he will almost invariably be made the worse by neglect, by being ignored or by insult . . . The missions and the traders have to be made more or less in unison.'[30]

The kind of redemption offered to the beachcomber by the missionary is not, however, represented within the fictional context of *The Ebb-Tide* as unambiguously positive. Davis, who becomes a cipher for Attwater's discourse, is an emasculated figure at the close of the novel, prepared to sacrifice the prospect of a return to wife and family in order to remain in a childlike role as 'Attwater's spoiled darling and pet penitent!'(301) Attwater's theology becomes, upon Davis's lips, a 'voluble and incoherent stream of prayer'(300): a form of nonsense, akin to the threatening gobbledegook of Huish's Cockney verbage. Herrick himself has earlier indicated an aptitude for Attwater's brand of redemption, which is discursive rather than ethical. His storytelling in the calaboose was already termed a 'parable'(179). Huish found it too redolent of sermon, commenting sarcastically: '"It's like the rot there is in tracts"'(180); '"it's like *Ministering Children!*"'(181) Indeed, Herrick's acquired sense of masculine purpose at the end of *The Ebb-Tide* reflects his resistance to complete conversion as much as it exemplifies the beachcomber's refashioning by the missionary.

'THE BEACH OF FALESĀ': TRADE SECRETS

Although Stevenson's lecture on missions discusses the potentially redemptive role of beachcombers – 'white men (by no means of the highest class) shipwrecked or stranded at random in these islands', his specific reference is to 'traders'. This slip, perhaps made for the benefit of an audience unfamiliar with the term *beachcomber* (which H. E. Maude claims is of 'genuine island coinage') elides an important distinction between the two roles, which reflects their potential to serve, as Stevenson advocates, the missionary cause. According to Maude, 'what really differentiated the beachcombers from other immigrants was the fact that they were essentially integrated into, and dependent for their livelihood on, the indigenous communities . . . To all intents and purposes they had voluntarily or perforce contracted out of the European monetary economy.'[31] Traders, on the other hand, were representatives of European and American commercial agendas. They operated at the nexus of Western and Pacific cultures, facilitating the two-way circulation of goods and produce. Traders manned the outposts of capitalist enterprise, and hence were more realistic candidates for appropriation to missionary colonialist agendas than the outcast beachcomber. They were not simply colluders, however; their role retained a certain ambivalence, falling in the unreliable territory between colonial representative and maverick entrepreneur.

'The Beach of Falesā', Stevenson's narrative of 'a South Seas Trader', is a story of divided allegiances. The trader, John Wiltshire, pits himself against and defeats his rival, the gentleman beachcomber Case, and in the process affirms his loyalty to the island community he has made his own. A text about the ethics of trade, 'The Beach of Falesā' is itself a product of transaction. It was published in book form in the volume *Island Nights' Entertainments*, with two other tales, 'The Bottle Imp' (originally published in the *New York Herald*, 8, 15, 22 February, 1 March 1891, and in *Black and White*, 28 March, 4 April 1891) and 'The Isle of Voices' (originally published in the *National Observer*, 4, 11, 18, 25 February 1893). Stevenson had wanted 'The Beach of Falesā' to be brought out as a single volume: the stories that came to accompany it were intended for a differently conceived 'Island Nights' Entertainments'. During preparation for printing, the 'Falesā' manuscript's idiosyncratic spellings and grammar were subject to correction by editors and proof-readers, and certain passages were censored. In his minutely documented study of these textual alterations, Barry Menikoff argues that editorial intervention effectively diluted the story's radical critique of colonial practice.[32] Menikoff draws attention to the subtle ways in which editors and publishers, aiming for the production of a smoothly literate text, ironed out disruptive effects that embodied Stevenson's attempt to transcribe the mixed language of his adopted context.

Stevenson's distance from metropolitan publishing centres slowed down negotiations over the text. The stages of publication become foregrounded in a dilatory series of questions, cross-decisions and re-evaluations, formulated in exchanges of letters across the Pacific. This slow-motion process provides a counterweight at the level of production to the readerly acceleration which, Menikoff argues, was edited into Stevenson's resistant text. He notes that 'the compositors and proof-readers . . . supplied substitutes which insured that a reader, when he passed over a sentence, would not have to pause or give a special ear to sound and meaning because a familiar word appeared in an unorthodox context. Instead he could glide gracefully over the page, automatically filling out the words and, on occasion, the clichés.' Physical distance acted as an impediment to production. Nor did this dynamic simply reinforce a familiar opposition between metropolitan advancement and peripheral obstruction: the urge towards acceleration coming from technologically advanced publishing centres, and resisted by an author from the Pacific wishing to preserve, as artefact, an 'authentic' piece of cultural transcription. The ultimate objective of Menikoff's study is to recuperate 'The Beach of Falesā' as a modernist, writerly text, whose aesthetic of difficulty has been attenuated by the conservative emendations of the literary establishment. He argues that

Falesā presented [compositors and proof-readers] with a more complex problem: it substituted ambiguity in language for certainty . . . The ambiguity was not merely that of an occasional word or syntactical construction but that of method and manner . . . It is as if the effort to communicate by mastering a clear style is contravened by the realisation that the style may not be a means for discovering any truth at all, except, paradoxically, that ambiguity and irresolution are the conditions of life.[33]

Despite his claims for 'The Beach of Falesā''s Modernism, Menikoff's project is essentially Romantic in its conception of authorship; motivated by a belief in the integrity of authorial creation that leads him back to the original, the signatory hand. His study describes the death of authorship that occurs when the sanctity of the text is violated by the philistine interventions of publishers. But while 'The Beach of Falesā' is clearly a product of transaction, there are alternative ways of interpreting the effects of negotiation. The editorial changes to Stevenson's manuscript disrupt a unified authorial intention, inscribing instead the process of the book's cross-cultural production. The negotiated printed text of 'The Beach of Falesā' makes manifest the contract implicit in all writing from oral cultural contexts, which may seek to remain faithful to the 'voice' of the exotic, but which remains financially dependent upon a metropolitan audience. The publishers' decision to print 'The Beach of Falesā' as part of *Island Nights' Entertainments* results in the production of a volume that makes explicit this dialogical impulse. The two halves of the book (the first story is novella length, and occupies slightly more than half the pages of the volume) demonstrate alternative traditions of storytelling. While the dedication of *Island Nights' Entertainments* to 'Three Old Shipmates Among the Islands' – friends from Stevenson's cruise aboard the *Janet Nichol* – explicitly situates the volume as a whole within the narrative context of the shipboard yarn, only 'The Beach of Falesā' actually exemplifies this mode of discourse. 'The Bottle Imp' and 'The Isle of Voices' have the aggregative format and rhythmical language of Polynesian oral compositions. Stevenson was an appreciative audience for, and a collector of, both these types of oral tradition. Graham Balfour observed that 'Well as Stevenson could himself tell a story, he was never tired of studying the methods of other men, and never failed to express his high appreciation of sailors' yarns.'[34]

Yet Stevenson opposed the combination of different narrative modes in a single volume, insisting in correspondence that 'The B. of F. is *simply not* to appear along with 'The Bottle Imp', a story of a totally different scope and intention, to which I have already made one fellow, and which I design for a substantive volume.'[35] A segregation was evident in the corpus of texts he produced from the Pacific, which can be divided between romances that retained a Scottish location, betraying only indirectly their context of production, and works of a local influence and setting. This discernible link between subject matter and genre reflects the fact that Stevenson's later writings were produced according to alternative criteria: on the one hand, continuing in the romance tradition, and on the other, offering Polynesian culture to the metropolitan reader as ethnographic artefact, a project which entailed an espousal of realism. He asserts that '['The Beach of Falesā'] is the first realistic South Sea story; I mean with real South Sea character and details of life; everybody else who has tried, that I have seen, got carried away by the romance and ended in a kind of sugar candy sham epic, and the whole effect was lost – there was no etching, no human grin, consequently no conviction.'[36] The contested juxtaposition of European and Polynesian oral narrative models in *Island Nights' Entertainments*, however, foregrounds implicit tensions and reciprocities between these traditions, reintroducing to the book as a whole the polyphonic and disjunctive structure that Menikoff seeks to recover for 'The Beach of Falesā'.

At the opening of 'The Beach of Falesā', Wiltshire arrives at a 'high island', after 'years on a low island near the line, living for the most part solitary among natives'.[37] The change of topographies offers him the promise of a cure: 'Here was a fresh experience; even the tongue would be quite strange to me; and the look of these woods and mountains, and the rare smell of them, renewed my blood.'(3) Like Stevenson making his first 'island landfall' in *In the South Seas*, Wiltshire has come to the high island in need of recuperation, but his illness is diagnosed as the lack of white society: 'I was sick for white neighbours after my four years at the line'.(5) This disablement is registered partly as a loss of technological dexterity. He spells out the effect of looking towards shore through a telescope, implying a defamiliarised relationship with the instrument: 'I took the glass; and the shores leapt nearer, and I saw the tangle of woods and the breach of the surf.'(3) This acquired technological naïveté echoes representations of native wonderment from early European accounts of the Pacific – compare Kotzebue's description of a Samoan chief looking through a telescope for the first time:

A telescope which I held in my hand attracted the observation of the chief, who took it for a gun. I directed him to look through it; but the sudden vision of the distant prospect brought so close to his eye that he could even distinguish the people on the strand, so terrified him, that nothing could induce him to touch the magic instrument again.[38]

As Wiltshire's story develops, technological facility is exposed as a force of exploitation.

The settler community that Wiltshire enters constitutes a predetermined narrative frame. It is populated by a cast of characters whose names have onomantic resonances. Wiltshire is not the first mercantile Adam to occupy this Edenic scene; his predecessor is 'old Adams'. The devil is represented by 'Black Jack', Case's accessory. 'Vigours', 'Whistling Jimmie' and 'Underhill' all meet apposite fates. This morality play cast also provides Stevenson with the opportunity for self-reflexive allusion. The villain of the piece, the gentleman beachcomber Case, offers an alternative model of the artist to Wiltshire, the plain-style storyteller. Case is a manipulator of devices and effects. His name signifies the subject both of detective fiction and, *avant la lettre*, of the psychoanalytic session.[39] These two discourses are, according to Walter Ong, typically literate. Ong claims that 'Detective plots are deeply interior . . . by contrast with the old oral narrative. The oral narrator's protagonist, distinguished typically for his external exploits, has been replaced by the interior consciousness of the typographic protagonist', while 'It would appear that the advent of modern depth psychology parallels the development of the character in drama and the novel, both depending on the inward turning of the psyche produced by writing and intensified by print.'[40] The name *Case* may also of course allude to the bag of tricks with which he keeps the population of Falesā in thrall. In the figure of Case, Stevenson associates malign technological wizardry with literate discourse.

Case's features are mask-like – 'He was yellow and smallish, had a hawk's nose to his face, pale eyes, and his beard trimmed with scissors' (5) – and he is a gifted actor and mimic – 'He could speak, when he chose, fit for a drawing room; and when he chose he could blaspheme worse than a Yankee boatswain, and talk smart to sicken a Kanaka. The way he thought would pay best at the moment, that was Case's way, and it always seemed to come natural, and like as if he was born to it.' (5–6) His facility reflects Stevenson's own capacity to register a multitude of different voices within his tale. As Menikoff observes:

In *Falesā* he possessed a subject that allowed him to meld the array of dialects and idioms that he had absorbed in his travels as an 'emigrant' across the continental United States, and on his cruises through the Pacific. At his command were American slang, Samoan, pidgin English (what the professional linguists call Beach-la-mar), and the ubiquitous sailor's talk, a range of terms and expressions that were commonplace at one extreme and required a glossary at the other.[41]

Case's authorship, however, produces a false text. He procures an attractive Falesān girl, Uma, for Wiltshire, and organises their 'marriage', writing the certificate, 'signatures and all, in a leaf out of the ledger'. (13) Case's document certifies that Uma 'is illegally married to Mr John Wiltshire for one week, and Mr John Wiltshire is at liberty to send her to hell when he pleases'. He manipulates a familiar scenario: the innocent native is duped by a writing that is fetishized without being comprehended. This section of the plot raises issues about the ethics of writing within which Stevenson is himself indirectly implicated. The marriage certificate can be contextualised by an episode from his travels. At church service in Butaritari, he observed a group of traders' wives, noting the 'unusually enviable' position they occupied within their community. He reports, however, that

the certificate of one, when she proudly showed it, proved to run thus, that she was 'married for one night', and her gracious partner was at liberty to 'send her to hell' the next morning; but she was none the wiser or the worse for the dastardly trick. Another, I heard, was married on a work of mine in a pirated edition; it answered the purpose as well as a Hall Bible.[42]

Stevenson's own writing, then, had occupied the space of the false text in the instance of deception on which Case's document is modelled. He points out, however, that the book employed was 'a pirated edition', from which he derived no profit; distinguishing his own authorship from self-serving literate impositions upon Pacific populations, and implying that he and the trader's wife are the mutual victims of literary exploitation. Case's false document was in turn the focus of censorship by Stevenson's editors. It was excised from *The Illustrated London News* and the 1892 copyright versions of the tale, and subsequently modified for publication (in the manuscript, 'week' had read as 'night') in accordance with perceptions of audience sensibilities.[43] The latter tussle of terminology appears so arbitrary as to represent primarily a contest of authority between writer and editors, subsumed into an ethical agenda.

The marriage certificates Stevenson mentions in *In the South Seas* represent a contract which is mutually beneficial. The trader gains a sexual partner, and his wife obtains both unlimited access to foreign commodities, and immunity by association from the tabus and curfews that restrict other members of her community. The marriage certificate in 'The Beach of Falesā' is similarly mutually binding, but it represents the deception of both parties. By signing, Wiltshire becomes united with a bride who turns out to have been tabued by her own community. The morning after his wedding night, the locals register that the trader's cynically achieved domesticity is also a performance in their eyes, by forming an audience outside his house: 'Some dozen young men and children made a piece of a half-circle, flanking my house . . . and they all sat silent, wrapped in their sheets, and stared at me and my house as straight as pointer dogs.'(17) Unable to speak their language, Wiltshire is at the mercy of Case as interpreter of this silent message. Case offers to discover from the village chiefs the story behind Wiltshire's alienation. The explanation he 'translates', however, is one of which he is in effect the author.

Case is not, then, simply a malign colonial exploiting a small island community. His success lies in his ability to negotiate between cultures, and to play upon mutual assumptions. His false certificate may manipulate Uma's innocent fetishisation of writing, but equally it plays upon Wiltshire's faith that, as a self-nominated 'British subject', writing will always be his tool, and, more broadly, on the trader's complacent ignorance of the codes and practices of his new community. Case accompanies his adoption of the role of Wiltshire's interpreter with the mimicked rhetoric of imperial duty: 'I count it the White Man's Quarrel.'(27) Wiltshire uncritically reiterates this discourse, instructing Case to declare to the chiefs: 'I'm a white man, and a British subject, and no end of a big chief at home; and I've come here to do them good, and bring them civilisation. . . . I demand the reason of this treatment as a white man and a British subject.'(29) Before he can overcome Case's treacherous influence, Wiltshire must cease to place confidence in false colonial kinship, and begin to identify with the interests of Falesā's indigenous community. In the early part of the story there is a clear division between the depiction of the Western settlers of Falesā, whose apposite names fix them, albeit grotesquely, in the mind of the reader, and the representation of the native population as inscrutably other, 'like graven images'(18), without individuated subjectivity. The exception here is of course Uma, who initially stands out among the 'Kanakas' of Falesā simply as the object of Wiltshire's voyeuristic sexual appraisal, but who forces her husband to recognise the integral humanity which is signalled by her own name ('Uma' is the core of the word *human*; in Samoan the word signifies wholeness and completeness).

Uma's affection for Wiltshire is prompted by her fetishisation of the written document. She believes the false marriage certificate to be authoritative: its textuality offers her a more substantial sign of her changed status than empty words. She tells Wiltshire:

'"White man, he come here, I marry him all-e-same Kanaka; very well then, he marry me all-e-same white woman. Suppose he no marry, he go 'way, woman he stop. All-e-same thief, empty-hand, Tonga-heart – no can love! Now you come marry me. You big heart – you no shamed island girl. That thing I love you far too much. I proud."'(39)[44] Yet her naïve faith in the deceptive document amounts also to a form of indirect authorship. Implicitly at Uma's dictation, Wiltshire transforms the false marriage certificate into the true sign that she believes it to be, and so begins his own course of redemption. He summons the local missionary, the Reverend Tarleton, to perform a genuine marriage ceremony, which is carried out in the language of the Polynesian bride rather than the English groom: '"And I guess you'd better do it in native"', Wiltshire orders the missionary, '"it'll please the old lady."'(44) Wiltshire gives way to an outburst of self-denigration that echoes and inverts his earlier, self-affirming imperialist rhetoric: '"I'm no missionary, nor missionary lover; I'm no Kanaka, nor favourer of Kanakas – I'm just a trader; I'm just a common low God-damned white man and British subject, the sort you would like to wipe your boots on."'(42) His recognition that British nationality does not guarantee authority coincides with the development of a more active role for his wife, who takes over the role of interpreter, becoming Wiltshire's accessory in unravelling the further plots of the villainous Case.

Although another Western character, the missionary, is required to bring the false marriage within the realm of law, his authority as guide and interpreter is simultaneously undermined. Tarleton, whose name (as well as being that of the most famous of the Elizabethan clowns), echoes 'charlatan', tells Wiltshire of his betrayal by a most promising convert, the teacher Namu. Namu's name signals to the English reader an inverted humanity, the reverse of Uma's. Tarleton has placed his faith in Namu as a genuine vessel of transcendent truth. He claims: 'All our islanders easily acquire a kind of eloquence, and can roll out and illustrate, with a great deal of vigour and fancy, second-hand sermons; but Namu's sermons are his own, and I cannot deny that I have found them means of grace.'(46) However Namu proves to be a mimic preacher. Under Case's influence, his discourse evolves into a pastiche of Protestant, Catholic and Polynesian superstition, undermining the claims of each religion to the status of absolute truth.

Its form remains indistinguishable from genuine Christian sermon, but its content is blasphemous, creating a tension that has been well analysed, in another context, by Homi Bhabha: 'A discourse at the crossroads of what is known and permissible and that which though known must be kept concealed; a discourse uttered between the lines and as such both against the rules and within them.'[45] Namu's false teaching recalls the destabilising mimicry practised by those Pacific cult leaders discussed earlier, and similarly incorporates a self-reflexive turn. In the following speech, reported by Tarleton, he explicitly professes the relative value of the sign:

'I reasoned thus: if this sign of the cross were used in a Popey manner it would be sinful, but when it is used only to protect men from a devil, which is a thing harmless in itself, the sign too must be harmless. For the sign is neither good nor bad. But if the bottle be full of gin, the gin is bad; and if the sign made in idolatry be bad, so is the idolatry.' And, very like a native pastor, he had a text apposite about the casting out of devils. (47)

Tarleton resists for too long the acknowledgement of Namu's defection, and with it the provisionality of his own discourse. He thus becomes implicated in a horror story of economic rivalry. Case has achieved ascendency as local trader by disposing of his rivals with the collusion of Namu. Old Adams is suspected of having been poisoned, Vigours survives, but is driven out, and Underhill is buried alive while paralysed by palsy, with Namu officiating. Tarleton has nonetheless determined upon a policy of wilful ignorance: 'At that moment, with Namu's failure fresh in my view, the work of my life appeared a mockery; hope was dead in me . . . Right or wrong, then, I determined on a quiet course.' (49) He resorts to commentary only in the indirect and contested language of scriptural allusion: 'On Sunday I took the pulpit in the morning, and preached from First Kings, nineteenth, on the fire, the earth-quake and the voice, distinguishing the true spiritual power, and referring with such plainness as I dared to recent events in Falesā.' (50) His textual exegesis is undermined by a performance which purports to expose the complicity between the discourse of the missionary and commercial profit. After the service, Case practices a simple magic trick, making believe to pluck a dollar out of Tarleton's head, and thus providing his local audience with apparent material evidence that the missionary's words are tainted at their source with lucre. Tarleton punningly recognises his text-bound impotence, in an oral cultural context in which such per-

formances achieve immediate authority: 'I wish I had learnt legerdemain instead of Hebrew, that I might have paid the fellow out
with his own coin.'(51)

Case creates a performance that turns to account the symbolic
imagination of cargo cult. Manipulating Polynesian modes of
understanding, he offers a critique of Western economic motiva-
tions: he is a two-faced mimic of settler and indigenous practices.
Earlier, when responding to Wiltshire's inquiries as to why the
islanders avoided his trade, Case feigned a respect for the uncanny
which gave way to the rhetoric of relativism: '"In short, I'm afraid,"
says he. ". . . The Kanakas won't go near you, that's all. And who's
to make 'em? We traders have a lot of gall, I must say; we make
these poor Kanakas take back their laws, and take up their taboos,
and that, whenever it happens to suit us."'(32) In Case, anti-colo-
nialist critique, as well as imperialist rhetoric, is destabilised.
Perhaps the only discourse that is redeemed within this story is the
transcendent discourse of love, as it is represented in the union
between the trader Wiltshire and the Polynesian woman Uma.
Stevenson's faith in such cross-cultural coupling did not extend,
however, to the production of his own text: he objected to the mis-
matching of a sailor's yarn, 'The Beach of Falesā', with his island
tales 'The Bottle Imp' and 'The Isle of Voices' in the *Island Nights'
Entertainments* volume.

Case's 'legerdemain' goes beyond sleight of hand. He successfully manipulates the myth of Western technological supremacy,
managing a personal cargo cult as theatre. In the woods behind
Falesā he has created a 'temple' of special effects with which he
keeps the village awed. He moves between the insider community
of the beach and this uncanny peripheral zone with the confidence of an actor stepping on to and off stage. Wiltshire's description of Case returning from a visit to the woods portrays him
emerging from behind curtains into a spotlight, in costume: 'I saw
the hanging front of the woods pushed suddenly open, and Case,
with a gun in his hand, step forth into the sunshine on the black
beach. He was got up in light pyjamas.'(56) Wiltshire's task
becomes, in turn, to expose the workings of Case's theatre. He
identifies Case's sham effects as they are shown up by the genuinely uncanny natural landscape. Exploring the woods, Wiltshire
encounters fantastical growth: 'lots of sensitive . . . ropes of liana
hanging down like a ship's rigging, and nasty orchids growing in

the forks like funguses'(61–2). Case's 'tyrolean harps', instruments which produce an eerie whistling sound, stand out among the rank fertility as non-organic in form. They are makeshift assemblages, incorporating identifiable items of trade: 'A box it was, sure enough, and a candle-box at that, with the brand upon the side of it; and it had banjo strings stretched so as to sound when the wind blew.' (64) Wiltshire pays a grudging tribute to Case's gift of fabrication: 'I must say I rather admired the man's ingenuity. With a box of tools and a few mighty simple contrivances he had made out to have a devil of a temple.' (66) Yet Case's theatre is also represented as a shoddy imposition. He has set up a gallery of masks on what appear to be the relics of a real 'temple'. This genuinely unearthly construction dwarfs the impact of his trademarked fright show:

There was a wall in front of me, the path passing it by a gap; it was tumbledown and plainly very old, but built of big stones very well laid; and there is no native alive today upon that island that could dream of such a piece of building! Along all the top of it was a line of queer figures, idols or scarecrows, or what not . . . And the singular thing was that all these bogies were as fresh as toys out of a shop. (65)

Local tales have also invested the landscape surrounding Falesā with uncanny resonances. Unlike Case's productions, these stories effectively incorporate the natural, and thus acquire a potency that remains undiminished at the end of Wiltshire's narrative. Uma tries to prevent her husband from entering the woods by recounting traditional superstitions. She tells of devil women who seduce the most promising Falesān youths, and of a boar 'with a man's thoughts'(61) that once chased her; two versions of the erotic turned horrific which invert the trajectory of Wiltshire's own love story, where the erotic is redeemed by law. The successful dénouement of Wiltshire's narrative depends implicitly upon this suppression, but Uma's stories, which reinvoke the threat of the erotic, are an unresolved moment within that narrative, describing a magic whose workings are never exposed. Her fantastic tales are incorporated directly into Wiltshire's narrative, rather than quoted as Uma's speech, implying his internalisation of a mode of belief which he explicitly rejects.

Before he can defeat Case's wizardry, Wiltshire must perform a task which gives him a practical insight into labour value. As he explains:

Of course we could get no labour, being all as good as tabooed, and the two women and I turned to and made copra with our own hands. It was copra to make your mouth water when it was done – I never understood how much natives cheated me till I had made that four hundred pounds of my own hand – and it weighed so light I felt inclined to take and water it myself. (53)

Once he has manufactured the genuine product, he is equipped not only to recognise 'native' duplicity, but to expose Case's false technologies. He approaches Case's sanctuary indirectly, from backstage: 'Digging off the earth with my hands, I found underneath tarpaulin stretched on boards, so that this was plainly the roof of a cellar. . . . The entrance was on the far side' (66). Evading the specular logic imposed by the architecture of Case's 'museum', Wiltshire is able to uncover its mode of construction, the workings by which its magical effects are produced. He exposes the material base of his rival's symbolic performance, the tools of his trade.

Having mastered Case's stagecraft, Wiltshire can declare himself exempt from the allegorical fate that has determined the histories of his predecessors. He warns Case: '"My name ain't Adams, and it ain't Vigours; and I mean to show you that you've met your match."' (68) He plans a nocturnal return visit to Case's sanctuary in order to explode Case's special effects in a triumphant spectacle of his own. When Uma tries to prevent him departing, he slips strategically into missionary rhetoric, claiming that he will be protected by the authority of the Bible: 'I turned to the title-page, where I thought there would likely be some English, and so there was. "There!" said I. "Look at that! '*London: Printed for the British and Foreign Bible Society, Blackfriars,*' and the date, which I can't read, owing to its being in three X's. There's no devil in hell can look near the Bible Society, Blackfriars."' (73) Uma responds with a scepticism which Wiltshire interprets as naïve literalism, and he is eventually compelled to substantiate his claims for the book by carrying it with him as a safeguard: 'I took to the road, laden like a donkey. First there was that Bible, a book as big as your head, which I had let myself in for by my own tomfoolery.' (74) Uma subsequently learns that Case has discovered Wiltshire's plan. She abandons her superstitious qualms to follow her husband into the woods and warn him of his danger. Wiltshire mines Case's temple, transforming the woods into an infernal landscape: 'the whole wood was scattered with red coals and brands from the explosion;

they were all round me on the flat, some had fallen below in the valley, and some stuck and flared in the tree-tops' (80). In this appropriate setting, the devilish Case meets his end.

Wiltshire's narrative concludes in pointed obfuscation. In his sermon at the burial of Case, the Reverend Tarleton refuses to acknowledge the incompatibility between practices of exploitation and the discourse of salvation. Wiltshire complains: 'what he ought to have done was to up like a man and tell the Kanakas plainly Case was damned, and a good riddance; but I never could get him to see it my way.' (84) Case leaves behind him a simple account, the pure economic subtext of his symbolic theatre: 'All they found was a bit of a diary, kept for a good many years, and all about the price of copra, and chickens being stolen, and that; and the books of the business and the will I told you of in the beginning.' (85) Wiltshire's grudging conversion to fair dealing is limited to his interaction with the community of Falesā, and fails to translate into general practice: 'I was half glad when the firm moved me on to another station, where I was under no kind of a pledge and could look my balances in the face.' (86) Uma's physical transformation, from the seductive feminine slightness which distinguishes her at the opening of the story, to a figure of bulk, disproportionate by English standards: 'She's turned a powerful big woman, and could throw a London bobby over her shoulder' (86), marks the successful integration of the erotic. Yet it is the problem posed by his half-caste daughters, the product of his legal union with Uma, which converts Wiltshire's paternalist conclusion into a question:

But what bothers me is the girls. They're only half-castes, of course; I know that as well as you do, and there's nobody thinks less of half-castes than I do, but they're mine, and about all I've got. I can't reconcile my mind to their taking up with Kanakas, and I'd like to know where I'm to find the whites?[46]

'THE BOTTLE IMP': DIMINISHING RETURNS

'The Bottle Imp' is a tale of fluctuating value. It has a certain mythical status within Stevenson's *œuvre*, but its originality has also been contested on several fronts. Biographers and scholars have repeatedly claimed that the story was first published in Samoan, as 'O Le Fagu Aitu', in the missionary journal *O le Sulu Samoa*.[47] In fact, the translation that came out in the May to December editions of the *Sulu* was preceded by the English original that appeared in the *New York Herald* and in *Black and White*. Nonetheless, copies of the relevant issues of the Samoan journal have subsequently acquired a greater value than the first English versions, since, as Isobel Strong explained in a letter to an inquirer, primitive printing conditions in Samoa rendered 'O Le Fagu Aitu' a particularly ephemeral text: 'I believe there are no copies extant. It was printed on paper of such particular vileness and flimsiness that we weren't even able to preserve our own set.'[48] The Samoan missionary J. E. Newell found, when he advertised for copies of the periodical shortly after Stevenson's death, that only two sets were forthcoming. He interpreted this reticence as follows: 'Apparently the Samoans who are the happy possessors of the first piece of foreign fiction they ever saw are reluctant to part with it.'[49] This depiction of blithe proprietorship contrasts, of course, with the anxieties produced by possession of the bottle within Stevenson's tale.

The confusion over initial publication reflects the tale's iconic status, as sign of the author's happy creative synthesis with Samoan culture. Newell notes that 'O Le Fagu Aitu' has a special status in Samoan literary history, as the first serial story to become available to a Samoan readership. According to Albert Lee, Newell's correspondent, it was the source of Stevenson's authorial reputation among the Samoans: 'as a result of its publication the natives ever afterwards called Stevenson "Tusitala" – the teller of tales'. In preparing the translation of the tale, Stevenson was able to test and extend his knowledge of the Samoan language. He worked with the missionary Arthur Claxton at drafting of the Samoan text: Claxton recalled that Stevenson 'seemed to enjoy the balancing of rival expressions in the Samoan idiom'.[50] The reminiscences of his tutor, the Reverend S. J. Whitmee, provide a fuller account of the legacies of Stevenson's ventures into Samoan. Referring to another of the author's projects – this time a full composition in Samoan – Whitmee emphasises Stevenson's appreciation of the nuances of the tongue:

Mr Stevenson wished to write a story in Samoan for the natives, and I suggested that he should bring a portion of his MS. for me to read. This exactly suited him. Those points in grammar and idiom, also the appropriateness of words, about which he was almost fastidious, could be discussed. I found him to be a keen student; and the peculiarities and niceties of the language greatly interested him. He thought the language was wonderful, and quite agreed with me that the Samoans must have descended from a much higher condition of intellectual culture, to possess such a tongue. The extent of the vocabulary, the delicate differences of form and expressive shades of meaning, the wonderful varieties of the pronouns and particles, astonished him.[51]

The history of a mutually productive and affirming exchange between the author and his peripheral literary audience, however, is undermined by alternative accounts of the tale's genesis and reception. In a prefatory note, Stevenson suggests that 'the fact that the tale has been designed and written for a Polynesian audience may lend it some extraneous interest nearer home'. Yet this 'extraneous interest' is clearly ethnographic rather than critical. Stevenson figured his Samoan audience as naïvely literalist, unable to distinguish between fantasy and history. In a letter to Arthur Conan Doyle, he digressed on the type of reception offered to fiction by a Samoan audience:

You might perhaps think that, were you to come to Samoa, you might be introduced as the Author of 'The Engineer's Thumb'. Disabuse yourself. They do not know what it is to make up a story. 'The Engineer's Thumb' (God forgive me) was narrated as a piece of actual and factual history. Nay, and more, I who write to you have had the indiscretion to perpetrate a trifling piece of fiction entitled 'The Bottle Imp'. Parties who come up to visit my unpretentious mansion, after having admired the ceilings by Vanderputty and the tapestry by Gobbling, manifest towards the end a certain uneasiness which proves them to be fellows of an infinite delicacy. They may be seen to shrug a brown shoulder, to roll up a speaking eye, and at last the secret bursts from them: 'Where is the bottle?'[52]

Stevenson jests patronisingly about life in a context without connoisseurship. Yet his acknowledgement of the spirit of delicacy that restrains the 'secret' question recognises a connection his Samoan audience has made between the wealth exhibited within Stevenson's colonial mansion and the magical bottle of his fiction. Effectively, the Bottle Imp of the story has been conflated with the story of 'The Bottle Imp'. Stevenson's literary output, the real source of his fortune, is elided with the immoral exchange represented by the fantastical bottle.

Attentiveness to sources has led 'sophisticated', as well as 'naïve' readers of 'The Bottle Imp' to interrogate the tale. Where Stevenson credits the source of his story in a deprecating manner

– 'Any student of that very unliterary product, the English drama of the early part of the century, will here recognise the name and the root idea of a piece once rendered popular by the redoubtable B. Smith' (88) – his critics have suggested that a more substantial literary background informed the writing of 'The Bottle Imp'. In an article in *Modern Language Notes* for January 1910, Joseph Beach traced the authorship of the original plot, first to a romance drama by the misremembered O. Smith, then to a volume entitled 'Popular Tales and Romances of the Northern Nations', published in 1823, and specifically to the tale of 'Das Galgenmännlein', by the Baron de Lamotte-Fouqué. Beach is concerned to emphasize, nonetheless, that the circulation of the tale ceases with Stevenson, who has rendered it all his own: 'In all details of the narrative, Stevenson is his own inimitable self.'[53] However, a more aggressive editorial in the New York *Sun* some years later questioned the originality of the 'Bottle Imp' narrative. This article referred to the same sources, the volume of northern tales and the tale by Lamotte-Fouqué, ironically failing to acknowledge the precedence of Beach's literary researches. The novelty of the editorial lies rather in the insistent pressure it places upon the issue of literary debt. The writer claims that Stevenson's effective plagiarism raises questions regarding 'the canons of artistic conscience, the ethics of appropriation and adaptation, and the equities of ownership'.[54] He is concerned to reclaim the story from its Pacific adaptation to its northern origin. His comments betray that sense of affront which recurs in European responses to Pacific appropriations of European culture, evidencing a comparable slippage between the discourses of aesthetics and economics. The easy shift from references to 'canons of artistic conscience' to questions of 'equities of ownership' suggests that the metropolitan writer, and not just the purportedly naïve Samoan, has confused real with fictional coinage.

A literalist reader is in fact constructed by the narration of 'The Bottle Imp', which repeatedly alludes to the non-fictional status of events and characters within the tale. The protagonist, for instance, is introduced under a pseudonym, as though to protect a living citizen from the imputations of fiction: 'There was a man of the island of Hawaii, whom I shall call Keawe; for the truth is, he still lives, and his name must be kept secret' (89). As the story progresses, the narrator continually avoids naming recipients of the bottle, who are implicated in its cycle of immoral gain: '(I must not tell his name)'; 'the name of a man, which, again, I had better not repeat' (107). It appears that those who have had dealings with the bottle have magically attained, in addition to wished-for wealth, a historical, rather than fictional, status.

The pseudonym Stevenson chooses for his protagonist is 'Keawe', a name resonant within Hawaiian heroic tradition. The story displays the hallmarks of oral composition. Sentences are rhythmically constructed, with the aggregative, repetitive, syntactically inverted format of oral discourse: 'This is a fine town, with a fine harbour, and rich people uncountable; and in particular, there is one hill which is covered with palaces.' Similes invoke a Pacific frame of reference: 'Keawe could see him as you see a fish in a pool upon the reef.' (89) Yet Keawe is also a product of the acquired culture of literacy: 'he could read and write like a schoolmaster'. A hero between oral and literate traditions, he represents the cultural moment at which his story is produced in the Pacific. He is a traveller between cultures, a sailor who, at the beginning of the tale, is on furlough in San Francisco. He journeys from California back to Hawaii and later between Polynesian islands, following the trajectory of Stevenson's own Pacific travels. The tale that critics have attempted to reclaim to northern European origins is shaped in both its form and content by the historical and geographical context of its production.

Keawe is strolling through the town of San Francisco, enjoying a tourist's taste of a foreign culture, when he espies a luxurious mansion, whose owner looks despondently from the window. The man invites Keawe into his home, and shows him the bottle which is the source of his enviable fortune. An imp dwells within the bottle, who will grant all its owner's wishes. If he or she dies with it in their possession, however, they are damned. The bottle can be sold, but only for less than its purchasing price; otherwise, it cannot be disposed of. The educated Keawe is sceptical of the man's claims, and is invited to put them to the test. He is thus tricked into purchasing the bottle. He attempts to sell it at a profit to a merchant of exotic items, whose wares include 'shells from the wild islands, old heathen deities, old coined money, pictures from China and Japan, and all manner of things that sailors bring in their sea-chests'. (94) The bottle cannot, of course, be assimilated upon advantageous terms among those cultural artefacts – themselves the relics of Pacific trade's uneven exchange. So Keawe returns to Hawaii with the imp still in his possession. The Polynesian has acquired a metropolitan article whose magical powers are not simply a figment of naïve imagination.

'The Bottle Imp' is in part a commentary on the representation of the gullible native, duped and over-impressed by foreign material culture, familiar from the early literature of the Pacific, and even from certain passages in Stevenson's own Pacific travel account. In Hawaii, Keawe uses the bottle to create a house furnished with remarkable objects:

As for the house, it was three stories high, with great chambers and broad balconies on each. The windows were of glass, so excellent that it was as clear as water and as bright as day. All manner of furniture adorned the chambers. Pictures hung upon the wall in golden frames – pictures of ships, and men fighting, and of the most beautiful women and singular places; nowhere in the world are there pictures of so bright a colour as those Keawe found hanging in his house. As for the knick-knacks, they were extraordinary fine: chiming clocks and musical boxes, little men with nodding heads, books filled with pictures, weapons of price from all quarters of the world, and the most elegant puzzles to entertain the leisure of a solitary man. And as no one would care to live in such chambers, only to walk through and view them, the balconies were made so broad that a whole town might have lived upon them in delight. (98)

The Pacific islander is depicted here, no longer as ethnographic object, but as the curator of a museum stocked with the artefacts of other cultures. Fascination with items of imported manufacture has graduated to connoisseurship. But such magnificence is for display rather than use, and the reality of Keawe's domestic existence shifts to the margins (or rather the balconies). This house recalls the many-windowed 'eidolon' on the Kona coast, which Stevenson described in *In the South Seas*. Where that mansion was depicted as epitomising a superficial display of foreign style that proved empty within, Keawe's rooms are replete with valuable acquisitions. Stevenson had felt that his own travels in Hawaii were overshadowed by the precedent of the deified Cook.[55] In 'The Bottle Imp', Keawe is told of the ways in which the bottle has shaped the course of European history: 'Napoleon had this bottle, and by it he grew to be king of the world; but he sold it at the last and fell. Captain Cook had this bottle, and by it he found his way to so many islands; but he, too, sold it, and was slain upon

Hawaii.'(91) In this reconciliation of myth with history, Cook's achievement becomes devil-work: he is less an overreacher than a fortunate recipient of magical assistance.

If the bottle embodies the ambivalent transactions of Western capitalism, it provides a reflection of other relationships of exchange. Like the reciprocal contract of Pacific gift-giving, it binds recipients even as it endows them. And like the object of tabu, it combines blessings with dangerous powers. The bottle represents a mixed blessing for the narrative itself. It precipitates action, creating scenarios of accelerated change, but in its offer of instant gratification, fails to satisfy that desire for the perpetuation of desire that motivates the act of storytelling. Instead, that particular desire is accommodated by a romantic plot which is interwoven with, and eventually transcends, those complex economic relationships motivating the tale of the bottle. Keawe falls in love with a beautiful woman named Kokua. Like Uma in 'The Beach of Falesā', Kokua is initially perceived voyeuristically, performing a reverse strip-tease: 'he was aware of a woman bathing at the edge of the sea; and she seemed a well-grown girl, but he thought no more of it. Then he saw her white shift flutter as she put it on, and then her red holoku, and she was all freshened with the bath, and her eyes shone and were kind.' (101) After wooing Kokua, Keawe notices that he is in the first stage of leprous infection. He decides to seek out the bottle once again, in order to heal himself, and become a fit husband. He travels to Honolulu, where he traces the bottle to its current owner, following a trail of duplicated luxury: '"No doubt I am upon the track," thought Keawe. "These new clothes and carriages are all the gifts of the little imp, and these glad faces are the faces of men who have taken their profit and got rid of the accursed thing in safety. When I see pale cheeks and hear sighing, I shall know that I am near the bottle."' (107–8) The value of the bottle has depreciated to a single cent. It lies in the possession of a man whose damnation is signalled by excessive whiteness: he is 'white as a corpse'. Keawe purchases it believing that further exchange has been precluded; willingly condemning himself in order to save his love for Kokua. The bottle thus serves as agent, not of material gain, but of sacrifice, and so begins to be transformed from a symbol of acquisitiveness into a touchstone of genuine emotion.

Kokua's qualities of humanity and intelligence are, like Uma's, quick to emerge. Her name signifies helper and comforter in Hawaiian.[56] Yet she is also the modern, literate Pacific islander: 'I was educated in a school in Honolulu; I am no common girl.'(112) Once she becomes aware of Keawe's plight, her education enables her to find a way of exploiting those very laws of circulation that seem to entrap him: '"What is this you say about a cent? But all the world is not America . . . Come, Keawe, let us go to the French islands; let us go to Tahiti, as fast as ships can bear us. There we have four centimes, three centimes, two centimes, one centime; four possible sales to come and go; and two of us to push the bargain."' Even from within the map of empire, Kokua is aware, exploitation can be delegated. The couple travel to Tahiti, equipped with costumes and props, and put on a calculated performance. Kokua packs 'the richest of their clothes and the bravest of the knick-knacks in the house. "For", said she, "we must seem to be rich folks, or who would believe in the bottle?"'(113) Their display is an investment in advertising, designed to create a market for their product. Yet they are regarded with suspicion, and fail to dispose of the bottle.

They resort, in turn, to self-sacrifice. Kokua secretly buys the bottle back from her husband, using as her agent a poor old man. Freed from the burden of damnation, Keawe succumbs to drunkenness. His companion in his lapse is a beachcomber: 'Now there was an old brutal Haole drinking with him, one that had been a boatswain of a whaler – a runaway, a digger in gold mines, a convict in prisons. He had a low mind and a foul mouth; he loved to drink and see others drunken; and he pressed the glass upon Keawe.'(120) The Haole (white man) encourages Keawe to suspect his wife of infidelity. In an attempt to prove her false, Keawe spies on Kokua, and finds her alone, not with a man, but with the feminine bottle, 'milk-white . . ., with a round belly and a long neck', now an object of virtue, the touchstone of her loyalty. He employs the beachcomber to buy the bottle back for him. However, the man subsequently refuses to return the bottle to Keawe, claiming '"I reckon I'm going anyway . . . and this bottle's the best thing to go with I've struck yet."'(124) In the beachcomber, the bottle locates its appropriate owner: a figure inhabiting the space between Western and Pacific systems of exchange; the unredeemed subject of the narrative.

'THE ISLE OF VOICES': COINED PHRASES

In 'The Isle of Voices', Hawaiian materialism is once again depicted as sourced in magic. This is a magician's nephew story, whose protagonist is Keola, son-in-law of the wizard Kalamake. Kalamake has legendary stature: 'It was rumoured that he had the art or the gift of the old heroes. Men had seen him at night upon the mountains, stepping from one cliff to the next; they had seen him walking in the high forest, and his head and shoulders were above the trees.'(127) He is represented as a figure deeply enshrined within Hawaiian oral tradition: '"Blind as Kalamake that can see across tomorrow" was a byword in the islands'(127); '"Bright as Kalamake's dollars" was another saying in the Eight Isles'(128). His powers, however, resemble those of the white settler in Hawaii rather than those of a Polynesian. He is a figure of civic authority and financial influence: 'no man was more consulted in all the Kingdom of Hawaii. Prudent people bought, sold and married, and laid out their lives by his counsels.' His enemies suffer a fate comparable to the genocide that followed European contact with Pacific societies: 'of his enemies, some had dwindled in sickness by virtue of his incantations, and some had been spirited away, the life and the clay both, so that folk looked in vain for so much as a bone of their bodies.' His house is built 'in the European style'(129), and he hides his wealth in a locked writing desk 'under the print of Kamehameha the fifth, and a portrait of Queen Victoria with her crown'(128). He is, indeed, 'more white to look upon than any foreigner'.(127)

Keola is fascinated by Kalamake's wealth, which materialises without apparent labour: 'he neither sold, nor planted, nor took hire – only now and then for his sorceries – and there was no source conceivable for so much silver coin'. As the internal rhyme here betrays, sorcery is the source of this mysterious fortune. Kalamake eventually takes Keola into his confidence. He requires his son-in-law's assistance in a magical ritual: a process of minting. Keola is transported on a woven mat from the high Hawaiian island of Molokai to a low Pacific atoll. Here he is instructed to burn a fire of leaves upon the mat's surface, while Kalamake gathers shells upon the beach. These transform to coins at the wizard's touch. As the flame expires, he jumps back upon the mat, and the pair return home, laden with money. This abundant

production in a reduced and alien landscape perhaps recalls
Stevenson's own account of his stay on the barren atoll of Fakarava,
a setting which yielded the author a wealth of fantastical narratives.
In the transformation of factual into fictional atoll landscape, the
location of subject matter becomes an act of false coinage.

Kalamake's magic is, like that of the bottle imp, the apotheosis
of cargo cult: the material object proves self-replicating. Like
Keawe, Keola functions as a Pacific empiricist, submitting to trial a
powerful system of circulation. But where Keawe had the heroic
capacity to transform the significance of the bottle, Keola is an
anti-hero, in the mould of the sorcerer's apprentice. His usurpa-
tion of power reflects merely a desire to occupy the position of his
master, while maintaining an iniquitous structure of production.
Keola falls under the misapprehension that his father-in-law's
authority is transferable, and can be used to serve himself – a delu-
sion he shares with Hawaiians who seek a stake in the power of
government. His wife Lehua recalls the fates of apparently influential figures within the Hawaiian administration, which illustrate
the consequences of dissent: "'Think of this person and that
person; think of Hua, who was a noble of the House of
Representatives, and went to Honolulu every year; and not a bone
or a hair of him was found. Remember Kamau, and how he wasted
to a thread, so that his wife lifted him with one hand."' (134) In this
parable of post-contact Hawaii, an imported mode of civil government is shown to be accompanied by a legacy of physical decline.
The Oedipal interactions of the father-in-law Kalamake and the
son-in-law Keola are paradigmatic of colonial relations. The son is
offered a partial entry into power, but in attempting to usurp
authority provokes the castrating wrath of the father. Kalamake
pretends to acquiesce to Keola's demand for a share of his power,
and invites him on a sea voyage that quickly becomes a nightmare.
Initially Kalamake affects phallic equality: 'the two sat in the stern
and smoked cigars' (135), but then, in a horrific tumescence, the
wizard reveals his authoritative stature, swelling to giant-size:
'behold – as he drew his finger from the ring, the finger stuck and
the ring was burst' (136), and mocking Keola's desire to appropriate the phallus: '"are you sure you would not rather have a flute?"'
He looms away across the ocean, and at once a trading vessel of
similar proportions appears, figuring the interchangeability of the
wizard's castrating power and that of capitalist venture.

Keola is rescued, and joins the boat's crew. He absconds at an atoll which turns out to be that same 'isle of voices' where the wizard gathers his coins. Keola joins a cannibalistic nomadic tribe whose members are making their annual sojourn upon the island. On his initial trip to the atoll, invisible and inviolable, he had observed the tribe with the immunity of an ethnographic field-worker, recording novel practices: '"they are not very particular about dress in this part of the country"'; '"these are strange manners."'(131) Now, however, visiting the island as flesh rather than spirit, he becomes aware that he is under physical threat. The atoll landscape is the space of the Pacific other: the reverse face of that Westernised Polynesia which is most successfully represented by Hawaiian civil society. The tribe's cannibalism renders its members the objects of a fearful fascination to Keola, the Hawaiian citizen. They belong to the mythical elsewhere of travellers' tales: 'He had heard tell of eaters of men in the South islands, and the thing had always been a fear to him; and here it was knocking at his door. He had heard besides, by travellers, of their practices.'(145) In fact the members of the tribe are themselves also model colonial subjects, whose annual reversion to traditional practices upon the atoll constitutes a return of the repressed:

'to tell you the truth, my people are eaters of men; but this they keep secret. And the reason they will kill you before we leave is because in our island ships come, and Donat-Kimiran comes and talks for the French, and there is a white trader there in a house with a verandah, and a catechist. Oh, that is a fine place indeed! The trader has barrels filled with flour; and a French warship once came in the lagoon and gave everybody wine and biscuit.'

The Eucharist of empire is only the public face of cannibalistic consumption – its 'civil' guise: '[Keola] judged they were too civil to be wholesome'.(142)

As anti-hero, Keola remains, unlike the protagonists of 'The Beach of Falesā' and 'The Bottle Imp', unredeemed by a unique love relationship. He is instead strategically assisted by two wives during the course of the story. His second wife, chosen for him by the tribe, alerts him to his physical danger. He departs for the ocean beach of the atoll, the fleshless realm of voice, where he dwells plagued by the whisperings of the invisible wizards. The tribe represents corporeal threat, disguised behind an accomplished discursive façade: 'The people of the tribe were very civil, as their way was. They were elegant speakers, and they made beautiful poetry, and jested at meals, so that a missionary must have died laughing. It was little enough that Keola cared for their fine ways; all he saw was the white teeth shining in their mouths.'(145) The other side of the atoll is, by contrast, a realm of disembodied tongues: 'All tongues of the earth were spoken there: the French, the Dutch, the Russian, the Tamil, the Chinese. Bodiless voices called to and fro; unseen hands poured sand upon the flames.'(146) For Keola, the Pacific subject, this intangibility represents the ungraspable power of global economics, to be explained as magical production, according to a logic of cargo cult: '"And to think how they have fooled me with their talk of mints," says he, "and that money was made there, when it is clear that all the new coin in all the world is gathered on these sands."'(147) The divided geography of the atoll landscape maps the split subjectivity of the Pacific anti-hero: on the one side consumed by a heritage of otherness, with its discourses of primitivity, cannibalism and savagery, and, on the other, absorbed within a system of economic circulation whose power and profit lie in foreign hands. In a final battle, wizards and tribe are left to their mutual destruction: the binary oppositions of flesh and spirit, savage and civilised, lock in annihilating contest.

Keola is rescued by his first wife, Lehua, who returns him to Molokai on the magic mat. Like 'The Beach of Falesā', 'The Isle of Voices' concludes with overt recantation. Keola consults the atlas and reassures himself that the wizard Kalamake has been safely relegated to a distant space: 'Keola knew by this time where that island was – and that is to say, in the Low or Dangerous Archipelago. So they fetched the atlas and looked upon the distance in the map, and by what they could make of it, it seemed a long way for an old gentleman to walk.'(150) He finds his appetite unaffected by recollections of his brush with cannibalism: 'he was mighty pleased to be home again in Molokai and sit down beside a bowl of poi – for . . . there was none in the Isle of Voices.'(149–50) The couple consult the local missionary, who admits, punningly, that he 'could make neither head nor tail' of the magical coinage. He willingly implicates his own endeavours, nonetheless, in the tainted transaction of its production, advising Keola 'to give some of it to the lepers and some of it to the missionary fund' as absolution. At the same time, he betrays the pair to the Hawaiian civil authorities, on the contradictory conviction that the money he has accepted is counterfeit: 'he warned the police at Honolulu that, by all he could make out, Kalamake and Keola had been coining false money, and it would not be amiss to watch them'. The coins thus retain their duplicitous status. Ambiguous signifiers, both true and false, valuable donation and worthless forgery, they expose the missionary's divided colonial loyalties.

In the press of events: Stevenson's Pacific history

In a letter to his literary adviser Sidney Colvin, which announced the completion of *The Wrecker*, Stevenson outlined a trio of new projects:

Now what am I to do next?

Lives of the Stevensons? *Historia Samoæ?* A History for Children? Fiction? I have had two damned hard months at fiction; I want a change. Stevensons? I am expecting some more material; perhaps better wait. Samoa; rather tempting; might be useful to the islands – and to me; for it will be written in admirable temper. I have never agreed with any party, and see merits and excuses in all; should do it (if I did) very slackly and easily, as if half in conversation. History for Children? This flows from my lessons to Austin: no book is any good . . . Now the difficulty is to give this general idea of man's place, growth, and movement, it is needful to tack it on a yarn. Now Scotch is the only history I know; it is the only history reasonably represented in my library; it is a very good one for my purpose, owing to two civilisations having been face to face throughout – or rather Roman civilisation face to face with an ancient barbaric life and government, down to yesterday, to 1750 anyway . . . I think I'll try; I really have some historic sense, I feel that in my bones. Then there's another thing: Scott never knew – never saw – the Highlands; he was always a Borderer. He has missed that whole, long, strange, pathetic story of our savages, and, besides his style is not very perspicuous to childhood.[1]

The successive proposals become shuffled here into aspects of a single enterprise: an engagement with the writing of history. Stevenson alternates between models of the historical – the personal and biographical, the local and political, the epic narrative – and with potential audiences – the literary, the Pacific, the juvenile. Yet such category distinctions are at the same time blurred. The history of forefathers is superseded in his imagination by a history for sons. The Samoan history suggests an oral mode of narration, 'half in conversation', which carries through to the projection of a Scottish history, albeit derived from the library.

Stevenson's purportedly non-partisan engagement with colonial politics in Samoa informs his reference to the 'savages' of Scotland: the discourse of empire sardonically applied to the partitions of homeland.

The plan to write a local history had developed from material Stevenson gathered towards a projected Samoan section of *In the South Seas*. As I noted in chapter 3, his Pacific travel account indicated to its initial audiences a shift in Stevenson's practice, away from storytelling, towards proto-ethnographic writing. Readers, commenting on the absence of motivating plot and on the unwieldy stockpiling of cultural information in early versions of the text, articulated a concern that diachronic narrative had been abandoned for a synchronic mode of detailing. In the event, *A Footnote to History* was the only part of this body of material that was published in book form during Stevenson's lifetime. A tightly plotted account of the last ten years of colonial history in Samoa, seeking to explain the present via the trajectory of the past, this was a declaratively diachronic text. Yet Stevenson was sceptical whether a Samoan history would meet his readers' demands for the reconciliation of narrative form and Pacific content, writing to Colvin, 'Will anyone ever read it? I fancy not; people don't read history for reading but for education and display – and who desires education in the history of Samoa with no population, no past, no future, or the exploits of Mata'afa, Muliaiga and Consul Knappe?'[2] He acknowledges a European perception that notions of historical development are incommensurate with the description of peripheral or 'primitive' cultures. His task emerges as the inherently vexed one of creating history from ostensibly ahistorical material.

For Stevenson, the author of historical romances, identifying a subject of writing would always, necessarily, involve identifying a historical subject. Countering scepticism in advance, he went so far as to assert that he had located in the Pacific the blueprint of the historical. 'Here under the microscope, we can see history at work', he enthused in a letter to Colvin from Samoa.[3] His subject matter, he claimed, amounted to pure history, breaking down distinctions between ancient and modern, myth and event, and conflating models of historical narrative:

Here is for the first time a tale of Greeks – Homeric Greeks – mingled with moderns, and all true; Odysseus alongside of Rajah Brooke, *proportion gardée*, and all true. Here is for the first time since the Greeks (that I remember) the history of a handful of men, where all know each other in the eyes and live close in a few acres, narrated at length and with the seriousness of history. Talk of the modern novel; here is a modern history. And if I had the misfortune to found a school, the legitimate historian might lie down and die, for he could never overtake his material.[4]

Stevenson moves swiftly here from the invocation to the slaying of historical forefathers. His peripheral history is legitimated by reference to elevated models of historical writing, only to emerge as an overreaching and subversive history that defeats the very narrative objective by which it is enabled.

The emergence of a Samoan historical narrative, invested with an archetypal historical status, out of the ethnographic context of Stevenson's travel account, challenges a methodological distinction that has continued to inform European writing about the Pacific in the twentieth century. Ethnography has become the dominant discourse for describing Pacific cultures; a development that in part constitutes a refusal to recognise the historical status of these cultures. The practice of ethnographic fieldwork privileges the synchronous, formulating social generalisations from evidence gathered in specific cross-cultural encounters which necessarily marginalise the impact of historical change. The geography of the Pacific islands renders them figuratively available to this model of scholarly appropriation, offering for ethnographic analysis microcosmic and apparently static societies isolated within the flux of the ocean. Change and history are represented as incursions from across the waves, negotiated at the sea borders of otherwise stable communities.

In opposition to the purportedly static social identity of the ethnographic subject, metropolitan culture has been figured as retaining the prerogative to history's diachronous narrative. Claude Lévi-Strauss formulates a distinction between 'cold' ('primitive') societies, which employ totemic classifications as explanatory models, and 'hot' ('modern') societies, which appeal to notions of historical development. Arguing in part from the evidence of Samoan myths of origin collected by the nineteenth-century missionary George Turner, Lévi-Strauss suggests that a resistance to historical explanation can be observed in the traditions of 'cold' societies. History, the entropy of events, is registered by such societies as a threat, which must be neutralised by assimilation to the repetitive and preordaining logic of myth and ritual.

'Hot' societies, on the other hand, are purportedly motivated by historical change, which is perceived as a dynamic force. Such societies display a corresponding capacity for projective, developmental thought: 'whereas so-called primitive societies are surrounded by the substance of history and try to remain impervious to it, modern societies interiorize history, as it were, and turn it into the motive power of their development'.[5] 'Primitive' societies, Lévi-Strauss implies, produce culture against history, where 'modern' societies produce culture by engaging with historical events.

Lévi-Strauss's resistance to acknowledging the historical status of certain cultures is accompanied by a suppression of the textual aspect of historical discourse. The metaphors by which he redescribes a conventional opposition between 'primitive' and 'civilised' societies – 'cold and hot', or, alternatively, 'mechanical and thermodynamic' – are resolutely material.[6] He argues that the writing which the historian holds most dear, that enshrined in the archive, has a primarily material status. In *The Savage Mind* he compares the *churinga*, or ancestor stones, of the Aranda tribes of Australia to the documents of the Western historical archive. For Lévi-Strauss, both serve equally as touchstones rather than texts, 'palpable proofs' of a historical reality. He refutes Durkheim's alternative suggestion 'that the churinga were sacred because they bore the totemic mark, drawn or engraved on them': that the value of the *churinga* as a historical record lies in their semi-textual status. Instead, he is concerned to refigure documents as artefacts, texts as objects, claiming that 'The virtue of archives is to put us in contact with pure historicity . . . They give a physical existence to history, for in them alone is the contradiction of a completed past and a present in which it survives, surmounted. Archives are the embodied essence of the event.'[7] The narrative status of the historical text is abolished, only to be subsequently recuperated by Lévi-Strauss as an inherent quality of the Western historicist ethos.

The distinction between 'cold' and 'hot' societies reads most immediately, however, as one between practices, rather than objects, of description. There is an inherent circularity to the location of static cultures via a discourse (ethnography) which suppresses the significance of the historical in describing cultures. Equally, it is perhaps unsurprising to find history ideologically embraced by societies whose tradition of writing impels them to shape all knowledge and experience as diachronous narrative.

The tendency to elide practice with interpretation recurs in descriptions of Pacific societies that are constructed from both anthropological and historical disciplinary perspectives. Margaret Mead, for instance, introduces the most famous twentieth-century Samoan ethnography as follows:

In complicated civilisations like those of Europe, or the higher civilisations of the East, years of study are necessary before the student can begin to understand the forces at work within them. A study of the French family alone would involve a preliminary study of French history, of French law, of the Catholic and Protestant attitudes towards sex and personal relations. A primitive people without a written language present a much less elaborate problem, and a trained student can master the fundamental structure of a primitive society in a few months.[8]

The European is figured here as situated within a complex historical context, whereas 'primitive' Pacific people save the anthropologist time by being timeless, and hence available for ethnographic description. Lacking writing, they dwell in the ever-present tense of speech acts. Similarly, J. W. Davidson commences his history of Samoa by invoking the post-contact incursions of what he describes, 'in the context of world history, as the European Age' upon a culture cognisant of its ethnographic epistemological identity: 'the Samoans were aware before the arrival of Europeans of the uniformities of their culture and of its differentiation from that of their neighbours'.[9] Where discrete Polynesian societies are represented as culturally paradigmatic, historical events tend inevitably to figure as intervention.[10]

A FOOTNOTE TO HISTORY: LITERARY HISTORY

The initial chapters of Stevenson's *A Footnote to History* are structured by the opposition between ethnographic and historical subjects. He divides his analysis of Samoan politics into 'Elements of Discord: native' and 'Elements of Discord: foreign': the former, static social practices; the latter, the incursions of historical change. The adoption of a conventional dichotomy between native culture and European history emerges in this context, however, as a method of introducing two conflicting narrative strategies, practised by, rather than merely upon, the subjects of this history. Stevenson confronts directly the ongoing problem of the elision of written and historical practices, describing a political

situation in which events are represented above all by the engagement between textual and oratorical strategies.

To establish the particular emphasis of Stevenson's account of
Samoan history, it is perhaps helpful to offer a summary of the
events he describes, which incorporates his prescient recognition
that the Pacific in the eighteenth and nineteenth centuries con-
stituted a historical trajectory, rather than a stable framework of
consolidated cultural systems.[11] As Ian Campbell has comprehen-
sively argued, European contact throughout Polynesia coincided
with a drive by ruling chiefs towards political centralisation and
state formation.[12] The interest of foreign settlers in establishing
stable Polynesian governments, which would provide a secure
environment for the introduction of plantation economies and
the facilitation of trade, coincided with pushes by different
Polynesian chiefs to obtain control in their island groups. In
Samoa, government was traditionally divided between the holders
of four paramount chiefly titles. There were, however, odd examples of unified rule. When all four chiefly titles were held by one
man, he became know as the *Tafa'ifā*, 'supported by the four', or
le Tupo o Samoa , 'paramount or highest-ranking chief of Samoa'.[13]
As Ralph Wardlaw Thompson, foreign secretary to the LMS during
Stevenson's residence in Samoa, noted however: 'When the white
man came on the scene, the strife between rival claimants of the
throne became more serious.' Settler nations sought 'to gain influence and advantage by supporting the claims of one or other of
the rival claimants for the chief place and kingly name'.[14]

During the course of the nineteenth century, the four highest
traditional Samoan titles were united by chiefs of the Malietoa
family. The three Western powers with commercial interests in the
area – Britain, the United States and Germany – sought to influence the course of government by promoting, alternately and
inconsistently, the cause of the ruling party or of contending
claimants. The Malietoa sovereignty was repeatedly resisted by the
Tupua family; in revolts in 1848 and 1869 Britain and the United
States supported Malietoa, while Germany supported Tupua.
During the 1870s, requests were made by Malietoa Laupepa that
Britain or the United States annex Samoa, which were declined.
By this time, German investment in Samoa was particularly large
in scale, represented by the copra trading firm of Goddefroy and
Sons, which went bankrupt in late 1878 and was replaced by the

Plate 5. Malietoa Laupepa.

Deutsche Handels- und Plantagen- Gesellschaft für Süd-See Inseln zu Hamburg. Just prior to Stevenson's arrival in the Pacific, the clerk of this firm, Captain Eugen Brandeis, encouraged Tupua Tamasese to usurp the Malietoa title. The German government in Samoa deported Malietoa Laupepa, and installed Tamasese as ruler. Mata'afa Iosefo continued to lead opposition against the Tupua government. Responding to this political tension, the Western powers increased their naval presence in Samoan waters. Three American and three German warships were destroyed by a hurricane in Apia harbour in March 1889. Following the disaster, the Samoa Act was signed by Germany, Britain and America in Berlin. This act reinstated Laupepa as king and formally recognised an independent Samoan government, subject to tripartite supervision. However there was much delay in implementing, or indeed even reporting, the Berlin provisions within Samoa, and against the inertia of European officialdom the *fono* (Samoan parliament) reasserted its authority. Shortly after the return of Malietoa Laupepa from exile, in early October 1889, Samoans elected to transfer the Malietoa title to Mata'afa, who was thus recognised as sovereign. A month later the British, American and German consuls in Samoa reversed the decision of the *fono* and proclaimed Laupepa king.

In Stevenson's account, the negotiation between Samoan systems of rank and capitalist imperatives – figured by contemporary commentators such as Wardlaw Thompson as the inevitable engagement of local tradition with the advancing course of global historical events – is represented primarily as a confrontation between literate and oral cultural politics. His introductory discussion of 'native' culture is characterised by a close attention to language: to the specific values of terminology and the power relationships inherent in Samoan speech practices. He notes, for instance, the ways in which Samoan discourse unravels British class distinctions – 'terms of ceremony fly thick as oaths on board a ship; commoners mylord each other when they meet' (71) – while also reinforcing traditional status – 'for the real noble a whole private dialect is set apart'.[15] The elusiveness of authority is represented for Stevenson by two Samoan institutions, the *fono* and the 'name'. The *fono* he depicts as a scene of competitive oratory, which renders official authority impotent: 'In the midst of these ineffective councils the chief sits usually silent: a kind of gagged audience

Plate 6. Tupua Tamasese.

for village orators . . . The chiefs of Samoa are surfeited with lip-honour, but the seat and extent of their actual authority is hard to find.' (72–3) The name, or title, is, as exposed by the performative politics of the *fono*, a formal rather than active index of power: 'the idea of a sovereign pervades the air. The name we have; the thing we are not so sure of.' (73) By succeeding to a title, the Samoan chief acquires an authority to command by letter and word that is self-mocking in its ineffectuality: 'He can now so sign himself on proclamations, which it does not follow that anyone will heed. He can summon parliaments; it does not follow they will assemble.' (74) In the *fono*, words are a powerful form of action: the letter of the title, on the other hand, renders its subject impotent if absolute.

This is a political scene, then, defined by linguistic relationships. The title is effectively Samoan culture's writing, displaying the capacity of writing to make objects of its subjects. In the oratory of the *fono*, however, speech hedges and controls formal authority. Nineteenth-century commentators were rarely so explicitly aware of the subtle negotiations of power taking place within the *fono*. The missionary George Turner portrays Samoan oratorical practice as a series of arbitrary conventions:

To a stranger the etiquette and delay connected with such meetings is tiresome in the extreme . . . It is quite well known, in most cases, who is to speak, but they must have this preliminary formality about it. At last, after an hour, or more, all have sat down but the one who is to speak; and, laden by them with the responsibility of speaking, he commences. He is not contented with a mere *word* of salutation, such as, 'Gentlemen', but he must, with great minuteness, go over the names and titles, and a host of ancestral references, of which they are proud. Another half hour is spent with this.[16]

Turner depicts the *fono* from the perspective of the 'stranger': a European observer who chafes at the constant balking of narrative momentum, the apparent absence of a Samoan sense of historical urgency. Yet his account also betrays the contest of power formalised in Samoan oratory. In the incantation of titles, traditional authority registers as at once an impediment to and a platform for performative politics.

Recent ethnographies have drawn attention to the integral connection between Samoan discursive and political practices. According to Alessandro Duranti, it is 'to language that we must

Plate 7. Mata'afa Iosefo.

. . . pay attention if we want to understand the past and make predictions about the political future of Samoan culture' since Samoan culture 'strongly identifies political acumen with verbal skills'. Duranti claims that Samoan politics can best be understood by examining the relationship between traditional oratorical structures and specific speech acts represented within the *fono*. The process and language of oratory serves to negotiate between official and contingent authority, between tradition and change. The *fono* can thus be seen to embody the dialectical engagement of continuous practice with historical events, rather than representing a theatre of cultural resistance to history. The nature of this engagement is moreover, Duranti shows, a highly self-reflexive one, involving the articulation of a relationship between events and the types of narrative which embed them, and between modes of political and discursive authority:

In an event such as the fono, which is largely defined by and through verbal performance (by professional speechmakers), the political struggle takes, to a large extent, the form of a linguistic problem. That is, much of the negotiation process is about how to tell or, in some cases, *not* to tell a story, how to mention or *not* to mention a given event or its agent(s).

In order to explicate this self-critical oratorical practice to a metropolitan audience, however, Duranti is forced to employ a highly literary framework of reference. For instance he describes the *lauga*, or opening speech in the *fono* – the subject of Turner's earlier impatient account – as the meeting point of an 'epic' and a 'novelistic' practice: ostensibly 'celebrat[ing] mythico-historical characters and places, eternal values and immutable heirarchies', but effectively giving expression to novel worldviews, to 'differences, disagreement, ugly facts, violations, faults, and individual and group responsibility'.[17] Refiguring Samoan oratory in literary terms, Duranti reinscribes a crucial distinction between oral and written epistemologies, which emerges within Stevenson's account as itself integral to the understanding of post-contact Samoan politics.

Bradd Shore's ethnography of crime and punishment, *Sala 'Ilua: a Samoan mystery*, also explores the complexities of discursive relationships, focusing on the same distinction that informed Stevenson's earlier account of the *fono*, between the authority of the *ali'i*, or titular chief, and the rhetorical power of the *tulāfale*, or chiefly orator. Shore describes these two roles as the 'potential and kinetic aspects' of authority, arguing that 'the relation of *tulāfale* to *ali'i* is that of function to form, or the execution of authority to the origin or seat of that authority'. They have, in turn, different moral implications:

> the more highly ranked *ali'i* are known as *sa'o*, which literally means 'the straight one' or 'the correct one', while orators are described (although never formally or publicly) as *pi'opi'o* (devious/meandering) and *kuluku* (from the English 'crooked'). As one informant volunteered, 'If a *tulāfale* isn't crooked, he isn't a good orator.' By 'crooked' is meant cunning or skilfully manipulative; orators are generally held to be not simply the repositories of genealogical and historical knowledge, but *par excellence* the professional manipulators of tradition with an eye to local or self-interest.[18]

There are clearly politicised inflections to these characterisations: the appellation *crooked* is taken 'from the English', and may reflect a post-literate distrust of oral facility. Yet they also serve to project an image of the historian that appears to be unmediated by Western notions of historical objectivity. The Samoan repositories of historical knowledge are also its manipulators: their discourse is verbal and strategic.[19] They operate within a cultural framework where subjectivity is regarded as performative: the person is an actor, whose character is cued by context. Practice, moreover, does not represent alienated tradition, but is consistently informed by self-reflexive intuition. Samoans are their own ethnographers, 'detached observer[s]' of their society, whose cultural self-assessments incorporate aesthetic agendas: 'New twists to old tales, local variants of ritual forms, and a proliferation of conflicting origin myths are all characteristic of the Samoan passion for the elaboration of cultural forms.'[20]

At the period of which Stevenson writes in *A Footnote to History*, traditional relationships of discursive authority within the Samoan *fono* were finding a reflection and field of application in the contests of empire in the Pacific. He depicts the town of Apia as a setting of subversive orality: 'Should Apia ever choose a coat of arms, I have a motto ready: "Enter Rumour painted full of tongues."'(84) Rumour is the shared language of settlers and Samoans: 'gossip is the common resource of all', 'everyone tells everything he knows'(84), 'tales fly'(85). However in this town of slippery tongues, according to Stevenson, the Germans are distinguished by their literalmindedness – by what emerges as a wilful faith in the power of the written word to resist interrogation: 'In the Germans alone, no trace of humour is to be observed, and their solemnity is accompanied by a touchiness often beyond belief.'(88) The incompatibility between this caricatured national ethos, which adds little to a received stereoptype, and the discursive requirements of the Samoan setting, is epitomised for Stevenson in a distinction between the cumbersome full title of the German firm, *Deutsche Handels und Plantagen Gesellschaft für Süd-See Inseln zu Hamburg*, and the range of subversive sobriquets, sitting more easily on the tongue, into which it has been locally translated: 'This piece of literature is (in practice) shortened to the D. H. and P. G., the Old Firm, the German Firm, the Firm, and (among humourists) the Long Handle Firm.'(86)

The Germans are shown to support humourless and literal Samoan chiefs as the mouthpieces of their commercial interests: first Laupepa Malietoa, the 'literal meaning' of whose name is 'Sheet of Paper'(110), then Tamasese, then Laupepa once more. Laupepa's name links him irrevocably with the introduction of print culture, and he appears to have been well characterised by the appellation. William Churchward wrote that 'he gave me the idea of a studious man, in which, as I afterwards found out, I was not mistaken. His distinctive name, "Laupepa" signifying sheet of paper, would point to that inference, but I never could satisfactorily ascertain whether it was given him on that account or not.'[21] As portrayed by Stevenson, 'Laupepa and Tamasese were both heavy, well-meaning, inconclusive men. Laupepa, educated for the ministry, still bears some marks of it in character and appearance; Tamasese was in private of an amorous and sentimental turn, but no one would have guessed it from his solemn and dull countenance. Impossible to conceive two less dashing champions for a threatened race.'(96) Laupepa, the 'Sheet of Paper' bearing the 'marks' of missionary education, and Tamasese, that most naïve reader, a private romantic, replace one another on the stage of Samoan history, while a suitable actor, Mata'afa the 'pretender', is overlooked: 'There was one thing requisite to the intrigue – a native pretender; and the very man, you would have said, stood waiting: Mata'afa, titular of Atua . . . Yet when . . . the curtain rose on the set scene of the coronation, Mata'afa was absent, and Tamasese stood in his place.'(97)

Where the Germans are represented as combining fidelity to law with ineffectual acting, the Samoans make an act of fidelity to the letter. The Western powers in Samoa have instigated a number of reforms designed to create the type of civil society in which their commercial projects can flourish. Samoans respond by altering the imported text in performance: 'These ideas most Polynesians have accepted in appearance, as they accept other ideas of the whites; in practice, they reduce it to a farce.'(93) The Germans answer Samoan passive resistance with documents – 'a trenchant state paper'(94), 'a new convention'(95) – affirming the sanctity of law and property. The Samoan countermove reduces the authority of signature to the farce of fraudulence. The chiefs, apparently unhampered by a sense of the liabilities of inscription, write secretly to offer sovereignty to Britain, even as they publicly sign the convention with Germany:

On the 5th November, 1885, accordingly, Laupepa, Tamasese, and forty-eight high chiefs met in secret, and the supremacy of Samoa was secretly offered to Great Britain for the second time in history. Laupepa and Tamasese still figured as king and vice-king in the eyes of Dr Stuebel [the German consul]; in their own they had secretly abdicated, were become private persons, and might do what they pleased without binding or dishonouring their country. On the morrow, accordingly, they did public humiliation in the dust before the consulate, and five days later signed the convention. (95–6)

While performing a public acquiescence to German law, on a date significant in English history for 'treason and plot', the Samoan chiefs are privately obedient to the law of the *fono*. They are in turn betrayed by the commodification of the document, when a Samoan scribe sells the text of the secret letter. The chiefs are exposed as actors, whose interpretation of the text of German law is performative rather than literal. The Germans in turn rewrite the Samoan discourse of the *fono*: speech becomes letter. Laupepa's supporters are summoned by threat. Stevenson reports the 'few and uncompromising'(109) words of Captain Brandeis: 'It is strictly forbidden that any discussion should take place as to whether it is good or not that Tamasese is king of Samoa, whether at this fono or at any future fono. I place for your signature the following.'(110) The etiquette of oratory is abandoned, and the signing of documents replaces discussion.

The villains Stevenson exhumes from the archives of foreign

government are figures who hold rigidly to the letter of the law. Consul Becker is depicted as a machiavellian writer of secret reports, who lacks the warmth of the active participant: '[Becker's] is not the language of a partisan. The tone of indifference, the easy implication that the case of Tamasese was already desperate, the hopes held secretly forth to Mata'afa and secretly reported to his government at home, trenchantly contrast with his external conduct.' (146) Consul Knappe's correspondence exemplifies the written word in decline, rendered contradictory and fragmented: 'Knappe, in the same despatch, confutes himself and confirms the testimony of his naval colleague . . . Plainly, then, he was not so much seeking to deceive others, as he was himself possessed; and we must regard the whole series of his acts and despatches as the agitations of a fever.' (192) Stevenson elsewhere employed the image of the obsessive German scribe to depict writing alienated through Samoan eyes. In the poem 'The Master of the House Tusitala', he ventriloquises the puzzled response of his servants to the spectacle of his own literary production, equating inscription with ailment:

> Brown, innocent aides in house and husbandry
> Wander askance. *What ails the Boss?* they ask
> . . . *Unthinkable Aladdin, dawn and dark,*
> *Scribbles and scribbles like a German clerk.*[22]

Among *A Footnote to History*'s German cast of frenzied literalists, however, the clerk Brandeis stands out as a figure distinguished by speech acts rather than texts. According to Stevenson, his discourse is characterised by flexibility, rather than legalism: 'he would legislate by word of mouth; sometimes forget what he had said; and on the same question arising in another province, decide it perhaps otherwise. I gather, on the whole, our artillery captain was not great in law.' (124–5)

By portraying a division between the frigid or feverish literalists and the passionate speakers of Samoan colonial history, Stevenson resurrects living characters from the cold words of the archive. Yet, implicitly, these figures are measured by the index of representation. They either testify to the author's ability to bring them back to life, or resist animation, remaining stubbornly text-bound. In the broader assembling of his narrative, individuals who have told Stevenson their own tales, or whose actions he has himself witnessed, are depicted more sympathetically than those whose stories are abstracted from documents. Stevenson characterises the two chiefs in the notes he made towards *A Footnote to History* according to a physiognomics of discourse. Mata'afa, the orator, 'shows many of his under teeth in speaking', while Malietoa, the textual subject, displays a 'face full of haggard lines'.[23] Mata'afa emerges as the hero of the published text because he upholds the value of spoken discourse enshrined in Samoan culture: 'He sits nightly at home before a semi-circle of talking-men from many quarters of the islands, delivering and hearing those ornate and elegant orations in which the Samoan heart delights.'(235) The American historian Henry Adams confirmed Mata'afa's oratorical supremacy, writing from Samoa in 1890 that 'The quiet restraint of their voice and manner in speaking is a study of art. King Malietoa spoke well, but Mata'afa's address was even more perfect.'[24] The manner in which Laupepa and Mata'afa tell their stories to Stevenson adumbrates a resolution of conflict: 'I heard them relate their various experience in the past; heard Laupepa tell with touching candour of the sorrows of his exile, and Mata'afa with mirthful simplicity of his resources and anxieties in the war.' The invocation of 'candour' and 'simplicity' in the residual context of discursive exchange contrasts with the portraits of German duplicity derived from the evidence of official documents and correspondence. As Stevenson punningly points out, such transcendent speech is not the matter of history: 'The relation was perhaps too beautiful to last.'(215)

Stevenson's history of the interaction between Western documentary and Samoan performative policy does not, however, simply affirm an essentialised opposition between oral and literate cultures. *A Footnote to History* is written from a transient historical perspective in which both written and oral discourses are held under reflected scrutiny in Pacific societies. It depicts Samoans and settlers testing the limits of their epistemological traditions, and negotiating with questions raised by other cultural practices. The German administration operates on the assumption that Samoans are still credulous readers, for whom documents are touchstones rather than texts. Samoan leadership responds by exploiting the role of naïve misreader, and failing to accord the requisite authority to an act of signature, which is rendered instead a political performance. By refusing Malietoa a copy of documentation for discussion prior to signing, the Germans deny him not only the opportunity to bring their demands before the traditional colloquy of the *fono*, but also the immediate critical response of readership. According to Churchward, Laupepa perceived that he was not accorded the recognition due to an educated reader: '[Malietoa] asked me whether it was a practice amongst white nations to make one another sign treaties without first reading and discussing their points . . . And before leaving, said that his Government had unanimously decided not to sign anything whatever without first being allowed a proper and dignified opportunity for discussion, with liberty of action.' Churchward confirms that German officials expected Malietoa unquestioningly to obey the authority of the written word. Both readerly consideration and written response were disallowed him: 'letters of the most peremptory nature were written to the King, whilst those from him complaining of the conduct of Mr Weber, who had recommenced his high-handed proceedings of former years, were not even acknowledged.'[25]

Yet Samoans are demonstrably astute readers, highly attuned to the literary implications of political interaction. Churchward observes, for instance, that the sum of thirty dollars, received as payment for the sale of the letter to Britain, had a biblical significance which was not lost on the well-versed Samoans: '[it] gained [the scribe] the name of Judas from the Samoans, who are most apt in bringing biblical incidents into comparison with latterday occurrences, and never miss an opportunity of doing so. Their Bible knowledge is extensive; and woe to the man who enters into discussion with them on such matters, for it is very certain to end in his confusion.'[26] In feigning public recognition of German sovereignty through an act of inscription, Churchward concludes, 'Samoan diplomacy was rather deeper than usual'; a politicised, rather than ingenuous, performance.[27] Stevenson expands this insight into prescription, advising European and American powers to recognise that Samoans are the addressees, and not merely the objects of their writing:

I am not asking what was intended by the gentlemen who sat and debated very benignly and, on the whole, wisely in Berlin; I am asking what will be understood by a Samoan studying their literary work, the Berlin act; I am asking what is the result of taking a word out of one state of society, and applying it to another, of which the writers know less than nothing, and no European knows much. (222)

Samoan affairs have reached a stalemate in which the documents of Western policy fail to work a reforming magic at the periphery. The texts of officialdom are, disconcertingly, being read and reinterpreted within the context to which they refer. Resistance operates between the lines of government.

Initially Stevenson describes a deadlock between mutual strategic misreadings. The Samoans make a farce of foreign law, and the Germans turn the *fono* into a signing of papers. But as *A Footnote to History* proceeds, written authority starts to break down. Mata'afa, the Samoan chief who poses the greatest threat to imperial power in Samoa, practises a strategy of formal acquiescence to Western policy:

Towards the provisions of the Berlin Act, his desire to be formally obedient is manifest. The Act imposed a tax. He has paid his taxes . . . The Act decreed the supreme court, and he sends his partisans to be tried at Mulinuu . . . From this literal conformity, in matters regulated, to the terms of the Berlin plenipotentiaries, we may plausibly infer, in regard to the rest, a no less exact observance of the famous and obscure 'laws and customs of Samoa'. (222)

Mata'afa negotiates between two incompatible texts, the laws of Berlin and the laws of Samoa, with a confounding literalism: 'Plainly, in the depths of his Samoan mind, he regards his attitude as regular and constitutional.'(221) His resistant conformity to the letter of government forces the German administration in turn to practise a novel somatic diplomacy: 'full of strange oaths, and gesticulating like semaphores; while over against them Mata'afa reposes smilingly obstinate'(223). Official documentation breaks into speech and movement: 'the pens screeching on paper, the messengers (you would think) running from consulate to consulate'(193).

If Samoan politics are figured as the interaction between strategically manipulated, rather than entrenched, oral and written practices, this in turn suggests a model for Stevenson's own historical method. *A Footnote to History* follows the example set by its Samoan protagonists: appearing to operate within and yet subtly manipulating discursive conventions; reconstituting imposed practice as indirect address. François Hartog has argued, using the example of that foundational text, Herodotus's *Histories*, that historical writing tends to invoke two alternative frameworks of authority. 'Original history', describing contemporary incidents, claims to be substantiated by the immediate witness of the eye. Positivist history, describing past events, acknowledges a debt to acts of reading and exchange:

The first form of history, the one Hegel calls 'original history', is organised around an 'I have seen' and, from the point of view of what is said, that 'I have seen' lends credibility to the statement insofar as I say what I have seen. Through my discourse I render visible what is invisible (for you). In contrast, in the second type of history, which we may as well call positivist, indicators as to who is speaking are deleted and frowned upon. The long chain of events is unrolled in the silence of the archives, stretching from the links that are causes to those that are consequences. Although indicators as to the source of the statement are absent, there are still hints – in the form of footnotes, for example, footnotes that signal 'I have read', that is to say, 'I too have read'. We both have read; I am credible, and you can recognise me as your peer.[28]

Stevenson plays at methodological naïveté, claiming that his history fails to meet both criteria of authorisation. It is largely unsupported by documentary evidence: 'This history is much from the outside; it is the digested report of eye-witnesses; it can be rarely corrected from state papers.'(97) He has instead based his account on the conflicting witness of duplicitous voices: 'The worth of native testimony is small, the worth of white testimony not overwhelming.' (187) In Apia, the town of rumour, Stevenson sifts shaky verbal evidence: 'Truth, in the midst of conflicting rumours and in the dearth of printed material, was often hard to ascertain, and since most of those engaged were of my personal acquaintance, it was often more than delicate to express.' Yet by sourcing his history in the spoken word, he simultaneously validates his account as the product of first-hand witness – according to an 'I have seen' – and as judiciously evaluated research. As Hartog points out, 'This superposition of layers of narrative and the interplay of utterances from different sources are fundamental to the narrative's ability to persuade the addressee to believe it. [The narrator] shows that he . . . is neither over-credulous nor a liar – in short, he demonstrates his own credibility.'[29] His very dependence on the unreliable evidence of spoken discourse authorises

Stevenson as the distiller of facts from lies. The self-deprecating title *A Footnote to History*, by contrast, situates the author among archival minutiae; at the edges, rather than in the centre of historical narrative. Yet Stevenson elevates his 'footnote', placing it above, rather than below, a text which itself incorporates all reference to sources and archival reading, and is demonstratively free of historiographical scaffolding.[30] The title *A Footnote to History* advertises a subversion of conventional historical method which anticipates criticisms about the historical unsuitability of Samoan material: its supplementarity to the main text of global events. The preface elaborates: 'An affair which might be deemed worthy of a note of a few lines in any general history has been here expanded to the size of a volume or large pamphlet.' (69) By creating a book from a footnote, Stevenson is less diminishing the scope of his subject matter than writing large that small print to which the history of peripheral societies is reduced in the grand historical narrative of empire.

By adopting the role of the historical novice, Stevenson frees himself from the demands of methodological consistency. His apologetic history destabilises distinctions between archival and eye-witness evidence, between text and speech. In Stevenson's version of history, to be on the scene is to enter the unreliable space of rumour. To examine the archive is to witness the breakdown of written authority. His attentiveness to the voice of rumour distinguishes his account from other Western versions of Pacific history, which strenuously denounce the subversive influence of gossip. William Churchward depicts Samoan rumour as sourced in unreliable feminine connections:

A great many of the alarming rumours which crop up every now and again have their origin with the old hands, who from their long residence pose as oracles, and authoritatively utter, for the benefit of more recent arrivals, certain information of what is to happen in the future . . . These men acquire their initial facts from their wives' relations, who are always visiting, and always ready to give any sort of news that they think will interest the 'old man'; and if they have heard no news, they will soon invent some.[31]

Settlers abjured Stevenson's method of building a historical text on the shaky foundations of the Polynesian word. Arthur Johnstone asserted, in his *Recollections of Robert Louis Stevenson*, that 'Those who have studied the Polynesians are well acquainted with the difficulty of securing reliable testimony from native witnesses on any matter, and especially in law cases where they are interested personally, or through some relationship, however remote.' A genuine first-hand experience of Pacific cultures, Johnstone argues, constitutes a form of 'study' which undermines testimony. He claims that it was Stevenson's literary investment in romance that made him a willing audience for Polynesian fabrication. In a chapter on the author's 'Unfitness for Political Life', Johnstone concludes that while Stevenson was 'a brilliant composer of sentences', this very facility ensured that 'he failed when it came to putting in place the facts composing the complex puzzle of life and government in Oceania'.[32]

Stevenson's literary audience, on the other hand, bemoaned the sacrifice of literary anecdote to historical fact. In the introduction to his edition of Stevenson's letters, Sidney Colvin wrote: 'he turned . . . from a sense of duty rather than from any literary inspiration, to the *Footnote to History*, a laboriously prepared and minutely conscientious account of recent events in Samoa'. A literary project characterised as 'laboriously prepared' may have addressed Stevenson's ongoing concerns regarding the value of literature as labour. However Colvin implies that laborious writing makes simply for onerous reading; that Stevenson's peripheral public concerns obstruct the unfolding of that private history which engages his metropolitan audience:

Later these interests [in the Vailima property] began to give place in his letters to those of the local politician, immersed in affairs which seemed to me exasperatingly petty and obscure, however grave the potential European complications which lay behind them. At any rate they were hard to follow from the other side of the globe; and it was a relief whenever his correspondence turned to matters literary or domestic, or humours of his own mind and character.

Colvin provides a potted history of Samoan colonial politics, which minimally contextualises the detailed local references within Stevenson's letters. His implication is that the political becomes relevant only as an aspect of a personal enthusiasm: 'For the love of Stevenson I will ask readers to take the small amount of pains necessary to grasp and remember the main facts of Samoan politics in the ten years 1889–99.'[33] Initial reviewers of *A Footnote to History* complained, like the first readers of *In the South Seas*, that Stevenson had sacrificed creative licence by harnessing his writing

to fact. William Archer inquired, in the *Pall Mall Gazette*, what 'a
born liar – one of the most convincing and accomplished of our
generation', was doing 'submitting to the tyranny of facts', and
suggested that the characters of Stevenson's history 'were not one
tithe as real as the most lightly sketched of his fictitious characters'.[34] A review in the *Graphic* expressed the hope that Stevenson
would again 'turn from history to romance'.[35]

Stevenson's historical text, then, appears to have forced his
critics to re-enact the crisis of inscription that it describes; to have
reduced their combined commentary to contradiction. Stevenson
in fact led the way in belittling his history as literature. He
referred insistently to his practice as one of journalism rather than
of literary composition, claiming to address merely the modest
ambition of accurate reportage: 'I do not go in for literature;
address myself to sensible people rather than to sensitive. And,
indeed, it is a kind of journalism . . . I am going to call it *A Footnote
to History: Eight Years of Trouble in Samoa*, I believe. I recoil from
serious names; they seem much too pretentious for a pamphlet.'[36]
However Stevenson's modest title, as I have already observed,
demonstrates that the rhetoric of self-deprecation can incorporate
new modes of authorisation. Writing as journalist rather than literary author, Stevenson embraces what he regards as a role of political agency. From a context in which historical events have a
primarily discursive status, he constructs his own writing as an
event. Stevenson intended *A Footnote to History* to contribute reliable information towards the revision of the Samoa Act, initially
scheduled for 1892, and feared that 'The book, with my best
expedition, may come just too late to be of use. In which case I will
have made a handsome present of some months of my life for
nothing and to nobody.'[37] He figures his text as dictated by the
imperatives of history, as immediately instrumental and ultimately
disposable. Divorced from literary ambitions, his history becomes
exempted from the imperatives of commerce. Stevenson anticipated that, as a text of use rather than market value, the *Footnote*
would not be a profitable venture, and was prepared to publish at
his own expense, writing to his New York publisher: 'to me it is not
business at all'.[38]

Stevenson addresses his history to a non-literary audience:
serious rather than effete, concerned with content rather than

form, with facts rather than their mediation. Yet its dénouement is a self-consciously literary and historically equivocal piece, describing the hurricane of 1889, in which three American and three German warships were wrecked in Apia harbour. In Stevenson's account, the disaster signals the intervention of a *deus ex machina* in Samoan affairs. Explicitly, he claims this narrative for history rather than literature, arguing that it was the policy of presence which dictated that American, German and British naval commanders risked leaving their vessels in Apia harbour when the hurricane menaced: 'that any modern war-ship, furnished with the power of steam, should have been lost in Apia, belongs not so much to nautical as to political history' (200). He cites historical repercussions: 'The so-called hurricane of March 16th made thus a marking epoch in world history; directly, and at once, it brought about the congress and the treaty of Berlin; indirectly, and by a process still continuing, it founded the modern navy of the [United] States. Coming years and other historians will declare the influence of that.' (211) However, the future historian, in the event, consigns this section of Stevenson's account from the realm of history to that of fiction. Kenneth MacKenzie isolates the hurricane chapter of *A Footnote to History* as 'of the variety of artistic licence', pointing out that the Berlin conference cannot in fact be linked to the meteorological event, since its organisation could only have been set in progress some time before news of the hurricane reached Europe.[39]

Stevenson portrays the hurricane as an implicitly textual event. 'The so-called hurricane' enables writing to continue: it represents 'a marking epoch', presiding at the birth of future histories. 'The Hurricane' is the chapter of Stevenson's history in which the duration of narrative and story are most compatible, in which telling keeps pace with events. Where previous chapters depicted writing in crisis, the hurricane results in one captain's superlative, absolving speech: 'a speech of unusual feeling and beauty, of which one who was present remarked to another, as they left the ship, "This has been a means of grace."' (210) With the force of natural disaster, the divine author has apparently intervened in the Samoan historical narrative, reintroducing the aesthetic and sentimental into discourse. Yet if Stevenson was determined to endow a literary set piece with historical causality, this was not because he was unaware of the strain it placed upon his narrative. In his correspondence, he expressed the fear that his depiction of the hurricane might undermine the overall use value of his account: 'The hurricane, a difficult problem; it so tempted one to be literary; and I feel sure the less of that there is in my little handbook, the more chance it has of some utility.'[40] Here he represents the intervention of the literary as lapse rather than redemption, recognising its complicity with the textualist politics his history criticises. Within *A Footnote to History* the hurricane is effectively an enactment of the problem of the literary. Its link with the Berlin conference is self-reflexive rather than causal: it correspondingly demonstrates the intervention of writing in Samoan affairs, even as it strategically addresses metropolitan literary expectations.

Rather than representing a resolution, the Berlin treaty, as I noted earlier, in fact instigated further ambiguity and contestation in Samoan politics. Therefore Stevenson's history moves from this exemplary literary moment into an inconclusive Samoan present of undramatic incidents and illegitimate discourse. Within Samoa the textual authority of the treaty, a metropolitan conclusion, is exposed by local superstition, as the written word accedes once more to the language of falsehood and rumour. The Samoans have credulously accepted the historical effectiveness of foreign words: 'they desired to see many fair speeches take on a body of deeds and works of benefit' (216–17). Their faith in the treaty's promise of a relative Samoan political autonomy is figured by Stevenson as a naïve belief in magical reanimation: the desire to produce a 'body' by incantation. This is superseded, more explicitly, by a 'sudden crop of superstitious stories . . . Rivers had come down red; unknown fishes had been taken on the reef and found to be marked with menacing runes; a headless lizard crawled among chiefs in council.' (216) The subversive discourse of superstition, which translates natural event into uncanny manifestation, implicitly refigures the hurricane's advent of grace as the intervention of supernatural menace, rather than divine authority, in Samoan history.

A Footnote to History concludes with a strategic address to European authority which appears to acknowledge that history is predicated on metropolitan intervention. Stevenson directs his message to Wilhelm II of Germany, a single ruler with the purported power to ajudicate divided rule at the periphery:

The future of Samoa should lie thus in the hands of a single man, on whom the eyes of Europe are already fixed. Great concerns press on his attention; the Samoan group, in his view, is but as a grain of dust; and the country where he reigns has bled on too many august scenes of victory to remember for ever a blundering skirmish in the plantations of Vailele. It is to him – to the sovereign of the wise Stuebel and the loyal Brandeis – that I make my appeal. (240)

Stevenson invokes an image of peripheral political stasis: 'With men so nearly balanced, it may be asked whether a prolonged successful exercise of power be possible for either . . . There is one way to peace and unity: that Laupepa and Mata'afa should be again conjoined on the best terms procurable.'(239) He sets out a policy of coalition that plays upon the assumption that a single Samoan ruler is insufficient to the task of self-government. Yet his excessively flattering rhetoric, and ambiguous references to two 'wise' and 'loyal' German officials, who have alone emerged unscathed among his representations of a German administration characterised by folly, signal that he is manipulating rather than acknowledging a European sense of historical agency. His formula for Samoan politics is in fact grounded in Samoan precedent; in a long-established model of divided chiefly rule.[41] Stevenson advocates a dialogical sovereignty, whose formalised structure of discursive exchange has in effect long been anticipated by the traditional government of the *fono*.

POLITICAL CORRESPONDENCE: AUTHORIAL INTERVENTION

Stevenson claimed that *A Footnote to History* was a work dictated by contemporary events, whose aim was to bring the 'footnote' of peripheral politics to metropolitan attention. His letters to the *Times* and other British newspapers reporting the state of affairs in Samoa met even more directly the criteria of intervention. The conviction that writing could represent active political involvement was heightened by the imperative created by postal deadlines, which produce a particular dynamic of addendum and recapitulation within the developing text of the correspondence. The letter is, Stevenson claims from the outset, an appropriately fragmentary medium for bulletins from the periphery: 'Sir, News from Polynesia is apt to come piecemeal, and thus fail of its effect, the first step being forgotten before the second comes to hand. For this reason I should like to be allowed to recapitulate a little of the past before I go on to illustrate the present extraordinary state of affairs in the Samoan Islands.'[42] This historical excursus is in turn cut short by the temporal exigencies of the post and the spatial exigencies of the addressed publication: 'but my time before the mail departs is very short, your space is limited, and in such a history must be only matter of conjecture'. Stevenson promises to write, in postal fashion, 'briefly'. Rather than the continuous narrative of history, with its authority of retrospection, the text of the letters is aleatory: significance becomes apparent gradually, interpretations are mooted, and then confirmed or rendered obsolete, conclusions can be supplanted. But if in this sense the letters are simply footnotes to *A Footnote to History*, the fragments of its narrative, the book is ultimately a footnote to the correspondence. The letters continue their political history up to the time of Stevenson's death: beyond the conclusions of *A Footnote to History*. They provide further commentary on the book's portrayal of a contest between oral and written, private and public discourse, which is informed by their own indeterminate discursive status.

Stevenson's task in the early letters, as in *A Footnote to History*, is to present to a distant public the contradictory documents of Western officialdom in Samoa, and to set beside these the disturbing text of local rumour. In his first letter to the *Times*, written from the Hawaiian islands before he had actually reached Samoa, Stevenson still combines the perspectives of Pacific insider and foreign commentator. From his Polynesian location, he has access to information unavailable to his metropolitan audience – 'I have had through my hands a file of consular proclamations, the most singular reading' – but he remains a relatively distanced reader, rather than an eye-witness of Samoan politics. According to Kenneth MacKenzie, this initial letter is effectively a romance text, full of subjective and ill-informed commentary, which was supplanted by the 'scope and realism' of Stevenson's later political correspondence from Samoa.[43] In the second letter, written from Vailima, first-hand involvement proves in the event to constitute further reading and writing. Stevenson's primary task is transcription: 'I beg leave to lay before your readers a copy of a correspondence, or (should that have reached you by another channel) to offer a few words of narrative and comment.'[44] In this dispatch, Stevenson includes copies of letters exchanged between 'certain residents of Apia and Baron Senfft von Pilsach', the president of Samoa, and chief officiary of the Berlin treaty. A party of five chiefs from the island of Manono, allied to Mata'afa, had strategically but peacefully surrendered. The Chief Justice of Samoa, Otto Waldemar Cedercrantz, pre-emptorily ordered that they be incarcerated for six months with certain 'gentlemanly' privileges. Rumour has it that when their supporters threatened to break down the jail, President Pilsach directed that the prison be mined with dynamite, to be detonated in the event of an attempted rescue. While by purely discursive standards rumour may be beneath response, this is a rumour of the unspeakable, and in the practical realm of colonial politics it requires confutation. The letters that Stevenson lays before the British public demonstrate the response of foreign settlers in Samoa to the report of Pilsach's treachery. They ask Pilsach to address directly the elusive voice of rumour: 'It is suggested for the President's consideration that rumours uncorrected or unexplained acquire almost the force of admitted truth.'[45] The signatories have made the initial move of translating rumour into text, thus according this slippery discourse official recognition. By publishing the exchange of letters in a metropolitan newspaper, Stevenson magnifies this publicising gesture to global scale.

Pilsach's response is precisely to refuse rumour the recognition demanded by the signatories. He exemplifies that literal-mindedness by which Stevenson characterises German officialdom, discrediting the form, rather than the content, of the report: 'with a view of successfully performing my official duties, I believe it is advisable for me to pay no attention to any anonymous rumour'. The signatories' letter is dismissed by Pilsach as an exercise in futility. It represents the text of rumour, and rumour can never be a text, since it credits no author:

I cannot forbear expressing my astonishment that in speaking to me so seriously in the name of 'the white residents' the subscribers of the address have deemed it unnecessary to acquaint me with their authorisation for doing so . . . This fact alone will justify me in objecting to the truth of the above-quoted statement so prominently set forth and so positively affirmed in the address. It will also justify me in abstaining from a reply to the further assertions of gentlemen who, in apostrophising me, care so little for the correctness of the facts they deal with.[46]

According to Pilsach, a letter cannot seek to substantiate the unauthorised discourse of rumour without becoming an unauthorised document, which henceforth absolves the addressee from the need to respond to its contentions. Commensurately, the wish to make official the discourse of rumour is also an attempt to undermine official discourse. Pilsach's response relegates the signatories to their position as objects, rather than subjects, of official discourse. Yet the literalist German president is also practising a policy of resistant readership that proves repeatedly effective in Samoan politics. As Arthur Johnstone observed: 'the signatories quite underestimated the diplomatic ability of Baron Von Pilsach'.[47]

The letter of the residents recognises the discursive constraints of the Samoan context: a small-scale, oral culture, within which the unofficial voice of rumour acquires authority. David Cohen has recently argued, using evidence from Mediterranean village societies, that 'Gossip . . . serves as a particularly effective form of social control since it is impossible to locate its exact source and eliminate it . . . Actors must constantly remain aware of the inferences which others might draw from their actions.' Within such communities, Cohen claims, a 'politics of reputation' can be observed to operate. Hyper-sensitivity to the ways in which actions can be read, to how 'one's words and deeds will be interpreted by others', dictates individual policy. Above all, conduct is motivated by a strong consciousness of shame: 'The moral perspective of shame involves evaluating oneself in significant measure according to the way in which one is seen by others.'[48] Bradd Shore refers to the operation of a similar social code in modern Samoa, noting that 'Many regulations are enforced . . . through the effects of informal social controls, such as gossip and public exposure of behaviour.'[49] In their second letter to Pilsach, the signatories affirm that it is shame which prompts their intervention:

It was not a sense of fear that moved [the signatories], but a sense of shame. It is their misfortune that they cannot address the President in his own language, or they would not now require to explain that the words 'tend to damage the white races in the native mind', quoted and misapplied by the President, do not express any fear of suffering by the hands of the Samoans, but in their good opinion, and were not the expression of any concern for the duration of peace, but of a sense of shame under what they conceived to be disgraceful imputations.[50]

The failure of communication that has taken place here, it is claimed, is not simply between the German and English languages, but between two different understandings of the politics of reputation, and between textual pedantry and discursive self-consciousness. Pilsach's response to their initial request for information, an affirmation of literate values, is, the signatories assert, 'foreign to the matter in hand'.

The President's disregard for the obligations of exchange reflects his sole appropriation of the disparate speaking positions of dialogic government. Stevenson reports that Pilsach has acquired funds by switching the receipt of customs revenue from the municipality to the government, a transferral managed simply by addressing a letter from and to himself, in his alternate capacities of adviser to the Samoan king and president. This circumlocutory manoeuvre demonstrates the complete self-enclosure of German policy:

The suit was brought by himself in his capacity (perhaps an imaginary one) of King's adviser; it was defended by himself in his capacity of President of the Council . . . Baron von Pilsach sat down (he told us) in his capacity of adviser to the King, and wrote to himself, in his capacity of President of the Council, an eloquent letter of reprimand three pages long; an unknown English artist clothed it for him in good language; and nothing remained but to have it signed by King Malietoa, to whom it was attributed. 'So long as he knows how to sign!' – a white official is said thus to have summed up, with a shrug, the qualifications necessary in a Samoan king.[51]

At the tail-end of nineteenth-century Pacific politics, the figure of the native duped by literate politics takes on a new particularity. Malietoa, the highly educated Samoan ruler, must here perform signature, not in literary ignorance, but under imperial pressure, as a front for a foreign government that addresses only itself. The circular authority exercised by the president alone, from a position of double sovereignty, replicates in reverse the double authority represented by the general will within Enlightenment political discourse. Geoffrey Bennington elaborates its operations, as they are set out in Rousseau's *Social Contract*, in the following terms: 'it seems possible to describe the general will as the sending of a letter (a circular letter) by the citizen as a member of the sovereign to that "same" citizen as subject . . . The citizen sends himself the law, and in this sending names himself as citizen: this structure is that of autonomy in general, and implies a concomitant autonomination.'[52] Pilsach's self-enclosed authority inverts the lineaments of this political rationale: he is depicted as a madman, talking to himself on paper. His chief symptom is his exaggerated respect for the authority of the printed word. He has thus, Stevenson reports, proved willing to spend a disproportionate share of the appropriated public funds covertly to acquire the local newspaper, the *Samoa Times.* Stevenson questions whether Pilsach and Cedercrantz 'were sent here with the understanding that they should secretly purchase, perhaps privately edit, a little sheet of two pages, issued from a crazy wooden building at the Mission gate'.[53] This printing house has echoes of the asylum: the Samoan press is, Stevenson implies, a marginal institution, whose significance is unduly magnified by textually obsessed officials.

An opposition is set up within the political correspondence between the true letter, Stevenson's, which publishes, and the false letter of German officialdom, which conceals. Stevenson's letters are demonstratively public: he plays the role of the private citizen, forced by personal disgust at the state of public affairs into making a public statement. This task involves publishing other documents, exposing the letters of corrupt officials, riddled with contradiction, as evidence of political duplicity. But Stevenson's letter is also false. While signing himself the private citizen, he plays upon his own publicity as author to create a space for himself within prominent British journals, and thus to gain the ear of the British reading public. While representing himself as a performer in the Samoan political context, he employs his writer's credentials to engage a metropolitan audience. He uses his authorial reputation to articulate a politics of reputation that privileges non-textual modes of discourse. He depicts himself, alternately, as the participant forced to write, and as the writer forced to participate in the political. Such role reversals are, he implies, the reflection of a society in which discourse is in chaos, writing has replaced action, and the wrong words are in the wrong mouths.

Stevenson is not, however, able to control the representation of a reigning discursive confusion. As he writes as the private citizen, so he increasingly fears that his words are received as private whim; as he speaks out as a writer, so he is accused of composing fictions.

Stevenson's fourth and fifth letters to the *Times* are occupied with this concern. He finds that he has established a ludicrous, rather than authoritative identity as a journalist: 'Sir, I read in a New Zealand paper that you published my last with misgiving. The writer then goes on to remind me that I am a novelist, and to bid me return to my romances and leave the affairs of Samoa to sub-editors in distant quarters of the world.'[54] His letters have served as the basis of a diagnosis of insanity – he has been accused of seeing things and of heightened passion:

> You observe the marks of passion in my letter, or so it seems to you. But your summary shows me that I have not failed to communicate with a sufficient clearness the facts alleged. Passion may have seemed to burn in my words; it has not at least impaired my ability to record with precision a plain tale. The 'cold language' of Consular reports (which you say you would prefer) is doubtless to be had upon inquiry in the proper quarter; I make bold to say it will be found to bear me out ... Let us have (as you propose) an inquiry; give to the Chief Justice and the President an opportunity to clear their characters, and to myself that liberty (which I am so often requested to take) of returning to my private business.[55]

Stevenson counters assumptions that cold textual facts outweigh in authority his own somatic engagement with Samoan politics, asserting that his heated interventions are themselves a performance designed to force official documentation to declare itself. He subsequently returns the accusations of madness to sender, describing political diagnoses made from abroad as 'the delusions of a fever'.[56]

At this time, one of the least publicised incidents of Stevenson's Samoan campaign threatened the very distinction between public writing and private statement. The Reverend Arthur Claxton adopted the resort of the textualist, and threatened Stevenson with a libel case for representing his political activities, within *A Footnote to History*, as morally compromising. Stevenson's correspondence with Baxter and Colvin refers at length to the affair. He writes to Baxter: 'An accursed ruffian, a missionary by the vile name of Arthur Claxton, of whom I narrated semi-anonymously a pleasing anecdote in the *Footnote to History*, has taken the thing amiss.' If Claxton is initially accused of having taken the public personally, Stevenson subsequently confesses that he cannot distinguish whether public or private discourse has been found matter for offence:

The exact nature of the man's action I cannot find out. The story told of him in the *Footnote* is the A. and B. story of the man who proposed a treachery to the American Consul, and I *suppose* it is on that issue he means to attack. I have never yet received any copy of the book and seem to have lost the proofs of that part; so that I cannot be certain of what words I used; still I believe I shall have a good chance to come scatheless, as the truth of the story can be proved and proved again. It is at the same time possible that he may intend to take action on a private letter to himself . . . On this, since I was unguarded enough to show a copy of it to one of the man's colleagues, I fear his action would be better grounded.[57]

The inefficient postal service between publishing centres and Samoa has brought Stevenson's text solely into the hands of a missionary keen to turn his words against him, while the author, lacking a copy, 'cannot be certain of what words I used'. His 'unguarded' attitude to private correspondence has also left him vulnerable, in a context in which his subjects are readers as well as characters, and in which any text belongs as much to its audience as to its author.

Ironically, it had been Claxton, among others, who had initially helped Stevenson to acquire fluency in Samoan. As the editor of *O le Sulu Samoa*, he helped Stevenson to translate 'The Bottle Imp' into Samoan for publication, recalling later: 'That is how it came to pass that this story was read in nearly every home in Samoa before it was published in English. By mutual agreement, Stevenson and I spent an evening together each month, going over each chapter before it was printed and discussing my translation.'[58] This image of harmonious literary collaboration is supplanted by one of political discord: in the brief note that Stevenson refers to as most likely having provoked the libel action, he informs the missionary 'that there can be in the future no relations between you and me', identifying Claxton as 'one of those men with whom I must either definitely break or cease to respect myself'.[59] Yet juxtaposed, the two texts represent the complex situation in which Stevenson's Samoan political writings found themselves entangled. Claxton chooses to invoke the official justice of libel laws, but he is also a facilitator of local discursive exchange. Stevenson may pretend that his written text has the status of innocent discourse – 'a pleasing anecdote' – whose form is so much less material than content that he 'cannot be certain of what words he used', yet as text his words can be turned against him. Having neglected to preserve his 'proofs', he must assert that, in the arena of events, 'the story can be proved and proved again'. Although Stevenson figured himself in public correspondence at this time as the exposer of treacherous letters, his private correspondence concerning the suit was among material suppressed in Colvin's edition of Stevenson's letters.

In metropolitan newspapers Stevenson struggled to attain recognition as a foreign correspondent: within Samoa his political campaign involved taking on the editorial role. To counter the unrivalled influence of the *Samoa Times* editor, Robert Thomas Chatfield, whom he had exposed as operating in the pay of the treaty officials, in November 1892 Stevenson helped to establish an alternative broadsheet, the *Samoan Weekly Herald*, which promoted itself as a vehicle of free speech. The leading article of the first edition argued, in provocative nationalist terms, that print should not respect public status:

This is an English paper, and the Anglo-Saxon races have different manners in one particular from what they have in Germany. With us, all public persons from the Queen or the President down, have to get criticized in the papers. They expect it; some of them like it; those who don't have just the one defence – they need not read it. We have the habit of this, though the Germans don't.[60]

In Britain, the leader claims, the distinction of rank is to become subject to the scrutiny of the media. Shortly after the *Samoan Weekly Herald* began publication, however, this claim to national freedom of comment was ironically undermined by a directive from the British High Commissioner, John Thurston, who issued a regulation in the pages of the *Samoa Times* stating that 'Any British Subject who shall be guilty of sedition towards the Government of Samoa shall be liable on conviction to a fine not exceeding ten pounds, or to imprisonment without hard labour for not more than three months', and further that 'The expression "Sedition towards the Government of Samoa" shall embrace all practices, whether by word, deed, or writing, having for their object to bring about in Samoa discontent or dissatisfaction, public disturbance, civil war, hatred or contempt towards the King or Government of Samoa or the laws or constitution of the country and generally to promote public disorder in Samoa.'[61]

Stevenson conceived this public declaration to constitute a primarily personal address. He wrote to the British *Times*, provoking questioning in the House of Commons.[62] In the person of 'The Beach of Falesā's protagonist, 'Plain John Wiltshire', he addressed a letter to the editor of the *National Observer*, in which he developed the implications of Thurston's declaration for 'a white man, and a British subject' in Samoa. The too forthright John Wiltshire, whose discourse had already once been censored during the publication of 'The Beach of Falesā', becomes, in this scenario, a shackled political correspondent: 'there's me with my letter about Mulinu'u half-written, and I can't finish it because I am a British Subject'.[63] Ventriloquising one of his own fictional creations, Stevenson employs his literary credentials duplicitously: Wiltshire's 'plain' speech is declaratively antithetical to literary intervention. The *Samoa Times* subsequently published an interview with Thurston, which endeavoured to highlight Stevenson's delusions of grandeur. It claimed that 'Sir John knows nothing of the novelist, apparently, and distinctly denies that he had him or any British subject in Samoa in view when drafting the Samoa Sedition Regulation lately published. All this controversy about the matter is an excellent advertisement for Mr Stevenson, who, doubtless, fully appreciates the situation.'[64] British etiquette ('we haven't been introduced') quashes Stevenson's belief that discourse requires an addressee. The High Commissioner presumably knows Stevenson by authorial reputation, but officialdom in Samoa is keen to devalue the politics of reputation. 'The novelist's' intervention is insidiously rendered a literary concern, motivated by a desire for self-publication. Thurston replicates the attitude of President Pilsach to political rumour, representing as vulgar interrogation Stevenson's invitation to participate in discursive exchange.

Stevenson is repesented as a literary meddler in political affairs, whose chief design is to increase his own publicity. In the same edition of the *Samoa Times* in which Thurston's interview appeared, the editor peruses the Imperial German White Book, 'to see where and in what respect its contents substantiate Mr R. L. Stevenson's sensational statements, contained in his letters to the *Times*'. Where his response to Thurston's declaration was depicted as mildly paranoid, here Stevenson is represented as actually seeing things which are not verified within the texts he cites; of

being an unreliable reader and incompetent political interpreter.
The editorial makes a virtue of its 'dry, and (to many) unin-
teresting criticism', in implicit contrast to the imaginative
constructions of Stevenson's own political dispatches. However
the Blue Book on Samoan Affairs, published by the British Foreign
Office on 13 May 1893, substantiated many of Stevenson's claims,
forcing British and colonial newspaper editors to retract equations
of authorial involvement with political naïveté. *The Times* con-
ceded:

Those who suspected that a master of historical romance and a humour-
ist of rare ingenuity has, on a slender basis of fact, constructed a story of
phantasy vying with the 'Treasure Island' should read the . . . Blue Book.
In official documents, some of them under the hand of . . . Pilsach
himself, he appears as absurd a personnage as in the letters from Mr
Stevenson which we have from time to time published. Far from being
the inventor of imaginary grievances and grotesque dignitaries, the latter
is only the spokesman of a community once amused, but long ago indig-
nant at the antics of the official comedians.[65]

The official text gives the ultimate authorisation: exposing officialdom's absurdity. From the swathe of confirming print
Stevenson emerges as community 'spokesman', as *tulāfale*: his
account validated. The romance writer has, after all, been a realist
in the political field.

Stevenson diagnoses a political crisis in which officialdom has
lost touch with exchange. Yet his own political commentary is
symptomatic of this condition: receiving official sanction, but
failing to communicate directly with its audience. His final letter
on Samoan politics can be seen as an attempt to retrieve this situation, by locating the private voice behind metropolitan government response, and so reconstituting official communication as
personal exchange. In early June and late July 1894, James Francis
Hogan twice queried the British government in the House of
Commons concerning the terms and conditions of Mata'afa's exile
in the Marshall Islands, citing Stevenson's correspondence to the
Times.[66] Stevenson responded to reports of this intervention by
directing a letter to Hogan in which he acknowledged that his
communications to metropolitan journals had been misjudged
ventures into the politics of literary reputation. He has earned the
name of a private enthusiast, a comic character, a writer of further
fictions:

Mata'afa is now known to be my hobby. People laugh when they see any mention of his name over my signature and *The Times*, while it still grants me hospitality, begins to lead the chorus. I know that nothing can be more fatal to Mata'afa's cause than that he should be made ridiculous, and I cannot help feeling that a man who makes his bread by writing fiction labours under the disadvantage of suspicion when he touches upon matters of fact.[67]

Mata'afa's 'name over my signature' is a reflection threatening not merely to the Samoan chief, but also, implicitly, to Stevenson, as the author expresses the fear that he has lost his audience. Mata'afa is a powerful speaker rendered the object of speculation. Communication has been cut off, an authoritative voice has been silenced: 'I can only speak of what I know here. It is impossible to send him or any of his chiefs either a present or a letter . . . communication is so completely sundered'. It is in the recognition of a comparable isolation that Stevenson appeals to the authorised politician for the support of another voice, urging Hogan, 'If I were even backed up before the world by one other voice, people might continue to listen, and in the end something might be done. But so long as I stand quite alone, telling the same story, which becomes, apparently, not only more tedious, but less credible by repetition, I feel that I am doing nothing good, possibly even some evil.' Stevenson's political activities have become a nightmare of authorial ineffectuality, in which he is left repeating a too familiar tale to a dwindling audience. His last request is to 'one other voice', to help him institute by example a metropolitan politics of dialogue.

THE ROMANCE OF POLITICS

Stevenson's historical writing and political correspondence are texts that register the impotence of textuality. In Britain, however, they provoked a commentary concerning issues of literary authority, which implicitly assumed that metropolitan authorial politics superseded peripheral power politics. His more localised involvement in Samoan politics, which was primarily discursive, similarly became appropriated to the question of genre by both the author and his audience. Stevenson described his activities to Sidney Colvin in romancist terms:

I have been wholly swallowed up in politics; a wretched business, with fine elements of farce in it too, which repay a man in passing, involving many dark and many moonlight rides, secret counsels which are at once divulged, sealed letters which are read aloud in confidence to the neighbours, and a mass of fudge and fun, which would have driven me crazy ten years ago and now makes me smile.[68]

In the essay 'A Gossip on Romance', Stevenson had some years earlier described the capacity of romance fiction to enable the child reader to enter the space of adventure, by offering a vicarious experience of the physical. 'Incident', he wrote, 'woos us out of our reserve . . . Then we forget the characters; then we push the hero aside; then we plunge into the tale in our own person and bathe in fresh experience; and then, and then only, do we say we have been reading a romance.' Romance literature is figured throughout this essay as the childhood perspective authorised: one whose imaginative vision is implicitly predicated on childhood's impotence (a powerlessness accentuated in Stevenson's particular case by early invalidism). Its pleasures are tinctured with a masochism that vicariously embraces death: 'there are lights in which we are willing to contemplate even the idea of our own death; ways in which it seems as if it would amuse us to be cheated, wounded or calumniated'.[69] The possibility of scripting his own death is part of the thrill Stevenson expresses in his Samoan political activities. 'If only I could secure a violent death, what a fine success!' he wrote to Colvin. 'I wish to die in my boots; no more Land of Counterpane for me. To be drowned, to be shot, to be thrown from a horse, – ay, to be hanged, rather than pass again through that slow dissolution.'[70] In *A Footnote to History* and the letters, he had depicted writing declining into fever and growing impotent: participation in Samoan warfare, on the other hand, is figured as enabling the ailing writer to experience a paradoxical revitalisation through violence. The readerly pleasure he had described in 'A Gossip on Romance' becomes inverted, with active engagement serving as the means of recuperating a literary experience. By participating in local politics, Stevenson re-enters the childhood frame of romance.

Attempts to distinguish the frivolous from the serious among Stevenson's different political activities are undermined by the fact that even the most officially-oriented of these is figured as play. Kenneth MacKenzie, concerned to rescue the author from a reputation as a literary dabbler in the world of real politics, has uncovered references in both British Foreign and Colonial Office records and private correspondence which indicate that Stevenson's name was circulated as a candidate for the office of Samoan consul.[71] If such evidence attests, as MacKenzie claims, to official recognition of the realism of his political commitment, Stevenson's own comments ludically dispel distinctions between realistic and romanticised political involvement, between official status and literary enjoyment. He writes to Colvin:

> supposing a vacancy to occur, I would condescend to accept the office of H.B.M.'s Consul with parts, pendicles and appurtenances. There is very little work to do except some little entertaining . . . The real reasons for the step are three: First, possibility of being able to do some good, or at least certainty of not being obliged to stand always looking on helplessly at what is bad. Second, Larks for the family who seem filled with childish avidity for the kudos. Third, and perhaps not altogether least, house in town and boat and boat's crew . . . Fourth, growing desire on the part of the old man virulent for anything in the nature of a salary – years seem to invest that idea with new beauty.[72]

Despite the emerging mature voice of financial concern in this extract, there is little to distinguish Stevenson's desire to provide 'larks' and to satiate his family's 'childish avidity', from his earlier attempt to play out a political romance in Butaritari: at that time, he wrote later, 'my family . . . bubbled with delight at the approach of trouble; and we sat deep into the night like a pack of school-boys'.[73]

MacKenzie, however, contrasts such political activity with what he regards as more irresponsible attempts to fabricate romance plots from Samoan political realities. In August 1892, Stevenson conducted Lady Margaret Jersey, wife of the governor of New South Wales, on a visit to Mata'afa's camp at Malie under alias, 'in a manner', Colvin comments, 'that seemed like the realisation of a chapter of a Waverley novel'.[74] The adventure was a diplomatically insensitive one, implying, as MacKenzie observes, acknowledgement of the rebel Mata'afa's authority by the wife of a British colonial official.[75] Anticipating this public inference, Margaret Jersey adopted the identity of Stevenson's cousin, Amelia Balfour, and Colvin claims that 'This transparent disguise was congenial to [Stevenson's] romantic instincts.'[76] Jersey soon afterwards published an extended account of her trip to Samoa, which detailed her adventure with Stevenson. She depicts the visit to Malie as a performance of which the Samoan rebels as well as their visitors were the elaborators. The element of farce involved in her adoption of a false identity was, she claims, enjoyed by all participants: 'though the eager inquiries for "the lady" overheard around gave reason to fear that my incognita was not a brilliant success, we sturdily carried through our little comedy'.[77] When a clash of interests arose between the performance of Polynesian ceremony and the performance of Western intrigue, however, the mask of Samoan complicity dropped. At the commencement of the kava ceremony, when the cup must be offered first to the guest of highest rank, it was proffered to Lady Jersey, the purported humble female cousin, who writes that, in turn, 'the difficulty of keeping our countenances was great'.[78]

Stevenson's charade, then, was scripted in a context in which performance was a shared language. It was an event not to be read literally: part of a mutual act of cultural role-playing and interpretation. Jersey was perhaps a more judicious ambassador than MacKenzie credits. She made diplomatically significant visits to the separate districts of Malietoa, Mata'afa and Tamasese Lealofi, the son of Tupua Tamasese, who had just succeeded to the Tupua title, and was offered in each case a particular performance: oratory at the residence of Malietoa; a traditional kava ceremony at the camp of Mata'afa; and a *siva*, or Samoan dance, at Tamasese's village. Such enactments were not simply displays, but ways of negotiating, either by defusing or making explicit, relationships of power. The ceremony at the official monarch's drew on the emblems of authority. In her written account, Jersey is careful to describe the positioning of each officiary, signifying rank, and is alert to the nuances of rhetorical phraseology. The visit to Malie is described immediately after this, so that the status of ceremony within Mata'afa's camp, as mimic authority, is highlighted: 'Having been duly presented to orthodox royalty, we were naturally anxious to invade the camp of Mataafa, commonly called the Rebel King.' Mata'afa's guard are 'strongly built men in native costume, for Mataafa has not followed the example of his cousin and rival by putting his army into regulation attire'. The kava ceremony was enlivened with 'small performances', which refer to traditional practice, and Lady Jersey opines that 'Mataafa probably keeps up these old customs with a view to maintaining the national spirit.'[79] As demonstrative repository of authentic Samoan custom, the 'Pretender' figures himself as authentic monarch. Finally

Tamasese, whose father Tamasese was known, for the brief period of his rule, as a German puppet, used the imitative framework of the *siva* to make puppets of the Germans: 'One series of gesticulations was supposed to represent "German fashion"; the imitation of walk and countenance was hardly complimentary to the supporters of the late Tamasese, but this may have been unintentional.'[80]

Traditionalist performance in Samoa at this time could clearly serve as a means of commenting on the political present. The appropriation of imported culture displayed a similar critical purpose. William Churchward describes how the game of cricket became politically charged theatre in 1880s Samoa:

The processions on match days are fearful and wonderful to behold. Headed by their Faamasinos, or judges, as they term their umpires, to the dulcet strains of the penny whistle and the drum, banners flaunting gaily in the breeze, dressed up in the latest novelty specially designed for the purpose – most likely gone tick for at their pet store – bewreathed and begarlanded to an outrageous extent, the players in single file march through the town in swaggering military order. Each one is armed with his bat, shouldered as though 'twere a war-club, and, at the word of command from their officers, goes through an entire special manual exercise whilst *en route* to the field. These officers are generally dressed in full naval uniform, with swords and cocked hats complete, and are continuously running up and down the ranks, keeping their men in place and showing them off to the fullest extent in their power.

The tone available for descriptions of such scenes is that of patronising amusement. Yet this is clearly more than natives mistaking the Englishman's sport for war, and indulging a penchant for costume and theatrics. It is a translation of the performance of sport into that of battle, which relies on the rhetoric of sportsmanship to disguise its manipulation of the politics of national allegiance. Churchward continues: 'It was the invariable practice of the Apia men on turning out for a match to halt in front of my Consulate, and drawn up in line receive word of command, "Salute the British Consul!" whereupon the whole line would perform a studied exercise with their bats and arms.' Cricket also served as a form of political procrastination at the time when the Samoans were waiting for a response to their missive offering sovereignty to Queen Victoria: 'They had officially written to England offering their country, and then, to avoid all complications or roughly exacted explanations, they determined to start a cricket match of such stupendous proportions that it would last until they got an answer from home.'[81] The public game in which they participate draws attention from the secret games of international diplomacy. 'Kirikiti' is a brazen metaphor, an explicit declaration of cultural loyalty.

Writing home from the Pacific, Stevenson frequently draws comparisons between Polynesian and Scottish contexts. There is another book to be written about the impact of his Samoan encounters upon those late fictions which he continued to set in Scotland: one that might focus, for instance, on the way in which, in the unfinished *Weir of Hermiston*, the lessons of *A Footnote to History* are translated into historical fiction. In this historical romance, ethnography and history serve as mutually reinforcing, rather than exclusive, discourses. It is a passage of ethnographic intervention, therefore, which characterises the historical self-consciousness of the Scottish subject: 'For that is the mark of the Scot of all classes: that he stands in an attitude towards the past unthinkable to an Englishman, and remembers and cherishes the memory of his forebears, good or bad.' The Scottish national traits that are emphasised in the late fiction are precisely those reinvoked for Stevenson by Pacific cultures. In *Weir of Hermiston*, narrative authority is partly delegated to the serving woman Kirstie Elliot, whose very existence, like that of the novel itself, is dependent upon the ability to narrate. An unmarried woman past the age of childbearing, she is aware that she embodies an oral cultural practice that will soon be superseded, and whose ephemerality is that of speech itself: 'again she had a vision of herself, the day over for her old-world tales and local gossip'. The succinct depiction of Kirstie as narrator recognises aspects of performance, mimicry and fantasy:

Like so many people of her class, she was a brave narrator; her place was on the hearthrug and she made it a rostrum, mimeing her stories as she told them, fitting them with vital detail, spinning them out with endless 'quo' he's' and 'quo' she's', her voice sinking into a whisper over the supernatural or the horrific.[82]

These emphases were absent from Stevenson's domesticated discussion of oral narration in the early essays 'Talk and Talkers' (1882), but seem to have achieved significance in the Polynesian context.

In *In the South Seas*, Stevenson compares the Marquesan historical present with the Scottish historical past:

Not much beyond a century has passed since [the Scottish Highlands and
Islands] were in the same convulsive and transitionary state as the
Marquesas of to-day. In both cases an alien authority enforced, the clans
disarmed, the chiefs deposed, new customs introduced, and chiefly that
fashion of regarding money as the means and object of existence. The
commercial age, in each, succeeding at a bound to an age of war abroad
and patriarchal communism at home.

More generally, he continues: 'points of similarity between a South
Sea people and my own folk at home ran much in my head in the
islands'.[83] When his inter-island tourism gave way to property
ownership, this sense of cultural kinship was displaced by a fantasy
that allowed Stevenson the settler to play the laird of his estate. He
referred to his arrival in Samoa as a type of home-coming, mixing
metaphors of the uncivilised: 'I shall probably return to Samoa
direct, having given up all idea of returning to civilisation in the
meanwhile. There, on my ancestral acres, which I purchased six
months ago from a blind Scots blacksmith, you will please address
me until further notice.'[84] In this broad equation of topographies
and cultures, the costumes and characters of Samoan and Scottish
colonial history are frequently made to merge. Stevenson
describes two Samoans among the cast of a dinner party in Apia in
the following terms: 'Henry was in a kilt of gray shawl, with a blue
jacket, white shirt and black neck tie, and looked like a dark
genteel guest in a Highland shooting box. Seumanu . . . is chief of
Apia, a rather big gun in this place, looking like a large, fatted military Englishman, bar the colour.'[85] It is, of course, skin colour
which remains the telling signifier of difference behind the perceived identity of national costume. Assumptions about the indel-
ibility of racial identity accompany Stevenson's ludic recognition
of the politics of adopted dress, just as the wider discourse of
Victorian empire continued to inform the theatrics of local resistance in Polynesia.

After-word: 'the impediment of tongues'

At the beginning of this book I looked at two anecdotes – one of the false, and one of the true reader – which I argued typified two alternative Western accounts of the reception of writing in the Pacific islands. To conclude, I want to turn to some visual images that aim to tell similar stories, and to add a footnote to the history which they confidently encapsulate. The first depicts the nemesis of false readership; of the wrongful appropriation of the written word. Entitled 'Eating the Mail', it offers the spectacle of a group of unconverted Micronesians committing the ultimate act of literary cannibalism; literally consuming the unfamiliar text. The second, 'Interior of the Chapel', portrays converted Polynesians transformed by the gift of literacy, receiving the printed word as sacrament. Juxtaposed, the two images illustrate a comforting teleology to Christian audiences. The islanders of the first picture display a primary savagery: semi-naked and out of doors, they misappropriate foreign letters which are explicitly addressed elsewhere. In the second picture dark-skinned child natives have been clothed uniformly in white, and enclosed beneath the familiar arches of a European-styled church. They are shown receiving with bowed heads the gift of texts that have been earned, from a missionary whose dark clothes and pale skin signify his sacred discrepancy from his flock.

The developmental narrative is in this instance, however, apocryphal. The scene represented in the second picture in fact slightly predates that of the former. Both illustrations are taken from missionary publications – the source of the majority of nineteenth-century representations of Pacific island life. Such images are generally clumsily proportioned woodcuts that depend on the text which surrounds them for exegesis. 'Interior of the Chapel' is the frontispiece to the same chapter of Aaron Buzacott's *Mission Life*

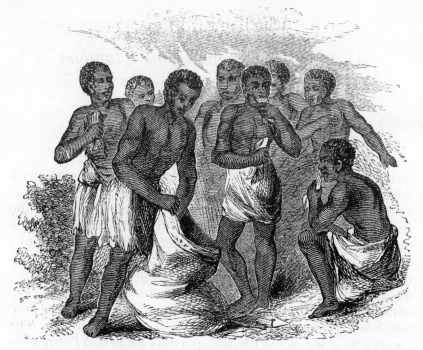

Plate 8. 'Eating the Mail', from Mrs Jane S. Warren, *The Morning Star.*

in which the story of the comical 'aged couple' reciting the English alphabet to excorcise a cat is retailed. It refers to a more encouraging subsequent period in the history of Rarotongan schooling, around the mid 1850s:

> The engraving at the head of this chapter, represents Mr Buzacott distributing prizes to the children belonging to his day and Sunday schools in the Coral Church, which he built in 1853 . . . Of course the schools varied somewhat in numbers and efficiency up to 1857; yet it is no exaggeration to state, that it would have been no easy matter to find a boy or girl at Avarua, of eight to ten years of age unable to read or write. In the upper classes were to be found boys who could write a beautiful hand, or who could read with fluency and correctness.[1]

Here a new Rarotongan literary confidence is depicted receiving its textual reward. The aged couple, fumbling with novel cabalistic signs, have been replaced by a generation of talented younger scholars. The emphasis of the illustration is emphatically on prestation, yet the scene also captures a curious equilibrium of

Plate 9. 'Interior of the Chapel', from J. P. Sunderland and A. Buzacott,
Mission Life in the Islands of the Pacific.

exchange. The book is not so much passed from the white hand of
the dark-clad missionary to the black hand of the white-clothed
schoolboy, as suspended indefinitely between the two figures.
Effectively each other's negative image, they embody the reciprocity of the literary transaction: the missionary endows the
native with the book, but in doing so, is himself legitimated as
donor. The book only has meaning in a context in which written
words have achieved a level of shared significance.

'Eating the Mail', on the other hand, encapsulates a story of
profit and loss, occurring a few years later than the Rarotongan
scene, at the periphery of the Pacific, in Micronesia. The illustration comes from Jane Warren's *The Morning Star*, an account
written for younger readers of the American missionary Hiram
Bingham's evangelical voyages among the Pacific islands. It is
accompanied by the following anecdote:

In February 1859, Mr Bingham heard from the natives a report that a
vessel, some two weeks before, had touched at a distant islet of the group,
and left there 'te-boki' – the native name for every thing made of paper.
He conjectured that it might be a mail designed for him, and set out

immediately to ascertain the facts, and, if possible, procure the precious package. The report was found to be true. The mail had been put on shore, but the savages opened it, and supposing the letters and papers to be some kind of food, had *eaten the greater portion of them!* A few whole ones and some fragments only remained, and for those he was obliged to pay. It is not stated whether the natives found the 'boki' to be a palatable diet. We can imagine what a disappointment this affair occasioned to the missionaries.[2]

As if to compensate for the act of desecration it depicts, the illustration is located in the centre of this page of words, almost swallowed by the surrounding text. This story echoes the anecdote of the 'aged couple' and the cat in its attempts to patronise its 'native' subjects: to highlight their limited vocabulary (they fail to recognise distinctions between different paper articles), and their crude appetites (they reveal an inordinate hunger for the printed word). But it also resonates with the tale of exploitation that formed a brief vignette in Stevenson's 'Authors and Publishers' manuscript. To quote once again: 'The late lamented Bully Hayes, the pirate of the Pacific, used to visit islands (where he was sure that nobody could read) the bearer of a letter, which he would obligingly read out himself to the local trader; and that innocent was usually convinced and handed out his oil.'[3] If the Micronesians of Warren's account are presented as more extreme versions of the illiterate trader, fetishising the written word to the extent that they seek to incorporate it as manna from a more developed world, they are equally versions of the crafty pirate, aware of the value of the text as commodity. They alone derive a profit from the cache of print; the missionaries who are its rightful educated recipients are in turn left to swallow their disappointment.

This book has tried to draw attention to the give and take of words in the history of the reception of writing in the Pacific islands. It has emphasised the complexity and the contingency that inform many apparently straightforward representations of intercultural transaction. Earlier chapters argued that a European tendency to figure native awe and wonderment at imported culture sat uneasily with depictions of the imaginative and politicised ways in which new technologies, and in particular the technology of writing, were integrated into Pacific societies. From this general discussion of a widespread representational practice, I proceeded to examine in detail Stevenson's perceptive fictional and factual writings on Polynesian subjects, concluding strategically rather than chronologically with his Samoan history. I argued that this text confronts immediate issues of authority raised for a wider politics of documentation by Samoan political manoeuvrings. *A Footnote to History* recognises that reading no longer takes place on one side of the world only. It is a text that takes account of the political nemesis of the literate Polynesian. Its battles are between writers and readers; its campaigns are instances of strategic misinterpretation; its negotiations occur between the letter and the enactment of the law. Concomitantly, it is a document produced in a context in which performance attains a new self-consciousness. In a post-literate society, tradition is reinvented and politicised. In representing himself as a repository of Samoan traditional values, the Pretender Mata'afa figures his opposition to the collusionist rule of King Laupepa. Yet both Mata'afa and Laupepa are educated subjects manipulating a particular relationship to an acquired culture of literacy in order to articulate opposing political agendas.

To focus on nineteenth-century Pacific history as the contested terrain of texts and voices is not, however, to neglect the immediate material impact of foreign imperialism. It is rather to interrogate a distinction between textual and material events which is repeatedly destabilised in the course of that history. To reinforce this point I want to look finally at a group of accounts whose common subject is the immediate ground of colonial contestation: the appropriation of land. In a letter to the *Times*, written in late April 1894 and published on 2 June, Stevenson reported the defeat and deportation of Mata'afa, and the incarceration of twenty-seven of his chiefly allies in Apia gaol.[4] These prisoners were gradually released in July and August, following concerted local campaigning by Stevenson. To show their gratitude for his efforts on their behalf, one group of chiefs, upon being freed from gaol, offered Stevenson a singular gift, the political complexities of which he detailed to Colvin in correspondence:

Up came Po'e, and some eight other chiefs, squatting in a big circle around the old dining-room floor . . . Then their talking man began. He said that they had been in prison, that I had always taken an interest in them, that they had now been set at liberty without condition whereas some of the other chiefs who had been liberated before them were still under bond to work upon the roads, and that this had set them considering what they might do to testify their gratitude. They had therefore agreed to work upon my road as a free gift.

Stevenson, although appreciative, initially regards this compliment as '(to one used with natives) . . . rather a hollow one. It meant only that I should have to lay out a good deal of money on tools and food and to give wages under the guise of presents to some workmen who were most of them old and in ill health.' He is delighted to discover, however, that unconventionally, he is only expected to provide tools for the job: the workers' families are to supply their rations. Stevenson is in fact expressly instructed to offer no reward for the labour: 'it was especially mentioned that I was to make no presents'.[5]

'The Road of Gratitude', as it was subsequently termed, is indeed, then, a free gift. It explicitly breaks the chain of reciprocity that underpins Polynesian systems of prestation, implying instead that the author's political activities have effectively paid for the gift in advance. For Stevenson, the road thus attains a primarily symbolic, rather than material, status. He concludes:

Now whether or not their impulse will last them through the road does not matter to me one hair. It is the fact they have attempted it, that they have volunteered and are now really trying to execute a thing that was never before heard of in Samoa. Think of it! It is road-making – the most fruitful cause (after taxes) of all rebellions in Samoa, a thing to which they could not be wiled with money nor driven by punishment. It does give one a sense of having done something for Samoa after all.[6]

The relationship between the act of construction and a wider metaphor of renewal and productivity is somewhat confused here. The road is at this stage a thought that counts rather than a trajectory, and appears in fact to have been more 'fruitful' as a sign of political non-compliance than as a project. In *A Footnote to History*, on the other hand, Stevenson had described a state of siege in which even already existing roads were sabotaged, so that attempts to visit Mata'afa's encampment, Malie, involved a negotiation of blocked trajectories which the author found particularly frustrating:

The road, one of the works of Brandeis, is now cut up by pig fences . . . Nothing can more thoroughly depict the worst side of the Samoan character than these useless barriers which deface their only road. It was one of the first orders issued by the government of Mulinuu after the coming of the chief justice, to have the passage cleared.[7]

Jacques Derrida has referred to 'writing as the possibility of the road', playing with imagery of paths beaten through 'the natural,

savage, salvage, forest', and claiming that 'it is difficult to imagine
that access to the possibility of a road-map is not at the same time
access to writing'.[8] In Stevenson's discussions of his particular
moment in Samoan history such connections appear to be more
than metaphoric. The blocked roads of Samoan warfare imply a
disruption of the advancing colonial narrative. The 'Road of
Gratitude', on the other hand, constitutes a new text, quickly converted by Stevenson into the subject of a political sermon. The
road was successfully completed by October 1894, and despite the
injunction not to reciprocate, Stevenson immediately invited the
chiefs to attend a feast, at which he gave a lengthy address that was
subsequently published. Throughout this speech he alludes
repeatedly to the status of the road as text. He claims that its value
is primarily as a 'lesson', to Samoa: 'I accepted, because I thought
the lesson of this road might be more useful to Samoa than a thousand breadfruit trees', that in it he 'read the promise of something
good for Samoa', and that the upkeep of the road amounts to an
act of publication: 'At least so long as my own life shall be spared,
it shall be here perpetuated; partly for my pleasure and in my gratitude; partly for others; to continually publish the lesson of this
road.'[9] In a recently literate Samoa, its value as text is integral to
Stevenson's recognition of the road as a virtuous production. The
chiefs had set up a board upon which they inscribed the title of the
road, 'The Road of Gratitude', and Stevenson draws attention to
this act of naming, paying tribute to the work as a symbolic achievement, a moral tale. However the question of publication is in turn
double-edged: in drawing a 'lesson' for Samoans, Stevenson also
provides himself with an opportunity for political self-promotion.
As he acknowledged in correspondence with Sidney Colvin: 'To
send this report to the papers is truly an act of self-advertisement,
and I dislike the thought . . . Do I wish to advertise? I think I do,
God help me! I have had hard times here, as every man knows who
mixes up with public business.'[10]

The substance of his speech, however, moves away from a focus
on what the road represents, to look at its value as an immediate
act of inscription. The road is embraced as an early sign, after the
destructive effects of warfare, of the productive reappropriation of
Samoan land by its first inhabitants. Stevenson draws parallels with
the colonial histories of Scotland and Hawaii, vehemently advo-
cating that 'there is but one way to defend Samoa. Hear it before

it is too late. It is to make roads, and gardens, and care for your trees, and sell their produce wisely, and, in one word, to occupy and use your country. If you do not, others will.'[11] He places his faith in the ability of the Land Commission set up under the Berlin Act to weigh the contradictory native and settler claims to land ownership in Samoa, to reach an equitable decision in which 'Much of your land will be restored to you, to do what you can with.'[12] (He had also spoken favourably of the work of this committee in the concluding pages of *A Footnote to History*.) Yet there is a circularity to Stevenson's definitions of productive use of the land, and to his appropriation of a road built to serve his own property as its primary symbol. The gift of the road remains embedded in a proto-colonial relationship, in which Samoans, as gratitude rather than punishment, work the land of the settler. On a wider scale, the very factors taken into account by the Land Commission in assessing land claims favoured particular types of use and occupation, of exploitation of local resources, which Stevenson adumbrated in his speech, but to the disservice of Samoan interests. Richard Gilson refers to 'the great importance of the factors of occupation and development in the establishment of foreign land titles in Samoa'.[13] According to Gilson, the Commission's estimations were invested in a particular reading of the Samoan landscape which favoured the interests of large-scale cultivators such as the *Deutsche Handels- und Plantagen- Gesellschaft*. As a result of its assessments, much land around Apia continued to be possessed by plantation owners: Samoa's political centre remained alienated.

Nonetheless, to interpret the bargain that the Road of Gratitude represents as a simple reinscription of a global colonial paradigm is to reduce to paperwork an even exchange whose very materiality was secondary to its ability to serve as a flexible symbol for both donor and recipient, articulated in the fluid back and forth of complimentary and elucidatory discourse. Paperwork, as we have seen, does not constitute the final story. In a passage from her travel account, Margaret Jersey depicts nineteenth-century land sales in Samoa as an equilibrium of duplicitous strategy and culpability. She observes that 'Forged deeds and fictitious purchases on the side of the foreigner are met by repeated re-sales to different individuals on the part of the native vendor.' Such transactions illustrate once again the relationship I have been describing between an imported culture of writing and a resistant Pacific readership. The settlers dupe the Samoans with forged pieces of paper, and the Samoans respond with a performed backwardness, refusing to acknowledge the signatory status of documents of contract, and so foregrounding and countering the venture of forgery. By the time that the Land Commission came to investigate claims of ownership, it was confronted, not with Stevenson's blank page, awaiting inscription with the lines of roads and the exemplary texts of productive agriculture, but with a map of Samoa spilling over its parameters, rendered redundant by subversive acts of superscription. As Jersey noted: 'An accurate computation shows that the amount of land claimed exceeds by some million of acres the total area of the islands.'[14] Samoa's colonial history, then, begins where this book ends, with the sorting of disputing accounts, the recognition of false transactions, the acknowledgement that the politics of discursive exchange in the Pacific exceed the frame of written record.

Notes

INTRODUCTION: ACTS OF READING

1 J. P. Sunderland and A. Buzacott, *Mission Life in the Islands of the Pacific*, London: John Snow, 1866; Suva, Fiji: Institute of Pacific Studies of the University of the South Pacific, 1985, pp. 64–5.

2 William Wyatt Gill, *From Darkness to Light in Polynesia*, London: n.p., 1894; Suva, Fiji: Institute of Pacific Studies of the University of the South Pacific, 1989, pp. 367–9.

3 Compare Matthew 23:25–7.

4 Stephen Greenblatt, *Marvelous Possessions: the wonder of the new world*, Oxford: Clarendon Press, 1991, p. 9.

5 Revd. John Williams, *A Narrative of Missionary Enterprises in the South Sea Islands, with remarks upon the natural history of the islands, origin, languages, traditions and usages of the inhabitants*, London: John Snow, 1837, p. 328.

6 Caroline Ralston, 'Early Nineteenth Century Polynesian Millennial Cults and the Case of Hawaii', *Journal of the Polynesian Society*, 94, 4 (1985), p. 311.

7 James Wilson, *A Missionary Voyage to the Southern Pacific Ocean, performed in the years 1796, 1797, 1798, in the Ship Duff*, London: published for the benefit of the society, printed by S. Gosnell for T. Chapman, 1799; reprinted (introduction Irmgard Moschner), New York: Frederick A. Praeger, n.d. (1979?), pp. 203–4.

8 Nicholas Thomas, *Entangled Objects: exchange, material culture and colonialism in the Pacific*, Cambridge, Mass.: Harvard University Press, 1991, pp. 86, 87.

9 See for instance Thomas, 'The Beautiful and the Damned', in Ann Stephen (ed.), *Pirating the Pacific: images of travel, trade and tourism*, Sydney: Powerhouse, 1993, pp. 44–59, and *Oceanic Art*, London: Thames and Hudson, 1995.

10 Barry Menikoff, *Robert Louis Stevenson and 'The Beach of Falesā: a study in Victorian publishing*, Edinburgh University Press, 1984, p. 9.

11 Letter to Edward Livermore Burlingame, 20 May 1889, Bradford A. Booth and Ernest Mehew (eds.), *The Letters of Robert Louis Stevenson*,

New Haven: Yale University Press, 1995, vol. VI, p. 300; to Burlingame, [18 June 1889], p. 319; to Burlingame, January– and 30th 1893, Booth and Mehew (eds.), *Letters*, vol. VIII, p. 14.

12 'American Rights and Wrongs', *Academy*, 20 March 1886, p. 203; 'International Copyright', *Times*, 2 April 1887, p. 6.

13 Stevenson, 'Authors and Publishers', New Haven, Beinecke Library, ms 5997; published in *The Lantern-Bearers and other essays*, selected and introduced by Jeremy Treglown, London: Chatto and Windus, 1988, pp. 261, 260.

14 Studies in this mode include Menikoff, *Robert Louis Stevenson and 'The Beach of Falesā'*, Robert Irwin Hillier, *The South Seas Fiction of Robert Louis Stevenson*, New York: Peter Lang, 1989, Patrick Brantlinger, *Rule of Darkness: British literature and imperialism, 1830–1914*, Ithaca, N.Y.: Cornell University Press, 1988, pp. 39–45.

15 Most thoroughly in Alan Sandison, *Robert Louis Stevenson and the Appearance of Modernism*, Macmillan, London, 1996; see also Barry Menikoff 'Introduction: Fable, Fiction, and Modernism', in Menikoff (ed.), Robert Louis Stevenson, *Tales from the Prince of Storytellers*, Evanston, Ill.: Northwestern University Press, 1993, pp. 1–37.

16 John Charles Olmstead (ed.), *A Victorian Art of Fiction: essays on the novel in British periodicals, 1870–1900*, New York and London: Garland, 1979, provides a selection of the seminal essays in this debate, in which Stevenson was an engaged participant. He defended romance writing in essays such as 'A Gossip on Romance', *Longman's*, November 1882, and 'A Humble Remonstrance', *Longman's*, December 1884, which are notable for the ways in which they seek to expand rather than delimit definitions of genre. The latter essay was a response to Henry James's realist manifesto 'The Art of Fiction', published in *Longman's*, September 1884. Stevenson continued to debate the practice of fiction with James in private correspondence: see Janet Adam Smith, *Henry James and Robert Louis Stevenson: a record of friendship and criticism*, London: Rupert Hart-Davis, 1948. The issues of the wider literary debate are elaborated in Kenneth Graham, *English Criticism of the Novel, 1865–1900*, Oxford: Clarendon Press, 1965. See also Christopher Caudwell, *Romance and Realism: a study in English bourgeoise literature*, Princeton University Press, 1970.

17 Robert Dixon, *Writing the Colonial Adventure: race, gender and nation in Anglo-Australian popular fiction, 1875–1914*, Cambridge University Press, 1995, p. 4. See also Martin Green, *Dreams of Adventure, Deeds of Empire*, London: Routledge and Kegan Paul, 1980, and Elaine Showalter, *Sexual Anarchy: gender and culture at the fin de siècle*, London: Bloomsbury, 1991, pp. 79–81.

18 Niel Rennie, *Far-Fetched Facts: the literature of travel and the idea of the*

South Seas, Oxford: Clarendon Press, 1995, offers a wide-ranging survey of the ways the Pacific was imaginitively prefigured in Europe before and immediately after its 'discovery'.

19 Gillian Beer, *The Romance*, London: Methuen, 1970, p. 9.

20 Joseph Bristow, *Empire Boys: adventures in a man's world*, London: Harper–Collins, 1991, pp. 121–3.

21 Letter to Robert Ross, 6 April, 1897, in Rupert Hart-Davis (ed.), *Selected Letters of Oscar Wilde*, Oxford University Press, 1979, p. 246.

22 Jean-Jacques Rousseau, *The Social Contract and Discourses*, trans. G. D. H. Cole, London: Everyman, 1991; Hoxie Neale Fairchild, *The Noble Savage: a study in romantic naturalism*, New York: Columbia University Press, 1928, pp. 120–39.

23 Bernard Smith, *European Vision and the South Pacific*, 2nd edition, London and New Haven: Yale University Press, 1985, pp. 5–6. An interesting discussion of Smith's model, which re-evaluates the complex interrelationship of idealist and realist discourses on the Pacific, is Christopher Herbert, *Culture and Anomie: ethnographic imagination in the nineteenth century*, University of Chicago Press, 1991, pp. 150–203.

24 Menikoff, *Robert Louis Stevenson and 'The Beach of Falesā'*, p. 8; George. L. McKay, *Some Notes on Robert Louis Stevenson: his finances and his agents and publishers*, New Haven: Yale University Library, 1958, pp. 30–43.

25 Graham Balfour, *The Life of Robert Louis Stevenson*, London: Methuen, 1901, vol. II, p. 89.

26 Letter to Charles Baxter, postmarked 11 March 1891, Booth and Mehew (eds.), *Letters*, vol. VII, p. 88.

27 Robert Louis Stevenson, *In the South Seas: Being an Account of Experiences and Observations in the Marquesas, Paumotus, and Gilbert Islands in the Course of Two Cruises, on the Yacht 'Casco' (1888) and the Schooner 'Equator'(1889)*, London: William Heinemann, 1924, pp. 182–3.

1 'A GIFT OF FABRICATION': THE BEACHCOMBER AS *BRICOLEUR*

1 William Diapea [Diaper], *Cannibal Jack: the true autobiography of a white man in the South Seas*, London: Faber and Gwyer, 1928, p. xvi.

2 A bibliography of these texts is to be found in H. E. Maude, *Of Islands and Men*, Oxford University Press, 1968, pp. 170–7. Bill Pearson, *Rifled Sanctuaries: some views of the Pacific islands in western literature*, Auckland University Press, 1984, pp. 59–70, discusses the more famous beachcomber narratives. Caroline Ralston examines the beachcomber as historical phenomenon, rather than literary subject, in *Grass Huts and Warehouses: Pacific beach communities of the*

nineteenth century, Canberra: Australian National University Press, 1977. I. C. Campbell explores the psychology of the beachcomber in his Ph.D. thesis 'European Transculturalists in Polynesia, 1789–*ca*.1840', University of Adelaide, 1976.

3 Maude, *Of Islands and Men*, pp. 151, 152, 163. Greg Dening, *Islands and Beaches*, Honolulu: University of Hawaii Press, 1980, p. 130.

4 J. H. Erskine *Journal of A Cruise among the Islands of the Western Pacific*, London: John Murray, 1853, p. 440; compare Maude, *Of Islands and Men*, pp. 150–1.

5 Bourdieu's suggestion that calculations of economic value cannot be divorced from notions of symbolic, or prestige, value is elaborated in *Outline of a Theory of Practice*, trans. Richard Nice, Cambridge University Press, 1977, pp. 171–83.

6 The beachcomber to whom textual records give us access is consistently a masculine subject. I have therefore employed the masculine pronoun throughout this chapter.

7 Dening, *Islands and Beaches*, p. 129.

8 Maude, *Of Islands and Men*, pp. 160, 161; Dening, *Islands and Beaches*, p. 136; cf. Campbell, 'European Transculturalists in Polynesia', p. 88.

9 H. Stonehewer Cooper, *Coral Lands*, London: Richard Bentley and Son, 1880, pp. 100–1, 172, 173.

10 T. Walter Herbert, *Marquesan Encounters: Melville and the meaning of civilisation*, Cambridge, Mass.: Harvard University Press, 1980, p. 155; Herman Melville, *Typee: a peep at Polynesian life, and Omoo: a narrative of adventures in the South Seas*, New York: Library of America, 1982.

11 Cooper, *Coral Lands*, p. 99.

12 Archibald Campbell, *A Voyage Round the World, from 1806 to 1812 . . . with an account of the present state of the Sandwich Islands, and a vocabulary of their language*, Edinburgh: Archibald Constable and Company, 1816, p. 140. As I. C. Campbell has pointed out, Hawaii under Kamehameha is somewhat exceptional for the systematic way in which skilled foreigners were utilised within the community: 'Whereas most island chiefs never passed beyond the use of beachcomber-artisans to repair and maintain muskets, Kamehameha actively recruited blacksmiths, carpenters and shipwrights, ropemakers and sailmakers, clerks, armourers, sailors, pilots, navigators and gardeners, as well as other highly specialized craftsmen.' 'European Transculturalists in Polynesia', pp. 320–1.

13 Diapea, *Cannibal Jack*, p. 4.

14 Campbell, *A Voyage Round the World*, pp. 140–1.

15 Claude Lévi-Strauss, *The Savage Mind*, Paris: Librairie Plon, 1962; London: Weidenfeld and Nicholson, (1966) 1989, pp. 16–17.

16 Ibid.

17 Ibid., p. 19.

18 Walter Benjamin, *Illuminations*, trans. Harry Zohn, New York: Schocken, 1969, p. 86.

19 Gananath Obeyesekere claims that the term *bricolage* as it is used by Lévi-Strauss refers simply to 'the shallow experimental skill of the European artisan', although Lévi-Strauss is quite precise in distinguishing between the *bricoleur* and the craftsman, and this is a distinction that translates to the realm of narrative practice. Gananath Obeyesekere, *The Apotheosis of Captain Cook: European mythmaking in the Pacific*, Princeton University Press, 1992, p. 15.

20 Chris Gregory, *Gifts and Commodities*, London: Academic Press, 1982, p. 19; Marcel Mauss, *The Gift: the form and reason for exchange in archaic societies*, trans. W. D. Halls, London: Routledge, 1990; Annette B. Weiner, *Inalienable Possessions: the paradox of keeping-while-giving*, Berkeley: University of California Press, 1992, pp. 40–54.

21 Diapea, *Cannibal Jack*, pp. xiii, 90–1, xxi–xxii. In fact, another fragment of Diaper's autobiography survives as 'Jackson's Narrative', appended to Erskine's *Journal of A Cruise*, London: John Murray, 1853. The identity of the author of the two narratives has been determined by Christopher Legge, see 'William Diaper: a biographical sketch', *Journal of Pacific History*, 1 (1966), pp. 79–90.

22 Diapea, *Cannibal Jack*, pp. 3, xv. William B. Churchward, *My Consulate in Samoa: a record of four years' sojourn in the Navigators Islands with personal experiences of King Malietoa Laupepa, his country, and his men*, London: Richard Bentley, 1887, pp. 31–2.

23 Diapea, *Cannibal Jack*, pp. xvii, xii, xvii.

24 William Arens, *The Man-Eating Myth: anthropology and anthropophagy*, Oxford University Press, 1979, p. 145.

25 Revd. William Wyatt Gill, *Jottings from the Pacific*, London: Religious Tract Society, 1885, pp. 241–2.

26 Owen Rutter, 'Introduction', James Morrison, *The Journal of James Morrison, Boatswain's Mate of the 'Bounty'*, London: Golden Cockerel Press, 1935, p. 12.

27 James F. O'Connell, *A Residence of eleven years in New Holland and the Caroline Islands* (Boston, 1836), ed. Saul H. Reisenberg, Honolulu: University Press of Hawaii, 1972, p. 18.

28 Peter Bays, *A Narrative of the Wreck of the 'Minerva' Whaler of Port Jackson, New South Wales, on Nicholson's Shoal, 24° S. 179°W . . .*, Cambridge: B. Bridges, 1831, p. 67.

29 Campbell, *A Voyage Round the World*, pp. 10–11.

30 John Martin, *An Account of the Natives of the Tonga Islands, in the South Pacific Ocean. With an original grammar and vocabulary of their language. Comp. and arranged from the extensive communications of Mr William Mariner, several years resident in those islands*, 2nd edition, London: John Murray, 1818, vol. I, pp. xxi–xxii.

31 Campbell, *A Voyage Round the World*, pp. 14, 10.
32 Otto von Kotzebue, *A New Voyage Round the World in the Years 1823, 24, 25, and 26*, London: Henry Colburn and Richard Bentley, 1830,vol. I, p. iv.
33 Campbell, *A Voyage Round the World*, p. 13; John Martin, *An Account of the Natives of the Tonga Islands*, 3rd edition, Edinburgh: Constable, 1827, p. xxii.
34 Martin, *Tonga Islands*, 1818, pp. xxxvii-xxxviii. Exact duplication could also figure, however, as the sign of duplicity. Early missionaries in the Pacific regarded an ability to testify in his or her own words as the sign of the genuine convert. Ebenezer Prout, *Memoirs of the Life of the Rev. John Williams*, London: John Snow, 1843, pp. 229–30.
35 Martin, *Tonga Islands*, 1818, p. xxx; Walter J. Ong, *Orality and Literacy: the technologising of the word*, London: Methuen, 1982, pp. 60–1.
36 Martin, *Tonga Islands*, 1818, pp. xlii–xliii, xliii.
37 James Wilson, *A Missionary Voyage to the Southern Pacific Ocean*, New York: Frederick A. Praeger, n.d. (1979?), p. iv.
38 Mrs Jane S. Warren, *The Morning Star: history of the children's missionary vessel, and of the Marquesan and Micronesian missions*, Boston: American Tract Society, 1860, p. 204.
39 Martin, *Tonga Islands*, 1818, pp. xi, vii, xxxi, xiv.
40 Ibid., pp. viii-ix, x.
41 Ibid., 1818, pp. xxxvii, x, xxxvii, xii.
42 O'Connell, *A Residence of Eleven Years*, pp. 49–50.
43 Ibid., p. 21.
44 Ibid., pp. 19, 22. The missionary turned beachcomber George Vason connects his comparable inability accurately to map the space he traversed in Tonga with the adoption of a local physical custom: 'I cannot, however, from my own knowledge, ascertain its proper extent, having been often much deceived respecting the relative distances of places, through the pain and fatigue of travelling barefoot: the natives never using any protection for the feet, in the form of bandage or sandal.' George Vason, *An Authentic Narrative of Four Years' Residence at Tongataboo*, London: Longman, Hurst, Rees and Orme, 1810, p. 185.
45 Bays, *A Narrative of the Wreck*, pp. 32, 6, 16, 28, 75, 32.
46 John P. Twyning, *Shipwreck and Adventures of John P. Twyning among the South Sea Islanders: giving an account of their feasts, massacres, etc., etc. . . .*, 2nd edition, enlarged, London: printed for the benefit of the author [1850], pp. 27, 57.
47 Vason, *An Authentic Narrative*, pp. vii-viii.
48 Ibid., p. 225.
49 Maude, *Of Islands and Men*, p. 142.
50 Niel Gunson, *Messengers of Grace: evangelical missionaries in the South*

Seas, 1797–1860, Melbourne: Oxford University Press, 1978, pp. 31–46.

51 Vason, *An Authentic Narrative*, p. 87.

52 Ibid., pp. 87, 90, 233–4.

53 Ibid., pp. 204–5, 179–80.

54 'Statement as to Puckey's Defection', in The Revd Thomas Haweis, *A collection of 38 draft letters and manuscripts many of which are in hand of the Rev. Thomas Haweis, dealing with the early missions to the South Seas, and including diaries sent by the missionaries to the London Missionary Society*, Sydney: Mitchell Library ms 4910X 1, 2.

55 Vason, *An Authentic Narrative*, pp. 230–1 (cf. p. 117).

56 Martin, *Tonga Islands*, 1818, pp. xxx-xxxi.

57 Vason, *An Authentic Narrative*, pp. 38, 17, 69.

58 Ibid., pp. 147, 93, 146, 148, 95.

59 Lincoln B. Faller, *Turned to Account: the forms and functions of criminal biography in late seventeenth- and early eighteenth-century England*, Cambridge University Press, 1987.

60 Cooper, *Coral Lands*, p. 100.

61 Diapea, *Cannibal Jack*, p. x.

62 Ibid., pp. ix-x, xxi, xii, xix.

63 Ibid., pp. xiv, xxii, 6–7.

64 Churchward, *My Consulate in Samoa*, pp. 31–2.

65 Maude, *Of Islands and Men*, p. 155.

66 Diapea, *Cannibal Jack*, pp. xx, xxii.

67 'Jackson's Narrative', in Erskine, *Journal of A Cruise*, pp. 411–77.

68 Diapea, *Cannibal Jack*, pp. xiv, 233, 232.

69 Samuel Patterson, *Narrative of the Adventures and Sufferings of Samuel Patterson* (1817), Fairfield, Washington: Ye Galleon Press, 1967, p. 3.

70 Campbell, *A Voyage Round the World*, pp. 127–8, 8.

71 Adolf Loos, 'Ornament und Verbrechen', quoted in Benedetto Gravagnuolo, *Adolf Loos: theory and works*, Milan: Idea Books Edizioni, 1982, p. 68. Alfred Gell discusses the relationship between traditional and Western subcultural tattooing in *Wrapping in Images: tattooing in Polynesia*, Oxford: Clarendon Press, 1993; compare Nicholas Thomas, *Oceanic Art*, London: Thames and Hudson, 1995, p. 100.

72 Wilson, *A Missionary Voyage*, p. 229.

73 Erskine, *Journal of a Cruise*, pp. 468–9.

74 Greg Dening (ed.), *The Marquesan Journal of Edward Robarts, 1797–1824*, Canberra: Australian National University Press, 1974, p. 8.

75 Dening, *Islands and Beaches*, pp. 139–40.

76 Robert Ker Porter, *Travelling Sketches in Russia and Sweden during the years 1805, 1806, 1807, 1808*, London: John Stockdale, 1813, vol. I, pp. 39–50, 42. See Markman Ellis, *The Politics of Sensibility: race,*

gender and commerce in the Sentimental Novel, Cambridge University Press, 1996, pp. 49–128, for a full account of the relationship between sentimental rhetoric and the discourse of otherness.

77 Jane Porter, 'The South Sea Chief', *Sydney Gazette*, 10 September 1829; Pearson, *Rifled Sanctuaries*, p. 59. Jane Porter was the author of the novel *Scottish Chiefs*, which Stevenson tells us, in the extract from *In the South Seas* that I quoted in the introduction, was absorbing Hawaiian readers at the time of his arrival in Hookena.

78 Dening, *Marquesan Journal*, p. 9n.

79 O'Connell, *A Residence of Eleven Years*, p. 43.

2   LIP SERVICE AND CONVERSION

1 Jean Comaroff and John Comaroff, *Of Revelation and Revolution: Christianity, colonialism, and consciousness in South Africa*, University of Chicago Press, 1991, vol. I, pp. 12–13.

2 Homi Bhabha, 'Of Mimicry and Man: the ambivalence of colonial discourse', *The Location of Culture*, London: Routledge, 1994, p. 86.

3 Revd Thomas Haweis, Letter, 19 January 1798, Sydney: Mitchell Library ms 4910X 1, 2.

4 For the historical background to missionary activity from 1797 to 1860, see Niel Gunson, *Messengers of Grace*, Melbourne: Oxford University Press, 1978, especially pp. 11–28; Revd.Thomas Smith, *The History and Origin of the Missionary Societies*, 2 vols. London: Thomas Kelly, 1838; Richard Lovett, *The History of the London Missionary Society, 1795–1895*, London: Henry Frowde, 1899; K. L. P. Martin, *Missionaries and Annexation in the Pacific*, Oxford University Press, 1924; Angus Ross, *New Zealand Aspirations in the Pacific in the Nineteenth Century*, Oxford: Clarendon Press, 1964.

5 Gunson, *Messengers of Grace*, p. 25.

6 John Williams, *A Narrative of Missionary Enterprises in the South Sea Islands . . .*, London: John Snow, 1837, p. 303.

7 George Brown, *Journal*, 1868, entries for 20 May and 1 July, Sydney: Mitchell Library ms A1686 9.

8 Smith, *History and Origin of the Missionary Societies*, pp. 4, 3.

9 An informative biographical portrait of Williams, which emphasizes the relationship between secular and spiritual advancement in Williams's career, is to be found in Gavan Daws, *A Dream of Islands: voyages of self-discovery in the South Seas*, New York: Norton, 1980, pp. 23–69.

10 James Wilson, *A Missionary Voyage to the Southern Pacific Ocean*, New York: Praeger, n.d. (1979?), p. 4.

11 Gunson, *Messengers of Grace*, pp. 32–42.

12 Williams, *Missionary Enterprises*, p. 588. Compare Ebenezer Prout, *Memoirs of the Life of the Rev. John Williams*, London: John Snow, 1843, p. 476, and Daws, *A Dream of Islands*, p. 58.

13 Niel Gunson, 'John Williams and his Ship: the bourgeoise aspirations of a missionary family', in D. P. Crook (ed.), *Questioning the Past:
a selection of papers in history and government*, University of Queensland
Press, 1972, p. 90.

14 Prout, *Memoirs*, p. 537.

15 Otto von Kotzebue, *A New Voyage Around the World in the Years 1823,
24, 25 and 26*, London: Colburn and Bentley, 1830, vol. II, pp.
258–9.

16 Prout, *Memoirs*, pp. 537, 538.

17 Asa Briggs, *Victorian Things*, London: Batsford, 1988, p. 135.

18 Williams, *Missionary Enterprises*, p. 156.

19 J. P. Sunderland and A. Buzacott, *Mission Life in the Islands of the
Pacific*, London: John Snow, 1866; Suva, Fiji: Institute of Pacific
Studies of the University of the South Pacific, 1985, p. 33.

20 Williams, *Missionary Enterprises*, pp. 328, viii.

21 Ibid., pp. 179, 75.

22 Ibid., p. 229.

23 Prout, *Memoirs*, pp. 475–6.

24 Daws, *A Dream of Islands*, p. 48; Prout, *Memoirs*, p. 256. Compare J.
Hadfield's claim for the narrative of William Diaper: 'His range of
experience was so wide that he had no need to draw on his imagination, as did Defoe.' William Diapea, *Cannibal Jack*, London: Faber
and Gwyer, 1928, p. xix.

25 Daniel Defoe, *Robinson Crusoe*, Oxford University Press, 1990, pp.
144, 68. For an extended discussion of the use of *Robinson Crusoe* as
a model in beachcomber and missionary literature, see Vanessa
Smith, 'Crusoe in the South Seas: beachcombers, missionaries and
the myth of the castaway', in Lieve Spaas and Brian Stimpson (eds.),
Robinson Crusoe: myths and metamorphoses, London: Macmillan, 1996,
pp. 62–77.

26 Williams, *Missionary Enterprises*, pp. 144, 148–9. Jonathan Culler
gives the traditional definition of metaphor as 'a substitution based
on resemblance'. *The Pursuit of Signs: semiotics, literature, deconstruction*, London: Routledge, 1981, p. 204.

27 Prout, *Memoirs*, p. 257.

28 I. C. Campbell, *A History of the Pacific Islands*, Christchurch:
University of Canterbury Press, 1992, p. 37.

29 Wilson, *A Missionary Voyage*, p. 226.

30 Prout, *Memoirs*, p. 189.

31 Gunson, 'John Williams and his Ship', pp. 86, 88.

32 Williams, *Missionary Enterprises*, pp. 167–8.

33 Sunderland and Buzacott, *Mission Life*, p. 36.

34 Prout, *Memoirs*, p. 257.

35 Williams, *Missionary Enterprises*, p. 108.

36 Ibid., p. 116.

37 Christopher Herbert, *Culture and Anomie*, University of Chicago Press, 1991, p. 169.

38 William Ellis, *Polynesian Researches, During a Residence of Nearly Six Years in the South Sea Islands* (1829), London: Dawsons of Pall Mall, 1967, vol. I, p. 379.

39 Ibid., pp. 353–7, 364–72.

40 Williams, *Missionary Enterprises*, pp. 491–5, 494–5. The breadfruit was appropriated to an extended purpose within the context of Empire: the project of Bligh's failed mission in the *Bounty* was to deliver breadfruit seedlings to the West Indies, where the fruit was intended to provide a cheap substitute for grain in the diet of slaves. Bligh eventually successfully carried out his commission, but slaves refused the Polynesian diet, and the project failed. Revd Thomas Boyles Murray, *Pitcairn: The Island, the People and their Pastor; with a short account of the mutiny of the Bounty*, London: SPCK, 1854, pp. 58–64; Greg Dening, *Mr Bligh's Bad Language: passion, power and theatre on the Bounty*, Cambridge University Press, 1992, p. 8; William Bligh, *Dangerous Voyage, containing an account of the wonderful and truly providential escape of Captain Bligh and a part of the crew of His Majesty's ship Bounty*, Dublin: Graisberry and Campbell, printers, 1817; William Bligh, *A Log of the proceedings of His Majesty's Ship Providence on a Second Voyage to the South Sea under the command of Captain William Bligh, to carry the bread-fruit plant from the Society Islands to the West Indies, written by himself* [2 vols.], 1791–2; Douglas Oliver, *Return to Tahiti: Bligh's second breadfruit voyage*, Melbourne University Press, 1988.

41 Prout, *Memoirs*, pp. 479–80.

42 Ibid., p. 66.

43 Williams, *Missionary Enterprises*, pp. 515–16.

44 Ibid, pp. 84–5.

45 James Frazer, 'Taboo: and the perils of the soul', *The Golden Bough (1913)*, London: Macmillan, 1990, vol. II, p. v.

46 Sigmund Freud, 'Totem and Taboo', *The Origins of Religion*, trans. James Strachey, London: Pelican, 1985, p. 71.

47 Compare Alain Babadzan's account of the missionary colonisation of the language of Rurutu:

the Manicheism of the first missionaries was able to put to good use one of the essential divisions in Polynesian dualism, the opposition of *ao* and *pō* – the world of light and life versus the world of night and death – consigning in one easy blow all that belonged (or was thought to belong) to the world of the pagans to the abject and perilous domain of *pō*.

'From Oral to Written: the *puta tupuna* of Rurutu', in Antony Hooper and Judith Huntsman (eds.), *Transformations of Polynesian Culture*, Auckland: Polynesian Society, 1985, p. 187.

48 Richard E. Lingenfelter, *Presses of the Pacific Islands, 1817–1867*, Los Angeles: Plantin Press, 1967.

49 G. S. Parsonson, 'The Literate Revolution in Polynesia', *Journal of Pacific History*, 2 (1967), pp. 44, 56.

50 Stephen Greenblatt, *Marvelous Possessions*, Oxford: Clarendon Press, 1991, p. 12.

51 Jack Goody, *The Logic of Writing and the Organization of Society*, Cambridge University Press, 1986, p. 5.

52 Ellis, *Polynesian Researches*, vol. I, pp. 426, 427.

53 Ibid., p. 262.

54 Prout, *Memoirs*, p. 89.

55 Ellis, *Polynesian Researches*, vol. I, p. 262.

56 Kotzebue, *A New Voyage*, vol. II, pp. 206, 259–60.

57 Ellis, *Polynesian Researches*, vol. I, pp. 427, 402–3.

58 Ibid., pp. 402, 391.

59 Williams, *Missionary Enterprises*, pp. 476–7.

60 Ellis, *Polynesian Researches*, vol. I, p. 138.

61 Ibid., pp. 407, 448–9.

62 Brown, *Journal*, 1860, entry for 7 April.

63 Ellis, *Polynesian Researches*, vol. I, pp. 406, 449, 430.

64 Ibid., pp. 398, 393, 394.

65 A letter in Tahitian from Pomare to a London Missionary Society printer, presumably Ellis, written during the first year of printing, is held in the National Library of Australia, ms 5674.

66 [Robert Southey,] Review of Polynesian Researches, *Quarterly Review*, 43, 85 (1830), p. 25. Compare Ellis, *Polynesian Researches*, vol. I, p. 397. For the other side of this coin– the relationship between colonial politics and technological demonstrations at metropolitan public fairs – see Paul Greenhalgh, *Ephemeral Vistas: the expositions universelles, great exhibitions and world's fairs, 1851–1939*, Manchester University Press, 1988.

67 Wilson, *A Missionary Voyage*, p. 174.

68 Ellis, *Polynesian Researches*, vol. I, pp. 325, 317, 330, 322.

69 Ibid., pp. 329, 330.

70 Prout, *Memoirs*, pp. 229–30, 432.

71 Ellis, *Polynesian Researches*, vol. I, p. 199.

72 William Ellis, *A Vindication of the South Sea Missions from the Misrepresentations of Otto von Kotzebue, captain in the Russian navy, with an appendix*, London: Frederick Westley and A. H. Davis, 1831, pp. 161, 159–60.

73 Herbert, *Culture and Anomie*, p. 168.

74 Nicholas Thomas, *Out of Time: history and evolution in anthropological discourse*, Cambridge University Press, 1989, pp. 71, 72. See also James A. Boutilier, Daniel T. Hughes and Sharon W. Tiffany (eds.), *Mission, Church, and Sect in Oceania*, Lanham, Md.: University Press of America, 1978.

75 Ellis, *Polynesian Researches*, vol. I, p. 185.
76 Gunson, *Messengers of Grace*, p. 319. See also Marjorie Tuainekore Crocombe, *Polynesian Missions in Melanesia: from Samoa, Cook Islands and Tonga to Papua New Guinea and New Caledonia*, Suva, Fiji: University of the South Pacific, 1982.
77 Quoted in Gunson, *Messengers of Grace*, p. 319.
78 Ellis, *Polynesian Researches*, vol. I, pp. 492–3.
79 Kotzebue, *A New Voyage*, vol. I, p. 153.
80 Ellis, *A Vindication*, p. 42.
81 Bhabha, 'Of Mimicry and Man', p. 87.
82 Nicholas Thomas, 'The Force of Ethnology: origins and significance of the Melanesia/Polynesia division', *Current Anthropology*, 30, 1 (1989), pp. 27–41, p. 31.
83 William Churchward, *My Consulate in Samoa*, London: Richard Bentley, 1887, pp. 81, 84.
84 William Arens, *The Man-Eating Myth*, Oxford University Press, 1979, pp. 33–5.
85 Gananath Obeyesekere, '"British Cannibals": contemplation of an event in the death and resurrection of James Cook, Explorer', *Critical Inquiry*, 18 (Summer 1992), p. 630n.
86 R. G. and Marjorie Crocombe (eds.), *The Works of Ta'unga: records of a Polynesian traveller in the South Seas, 1833–1896*, Canberra: Australian National University Press, 1968, pp. 21, 14, 31, 64, 91, 19, 40, 78.
87 Ibid., pp. xviii, 74, 61.
88 Ibid., pp. 1, 138, 145.
89 Peter Worsley, *The Trumpet Shall Sound*, London: Macgibbon and Kee, 1957.
90 Caroline Ralston, 'Early Nineteenth Century Polynesian Millennial Cults', *Journal of the Polynesian Society*, 94, 4 (1985), pp. 307–31.
91 Martha Kaplan, *Neither Cargo nor Cult: ritual politics and the colonial imagination in Fiji*, Durham, N.C., and London: Duke University Press, 1995.
92 Jukka Siikala, *Cult and Conflict in Polynesia: a study of traditional religion, Christianity and nativistic movements*, Helsinki: Academica Scientiarum Fennica, 1982, pp. 56, 197.
93 Revd George Turner, *Nineteen Years in Polynesia*, London: John Snow, 1861, p. 109.
94 Sunderland and Buzacott, *Mission Life*, p. 127.
95 [Revd George Brown,] 'Old Hands and Old Times in the South Seas', Mitchell Library ms 1119.
96 J. D. Freeman, 'The Joe Gimlet or Siovili Cult: an episode in the religious history of early Samoa', in J. D. Freeman and W. R. Geddes (eds.), *Anthropology in the South Seas*, New Plymouth, N.Z.: Thomas Avery, 1959, pp. 196–7.
97 Siikala, *Cult and Conflict*, p. 197; Freeman, 'The Joe Gimlet or Siovili Cult', p. 193.

98 Freeman, 'The Joe Gimlet or Siovili Cult', p. 191.
99 Siikala, *Cult and Conflict*, p. 199.
100 Quoted in Bhabha, 'Sly Civility', *The Location of Culture*, p. 101.
101 Siikala, *Cult and Conflict*, p. 201; compare Freeman, 'The Joe Gimlet or Siovili Cult', p. 196.
102 Freeman, 'The Joe Gimlet or Siovili Cult', pp. 191n, 196.
103 The return to proscribed practices was justified by millennial cults in terms of what amounted to a doctrine of perfectibility: according to the Mamaia of Tahiti, the commencement of the Millennium had invalidated law. Such attitudes reflected nineteenth-century millenarian heresies in Britain, which had been rejected by early LMS missionaries in the 'godly mechanic' tradition. Niel Gunson, 'An Account of the Mamaia or Visionary Heresy of Tahiti, 1826–1841', *Journal of the Polynesian Society*, 71 (1962), p. 215.
104 Wilson, *A Missionary Voyage*, pp. 165–6.
105 Frederick Debell Bennett, *Narrative of a Whaling Voyage round the globe, from the year 1833 to 1836. Comprising sketches of Polynesia, California, the Indian Archipelago, etc. with an account of Southern whales, the sperm whale fishery, and the natural history of the climates visited*, London: Richard Bentley, 1840, vol. II, pp. 155–6.
106 Turner, *Nineteen Years*, p. 107.
107 Siikala, *Cult and Conflict*, p. 200.
108 Freeman, 'The Joe Gimlet or Siovili Cult', p. 193; Siikala, *Cult and Conflict*, p. 200.
109 Freeman, 'The Joe Gimlet or Siovili Cult', p. 193n.
110 Bhabha, 'Signs Taken for Wonders', *The Location of Culture*, p. 103.
111 Gauri Viswanathan, *Masks of Conquest: literary study and British rule in India*, London: Faber, 1989, p. 96.
112 Bhabha, 'Of Mimicry and Man', p. 92.
113 Siikala, *Cult and Conflict*, pp. 239, 241.
114 Gunson, 'An Account of the Mamaia', p. 209. The missionaries were here equally exploiting the competitive aspect of the performance aesthetic.
115 Ibid., pp. 210, 223, 240. Peter Hulme discusses the complicity between the discourses of communion and cannibalism in early modern Europe in *Colonial Encounters: Europe and the native Caribbean, 1492–1797*, London: Methuen, 1986, p. 85. See also Maggie Kilgour, *From Communion to Cannibalism: an anatomy of metaphors of incorporation*, Princeton University Press, 1990.
116 Gunson, 'An Account of the Mamaia', p. 239; Siikala, *Cult and Conflict*, p. 241.
117 Gunson, 'An Account of the Mamaia', pp. 238, 241, 242.
118 I. C. Campbell, 'European Transculturalists in Polynesia', Ph.D. thesis, University of Adelaide, 1976, p. 346.
119 Williams, *Missionary Enterprises*, p. 419.

120 Sunderland and Buzacott, *Mission Life*, p. 126.
121 Williams, *Missionary Enterprises*, pp. 464, 463.
122 Ibid., pp. 222–3.

3 'OTHER PEOPLE'S BOOKS': STEVENSON'S PACIFIC TRAVELS

1 Letter to Samuel Sidney McClure, 19 July 1890, Bradford A. Booth and Ernest Mehew (eds.), *The Letters of Robert Louis Stevenson*, New Haven: Yale University Press, 1995, vol. VI, pp. 394–5.
2 Sidney Colvin to Charles Baxter, 4 February 1891, New Haven, Beinecke Library, ms 4207.
3 Roger Swearingen, *The Prose Writings of Robert Louis Stevenson: a guide*, London: Macmillan, 1980, p. 143.
4 Fanny Stevenson, letter to Sidney Colvin, 21 May [1889], Booth and Mehew (eds.), *Letters*, vol. VI, pp. 303–4.
5 The details of this debate about anthropological practice are rehearsed in George W. Stocking, *Victorian Anthropology*, New York: Macmillan, 1987, pp. 286–329, and James Clifford, *The Predicament of Culture: twentieth-century ethnography, literature, and art*, Cambridge, Mass. and London: Harvard University Press, 1988, pp. 26–41.
6 Fanny Stevenson, letter to Sidney Colvin, January 1890, Beinecke Library, ms 3674.
7 Robert Louis Stevenson, *In the South Seas*, London: William Heinemann, 1924, p. 10. All subsequent references are to this edition.
8 Jenni Calder (ed.), *RLS: a life study*, London: Hamish Hamilton, 1980, pp. 247–8.
9 Charles Warren Stoddard, *The Island of Tranquil Delights*, London: Grant Richards, 1904, p. 13. *South Sea Idyls*, Boston: James R. Osgood, 1873.
10 Mark Twain, *Letters from the Sandwich Islands: written for the Sacramento Union*, Stanford University Press, 1938.
11 Pratt, Mary Louise, 'Fieldwork in Common Places', in James Clifford and George E. Marcus (eds.), *Writing Culture: the poetics and politics of ethnography*, Berkeley: University of California Press, 1986, pp. 35, 36; Raymond Firth, *We, the Tikopia: a sociological study of kinship in primitive Polynesia*, London: Allen & Unwin, 1957, pp. 1–2. Firth's introductory scene has also provided material for Clifford Geertz's reflections upon anthropological authorship. Clifford Geertz, *Works and Lives: the anthropologist as author*, Cambridge: Polity, 1989, pp. 11–17.
12 Nicholas Thomas provides an account of the complex local agendas articulated through the activities of barter in the Marquesas in *Entangled Objects*, Cambridge, Mass.: Harvard University Press, 1991, pp. 83–103.

13 Emmanuel Le Roy Ladurie has written of the 'unification of the globe by disease', analysing, in the American colonial experience, the causal link between imported disease and the genocide of indigenous populations. Emmanuel Le Roy Ladurie, 'A Concept: the unification of the globe by disease (fourteenth to seventeenth centuries)', *The Mind and Method of the Historian*, trans. Sian and Ben Reynolds, Sussex: Harvester, 1981. Raeburn Lange has developed Ladurie's argument for the critical role of disease in colonial history in the Pacific context. Raeburn Lange, 'European Medicine in the Cook Islands', in Roy MacLeod and Milton Lewis (eds.), *Disease, Medicine and Empire: perspectives on Western medicine and the experience of European expansion*, London: Routledge, 1988; 'Plagues and Pestilence in Polynesia: the nineteenth century Cook Islands experience', *Bulletin of the History of Medicine*, 58 (1984), pp. 325–46. Cluny and La'avasa Macpherson, *Samoan Medical Belief and Medical Practice*, Auckland University Press, 1990, examines the ways in which the traditional medical practices of one Pacific culture responded to the illnesses introduced by contact.

14 Stevenson took up the theme of the spread of foreign disease in a story entitled 'Talofa, Togarewa!', which may have been published in the Samoan missionary paper *O le Sulu Samoa*. The tale is a thinly fictionalised polemic arguing for the segregation of lepers in Samoa, in the light of the disturbing examples of contagion he had witnessed elsewhere in the Pacific. He clearly had little authorial investment in the piece: in an appended note to the editor he writes: 'Please yourself about whether it should be signed or not.' 'Talofa, Togarewa', Beinecke Library, ms 6958.

15 William Arens, *The Man-Eating Myth*, Oxford University Press, 1979, p. 159.

16 Fanny Stevenson, letter to Sidney Colvin, 18 August 1888, Marquesas, Beinecke Library, ms 3669, published in *Scribner's Magazine*, 75, 4 (April, 1924), pp. 408–10.

17 Michel Butor, 'Travel and Writing', *Mosaic*, 8 (1974), pp. 1–16.

18 Dean MacCannell, *The Tourist: a new theory of the leisure class*, London: Macmillan, 1976; Georges van den Abbeele, 'Sightseers: the tourist as theorist', *Diacritics*, 10, 4 (1980), pp. 3–15.

19 Jonathan Culler, 'Semiotics of Tourism', *American Journal of Semiotics*, 1, 1/2 (1981), p. 133.

20 Criticism that attacks the mythologising of an 'authentic' oral tradition tends to propose in its place a hyperliterate touristic experience. John Frow, for instance, claims that MacCannell reiterates an opposition between modern and traditional which 'is closely bound up with the construction of a cultural Other – a mythology of "the primitive, the folk, the peasant, and the working class," who "speak without self-consciousness, without criticism, and without affecta-

tion"'. Frow would push MacCannell's theory 'that the marker is constitutive of the sight' to its logical conclusion: 'The sight would itself be a further marker within a chain of supplementarity.' John Frow, 'Tourism and the Semiotics of Nostalgia', *October*, 57 (1991), pp. 129, 131; compare Susan Stewart, *On Longing: narratives of the miniature, the gigantic, the souvenir, the collection*, Baltimore: Johns Hopkins University Press, 1984, p. 16.

21 Edmund Gosse, *Father and Son* (1907), Gloucester: Alan Sutton, 1984, pp. 82–7.

22 Richard Handler and Jocelyn Linnekin, 'Tradition, Genuine or Spurious', *Journal of American Folklore*, 97, 385 (1984), pp. 273–90.

23 John Carroll has referred to 'Cook fantasies' in his typology of the myths which invest the travels of the modern tourist. John Carroll, *Sceptical Sociology*, London: Routledge, 1980, p. 146.

24 Marshall Sahlins, *Islands of History*, London: Tavistock, 1987, p. 148; also *Historical Metaphors and Mythical Realities*, Ann Arbor: University of Michigan Press, 1981.

25 Gananath Obeyesekere, *The Apotheosis of Captain Cook*, Princeton University Press, 1992, p. 177.

26 Marshall Sahlins, *How Natives Think: about Captain Cook, for example*, University of Chicago Press, 1995. An astute discussion of the debate between Sahlins and Obeyesekere is Clifford Geertz, 'Culture War', *New York Review*, 30 November 1995, pp. 4–6.

27 Twain, *Letters from the Sandwich Islands*, pp. 155, 156.

28 Marshall Sahlins, *Anahulu: the anthropology of history in the kingdom of Hawaii*, University of Chicago Press, 1992, vol. I, *Historical Ethnography*, pp. 76–7.

29 Gavan Daws, 'Honolulu in the Nineteenth Century: notes on the emergence of urban society in Hawaii', *Journal of Pacific History*, 2 (1967), p. 81.

30 Dean MacCannell, 'Staged Authenticity: arrangements of social space in tourist settings', *American Journal Of Sociology*, 79, 3 (1974), p. 591.

31 In fact Stevenson slightly misquotes and fails to do justice to the detailed reticence with which Ellis constructs himself as viewer of the forbidden. Compare William Ellis, *Narrative of a Tour Through Hawaii, or, Owhyhee; with remarks on the history, traditions, manners, customs and language of the inhabitants of the Sandwich Islands*, London: H. Fisher, Son, and P. Jackson, 1826, pp. 136–7.

32 Sahlins, *Anahulu*, p. 69.

33 Jocelyn Linnekin, *Sacred Queens and Women of Consequence: rank, gender and colonialism in the Hawaiian Islands*, Ann Arbor: University of Michigan Press, 1990, pp. 70–1.

34 These letters are reprinted in Stevenson, *Vailima Papers*, London: William Heinemann, 1924, pp. 317–41.

35 H. E. Maude, introduction to Dorothy Shineberg (ed.), *The Trading Voyages of Andrew Cheyne, 1841–1844*, Canberra: Australian National University Press, 1971, p. viii.

36 A shift has been notable in recent accounts of barter between metropolitan and peripheral societies, from the representation of the inevitable triumph of global capitalism, to the depiction of the modifying impact of local agendas. See in particular Thomas, *Entangled Objects*, Sahlins, *Anahulu*, and Caroline Humphrey and Stephen Hugh-Jones (eds.), *Barter, Exchange and Value*, Cambridge University Press, 1992.

37 Ernest Osbourne, 'Stevenson's House on Butaritari Island Where 'T'Imatan Ni Kore Boki' Tarried Awhile', *Pacific Islands Monthly*, 20 September 1933, pp. 34–35.

38 Letter to Charles Baxter, postmarked 7 June 1889, Honolulu, Booth and Mehew (eds.), *Letters*, vol. VI, p. 315.

39 H. E. Maude, 'Baiteke and Binoka of Abemama: arbiters of change in the Gilbert Islands', in J. W. Davidson and Deryck Scarr (eds.), *Pacific Island Portraits*, Canberra: Australian National University Press, 1970, pp. 223, 224, 218, 219. Maude's sources include Stevenson's account, which he considers to be a somewhat softened, but 'with this reservation, a perceptive and, considering his limited social contacts, an accurate one'.

40 Ibid., p. 213.

41 Jean Baudrillard, 'The System of Collecting', in John Elsner and Roger Cardinal (eds.), *The Cultures of Collecting*, London: Reaktion, 1994, p. 9.

42 *Autograph Letters, original manuscripts, books, portraits and curios from the library of the late Robert Louis Stevenson consigned by the present owner Mrs Isobel Strong*, New York: Anderson Auction Company, 1914, part 1, p. 84.

43 Elsner and Cardinal (eds.), *The Cultures of Collecting*, p. 3. For further discussion of the politics of collecting see George W. Stocking (ed.), Objects and Others: essays on museums and material culture, *History of Anthropology*, Madison: University of Wisconsin Press, 1985, volume III.

44 Maude, 'Baiteke and Binoka of Abemama', p. 215.

45 Hyde's letter was reproduced by Stevenson within his reply. See 'Father Damien: an open letter to the Reverend Dr Hyde of Honolulu', in *Vailima Papers*, p. 28.

46 Ibid., p. 32.

47 Fanny Stevenson, preface to Robert Louis Stevenson, *Lay Morals and Other Papers*, London: Chatto and Windus, 1911, p. xi.

48 Letter to Baxter, 12 March [1890], Booth and Mehew (eds.), *Letters*, vol. VI, pp. 377–8.

49 Letter to Andrew Chatto, [September 1890,] ibid., p. 424.

50 *Pacific Commercial Advertiser*, 21 May 1890.
51 Stevenson, 'Father Damien', p. 29.
52 Harold Winfield Kent, *Dr Hyde and Mr Stevenson: the life of the Revd Dr Charles McEwen Hyde including a discussion of the Open Letter of Robert Louis Stevenson* Vermont: Charles E. Tuttle, 1973, is a more recent defence of Hyde.
53 Arthur Johnstone, *Recollections of Robert Louis Stevenson in the Pacific*, London: Chatto and Windus, 1905, pp. 77, 78.
54 Stevenson, 'Father Damien', p. 28.
55 Ibid., p. 40.
56 Johnstone, *Recollections of Robert Louis Stevenson*, pp. 81, 82.
57 Ibid., pp. 82, 81.
58 Robert Louis Stevenson, 'Missions in the South Seas', Sydney: State Library of N.S.W., AS25/19, p. 1. Published with slight variation in Graham Balfour, *The Life of Robert Louis Stevenson*, London: Methuen, 1901, vol. II, pp. 193–5.
59 *Vailima Papers*, pp. 1, 2.
60 Revd S. J. Whitmee, 'Tusitala: a new reminiscence of R. L. S.', in Rosaline Masson (ed.), *I Can Remember Robert Louis Stevenson*, Edinburgh: W. and R. Chambers, 1922, p. 232.
61 'O Le Tala Ia Eatuine O Teira O Le Tala Moni'; 'O Mana'o e Tolu', 'O Tuapi'o e Toalua', Beinecke Library, ms 6662, 6663, 6668. Samoan vocabulary, Beinecke Library, ms 6827. Only the latter of these terms is listed in a recent Samoan dictionary, where it is rendered as 'Be shaky, unstable'. G. B. Milner, *Samoan Dictionary*, Auckland: Polynesian Press, (1966) 1993, p. 173.
62 Revd George Pratt, *A Grammar and Dictionary of the Samoan Language, With English and Samoan Vocabulary*, 3rd revised edition, London: Religious Tract Society, 1893; Stevenson's signature copy, Beinecke Library, ms 2568.
63 See Felix and M. Keesing, *Elite Communication in Samoa*, Stanford University Press, 1954, and G. B. Milner, 'The Samoan Vocabulary of Respect', *Journal of the Royal Anthropological Institute of Great Britain and Ireland*, 91, 2 (1961), pp. 296–317.
64 Stevenson, 'Address to Students at Malua Institution, Upolu, Samoa', [January 1890], Beinecke Library, ms 5940. Published with slight variation in Balfour, *The Life of Robert Louis Stevenson*, vol. II, pp. 187–92.
65 Stevenson, 'A Malaga in Samoa', [December 1889 –January 1890], Beinecke Library, ms 6556, p. 2. A section of this manuscript (excluding the above quotation), is published in Balfour, *The Life of Robert Louis Stevenson*, vol. II, pp. 85–8.
66 Beinecke Library, ms 6485, 6885, 6886, 6887, 6888, 6893. The relationship between Stevenson and the Tahitian chief is the topic of some of the many minor travel articles and recollections which

attest to an early twentieth-century Stevenson cult. See for example Sir Edmund Radcliffe Pears, 'Some Recollections of Robert Louis Stevenson with a Visit to his Friend Ori, at Tahiti', *Scribners Magazine*, 73, 1 (January 1923), pp. 3–18; Robert Keable, 'Bohemian and Rebel in the World's Garden: how Stevenson found a brother in the Tahitian and Gauguin sought him in living art', *ASIA* (November 1924), pp. 892–97; Paul Gooding, 'Stevenson's Tahitian "Brother"', *Overland Monthly* (July 1915), pp. 64–69.

67 Gooding, 'Stevenson's Tahitian "Brother"', p. 64n. For discussion of the politics of Tahitian ceremonies of adoption, see Robert I. Levy, 'Tahitian Adoption as a Psychological Message', in Vern Carroll (ed.), *Adoption in Eastern Oceania*, Honolulu: University of Hawaii Press, 1970, pp. 71–87.

68 'Song of Clan Departure', Beinecke Library, ms 6885.

69 Stevenson, *Poems*, London: William Heinemann, 1924, vol. II, pp. 75, 3, 77, 78.

4 PIRACY AND EXCHANGE: STEVENSON'S PACIFIC FICTION

1 Robert Louis Stevenson, Autograph Manuscript of Imaginary Dispatches [1885], Beinecke Library, ms 5957.

2 Letter to Will H. Low, 15 January [1894], Bradford A. Booth and Ernest Mehew (eds.), *The Letters of Robert Louis Stevenson*, New Haven: Yale University Press, 1995, vol. VIII, p. 235.

3 Will H. Low, *Concerning a Painting of Robert Louis Stevenson*, Bronxville, New York: Bronx Valley Press, 1924.

4 Robert Louis Stevenson, 'The Barbizon Free-Trading Company, unlimited', typescript, 3pp., Beinecke Library, ms 6002.

5 George L. McKay, *A Stevenson Library Catalogue of a collection of writings by and about Robert Louis Stevenson formed by Edwin J. Beinecke*, New Haven: Yale University Press, 1961, vol. V, p. 1729.

6 Stevenson pays tribute to his paternal heritage in *Records of a Family of Engineers*, London: William Heinemann, 1924.

7 These were *The Wrong Box* (1889), *The Wrecker* (1892), and *The Ebb-Tide* (1894). The pair had been involved in 'literary' collaboration since Osbourne's childhood. James D. Hart, *The Private Press Ventures of Samuel Lloyd Osbourne and R. L. S.*, Los Angeles: Book Club of California, 1966.

8 'It's a machine, you know; don't expect aught else: a machine, and a police machine.' Letter to Henry James [?25 May 1892], Booth and Mehew (eds.), *Letters*, vol. VII, p. 292.

9 Robert Louis Stevenson and Lloyd Osbourne, *The Wrecker*, London: Cassell and Company, 1893, p. 17. Subsequent references are to this edition.

10 Letter to Burlingame, 11 March [1890], Booth and Mehew (eds.), *Letters*, vol. VI, p. 375.

11 Letter to Lloyd Osbourne, [5 November 1890], ibid., vol. VII, p. 35; compare Colvin to Baxter, 26 May 1893, Beinecke Library, ms 4247.

12 Letter to Charles Baxter, [30 March 1892], Booth and Mehew (eds.), *Letters*, vol. VII, p. 258.

13 William Diapea, *Cannibal Jack*, London: Faber and Gwyer, 1928, pp. 232–3.

14 Letter to Sidney Colvin, [3] November 1890, Booth and Mehew (eds.), *Letters*, vol. VII, p. 20.

15 Oscar Wilde to Robert Ross, 6 April 1897, Rupert Hart-Davis (ed.), *Selected Letters of Oscar Wilde*, Oxford University Press, 1979, p. 246.

16 Kenneth Graham, *English Criticism of the Novel, 1865–1900*, Oxford: Clarendon Press, 1965, pp. 4–5.

17 Peter Keating, *The Haunted Study: a social history of the English novel, 1875–1914*, London: Fontana, 1989, pp. 11–12.

18 Letter to A. Trevor Haddon, 5 July 1883, Booth and Mehew (eds.), *Letters*, vol. IV, pp. 140–1.

19 Christopher Morley, 'Notes on a Painting', reprinted from the *New York Evening Post*, 18 October 1923, in Low, *Concerning a Painting*, p. 7.

20 Letter to Lloyd Osbourne, 29 September 1890, Booth and Mehew (eds.), *Letters*, vol. VII, p. 9.

21 Letter to Robert Alan Mowbray Stevenson, [*c.* 9 September 1894], ibid., vol. VIII, p. 364.

22 Letter to Sidney Colvin, 16 May 1893; compare letter to Colvin, 27 May–18 June 1893; ibid., vol. VIII, pp. 68; 87–94.

23 Review in the *Speaker*, 29 September 1894, quoted in Paul Maixner (ed.), *Robert Louis Stevenson: the critical heritage*, London: Routledge, 1981, p. 450.

24 Alastair Fowler, 'Parable of Adventure: the debatable novels of Robert Louis Stevenson', in Ian Campbell (ed.), *Nineteenth-Century Scottish Fiction: critical essays*, Manchester: Carcanet, 1979, p. 116.

25 Robert Louis Stevenson, 'The Ebb-Tide', in *Dr Jekyll and Mr Hyde and other stories*, London: Penguin, 1987, pp. 188–9. All subsequent references are to this text.

26 T. Walter Herbert, *Marquesan Encounters*, Cambridge, Mass.: Harvard University Press, 1980, p. 155.

27 Herman Melville, *Omoo*, New York: Library of America, 1982, pp. 334, 336, 337.

28 Robert Hillier, *The South Seas Fiction of Robert Louis Stevenson*, New York: Peter Lang, 1989, p. 137.

29 Stevenson, 'Missions in the South Seas', Sydney: State Library of N.S.W., AS25/19, p. 1.

30 Ibid., p. 4.

31 H. E. Maude, *Of Islands and Men*, Oxford University Press, 1968, p. 135.

32 Barry Menikoff, *Robert Louis Stevenson and 'The Beach of Falesā'*, Edinburgh University Press, 1984, p. 59.

33 Ibid., pp. 72, 64–5.

34 Graham Balfour, 'A South Sea Trader', *Macmillan's* (November 1896), p. 67.

35 Letter to Charles Baxter, 11 August 1892, Booth and Mehew (eds.), *Letters*, vol. VII, p. 350.

36 Letter to Sidney Colvin, 28 September 1891, ibid., p. 161.

37 Stevenson, *Island Nights' Entertainments*, London: Hogarth Press, 1987, p. 3. Subsequent references are to this edition.

38 Otto von Kotzebue, *A New Voyage Round the World in the Years 1823, 24, 25, and 26*, London: Colburn and Bentley, 1830, vol. I, pp. 282–3.

39 Stephen Heath, 'Psychopathia sexualis': Stevenson's *Strange Case*', in *Futures for English* (ed. Colin MacCabe), Manchester University Press, 1988, explores the nuances of the term 'case' in Stevenson's *Strange Case of Dr Jekyll and Mr Hyde*. Recent critics have focused on the psychology of the narrator in attempting to recuperate 'The Beach of Falesā' for modernity and post-modernity. Menikoff represents Wiltshire's narrative as a failed psychoanalytic session: 'This, of course, is the underlying quest of Wiltshire throughout the novel – to discover meaning and order, and to find some vindication for his own life. That he cannot is one of the basic ironies of the story', while Lisa St Aubin de Terán claims that: 'Stevenson is quick to show that he is offering us an adventure story which is the mask for a case study in neurosis.' Case is, in a practical sense, Wiltshire's object of study. Menikoff, *Robert Louis Stevenson and 'The Beach of Falesā'*, p. 69; Lisa St Aubin de Terán, introduction to *Island Nights' Entertainments*, p. ii.

40 Walter J. Ong, *Orality and Literacy: the technologizing of the word*, London: Methuen, 1982, pp. 149–50, 154.

41 Menikoff, *Robert Louis Stevenson and 'The Beach of Falesā'*, p. 58.

42 Stevenson, *In the South Seas*, p. 267; compare Menikoff, *Robert Louis Stevenson and 'The Beach of Falesā'*, p. 85.

43 Menikoff, *Robert Louis Stevenson and 'The Beach of Falesā'*, pp. 83–90.

44 According to Stevenson's Samoan vocabulary lists, *Fa'alototoga*, or 'to have the heart of a Tongan' means 'to be without love, greedy, revengeful'.

45 Homi Bhabha, 'Of Mimicry and Man', *The Location of Culture*, London: Routledge, 1994, p. 89.

46 The problem of the half-caste daughter is playfully developed in a manuscript of an unpublished drama written at Vailima. In this fragment, which gestures towards a reversal of the typical scenario of South Seas seduction, a sailor, Henderson, turns up in Samoa to claim the adopted baby daughter of his wealthy uncle. The girl, Fanua, who has reached an attractive puberty, is repelled by the idea of removing to England, where women are forced to wear stays and

spend their time idly making calls. She is only convinced of the appeal of the idea once Henderson has presented himself as a suitor, with 'no use for corsets.' Play (untitled). Portion. New Haven, Beinecke Library, ms 6722, p. 8.

47 For instance Balfour, *The Life of Robert Louis Stevenson*, vol. II, p. 130; Joseph Beach, 'The Sources of Stevenson's "Bottle Imp"', *Modern Language Notes* 25 (1910), p. 12.

48 Quoted in Albert Lee, '"Black and White" and "O Le Sulu Samoa"', *Black and White*, 6 February 1897, p. 175.

49 Ibid. Original ms in Beinecke Library.

50 Revd A. E. Claxton, 'Stevenson as I Knew Him in Samoa', in Rosaline Masson (ed.), *I Can Remember Robert Louis Stevenson*, Edinburgh: W. and R. Chambers, 1922, p. 249; reprinted from *Chambers's Journal* (October 1922).

51 Revd S. J. Whitmee, 'Tusitala: A New Reminiscence of R. L. S.', in Masson (ed.), *I Can Remember Robert Louis Stevenson*, p. 232.

52 Letter to Arthur Conan Doyle, 23 August 1893, Booth and Mehew (eds.), *Letters*, vol. VIII, p. 155; compare Beach, 'The Sources of Stevenson's "Bottle Imp"', p. 12; H. J. Moors, *With Stevenson in Samoa*, London: T. Fisher Unwin, 1911, p. 97.

53 Beach, 'The Sources of Stevenson's 'Bottle Imp"', p. 17.

54 The editorial is summarised and quoted under the title 'Stevenson's Borrowed Plot' in *The Literary Digest*, 18 July 1914, pp. 105–6.

55 *In the South Seas*, pp. 191, 183.

56 Mary Kawena Pukui and Samuel H. Elbert (eds.), *Hawaiian–English Dictionary*, Honolulu: University of Hawaii Press, 1957.

5 IN THE PRESS OF EVENTS: STEVENSON'S PACIFIC HISTORY

1 Letter to Sidney Colvin, October/November 1891, Bradford A. Booth and Ernest Mehew (eds.), *The Letters of Robert Louis Stevenson*, New Haven: Yale University Press, 1995, vol. VII, pp. 182–3.

2 Letter to Sidney Colvin, 1 January 1892; ibid., p. 218.

3 Letter to Sidney Colvin, [19 April] 1891, ibid., p. 100.

4 Letter to Edward Livermore Burlingame, [November 1891], ibid., p. 196.

5 Georges Charbonnier (ed.), *Conversations with Claude Lévi-Strauss*, trans. John and Doreen Weightman, London: Jonathan Cape, (1961) 1969, p. 39; Lévi-Strauss, *The Savage Mind*, London: Weidenfeld and Nicholson, 1989, pp. 233–4; compare Lévi-Strauss, *Structural Anthropology Volume II*, trans. Monique Layton, London, Allen Lane, (1973) 1977, pp. 28–30.

6 Charbonnier, *Conversations*, pp. 32–3.

7 Lévi-Strauss, *The Savage Mind*, pp. 239, 242.

8 Margaret Mead, *Coming of Age in Samoa*, London: Penguin, (1928) 1966, p. 14.

9 J. W. Davidson, *Samoa mo Samoa: the emergence of the Independent State of Western Samoa*, Melbourne: Oxford University Press, 1967, p. ix.

10 Compare Robert Borofsky and Alan Howard, 'The Early Contact Period', in Alan Howard and Robert Borofsky (eds.), *Developments in Polynesian Ethnology*, Honolulu: University of Hawaii Press, 1989, pp. 243–7, and Nicholas Thomas, 'Partial Texts: representation, colonialism and agency in Pacific history', *Journal of Pacific History*, 25, 2 (1990), pp.139–58.

11 I am indebted here primarily to *A Footnote to History* itself, but also to two excellent recent histories, R. P. Gilson's *Samoa 1830 to 1900: the politics of a multicultural community*, Melbourne: Oxford University Press, 1970, and more generally, I. C. Campbell's *A History of the Pacific Islands*, Christchurch: University of Canterbury Press, 1992. Above all, Kenneth MacKenzie's scrupulously researched 'Robert Louis Stevenson and Samoa, 1888–94', unpublished Ph.D. dissertation, Dalhousie University, 1974, has provided invaluable detailed information concerning both Stevenson's political involvements in Samoa and metropolitan responses to his history and correspondence.

12 Campbell, *A History of the Pacific Islands*, p. 40.

13 MacKenzie, 'Robert Louis Stevenson and Samoa', p. 45.

14 R. Wardlaw Thompson, 'Samoa', *Contemporary Review*, 77 (1900), pp. 233, 34.

15 Stevenson, 'A Footnote to History: eight years of trouble in Samoa', *Vailima Papers*, London: William Heinemann, 1924, p. 71. Subsequent references are to this edition.

16 Revd George Turner, *Nineteen Years in Polynesia: missionary life, travels, and researches in the islands of the Pacific*, London: John Snow, 1861, p. 289.

17 Alessandro Duranti, *From Grammar to Politics: linguistic anthropology in a Western Samoan village*, Berkeley: University of California Press, 1994, pp. 176, 3, 100, 103. See also Alessandro Duranti, 'Doing Things with Words: conflict, understanding, and change in a Samoan fono', in Karen Ann Watson-Gegeo and Geoffrey M. White (eds.), *Disentangling: conflict discourse in Pacific societies*, Stanford University Press, 1990, pp. 459–89.

18 Bradd Shore, *Sala'Ilua: a Samoan mystery*, New York: Columbia University Press, 1982, pp. 241, 243.

19 William B. Churchward, British consul in Samoa from 1881 to 1885, uses a more conventional image of the historian, as conscientious student of cultural archives, to depict the authority of the *tulāfale*: 'invariably men of more than ordinary intellectual parts[, t]hese men make early Samoan precedent their careful study; for the more they can illustrate present affairs by ancient references, the stronger

they are in leading public opinion'. William Churchward, *My Consulate in Samoa*, London: Richard Bentley, 1887, p. 25.

20 Shore, *Sala'Ilua*, pp. 186, 169.
21 Churchward, *My Consulate in Samoa*, p. 63.
22 'The Master of the House Tusitala', Beinecke Library, ms 6566, 6567.
23 Portion of notes used in preparation of *A Footnote to History*, Beinecke Library, ms 6224, p. 85.
24 Henry Adams, letter to John Hay, Vaiale, [Samoa], 16 October 1890, in *Henry Adams and His Friends: a collection of his unpublished letters. Compiled with a biographical introduction [and notes] by Harold Dean Cater*, Boston: Houghton Mifflin, 1947, p. 199.
25 Churchward, *My Consulate in Samoa*, pp. 374, 378.
26 Ibid., p. 83. In *A Footnote to History*, Stevenson inaccurately claims that 'Consul Churchward states with precision that the document was sold by a scribe for thirty-six dollars.' (96)
27 Churchward, *My Consulate in Samoa*, p. 373.
28 François Hartog, *The Mirror of Herodotus: the representation of the other in the writing of history*, trans. Janet Lloyd, Berkeley: University of California Press, 1988, pp. 267.
29 Ibid., p. 294.
30 Steve Nimis has discussed the use of the footnote as mode of authorisation, in 'Fussnoten: das Fundament der Wissenschaft', *Arethusa*, 17, 2 (1984), p. 105.
31 Churchward, *My Consulate in Samoa*, p. 163.
32 Arthur Johnstone, *Recollections of Robert Louis Stevenson in the Pacific*, London: Chatto and Windus, 1905, pp. 149, 148.
33 Sidney Colvin, introductory material, *The Letters of Robert Louis Stevenson* ed. Sidney Colvin, London: William Heinemann, 1924, vol. IV, pp. 4, 5.
34 *Pall Mall Gazette*, 20 September 1892; quoted in MacKenzie, 'Robert Louis Stevenson and Samoa', p. 213.
35 Charles Whibley in the *Graphic*, September, 1892; quoted in ibid., p. 211.
36 Letter to Sidney Colvin, 29 November 1891, Booth and Mehew (eds.), *Letters*, vol. VII, p. 201. According to the notes accompanying this edition of the letters, Stevenson crossed out the humorous title he had initially written here, *A Tempest in a Teapot*. See also letter to E. L. Burlingame, 2 January 1892; letter to Sidney Colvin, 30 March 1892, ibid., pp. 225, 252.
37 Letter to Sidney Colvin, 29 March 1892, ibid., p. 252.
38 Letter to E. L. Burlingame, [late November] 1891, ibid., p. 196.
39 MacKenzie, 'Robert Louis Stevenson and Samoa', p. 199.
40 Letter to Sidney Colvin, 29 March 1892, Booth and Mehew (eds.), *Letters*, vol. VII, p. 252.
41 Compare MacKenzie, 'Robert Louis Stevenson and Samoa', pp. 180–1.

42 To the editor of the 'Times', 10 February 1889; published in *The Times*, 11 March 1889, Booth and Mehew (eds.), *Letters*, vol. V, pp. 250–1.

43 MacKenzie, 'Robert Louis Stevenson and Samoa', pp. 58–9.

44 To the editor of the 'Times', 12 October 1891; published in *The Times*, 17 November 1891, Booth and Mehew (eds.), *Letters*, vol. VII, p. 169.

45 Stevenson, E. W. Gurr and signatories to Pilsach, 28 September 1891; published in *The Times*, 17 November 1891, ibid., p. 173.

46 Pilsach to Stevenson, E. W. Gurr and signatories, 2 October 1891; published in *The Times*, 17 November 1891, ibid., p. 175.

47 Johnstone, *Recollections of Robert Louis Stevenson*, p. 161.

48 David Cohen, *Law, Sexuality, and Society: the enforcement of morals in classical Athens*, Cambridge University Press, 1991, pp. 51, 59, 58.

49 Shore, *Sala'Ilua*, p. 178.

50 Stevenson, E. W. Gurr and signatories to Pilsach, 9 October 1891; published in *The Times*, 17 November 1891, Booth and Mehew (eds.), *Letters*, vol. VII, p. 176.

51 To the editor of the 'Times', 9 April 1892; published in *The Times*, 4 June 1892, ibid., p. 261.

52 Geoffrey Bennington, 'Postal Politics and the Institution of the Nation', in *Nation and Narration*, ed. Homi K. Bhabha, London: Routledge, 1990, p. 129.

53 To the editor of the 'Times', 12 April 1892; published in *The Times*, 4 June 1892, Booth and Mehew (eds.), *Letters*, vol. VII, p. 265.

54 To the editor of the 'Times', 22 June 1892; published in *The Times*, 23 July 1892, ibid., p. 320.

55 To the editor of the 'Times', 19 July 1892; published in *The Times*, 19 August 1892, ibid., p. 338.

56 To the editor of the 'Times', 22 May 1894; published in *The Times*, 30 June 1894, ibid., vol. VIII, p. 297.

57 Letter to Baxter, 7 October 1892, ibid., vol. VII, pp. 395, 396.

58 Revd A. E. Claxton, 'Stevenson as I Knew Him in Samoa', in Rosaline Masson (ed.), *I Can Remember Robert Louis Stevenson*, Edinburgh, W. and R. Chambers, 1922, p. 248; reprinted from *Chambers's Journal* (October 1922).

59 Letter to A. E. Claxton, 1 October 1892, Booth and Mehew (eds.), *Letters*, vol. VII, p. 391.

60 *Samoan Weekly Herald*, 26 November 1892; MacKenzie attributes the piece to Stevenson, 'Robert Louis Stevenson and Samoa', p. 244.

61 John B. Thurston, 'A Regulation', *Samoa Times*, Saturday, 1 April 1893; the regulation was reprinted weekly in this newspaper from late January 1893.

62 'Cables Relative to Samoa', *Samoa Times*, 29 April 1893.

63 Stevenson, *Plain John Wiltshire on the Situation*, ed. William Fuller

Kirkpatrick, Midland, Texas: French Publishing Corporation, 1989, p. 29.
64 Leader, *Samoa Times*, 29 April 1893.
65 'Official Justification of Mr R. L. Stevenson', *The Times*, 18 May 1893; quoted in MacKenzie, 'Robert Louis Stevenson and Samoa', p. 338.
66 Ibid., pp. 400–1.
67 To J. F. Hogan, Esq., MP, 7 October 1894; published in the *Daily Chronicle*, 18 March 1895, Booth and Mehew (eds.), *Letters*, vol. VIII, p. 374.
68 Letter to Sidney Colvin, 13 October 1891, ibid., vol. VII, pp. 163.
69 Stevenson, 'A Gossip on Romance', *Memories and Portraits*, London: William Heinemann, 1924, pp. 128, 129.
70 Letter to Sidney Colvin, 27 [25] May 1892, Booth and Mehew (eds.), *Letters*, vol. VII, p. 287.
71 MacKenzie, 'Robert Louis Stevenson and Samoa', pp. 239–40, 335–7, 358.
72 Letter to Colvin, 21 June 1892, Booth and Mehew (eds.), *Letters*, vol. VII, pp. 310, 311.
73 Stevenson, *In the South Seas*, p. 252.
74 Sidney Colvin, introductory material, *The Letters of Robert Louis Stevenson*, vol. IV, p. 142.
75 MacKenzie, 'Robert Louis Stevenson and Samoa', pp. 164–6.
76 Colvin, introductory material, *The Letters of Robert Louis Stevenson*, vol. IV, p. 216.
77 M. E. Jersey, 'Three Weeks in Samoa' part 1, *Nineteenth Century* (January 1893), p. 59.
78 Ibid., p. 61.
79 Ibid., pp. 58, 59, 63, 64.
80 M. E. Jersey, 'Three Weeks in Samoa' part 2, *Nineteenth Century* (February 1893), p. 253.
81 Churchward, *My Consulate in Samoa*, pp. 144, 145, 146.
82 Stevenson, *Weir of Hermiston and other stories*, London: Penguin, 1979, pp. 104, 161, 104.
83 Stevenson, *In the South Seas*, pp. 12, 13.
84 Letter to Edward Livermore Burlingame, 13 July 1890, Booth and Mehew (eds.), *Letters*, vol. VI, p. 393.
85 Letter to Sidney Colvin, 13 October 1891, ibid., vol. VII, p. 163.

AFTER-WORD: 'THE IMPEDIMENT OF TONGUES'

1 J. P. Sunderland and A. Buzacott, *Mission Life in the Islands of the Pacific*, Suva, Fiji: Institute of Pacific Studies of the University of the South Pacific, 1985, p. 71.
2 Mrs Jane Warren, *The Morning Star*, Boston: American Tract Society, 1860, pp. 254–6.

3 Stevenson, 'Authors and Publishers', *The Lantern-Bearers*, London: Chatto and Windus, 1988, p. 261.

4 To the editor of the 'Times', 23 April 1894; published in *The Times*, 2 June 1894; Bradford A. Booth and Ernest Mehew (eds.), *The Letters of Robert Louis Stevenson*, New Haven: Yale University Press, 1995, p. 268.

5 Stevenson to Sidney Colvin, 10 September 1894, ibid., p. 358. The story of the gift of the road is told by J. C. Furnas in 'The Road of the Loving Heart: Robert Louis Stevenson in Samoa', *Atlantic* (September 1951), pp. 33–44.

6 Stevenson to Sidney Colvin, 10 September 1894, Booth and Mehew (eds.), *Letters*, vol. VIII, p. 359.

7 Stevenson, 'A Footnote to History', *Vailima Papers*, London: William Heinemann, 1924, p. 234.

8 Jacques Derrida, 'The Violence of the Letter', *Of Grammatology*, trans. Gayatri Spivak, Baltimore: Johns Hopkins University Press, 1982, pp. 107–8.

9 Stevenson, 'Address of R. L. Stevenson to the Chiefs, on the Opening of the Road of Gratitude, October, 1894', Sidney Colvin (ed.), *The Letters of Robert Louis Stevenson*, London, William Heinemann, 1924, vol. V, pp. 190–1.

10 Stevenson to Sidney Colvin, 6 October 1894, Booth and Mehew (eds.), *Letters*, vol. VIII, p. 371.

11 Stevenson, 'Address of R. L. Stevenson to the Chiefs', p. 191.

12 Ibid., p. 193.

13 Richard Gilson, *Samoa 1830 to 1900*, Melbourne: Oxford University Press, p. 414.

14 Margaret Jersey, 'Three Weeks in Samoa' part 1, *Nineteenth Century* (January 1893), pp. 56–7.

Bibliography

MANUSCRIPT SOURCES

The Edwin J. Beinecke collection of writings by and about Robert Louis
Stevenson, New Haven, Yale University Library (individual
references cited in text)
Brown, Revd George, *Journal, 1 January 1867–28 May 1871*, Sydney,
Mitchell Library, ms A1686–9
  Journal, 4 September 1860–31 December 1866, Sydney, Mitchell Library,
ms A1686–8
Dawson, T. Madison (of Apia, Samoa), *Poems, 1877–1882*, Sydney,
Mitchell Library, ms A500
Haweis, Revd Thomas, *A Collection of 38 Draft Letters and Manuscripts
Many of Which are in Hand of the Revd Thomas Haweis, Dealing with the
Early Missions to the South Seas, and Including Diaries Sent by the
Missionaries to the London Missionary Society*, Sydney, Mitchell
Library, ms 4910X 1, 2
Stair, Revd John B., *Early Samoan Voyages and Settlement*, 1895, Sydney:
Mitchell Library, ms A229
Stevenson, Robert Louis, 'Missions in the South Seas', Sydney: State
Library of N.S.W., AS25/19

PRINTED SOURCES

Abbeele, Georges van den, 'Sightseers: the tourist as theorist', *Diacritics*,
10, 4 (1980)
Adam Smith, Janet (ed.), *Henry James and Robert Louis Stevenson: a record
of friendship and criticism*, London: Rupert Hart-Davis, 1948
Adams, Henry, *Henry Adams and His Friends: a collection of his unpublished
letters. Compiled with a biographical introduction [and notes] by Harold
Dean Cater*, Boston: Houghton Mifflin, 1947
Adventures in the South Pacific, by One who was Born There, 3rd edition,
London, Religious Tract Society, n.d.
Anderson, Charles Roberts, *Melville in the South Seas*, New York:
Columbia University Press, 1939

Andrews, Lorrin, *A Dictionary of the Hawaiian Language*, Honolulu:
    Henry M. Whitney, 1865
Appadurai, Arjun (ed.), *The Social Life of Things: commodities in cultural
    perspective*, Cambridge University Press, 1986
Archetti, Eduardo P. (ed.), *Exploring the Written: anthropology and the
    multiplicity of writing*, Oslo: Scandinavian University Press, 1994
Arens, W., *The Man-Eating Myth : anthropology and anthropophagy*, Oxford
    University Press, 1979
Arnold, David (ed.), *Imperial Medicine and Indigenous Societies*,
    Manchester University Press, 1988
Asad, Talal, *Anthropology and the Colonial Encounter*, London: Ithaca, 1973
*Autograph Letters, Original Manuscripts, Books, Portraits and Curios from the
    Library of the Late Robert Louis Stevenson Consigned by the Present Owner
    Mrs Isobel Strong*, New York: Anderson Auction Company, 1914
Aylmer, Captain Fenton (ed.), *A Cruise in the Pacific. From the log of a
    naval officer*, 2 volumes, London: Hurst and Blackett, 1860
Babadzan, Alain, 'From Oral to Written: the *puta tupuna* of Rururu', in
    Hooper, Antony and Judith Huntsman (eds.), *Transformations of
    Polynesian Culture*, Auckland: Polynesian Society, 1985
Balfour, Graham, *The Life of Robert Louis Stevenson*, 2 volumes, London:
    Methuen, 1901
'A South Sea Trader', *Macmillan's* (November 1896)
Bann, Stephen, *The Clothing of Clio: a study of the representation of history in
    nineteenth-century Britain and France*, Cambridge University Press,
    1984
Barker, Francis, and Peter Hulme, Margaret Iversen, Diana Loxley
    (eds.), *Europe and its Others: proceedings of the Essex Conference on the
    Sociology of Literature, July 1984*, Colchester: University of Essex, 1985
Barrow, Sir John, *Eventful History of the Mutiny and Piratical Seizure of the
    H.M.S. Bounty: its cause and consequence*, London: Murray, 1831
Barrow, Terence, *Art and Life in Polynesia*, London: Pall Mall Press, 1972
Baudrillard, Jean, 'The System of Collecting', in Elsner and Cardinal
    (eds.), *The Cultures of Collecting*
Bays, Peter, *A Narrative of the Wreck of the 'Minerva' Whaler of Port Jackson,
    New South Wales, on Nicholson's Shoal, 24°S. 179°W*, Cambridge: B.
    Bridges, 1831
Beach, Joseph, 'The Sources of Stevenson's "Bottle Imp"', *Modern
    Language Notes* 25 (1910)
Beaglehole, J. C., *The Exploration of the Pacific*, 3rd edition, London:
    Adam and Charles Black, 1966
Beer, Gillian, *The Romance*, London: Methuen, 1970
'Can the Native Return?', *The Hilda Hume Lecture 1988*, London:
    University of London, 1989
'Speaking for the Others: relativism and authority in Victorian
    anthropological literature', in Fraser (ed.), *Sir James Frazer and the
    Literary Imagination*

Beidelman, T. O., *Colonial Evangelism: a socio-historical study of an East African mission at the grassroots*, Bloomington: Indiana University Press, 1982

Bell, Ian, *Robert Louis Stevenson: dreams of exile*, Edinburgh: Mainstream, 1992

Bellwood, Peter, *The Polynesians: prehistory of an island people*, London: Thames and Hudson, 1987

Benjamin, Walter, *Illuminations*, trans. Harry Zohn, New York: Schocken, 1969

Bennett, Frederick Debell, *Narrative of a Whaling Voyage Round the Globe, from the Year 1833 to 1836. Comprising sketches of Polynesia, California, the Indian Archipelago, etc. with an account of southern whales, the sperm whale fishery, and the natural history of the climates visited*, 2 volumes, London: Richard Bentley, 1840

Bennington, Geoffrey, 'Postal Politics and the Institution of the Nation', in Bhabha (ed.), *Nation and Narration*

Bhabha, Homi K., *The Location of Culture*, London: Routledge, 1994

Bhabha, Homi K. (ed.), *Nation and Narration*, London: Routledge, 1990

Bingham, Hiram, *A Residence of Twenty-one Years in the Sandwich Islands; or the civil, religious, and political history of those islands: comprising a particular view of the missionary operations connected with the introduction and progress of Christianity and civilization among the Hawaiian people*, 2nd edition, Hartford: Hezekiah Huntingtin, 1848

Bingham, Hiram, Jr, *Story of the Morning Star, the children's missionary vessel*, Boston: American Board, 1866

Bligh, William, *A Dangerous Voyage, Containing an Account of the Wonderful and Truly Providential Escape of Captain Bligh and a Part of the Crew of His Majesty's Ship Bounty*, Dublin: Graisberry and Campbell, printers, 1817
  Log of the Proceedings of His Majesty's Ship Providence on a Second Voyage to the South Sea Under the Command of Captain William Bligh, to carry the Bread-fruit Plant from the Society Islands to the West Indies, Written by Himself, 2 volumes, 1791–2

Boon, James A., *Other Tribes, Other Scribes: symbolic anthropology in the comparative study of cultures, histories, religions and texts*, Cambridge University Press, 1987

Booth, Bradford A., and Ernest Mehew (eds.), *The Letters of Robert Louis Stevenson*, 8 volumes, New Haven: Yale University Press, 1994–5

Borofsky, Robert, and Alan Howard, 'The Early Contact Period', in Howard and Borofsky (eds.), *Developments in Polynesian Ethnology*

Bourdieu, Pierre, *Distinction: a social critique of the judgement of taste*, trans. Richard Nice, London: Routledge, 1989
  Outline of a Theory of Practice, trans. Richard Nice, Cambridge University Press, 1977

Boutilier, James A., Daniel T. Hughes and Sharon W. Tiffany (eds.),

Mission, Church, and Sect in Oceania, Lanham, Md.: University Press of America, 1978

Boyarin, Jonathan (ed.), *The Ethnography of Reading*, Berkeley: University of California Press, 1992

Brantlinger, Patrick, *Rule of Darkness: British literature and imperialism, 1830–1914*, Ithaca, N.Y.: Cornell University Press, 1988

Bratton, J. S., *The Impact of Victorian Children's Fiction*, London: Croom Helm, 1981

Briggs, Asa, *Victorian Things*, London: Batsford, 1988

Bristow, Joseph, *Empire Boys: adventures in a man's world*, London: Harper Collins, 1991

Brown, G. Gordon, 'Missions and Cultural Diffusion', *American Journal of Sociology*, L, 3 (1944)

'Some Problems of Culture Contact with Illustrations from East Africa and Samoa', *Human Organization*, 16, 3 (1957)

Brown, Revd George, *Melanesians and Polynesians: their life-histories described and compared*, London: Macmillan, 1910

'Life History of a Savage', *Report of the Seventh Meeting of the Australasian Association for the Advancement of Science*, Sydney: published by the Association, 1898

'Proverbs, Phrases, and Similes of the Samoans', *Report of the Australasian Association for the Advancement of Science*, 14 (1919)

Brownlie, Ian, *Treaties and Indigenous Peoples*, Oxford: Clarendon Press, 1992

Burlingame, Roger, *Of Making Many Books: a hundred years of reading, writing and publishing*, New York: Scribner's, 1946

Butor, Michel, 'Travel and Writing', *Mosaic*, 8 (1974),

'Cables Relative to Samoa', *Samoa Times*, 29 April 1893

Calder, Jenni, *RLS: a life study*, London: Hamish Hamilton, 1980

Calder, Jenni (ed.), *Island Landfalls: reflections from the South Seas*, Edinburgh: Canongate, 1987

Stevenson and Victorian Scotland, Edinburgh: Edinburgh University Press, 1981

Campbell, Archibald, *A Voyage Round the World, from 1806 to 1812 . . . with an account of the present state of the Sandwich Islands, and a vocabulary of their language*, Edinburgh: Archibald Constable and Company, 1816

Campbell, Ian (ed.), *Nineteenth-Century Scottish Fiction: critical essays*, Manchester: Carcanet, 1979

Campbell, I. C., *A History of the Pacific Islands*, Christchurch: University of Canterbury Press, 1992

'European Transculturalists in Polynesia, 1789–ca.1840', Ph.D. thesis, University of Adelaide, 1976

Campbell, John, *Maritime Discovery and Christian Missions, Considered in their Mutual Relations*, London: John Snow, 1840

The Martyr of Erromanga or the Philosophy of Missions: illustrated from the labours, death and character of the late Rev. John Williams, London: John Snow, 1842

Carroll, John, *Sceptical Sociology*, London: Routledge, 1980

Carroll, Vern (ed.), *Adoption in Eastern Oceania*, Honolulu: University of Hawaii Press, 1970

Carter, Paul, *Living in a New Country: history, travelling and language*, London: Faber and Faber, 1992

The Road to Botany Bay: an essay in spatial history, London: Faber and Faber, 1987

Caudwell, Christopher, *Romance and Realism: a study in English bourgeoise literature*, Princeton University Press, 1970

Certeau, Michel de, *Heterologies: discourse on the other*, trans. Brian Massumi, Manchester University Press, 1986

Charbonnier, Georges (ed.), *Conversations with Claude Lévi-Strauss*, trans. John and Doreen Weightman, London: Jonathan Cape, (1961) 1969

Charlot, John, 'The War Between the Gods of Upolu and Savai'i: a Samoan story from 1890', *Journal of Pacific History*, 23, 1 (1988)

Churchward, William B., *My Consulate in Samoa: a record of four years' sojourn in the Navigators Islands with personal experiences of King Malietoa Laupepa, his country, and his men*, London: Richard Bentley, 1887

Claxton, Revd A. E., 'Stevenson as I Knew Him in Samoa', in Masson (ed.), *I Can Remember Robert Louis Stevenson*

Clifford, James, *The Predicament of Culture: twentieth-century ethnography, literature, and art*, Cambridge, Mass. and London: Harvard University Press, 1988

Clifford, James, and George E. Marcus (eds.), *Writing Culture: the poetics and politics of ethnography*, Berkeley: University of California Press, 1986

Cohen, David, *Law, Sexuality and Society: the enforcement of morals in classical Athens*, Cambridge University Press, 1991

Cohen, Erik, 'Authenticity and Commoditization in Tourism', *Annals of Tourism Research*, 15, 3 (1988)

Colvin, Sidney (ed.), *The Letters of Robert Louis Stevenson*, 5 volumes, London: William Heinemann, 1924

Colvin, Sidney, *Robert Louis Stevenson: his work and his personality*, London: Hodder and Stoughton, 1924

Comaroff, Jean, and John Comaroff, *Of Revelation and Revolution: christianity, colonialism, and consciousness in South Africa*, volume I, University of Chicago Press, 1991

Cooper, H. Stonehewer, *Coral Lands*, London: Richard Bentley and Son, 1880

Cousins, George, *From Island to Island in the South Seas: or The Work of a*

Missionary Ship, 2nd edition, London: London Missionary Society,
1894

The Story of the South Seas, London: London Missionary Society, 1894

Crawford, Robert, *Devolving English Literature*, Oxford, Clarendon Press,
1992

Crocombe, Marjorie Tuainekore, *Polynesian Missions in Melanesia: from
Samoa, Cook Islands and Tonga to Papua New Guinea and New
Caledonia*, Suva, Fiji: University of the South Pacific, 1982

Crocombe, R. G., and Marjorie Crocombe (eds.), *The Works of Ta'unga:
records of a Polynesian traveller in the South Seas, 1833–1896*,
Canberra: Australian National University Press, 1968

Crook, D. P. (ed.), *Questioning the Past: a selection of papers in history and
government*, University of Queensland Press, 1972

Culler, Jonathan, *The Pursuit of Signs: semiotics, literature, deconstruction*,
London: Routledge, 1981

'Semiotics of Tourism', *American Journal of Semiotics*, 1, 1/2 (1981)

Curtin, Philip D., *Cross-Cultural Trade in World History*, Cambridge
University Press, 1992

Davidson, J. W., and Deryck Scarr (eds.), *Pacific Island Portraits*,
Canberra: Australian National University Press, 1970

Davidson, J. W., *Samoa mo Samoa: the emergence of the Independent State of
Western Samoa*, Melbourne: Oxford University Press, 1967

[Davies, John], *A Tahitian and English Dictionary, with introductory remarks
on the Polynesian language and a short grammar of the Tahitian dialect:
with an appendix containing a list of foreign words used in the Tahitian
Bible, in commerce, etc., with the sources from whence they have been
derived*, Tahiti: London Missionary Society Press, 1851; New York:
AMS Press, 1978

Daws, Gavan, *A Dream of Islands: voyages of self-discovery in the South Seas*,
New York and London: Norton, 1980

'Honolulu in the Nineteenth Century: notes on the emergence of
urban society in Hawaii', *Journal of Pacific History*, 2 (1967)

Day, A. Grove and Albertine Loomis, *Ka Pa'i Palapala: early printing in
Hawaii*, Honolulu: Printing Industries of Hawaii, 1973

Defoe, Daniel, *Robinson Crusoe*, 1719; Oxford University Press, 1990

Dening, Greg, *Islands and Beaches: discourse on a silent land, Marquesas,
1774–1880*, Honolulu: University of Hawaii Press, 1980

Mr Bligh's Bad Language: passion, power and theatre on the Bounty,
Cambridge University Press, 1992

'Ethnohistory in Polynesia: the value of ethnohistorical evidence',
Journal of Pacific History, 1 (1966)

'Possessing Tahiti', *Archaeology in Oceania*, 21 (1986)

Dening, Greg, (ed.), *The Marquesan Journal of Edward Robarts,
1797–1824*, Canberra: Australian National University Press, 1974

Derrida, Jacques, *Of Grammatology*, trans. Gayatri Spivak, Baltimore:
Johns Hopkins University Press, 1982

Diapea, William, *Cannibal Jack : the true autobiography of a white man in the South Seas*, London: Faber and Gwyer, 1928

Dirks, Nicholas B. (ed.), *Colonialism and Culture*, Ann Arbor: University of Michigan Press, 1992

Dixon, Robert, *Writing the Colonial Adventure: race, gender and nation in Anglo-Australian popular fiction, 1875–1914*, Cambridge University Press, 1995

Dodge, Ernest S., *Islands and Empires: Western impact on the Pacific and East Asia*, Minneapolis: University of Minnesota Press, 1976

Douglas, Mary, *Implicit Meanings: essays in anthropology*, London: Routledge, 1975

Dunae, Patrick A., 'Boys' Literature and the Idea of Empire, 1870–1914', *Victorian Studies*, 24, 1 (1980)

Duranti, Alessandro, *From Grammar to Politics: linguistic anthropology in a Western Samoan village*, Berkeley: University of California Press, 1994

The Samoan Fono: a sociolinguistic study, Canberra: Australian National University Press, 1981

Eagleton, Terry, *Exiles and Emigrés: studies in modern literature*, London: Chatto and Windus, 1970

Eigner, Edwin M., *Robert Louis Stevenson and Romantic Tradition*, Princeton University Press, 1966

Ellis, Markman, *The Politics of Sensibility: race, gender and commerce in the sentimental novel*, Cambridge University Press, 1996

Ellis, William, *Narrative of a Tour Through Hawaii, or, Owhyhee; with Remarks on the History, Traditions, Manners, Customs and Language of The Inhabitants of the Sandwich Islands*, London: H. Fisher, Son, and P. Jackson, 1826

Polynesian Researches, During a Residence of Nearly Six Years in the South Sea islands, 1829; 2 volumes, London: Dawsons of Pall Mall, 1967

A Vindication of the South Sea Missions from the Misrepresentations of Otto von Kotzebue, Captain in the Russian Navy, with an Appendix, London: Frederick Westley and A. H. Davis, 1831

Elsner, John and Roger Cardinal (eds.), *The Cultures of Collecting*, London: Reaktion, 1994

Erskine, John Elphinstone, *Journal of A Cruise Among the Islands of the Western Pacific, including the Feejees and others inhabited by the Polynesian negro races, in her majesty's ship Havannah*, London: John Murray, 1853

Fabian, Johannes, *Time and the Other: how anthropology makes its object*, New York: Columbia University Press, 1983

'Keep Listening: ethnography and reading', in Boyarin (ed.), *The Ethnography of Reading*

Fairchild, Hoxie Neale, *The Noble Savage: a study in romantic naturalism*, New York: Columbia University Press, 1928

Faller, Lincoln B., *Turned to Account: the forms and functions of criminal biography in late seventeenth- and early eighteenth-century England,* Cambridge University Press, 1987

Finnegan, Ruth, *Oral Traditions and the Verbal Arts: a guide to research practices,* London: Routledge, 1992

Firth, Raymond, *Primitive Polynesian Economy,* London: Routledge and Kegan Paul, 1967

Symbols: public and private, London: Allen and Unwin, 1973

We, the Tikopia: a sociological study of Kinship in primitive Polynesia, London: Allen and Unwin, 1957; Boston: Beacon Press, 1963

Fowler, Alastair, *Kinds of Literature: an introduction to the theory of genres and modes,* Oxford: Clarendon Press, 1982

'Parable of Adventure: the debatable novels of Robert Louis Stevenson', in Campbell (ed.), *Nineteenth-Century Scottish Fiction*

Fraser, Robert (ed.), *Sir James Frazer and the Literary Imagination: essays in affinity and influence,* London: Macmillan, 1990

Frazer, James George, *The Golden Bough: a study in magic and religion,* 1913; London: Macmillan, 1990

Freeman, J. D. and W. R. Geddes (eds.), *Anthropology in the South Seas,* New Plymouth, N.Z.: Thomas Avery, 1959

Freeman, J. D., 'The Joe Gimlet or Siovili Cult: an episode in the religious history of early Samoa', in Freeman and Geddes (eds.), *Anthropology in the South Seas*

Freud, Sigmund, 'Totem and Taboo', *The Origins of Religion,* trans. James Strachey, London: Pelican, 1985

Frow, John, 'Tourism and the Semiotics of Nostalgia', *October,* 57 (1991)

Furnas, J. C., *Voyage to Windward: the life of Robert Louis Stevenson,* London: Faber and Faber, 1952

'The Road of the Loving Heart: Robert Louis Stevenson in Samoa', *Atlantic,* (September 1951)

'Stevenson and Exile', in Calder (ed.), *Stevenson and Victorian Scotland*

Garrett, John, *Footsteps in the Sea: Christianity in Oceania to World War II,* Suva, Fiji: Institute of Pacific Studies, 1992

Gates, Henry Louis, Jr., *'Race', Writing and Difference,* University of Chicago Press, 1986

Geertz, Clifford, *Local Knowledge: further essays in interpretive anthropology,* New York: Basic Books, 1983

Works and Lives: the anthropologist as author, Cambridge: Polity, 1988

'Culture War', *New York Review,* 30 November 1995

Gell, Alfred, *Wrapping in Images: tattooing in Polynesia,* Oxford: Clarendon Press, 1993

Giles, W. E., *A Cruize in a Queensland Labour Vessel to the South Seas,* ed. Deryck Scarr, Canberra: Australian National University Press, 1968

Gill, Revd William Wyatt, *From Darkness to Light in Polynesia,* London: n.p., 1894; Suva, Fiji: Institute of Pacific Studies, 1989

Historical Sketches of Savage Life in Polynesia, Wellington: George
    Didsbury, 1880
Jottings from the Pacific, London: Religious Tract Society, 1885
*Life in the Southern Isles, or Scenes and Incidents in the South Pacific and
    New Guinea*, London: Religious Tract Society, 1862
Myths and Songs from the South Pacific, London: Henry S. King, 1876
Gilman, Sander L., *Difference and Pathology: stereotypes of sexuality, race,
    and madness*, Ithaca, N.Y.: Cornell University Press, 1985
Gilson, R. P., *Samoa 1830 to 1900: the politics of a multi-cultural community*,
    Melbourne: Oxford University Press, 1970
Goldman, Irving, *Ancient Polynesian Society*, University of Chicago Press,
    1970
Gooding, Paul, 'Stevenson's Tahitian "Brother"', *Overland Monthly* (July
    1915)
Goody, J. R. (ed.), *The Interface Between the Written and the Oral*,
    Cambridge University Press, 1987
Literacy in Traditional Societies, Cambridge University Press, 1968
The Logic of Writing and the Organization of Society, Cambridge
    University Press, 1986
Gosse, Edmund, *Father and Son*, 1907; Gloucester: Alan Sutton, 1984
'The Tyranny of the Novel', *National Review*, 19, (April 1892)
Graff, Harvey J., *The Literacy Myth: literacy and social structure in the
    nineteenth-century city*, New York: Academic Press, 1979
Graham, Kenneth, *English Criticism of the Novel, 1865–1900*, Oxford:
    Clarendon Press, 1965
Grant, Damian, *Realism*, London: Methuen, 1970
Gravagnuolo, Benedetto, *Adolf Loos: theory and works*, Milan: Idea Books,
    1982
Green, Martin, *Dreams of Adventure, Deeds of Empire*, London: Routledge
    and Kegan Paul, 1980
Greenblatt, Stephen, *Marvelous Possessions: the wonder of the new world*,
    Oxford: Clarendon Press, 1991
Greenhalgh, Paul, *Ephemeral Vistas: the expositions universelles, great
    exhibitions and world's fairs, 1851–1939*, Manchester University
    Press, 1988
Gregory, C. A., *Gifts and Commodities*, London: Academic Press, 1982
Gunson, Niel, *Messengers of Grace: evangelical missionaries in the South Seas,
    1797–1860*, Melbourne: Oxford University Press, 1978
'An Account of the Mamaia or Visionary Heresy of Tahiti,
    1826–1841', *Journal of the Polynesian Society*, 71 (1962)
'John Williams and his Ship: the bourgeoise aspirations of a
    missionary family', in Crook (ed.), *Questioning the Past*
'Victorian Christianity in the South Seas: a survey', *Journal of Religious
    History*, 8 (1974)
Gunson, Niel (ed.), *The Changing Pacific*, Melbourne: Oxford University
    Press, 1978

Gutch, John, *Beyond the Reefs: the life of John Williams, missionary*, London: Macdonald, 1974

Hale, Horatio, 'Ethnography and Philology', Charles Wilkes (ed.), *United States Exploring Expedition*, vol. VI, Philadelphia: Lea and Blanchard, 1846

Hammond, J. R., *A Robert Louis Stevenson Companion: a guide to the novels, essays and short stories*, London: Macmillan, 1984

Handler, Richard, and Jocelyn Linnekin, 'Tradition, Genuine or Spurious', *Journal of American Folklore*, 97, 385 (1984)

Harding, Thomas, and Ben J. Wallace (eds.), *Cultures of the Pacific*, New York: Free Press, 1970

Hart, James D., *The Private Press Ventures of Samuel Lloyd Osbourne and R. L. S.*, Los Angeles: Book Club of California, 1966

Hart-Davis, Rupert (ed.), *Selected Letters of Oscar Wilde*, Oxford University Press, 1979

Hartog, François, *The Mirror of Herodotus: the representation of the other in the writing of history*, trans. Janet Lloyd, Berkeley: University of California Press, 1988

Heath, Stephen, 'Psychopathia sexualis': Stevenson's *Strange Case*', in *Futures for English*, ed. Colin MacCabe, Manchester University Press, 1988

Hempenstall, Peter J., *Pacific Islanders Under German Rule: a study in the meaning of colonial resistance*, Canberra: Australian National University Press, 1978
  Protest and Dissent in the Colonial Pacific, Suva, Fiji: Institute of Pacific Studies, 1984
  'Protest or Experiment?: theories of "cargo cults"', occasional paper no. 2, Research Centre for Southwest Pacific Studies, Melbourne: La Trobe University, 1981

Hennessy, James Pope, *Robert Louis Stevenson*, London: Jonathan Cape, 1974

Herbert, Christopher, *Culture and Anomie: ethnographic imagination in the nineteenth century*, University of Chicago Press, 1991

Herbert, T. Walter, *Marquesan Encounters: Melville and the meaning of civilization* Cambridge, Mass.: Harvard University Press, 1980

Highland, G. (ed.), *Polynesian Culture History*, Honolulu: Bishop Museum Press, 1967

Hillier, Robert Irwin, *The South Seas Fiction of Robert Louis Stevenson*, New York: Peter Lang, 1989

Hogg, Garry, *Cannibalism and Human Sacrifice*, London: Robert Hale, 1958

Holden, Horace, *A Narrative of the Shipwreck, Captivity and Sufferings of Horace Holden and Benj. H. Nute; who were cast away in the American ship 'Mentor', on the Pelew Islands, in the year 1832; and for two years afterwards were subjected to unheard-of sufferings among the barbarous inhabitants of Lord North's Island*, Boston: Russell, Shattuck and Co., 1836

Hooper, Antony, and Judith Huntsman, 'History and the Representation of Polynesian Societies', in Siikala (ed.), *Culture and History in the Pacific*

Hooper, Antony, and Judith Huntsman (eds.), *Transformations of Polynesian Culture*, Auckland: Polynesian Society, 1985

Howard, Alan, and Robert Borofsky (eds.), *Developments in Polynesian Ethnology*, Honolulu: University of Hawaii Press, 1989

Howe, K. R., 'Pacific Islands Historiography in the 1980's: new directions or monograph myopia?', *Pacific Studies* 3 (1979)

Hulme, Peter, *Colonial Encounters: Europe and the native Caribbean, 1492–1797*, London: Methuen, 1986

Humphrey, Caroline, and Stephen Hugh-Jones (eds.), *Barter, Exchange and Value*, Cambridge University Press, 1992

Ii, John Papa, 'Ancient Idolatrous Customs and Kapus of the Hawaiian People', *Hawaiian Almanac*, (1890)

Fragments of Hawaiian History, trans. M. K. Pukui, ed. D. B. Barrère, Honolulu: Bernice P. Bishop Museum Press, 1959

Im Thurn, Sir Everard, and Leonard C. Wharton (eds.), *The Journal of William Lockerby, Sandalwood Trader in the Fijian Islands During the Years 1808–1809*, London: Hakluyt Society, 1925

Jersey, M. E., 'Three Weeks in Samoa', *Nineteenth Century* (January and February 1893)

Johnstone, Arthur, *Recollections of Robert Louis Stevenson in the Pacific*, London: Chatto and Windus, 1905

[Jones, John D.,] *Life and Adventure in the South Pacific, by A Roving Printer*, London: Sampson, Low and Son, 1861

Kamakau, Samuel Manaiakalani, *Ka Po'e Kahiko: the people of old*, translated from the newspaper *Ke Au 'Oko'a* by Mary Kawena Pukui, ed. Dorothy B. Barrère, Honolulu: Bernice P. Bishop Museum Press, 1964

Kaplan, Martha, *Neither Cargo nor Cult: ritual politics and the colonial imagination in Fiji*, Durham, N.C. and London: Duke University Press, 1995

Keable, Robert, 'Bohemian and Rebel in the World's Garden: how Stevenson found a brother in the Tahitian and Gauguin sought him in living art', *ASIA* (November 1924)

Keate, George, *An Account of the Pelew Islands, Situated in the Western Part of the Pacific Ocean; composed from the journals and communications of Captain Henry Wilson, and some of his officers, who, in August, 1783, were there shipwrecked, in the 'Antelope', a packet belonging to the Honourable East India Company*, London: printed for Captain Wilson, 1788

Keating, Peter, *The Haunted Study: a social history of the English novel, 1875–1914*, London: Fontana, 1989

Keesing, Felix and M. Keesing, *Elite Communication in Samoa*, Stanford University Press, 1954

Kent, Harold Winfield, *Dr Hyde and Mr Stevenson: the life of the Revd Dr Charles McEwen Hyde including a discussion of the open letter of Robert Louis Stevenson* Vermont: Charles E. Tuttle, 1973

Kern, Stephen, *The Culture of Time and Space, 1880–1918*, London: Weidenfeld and Nicholson, 1983

Kiely, Robert, *Robert Louis Stevenson and the Fiction of Adventure*, Cambridge, Mass.: Harvard University Press, 1964

Kilgour, Maggie, *From Communion to Cannibalism: an anatomy of metaphors of incorporation*, Princeton University Press, 1990

Kirch, Patrick Vinton, *The Evolution of the Polynesian Chiefdoms*, Cambridge University Press, 1984

Knight, Alanna (ed.), *R. L. S. In the South Seas: an intimate photographic record*, Edinburgh: Mainstream, 1986

  Robert Louis Stevenson Treasury, London: Shepheard-Walwyn, 1985

Korn, Alfons L., *The Victorian Visitors: an account of the Hawaiian Kingdom, 1861–1866, including the journal letters of Sophia Cracroft, extracts from the journals of Lady Franklin, and diaries and letters of Queen Emma of Hawaii*, Honolulu: University of Hawaii Press, 1958

Kotzebue, Otto von, *A New Voyage Round the World in the Years 1823, 24, 25, and 26*, 2 volumes, London: Henry Colburn and Richard Bentley, 1830.

  A Voyage of Discovery, Into the South Sea and Beering's Straits, for the Purpose of Exploring a North-East Passage, Undertaken in the Years 1815–1818, at the Expense of His Highness the Chancellor of the Empire, Count Romanzoff, in the Ship Rurick, Under the Command of the Lieutenant in the Russian Imperial Navy, Otto von Kotzebue, 3 volumes, London: Longman, Hurst, Rees, Orme, and Brown, 1821

Krusenstern, A. J. von, *Voyage round the World in the Years 1803 . . . 1806*, trans. Richard Belgrave Hoppner, London: John Murray, 1813

Kuper, Adam, *The Invention of Primitive Society: transformations of an illusion*, London: Routledge, 1988

Lack, C. ' Pirates, Blackbirders and other Shady Characters', *Journal of the Royal Historical Society of Queensland*, 6 (1959–60)

Lamont, E. H., *Wild Life Among the Pacific Islanders*, London: Hurst and Blackett, 1867

Lang, Andrew, 'Are Savage Gods Borrowed from Missionaries?', *Nineteenth Century*, 45 (1899)

  'Realism and Romance', *Contemporary Review*, 51 (1887)

Lange, Raeburn, 'European Medicine in the Cook Islands', in MacLeod and Lewis (eds.), *Disease, Medicine and Empire*

  'Plagues and Pestilence in Polynesia: the nineteenth century Cook Islands experience', *Bulletin of the History of Medicine*, 58 (1984)

Langsdorff, Georg H. von, *Voyages and Travels in Various Parts of the*

World, During the Years 1803, 1804, 1805, 1806, and 1807, London: H. Colburn, 1813–14

Lee, Albert, '"Black and White" and "O Le Sulu Samoa"', *Black and White*, 6 February 1897

Legge, Christopher, 'William Diaper: a biographical sketch', *Journal of Pacific History*, 1 (1966)

Le Roy Ladurie, Emmanuel, 'A Concept: the unification of the globe by disease (fourteenth to seventeenth centuries)', in *The Mind and Method of the Historian*, trans. Sian and Ben Reynolds, Sussex: Harvester, 1981

Letley, Emma, *From Galt to Douglas Brown: nineteenth-century fiction and Scot's language*, Edinburgh: Scottish Academic Press, 1988

Lévi-Strauss, Claude, *The Savage Mind*, Paris: Librarie Plon, 1962; London: Weidenfeld and Nicholson, (1966) 1989
 Structural Anthropology, trans. Claire Jacobsen, London: Allen Lane, 1969
 Structural Anthropology, volume II, trans. Monique Layton, London: Allen Lane, 1977
 Tristes Tropiques, trans. John and Doreen Weightman, London: Picador, 1989

Levine, George, *The Realistic Imagination: English fiction from Frankenstein to Lady Chatterley*, University of Chicago Press, 1981

Levy, Robert I., 'Tahitian Adoption as a Psychological Message', in Carroll (ed.), *Adoption in Eastern Oceania*

Lingenfelter, Richard E., *Presses of the Pacific Islands, 1817–1867: a history of the first half century of printing in the Pacific islands*, Los Angeles: Plantin Press, 1967

Linnekin, Jocelyn, *Sacred Queens and Women of Consequence: rank, gender and colonialism in the Hawaiian Islands*, Ann Arbor: University of Michigan Press, 1990
 'Structural History and Political Economy: the contact encounter in Hawaii and Samoa', *History and Anthropology*, 5 (1991)

Linton, Ralph, 'Nativistic Movements', *American Anthropologist*, 45, 1

Lisiansky, Urey, *A Voyage Round the World in the Years 1803, 1804, 1805 and 1806, performed by order of his Imperial Majesty Alexander the First, Emperor of Russia, in the ship Neva*, London: Longman, Hurst, Rees, Orme and Brown, 1814

Lovett, Richard, *The History of the London Missionary Society, 1795–1895*, London: Henry Frowde, 1899

Low, Will H., *Concerning a Painting of Robert Louis Stevenson*, Bronxville, New York: Bronx Valley Press, 1924

MacCannell, Dean, *The Tourist: a new theory of the leisure class*, London: Macmillan, 1976
 'Staged Authenticity: arrangements of social space in tourist settings', *American Journal of Sociology*, 79, 3 (1974)

MacKay, David, *In the Wake of Cook: exploration, science and empire, 1780–1801*, London: Croom Helm, 1981

MacKenzie, Donald A., *Myths and Traditions of the South Seas*, London: Gresham, 1930

MacKenzie, John M., *Propaganda and Empire: the manipulation of British public opinion, 1880–1960*, Manchester University Press, 1984

MacKenzie, Kenneth Starr, 'Robert Louis Stevenson and Samoa 1888–94', Ph.D. dissertation, Dalhousie University, 1974

MacLeod, Roy, and Milton Lewis (eds.), *Disease, Medicine, and Empire: perspectives on Western medicine and the experience of European expansion*, London and New York: Routledge, 1988

Macpherson, Cluny and La'avasa, *Samoan Medical Belief and Medical Practice*, Auckland University Press, 1990

Maixner, Paul (ed.), *Robert Louis Stevenson: the critical heritage*, London: Routledge, 1981

Mangan, J. A. and James Walvin (eds.), *Manliness and Morality: middle-class masculinity in Britain and America, 1800–1940*, Manchester University Press, 1987

Marcus, George E. and Michael M. J. Fischer, *Anthropology as Cultural Critique: an experimental moment in the human sciences*, Chicago and London: University of Chicago Press, 1986

Martin, John, *An Account of the Natives of the Tonga Islands, in the South Pacific Ocean. With an original grammar and vocabulary of their language. Comp. and arranged from the extensive communications of Mr William Mariner, several years resident in those islands*, 2 volumes, London: printed for the author, 1817; 2nd edition, 2 volumes, London: John Murray, 1818; 3rd edition, 2 volumes, Edinburgh: Constable, 1827

Martin, K. L. P., *Missionaries and Annexation in the Pacific*, Oxford University Press, 1924

Masson, Rosaline (ed.), *I Can Remember Robert Louis Stevenson*, Edinburgh: W. and R. Chambers, 1922

Maude, H. E., *Of Islands and Men*, Oxford University Press, 1968
Slavers in Paradise: the Peruvian slave trade in Polynesia, 1862–1864, Stanford University Press, 1981
'Baiteke and Binoka of Abemama: arbiters of change in the Gilbert Islands', in Davidson and Scarr (eds.), *Pacific Island Portraits*

Mauss, Marcel, *The Gift : the form and reason for exchange in archaic societies*, trans. W.D. Halls, London: Routledge, 1990

McFarlane, Revd S., *The Story of the Lifu Mission*, London: James Nisbet and Co., 1873

McGrane, Bernard, *Beyond Anthropology: society and the other*, New York: Columbia University Press, 1989

McKay, George L., *Some Notes on Robert Louis Stevenson: his finances and his agents and publishers*, New Haven: Yale University Library, 1958
A Stevenson Library Catalogue of a collection of Writings By and About

Robert Louis Stevenson Formed by Edwin J. Beinecke, 5 volumes, New
Haven: Yale University Press, 1961

McKenzie, D. F., *Oral Culture, Literacy and Print in Early New Zealand: the
Treaty of Waitangi*, Wellington: Victoria University Press, 1985

McLynn, Frank J., *Robert Louis Stevenson: a biography*, London:
Hutchinson, 1993

Mead, Margaret, *Coming of Age in Samoa*, 1928; London: Penguin, 1966

Melville, Herman, *Typee: a peep at Polynesian life; Omoo: a narrative of
adventures in the South Seas; Mardi and a Voyage Thither*, New York:
Library of America, 1982

Menikoff, Barry, *Robert Louis Stevenson and 'The Beach of Falesā': a study in
Victorian publishing*, Edinburgh University Press, 1984

Menikoff, Barry (ed.), Robert Louis Stevenson, *Tales from the Prince of
Storytellers*, Evanston, Ill.: Northwestern University Press, 1993

*Missionary Sketches: for the use of the weekly and monthly contributors to the
Missionary Society*, 1–73 (April 1818–April 1836)

Milner, G. B., *Samoan Dictionary*, 1966; Auckland: Polynesian Press, 1993

'The Samoan Vocabulary of Respect', *Journal of the Royal
Anthropological Institute of Great Britain and Ireland*, 91, 2 (1961)

Moors, H. J., *With Stevenson in Samoa*, London: T. Fisher Unwin, 1911

Morrell, Benjamin, *A Narrative of Four Voyages, to the South Sea, North and
South Pacific Ocean, Chinese Sea, Ethiopia and South Atlantic Ocean,
Indian and Antarctic Ocean, from the year 1822 to 1831*, New York: J.
and J. Harper, 1832

Morrison, James, *The Journal of James Morrison, Boatswain's Mate of the
'Bounty', Describing the Mutiny and Subsequent Misfortunes of the
Mutineers, Together with an Account of the Island of Tahiti*, London:
Golden Cockerel Press, 1935

Moss, Frederick J., *Through Atolls and Islands in the Great South Sea*,
London: Sampson, Low, Marston, Searle and Rivington, 1889

Moyle, Richard (ed.), *The Samoan Journals of John Williams*, Canberra:
Australian National University Press, 1984

Murray, A. W., *The Martyrs of Polynesia. Memorials of missionaries, native
evangelists, and native converts, who have died by the hand of violence,
from 1799 to 1871*, London: Elliot Stock, 1885

*Missions in Western Polynesia, being historical sketches of these missions, from
their commencement in 1839 to the present time*, London: John Snow,
1863

Murray, Revd Thomas Boyles, *Pitcairn: the island, the people and their
pastor; with a short account of the mutiny of the Bounty*, 3rd edition,
London: printed for the SPCK, 1854

Myers, Fred, and Donald L. Brenneis (eds.), *Dangerous Words: language
and politics in the Pacific*, New York University Press, 1984

Nimis, Steve, 'Fussnoten: das Fundament der Wissenschaft', *Arethusa*,
17, 2 (1984)

Noble, Andrew (ed.), *Robert Louis Stevenson*, London: Vision, 1983

Nystrand, Martin (ed.), *What Writers Know: the language, process, and structure of written discourse*, New York: Academic Press, 1982

Obeyesekere, Gananath, *The Apotheosis of Captain Cook: European mythmaking in the Pacific*, Princeton University Press, 1992

'"British Cannibals": contemplation of an event in the death and resurrection of James Cook, Explorer', *Critical Inquiry*, 18 (Summer 1992)

O'Connell, James F., *A Residence of Eleven Years in New Holland and the Caroline Islands*, 1830; ed. Saul H. Riesenberg, Honolulu: University of Hawaii Press, 1972

Oliver, Douglas, *Return to Tahiti: Bligh's second breadfruit voyage*, Melbourne University Press, 1988

Olmstead, John Charles (ed.), *A Victorian Art of Fiction: essays on the novel in British periodicals, 1870–1900*, New York and London: Garland, 1979

Ong, Walter J., *Orality and Literacy: the technologising of the word*, London: Methuen, 1982

Orange, James, *Narrative of the Late George Vason, of Nottingham. One of the first missionaries sent out by the London Missionary Society, in the ship Duff, Captain Wilson, 1796. Giving an account of his voyage outward, settlement in Tongataboo, apostacy, heathen life, escape from the island, return to England, subsequent life, and death in 1838, aged 66 years. With a preliminary essay, on the geography of the South Sea Islands, also a description of the manners, habits, customs, traditions, &c. &c. of the inhabitants, and a succinct account of the South Sea Island Mission*, Derby: Henry Mozley, 1840

Osbourne, Ernest, 'Stevenson's House on Butaritari Island where "T'Imatan Ni Kore Boki" Tarried Awhile', *Pacific Islands Monthly*, 20 September 1933

Pacific Commercial Advertiser, 21 May 1890

Pagden, Anthony, *The Fall of Natural Man: the American Indian and the origins of comparative ethnology*, Cambridge University Press, 1986

Parry, Benita, 'Problems in Current Theories of Colonial Discourse', *Oxford Literary Review*, 9, 1–2 (1987)

Parsonson, G. S., 'The Literate Revolution in Polynesia', *Journal of Pacific History*, 2 (1967)

Patterson, Samuel, *Narrative of the Adventures and Sufferings of Samuel Patterson, experienced in the Pacific Ocean, and many other parts of the world, with an account of the Feegee, and Sandwich Islands*, 1817; Fairfield, Washington: Ye Galleon Press, 1967

Pears, Sir Edmund Radcliffe, 'Some Recollections of Robert Louis Stevenson with a visit to his friend Ori, at Tahiti', *Scribners Magazine*, 73, 1 (January 1923)

Pearson, Bill, *Rifled Sanctuaries: some views of the Pacific islands in Western literature*, Auckland University Press, 1984

Penisimani, *Samoan Stories, Collected and Partly Edited by Rev. George Brown*, 2 volumes, 1861–70; Sydney: Mitchell Library, ZA1686 25–6

Phillips, Revd Charles, *Samoa: past and present: a narrative of missionary work in the South Seas*, London: John Snow, 1890

Porteous, Stanley D., *The Restless Voyage, being an account by Archibald Campbell, seaman, of his wanderings in five oceans from 1806 to 1812 . . . supplemented and re-indited in 1948 from documents dealing with his further history in Scotland and America*, London and Sydney: Harrap and Australian Publishing Company, 1948

Porter, Jane, 'The South Sea Chief', *Sydney Gazette*, 10 September 1829

Porter, Robert Ker, *Travelling Sketches in Russia and Sweden During the Years 1805, 1806, 1807, 1808*, 2nd edition, 2 volumes, London: John Stockdale, 1813

Pratt, Revd George, *A Grammar and Dictionary of the Samoan Language, with English and Samoan Vocabulary*, 3rd, revised edition, London: Religious Tract Society, 1893

Pratt, Mary Louise, *Imperial Eyes: travel writing and transculturation*, London: Routledge, 1992

'Fieldwork in Common Places', in Clifford and Marcus (eds.), *Writing Culture*

Pritchard, George, *The Missionary's Reward; or, the success of the gospel in the Pacific*, London: John Snow, 1844

Pritchard, W. T., *Polynesian Reminiscences: or, Life in the South Pacific Islands*, London: Chapman and Hall, 1866

Progress of the Gospel in Polynesia. (Southern Group) Georgian, Society, & Harvey (sic) Islands, Edinburgh: Waugh and Innes, 1831

Prout, Ebenezer, *Memoirs of the Life of the Rev. John Williams*, London: John Snow, 1843

Pukui, Mary Kawena, and Samuel H. Elbert (eds.), *Hawaiian–English Dictionary*, Honolulu: University of Hawaii Press, 1957

Ralston, Caroline, *Grass Huts and Warehouses: Pacific beach communities of the nineteenth century*, Canberra: Australian National University Press, 1977

'Early Nineteenth Century Polynesian Millennial Cults and the Case of Hawaii', *Journal of the Polynesian Society*, 94, 4 (1985)

Rankin, Nicholas, *Dead Man's Chest: travels after Robert Louis Stevenson*, London: Faber and Faber, 1987

Rennie, Neil, *Far-Fetched Facts: the literature of travel and the idea of the South Seas*, Oxford: Clarendon Press, 1995

Richstad, Jim, and Miles M. Jackson, *Publishing in the Pacific Islands*, Honolulu: University of Hawaii Press, 1984

Robie, David (ed.), *Nius Bilong Pasifik: mass media in the Pacific*, Port Moresby: University of Papua New Guinea Press, 1995

Ross, Angus, *New Zealand Aspirations in the Pacific in the Nineteenth Century*, Oxford: Clarendon Press, 1964

Rousseau, Jean-Jacques, *The Social Contract and Discourses*, trans G. D. H.
    Cole, London: Everyman, 1991
Sahlins, Marshall, *Anahulu: the anthropology of history in the kingdom of
    Hawaii*, vol. I, *Historical Ethnography*, University of Chicago Press,
    1992
    *Historical Metaphors and Mythical Realities: structure in the early history of
    the Sandwich Islands kingdom*, Ann Arbor: University of Michigan
    Press, 1981
    How Natives Think: about Captain Cook, for example, University of
    Chicago Press, 1995
    Islands of History, London: Tavistock, 1987
    Stone Age Economics, London: Tavistock, 1974
Said, Edward, *Culture and Imperialism*, London: Chatto and Windus, 1993
    Orientalism, London: Penguin, 1978
Sandison, Alan, *Robert Louis Stevenson and the Appearance of Modernism*,
    London: Macmillan, 1996
    'Robert Louis Stevenson: a Modernist in the South Seas', *Durham
    University Journal*, 83, 1 (1991)
Schousboe, Karen, and Mogens Trolle Larsen, *Literature and Society*,
    Copenhagen: Akademisk Forlag, 1989
Sharrad, Paul, 'Imagining the Pacific', *Meanjin*, 49 (1990)
Shineberg, Dorothy, *They Came for Sandalwood: a study of the sandalwood
    trade in the south-west Pacific, 1830–1865*, Melbourne University
    Press, 1967
Shineberg, Dorothy (ed.), *The Trading Voyages of Andrew Cheyne,
    1841–1844*, Canberra: Australian National University Press, 1971
Shoberl, Frederick (ed.), *South Sea Islands: being a description of the
    manners, customs, character, religion, and state of society among the
    various tribes scattered over the great ocean, called the Pacific, or the South
    Sea: illustrated with twenty-six coloured engravings*, 2 volumes, London:
    R. Ackermann, n.d.
Shore, Bradd, *Sala'Ilua: a Samoan mystery*, New York: Columbia
    University Press, 1982
Showalter, Elaine, *Sexual Anarchy: gender and culture at the fin de siècle*,
    London: Bloomsbury, 1991
Siikala, Jukka, *Cult and Conflict in Polynesia: a study of traditional religion,
    Christianity and nativistic movements*, Helsinki: Academica
    Scientiarum Fennica, 1982
Siikala, Jukka (ed.), *Culture and History in the Pacific*, Helsinki: Finnish
    Anthropological Society, 1990
Smith, Bernard, *European Vision and the South Pacific*, 2nd edition,
    London and New Haven: Yale University Press, 1985
    Imagining the Pacific: in the wake of the Cook voyages, New Haven and
    London: Yale University Press, 1992
Smith, Revd Thomas, *The History and Origin of the Missionary Societies;
    containing faithful accounts of the voyages, travels, labours, and happy*

results of the various missionaries who have been sent out for the purposes
of evangelizing the heathen, and other unenlightened nations, in different
parts of the habitable globe, 2 volumes, London: Thomas Kelly, 1838
Smith, Valene L. (ed.), *Hosts and Guests: the anthropology of tourism*,
Oxford: Basil Blackwell, 1978
Smith, Vanessa, 'Crusoe in the South Seas: beachcombers, missionaries
and the myth of the castaway', in Spaas and Stimpson (eds.),
Robinson Crusoe: myths and metamorphoses
Snow, Philip, and Stefanie Waine, *The People from the Horizon: an
illustrated history of the Europeans among the South Sea islanders*,
Oxford: Phaidon, 1979
[Southey, Robert,] Review of *Polynesian Researches, during a residence of
nearly six years, in the South Sea islands; including descriptions of the
natural history and scenery of the islands; with remarks on the history,
mythology, traditions, government, arts, manners, and customs of the
inhabitants. By William Ellis, missionary to the Society and Sandwich
islands, and author of the 'Tour of Hawaii'*, *Quarterly Review*, 43,
85(1830)
Spaas, Lieve, and Brian Stimpson (eds.), *Robinson Crusoe: myths and
metamorphoses*, London: Macmillan, 1996
Sperber, Dan, *Rethinking Symbolism*, trans. Alice L. Morton, Cambridge
University Press, 1975
Spivak, Gayatri Chakravorty, *In Other Worlds: essays in cultural politics*,
New York and London: Methuen, 1987
Stephen, Ann (ed.), *Pirating the Pacific: images of travel, trade and tourism*,
Sydney: Powerhouse, 1993
Stevenson, Fanny, letter to Sidney Colvin, *Scribner's Magazine*, 75, 4
(April 1924)
Stevenson, Fanny and Robert Louis, *Our Samoan Adventure*, ed. Charles
Neider, London: Weidenfeld and Nicolson, 1956
Stevenson, Mrs R. L., *The Cruise of the 'Janet Nichol' Among the South Sea
Islands*, London: Chatto and Windus, 1915
Stevenson, Robert Louis, *Dr Jekyll and Mr Hyde and other stories*, London:
Penguin, 1987
  Essays Literary and Critical, London: William Heinemann, 1924
  Familiar Studies of Men and Books, London: William Heinemann, 1924
  *In the South Seas: being an account of experiences and observations in the
  Marquesas, Paumotus, and Gilbert islands in the course of two cruises, on
  the yacht 'Casco' (1888) and the schooner 'Equator' (1889)*, London:
  William Heinemann, 1924
  Island Nights' Entertainments, London: Hogarth Press, 1987
  The Lantern-Bearers and other essays, selected and introduced by Jeremy
  Treglown, London: Chatto and Windus, 1988
  Lay Morals and other papers, London: Chatto and Windus, 1911
  Memoir of Fleeming Jenkin and Records of a Family of Engineers, London:
  William Heinemann, 1924

Memories and Portraits, Memoirs of Himself, Selections from his Notebooks, London: William Heinemann, 1924

Plain John Wiltshire on the Situation, ed. William Fuller Kirkpatrick, Midland, Texas: French Publishing Corporation, 1989

Poems, volume II, London: William Heinemann, 1924

Treasure Island, Oxford University Press, 1985

Vailima Papers, London: William Heinemann, 1924

Weir of Hermiston and other stories, London: Penguin, 1979

'American Rights and Wrongs', *Academy*, 20 March 1886

'International Copyright', *Times*, 2 April 1887

Stevenson, Robert Louis, and Lloyd Osbourne, *The Wrecker*, London: Cassell and Co., 1893

'Stevenson's Borrowed Plot' *Literary Digest*, 18 July 1914

Stewart, Susan, *On Longing: narratives of the miniature, the gigantic, the souvenir, the collection*, Baltimore: Johns Hopkins University Press, 1984

Stocking, George W., *Victorian Anthropology*, New York: Macmillan, 1987

Stocking, George W. (ed.), *Objects and Others : essays on museums and material culture*, History of Anthropology, volume III, Madison: University of Wisconsin Press, 1985

Romantic Motives: Essays on Anthropological Sensibility, History of Anthropology, volume VI, Madison: University of Wisconsin Press, 1989

Stoddard, Charles Warren, *The Island of Tranquil Delights: a South Sea idyl*, London: Grant Richards, 1904

The Lepers of Molokai, Notre Dame, Ind.: Ave Maria Press, 1885

South Sea Idyls, Boston, James R. Osgood, 1873

Summer Cruising in the South Seas, 1874; London: Chatto and Windus, 1905

A Trip to Hawaii . . . with descriptive introduction, 2nd edition, San Francisco: Oceanic Steamship Company, 1892

Strathern, Marilyn, 'Artefacts of History: events and the interpretation of images', in Siikala (ed.), *Culture and History in the Pacific*

'Partners and Consumers: making relations visible', *New Literary History*, 22, 3 (1991)

Street, Brian V. (ed.), *Cross-Cultural Approaches to Literacy*, Cambridge University Press, 1993

Sunderland, J. P. and A. Buzacott, *Mission Life in the Islands of the Pacific*, London: John Snow, 1866; Suva, Fiji: Institute of Pacific Studies, 1985

Swearingen, Roger, *The Prose Writings of Robert Louis Stevenson: a guide*, London: Macmillan, 1980

Thomas, Julian ('The Vagabond'), *Cannibals and Convicts: notes of personal experiences in the Western Pacific*, London: Cassell, 1886

Thomas, Nicholas, *Entangled Objects: exchange, material culture and colonialism in the Pacific*, Cambridge, Mass.: Harvard University Press, 1991

Oceanic Art, London: Thames and Hudson, 1995

Out of Time: history and evolution in anthropological discourse, Cambridge University Press, 1989

'The Beautiful and the Damned', in Stephen (ed.), *Pirating the Pacific*

'The Force of Ethnology: origins and significance of the Melanesia/Polynesia division', *Current Anthropology* 30, 1 (1989)

'Partial Texts: representation, colonialism and agency in Pacific history', *Journal of Pacific History*, 25, 2 (1990)

Thompson, Harold W. (ed.), *The last of the 'Logan'. The true adventures of Robert Coffin mariner in the years 1854 to 1859 wherein are set forth his pursuit of the whale, his shipwreck on Rapid Reef, his life among the cannibals of Fiji, and his search for gold in Australia, as told by himself and now first published*, Ithaca, N.Y.: Cornell University Press, 1941

Thompson, Ralph Wardlaw , 'Samoa', *Contemporary Review*, 77 (1900)

Thurston, John B., 'A Regulation', *Samoa Times*, 1 April 1893

Tippett, Alan R., *People Movements in Southern Polynesia: studies in the dynamics of church-planting and growth in Tahiti, New Zealand, Tonga, and Samoa*, Chicago: Moody Press, 1971

Tui, Tātupu Fa'afetai Matā'afa, *Lāuga: Samoan Oratory*, National University of Samoa, 1987

Turner, Revd George, *Nineteen Years in Polynesia: missionary life, travels, and researches in the islands of the Pacific*, London: John Snow, 1861

Samoa: a hundred years ago and long before, London, 1884; Suva, Fiji: Institute of Pacific Studies, 1989

Turner, Louis, and John Ash, *The Golden Hordes: international tourism and the pleasure periphery*, London: Constable, 1975

Twain, Mark, *Letters from the Sandwich Islands: written for the Sacramento Union*, Stanford University Press, 1938

Twyning, John P., *Shipwreck and Adventures of John P. Twyning Among the South Sea Islanders: giving an account of their feasts, massacres, etc.*, London: printed for the author [1850]

Tyerman, Daniel, and George Bennet, *Voyages and Travels Round the World, by the Rev. Daniel Tyerman and George Bennet, Esq. deputed from the London Missionary Society to visit their various stations in the South Sea Islands, Australia, China, India, Madagascar, and South Africa, between the years 1821 and 1829. Compiled from original documents by James Montgomery*, 2nd edition, corrected, London: John Snow, 1840

Urry, John, *The Tourist Gaze: leisure and travel in contemporary societies*, London: Sage, 1990

Varigny, Charles de, *Fourteen Years in the Sandwich Islands, 1855–1868*, trans. Alfons L. Korn, Honolulu: University of Hawaii Press, 1981

Vason, George, *An Authentic Narrative of Four Years' Residence at*

Tongataboo, one of the Friendly Islands, in the South Sea, by – who went there in the 'Duff', under Captain Wilson, in 1796, London: Longman, Hurst, Rees and Orme, 1810

Viswanathan, Gauri, *Masks of Conquest: literary study and British rule in India*, London: Faber, 1989

Wagner, Roy, *The Invention of Culture*, New Jersey: Prentice-Hall, 1975

Ward, R. G. (ed.), *Man in the Pacific Islands*, Oxford: Clarendon Press, 1972

Warren, Mrs Jane S., *The Morning Star: history of the children's missionary vessel, and of the Marquesan and Micronesian missions*, Boston: American Tract Society, 1860

Watson-Gegeo, Karen Ann, and Geoffrey M. White (eds.), *Disentangling: conflict discourse in Pacific societies*, Stanford University Press, 1990

Weiner, Annette B., *Inalienable Possessions: the paradox of keeping-while-giving*, Berkeley: University of California Press, 1992

West, Francis J., *Political advancement in the South Pacific: a comparative study of colonial practice in Fiji, Tahiti and American Samoa*, Melbourne: Oxford University Press, 1961

White, Geoffrey M., and John Kirkpatrick, *Person, Self and Experience: exploring Pacific ethnopsychologies*, Berkeley: University of California Press, 1985

Whitmee, Revd S. J., *A Missionary Cruise in the South Pacific, being the report of a voyage amongst the Tokelau, Ellice, and Gilbert Islands, in the missionary barque 'John Williams', during 1870*, Sydney: Joseph Cook, 1871

'Tusitala: a new reminiscence of R. L. S.', in Masson (ed.), *I Can Remember Robert Louis Stevenson*

Wilkes, Charles, *Narrative of the United States Exploring Expedition*, 5 volumes, Philadelphia: Lea and Blanchard, 1845

Williams, F. E., *'The Vailala Madness' and other essays*, ed. Erik Schwimmer, St. Lucia: University of Queensland Press, 1976

Williams, John, *A Narrative of Missionary Enterprises in the South Sea Islands, with remarks upon the natural history of the islands, origin, languages, traditions and usages of the inhabitants*, London: John Snow, 1837

Wilson, James, *A Missionary Voyage to the Southern Pacific Ocean, performed in the years 1796, 1797, 1798, in the ship Duff, commanded by Captain James Wilson*, London: published for the benefit of the society, printed by S. Gosnell for T. Chapman, 1799; reprinted with an introduction by Irmgard Moschner, New York: Frederick A. Praeger, n.d. (1979?)

Worsley, Peter, *The Trumpet Shall Sound: a study of 'cargo' cults in Melanesia*, London: Macgibbon and Kee, 1957

Young, Robert, *White Mythologies: writing history and the West*, London: Routledge, 1990

Index

293

CAMBRIDGE STUDIES IN NINETEENTH-CENTURY LITERATURE AND CULTURE

General Editors
Gillian Beer, *University of Cambridge*
Catherine Gallagher, *University of California, Berkeley*

Titles published